Professional
Healthy
Cooking

Professional
Healthy
Cooking

Sandy Kapoor, Ph.D., M.P.H, R.D.
California State Polytechnic University

JOHN WILEY & SONS, Inc.
New York ◆ Chichester ◆ Brisbane ◆ Toronto ◆ Singapore

Library of Congress Cataloging-in-Publication Data:
Kapoor, Sandy, 1952–
    Professional healthy cooking / Sandy Kapoor.
      p.   cm.
    Includes bibliographical references (p.   ).
    ISBN 0-471-53839-6 (cloth : acid-free paper)
    1. Quantity cookery.   2. Low-fat diet—Recipes.   3. Salt-free
diet—Recipes.   4. Sugar-free diet—Recipes.   5. Low-calorie diet—
Recipes.   I. Title.
TX820.K35   1995
641.5′63—dc20   94-37924

Printed in the United States of America

10 9 8 7 6 5 4 3 2 1

To my Mom for teaching me to cook before I could print the alphabet, my Dad for cultivating my appreciation of "good" food, and my husband for his continuous encouragement.

Acknowledgments

The concepts formulated in *Healthy Professional Cooking* are the results of six years of research in healthy recipe development. Many talented, creative, and diligent California State Polytechnic University, School of Hotel and Restaurant Management (SHRM) student research assistants have participated in this project. There is only one word for their many contributions—awesome! I would like to thank all of them, the SHRM, and the University for their ongoing support of this project.

Tim Allison
Chris Carlson
Jackson Chuang
Chris Cuffari
Gary Dahl
Shelley Doonan
Sondra Dreis
Jeff Durham
Kathy Farnsworth
Paul Findly
Karen Fitzgerald
Christine Garboski
Leticia Gonzales
Cheryl Goodrich
Sean Grovier
Jeff Haines
Terry Jackson

Katie Kehoe
Blair Kerley
KC Knauer
Brian Knirk
Diane Knirk
Bibi Leung
Derin Lewis
Genevieve Lorenzo
Rajeev Maini
Stacy Medrano
Lisa Milton
Karen Moses
Victoria Mylne
Kelly Potter
Saijai (April) Pradipnathalang
Alicia Rowan
Susan Serdarusich
Byron Takeuchi
Vicki Tan
Robert Trummeter
Michele Tune
Paula Zahursky

I am also most appreciative to Stephan Fernald, CCC, Director of Education for the American Culinary Federation, and Nancy Graves, Assistant Professor, Conrad N. Hilton College of Hotel and Restaurant Management, University of Houston, for their careful reviews of the manuscript and helpful suggestions.

Finally, I am grateful to my editor Claire Thompson for continuing to believe in me, and to the staff at John Wiley & Sons.

Contents

7

Making Magic with Recipe Modifications   257

APPENDIX 1

APPENDIX 2

APPENDIX 3

Introduction

The term "healthy food" has many connotations. Some diners believe healthy food to be low in fat, cholesterol, sodium, sugar, and calories and rich in complex carbohydrates, vitamins, and minerals. Others consider healthy foods to be those which are organically grown and "natural" such as brown rice and free-range chicken. Many recognize healthy food to be all food. They believe there are no good or bad foods but that it is more important to eat a balanced diet containing a variety of foods.

Recently, the U.S. Food and Drug Administration (FDA) and the U.S. Department of Agriculture (USDA) published final rules defining what the term healthy means when used as a nutrient content claim on food labels (Federal Register, May 10, 1994). The FDA's rule was effective May 8, 1994 but manufacturers of existing products have until January 1, 1996 to comply. USDA's rule takes effect November 10, 1995. The rules define "healthy" and its derivatives "healthfully," "healthier," and "healthiness." The claim that an individual food is "healthy" can be made if the food is first, low in fat, saturated fat, cholesterol, and sodium and second, the food contains at least 10% of the Daily Value for one of the following: vitamin A, vitamin C, iron, calcium, protein, or fiber. This prevents foods like candy, popsicles, and soft drinks from being called healthy just because they are low in fat and sodium.

Eating Healthfully Outside the Home

Now more than ever before, Americans want to eat healthfully when dining outside the home. The six nutritional requests they make most frequently when dining out are for selections which contain

- Reduced amounts of total fat, saturated fat, and cholesterol
- Increased amounts of the complex carbohydrates, starch, and fiber
- Less sodium/salt
- Less sugar
- Nonred meat sources of protein
- Fewer calories

Dietary Guidelines

Whether eating at home or away from home, nutrition authorities agree that following these six practices along with a few others can help make and keep Americans healthy. Their healthy eating recommendations are stated in the USDA and U.S. Department of Health and Human Services Dietary Guidelines. The Dietary Guidelines are:

- Eat a variety of foods
- Maintain healthy weight
- Choose a diet low in fat, saturated fat, and cholesterol
- Choose a diet with plenty of vegetables, fruits, and grain products
- Use sugars only in moderation
- Use salt and sodium only in moderation
- If you drink alcoholic beverages, do so in moderation

Purpose of Professional Healthy Cooking

The purpose of this book is to teach food service professionals and students how to cook healthy cuisine that is satisfying and appealing. Healthy food has gained a reputation for being tasteless and boring. This does not need to be the case. The goal when developing healthy recipes is that they be delicious and of a quality that will cause food service patrons to return. Their nutritional attributes should be considered an added benefit.

The first six chapters of this text provide detailed strategies on how to prepare delicious tasting food that addresses diners' nutritional requests when eating outside the home. At the same time, the following are described in these six chapters: how to prepare flavorful food that (1) might be called healthy by diners holding varied meanings of the term, (2) meets USDA and FDA's recent rules defining what healthy food is, and (3) enables diners to eat a diet that will help them to be healthy as described in the Dietary Guidelines. At the end of each chapter, a few sample recipes are offered. These illustrate the principles of healthy cooking discussed in the chapter.

Chapter 7 includes 10 traditional recipes, with instructions for adjustments to reduce total fat, saturated fat, cholesterol, sodium, and calories and to increase fiber, complex carbohydrates, and nutrients. These examples are designed to serve as training tools for food service professionals seeking to offer more healthful selections on their menus.

Following the seven chapters, Appendices 1–4 offer charts of substitutions for healthier recipes. The charts provide a quick and easy reference on the cooking techniques and ingredients that can be used to cook healthy cuisine. In Appendices 5–9, sample answers are given to the activities following each chapter.

1

Cut the Fat—Keep the Flavor

Fat in the Body and in Food

The Effects of a High-Fat Diet

Fat has long been a topic of discussion. Sadly, most of its recent attention has been negative. It has been linked with high blood pressure, heart attack, diabetes, cancer, and obesity. As the Surgeon General's Report states, too much is likely to be hazardous to health.

Functions of Fat in Cooking

On the other hand, fat is a blessing to the chef or cook. It performs many valuable functions in food. It makes pastry and pie crusts flaky, gives cookies their crisp texture, and tenderizes cakes and breads. In frying, fat provides an extremely high moist-free environment. It is responsible for the crisp, browned products millions of Americans crave, ranging from potato chips to batter-coated chicken wings and breaded zucchini.

To prevent sticking, pots and pans are frequently coated with shortening, oil, margarine, or butter before baking or cooking. Further, fat produces aroma. Imagine the delicious smell of bacon frying or butter sizzling in a pan. Fat also adds and carries flavor. Consider a slice of pumpkin pie. It may be fine as is, but a dollop of whipped cream will make it really good, or picture a steak hot off the grill. But to make it even better, it might be topped with a slice

EXAMPLE

Calculating the Percentage of Fat

One serving of item A
Fat and calorie information on the label or in a food composition table.

Grams of fat = 5
Calories per serving = 100

Formula:
5 grams of fat × 9 calories/gram of fat = 45 fat calories

$$\frac{45 \text{ fat calories}}{100 \text{ calories/serving}} \times 100 = 45\% \text{ calories from fat}$$

of melting maitre d'hotel butter (melted butter cooked with lemon juice, chopped parsley, and seasonings). Fat enhances the mouth-feel of food too. For example, rate a scoop of frozen ice milk against one of rich, high-fat ice cream. There's no question which tastes better.

Functions of Fat in the Body

Fat also performs valuable functions in the body. It provides energy, is a source of essential fatty acids, and serves as a carrier of the fat-soluble vitamins A, E, D, K. To meet this need and stay healthy, humans require fat in the diet but only a small amount. About a tablespoon of polyunsaturated vegetable oil per day will suffice.

CALORIC VALUE OF FAT

The term fat includes both fats and oils. They are the richest source of calories in the diet. Each gram (about ⅛ teaspoon oil or ¼ teaspoon butter) provides 9 calories. This is more than double the 4 calories per gram in carbohydrates and protein. For this reason, it is often necessary to reduce the fat content of an item to lower its calories.

CALCULATING THE PERCENTAGE OF FAT IN FOOD

The percentage of calories from fat in an item can be determined by a simple calculation. First, identify the grams of fat and calories in one serving of the product. These figures can be found on the product's label or in a food composition table. Second, multiply the product's grams of fat by 9 or the number of calories per gram of fat. Third, divide the calories from fat in the product by the number of calories per serving. Finally, multiply this figure by 100 to obtain the percent of calories from fat in the item.

Sources of Fat in Food

Fat is found in many foods (see Table 1.2). Sometimes it is visible and sometimes not. It's apparent that butter, margarine, oil, salad dressing, lard, and bacon are rich in fat. However, the fat in some foods is almost hidden. For instance, even if all the visible fat was removed from a piece of meat, its muscle tissues would still be surrounded by fat in the form of marbling. The fat in olives, avocados, and nuts isn't readily apparent either, yet the fat in three ripe olives provides about 70% or 11 of their 15 calories, and nearly 90% or 135 of the 155 calories in half of an avocado is from fat.

Nuts aren't quite as bad but still very high in fat, with around 80% of their calories from fat.

Saturation of Fats

The diet commonly contains a mixture of both saturated and unsaturated fats.

SATURATED FATS

Saturated fats are generally found in animal foods and are solid at room temperature. For example, lard, suet (solid white fat from cattle, sheep, and other animals), butter, and the fat in milk, cheese, cream, chicken, and bacon are high in saturated fats.

UNSATURATED FATS

On the other hand, unsaturated fats, both mono- and polyunsaturated, tend to come from plant foods and be liquid at room temperature. For example, vegetable oils like safflower, sunflower, soybean, cottonseed, and corn are high in polyunsaturated fats, while peanut, olive, avocado, almond, hazelnut, rice bran, and canola are rich in monounsaturated fats.

FISH AND TROPICAL OILS

Note: technically, a fat is not completely mono- or polyunsaturated or saturated. While fats from plant foods are mostly unsaturated and those from animal foods mostly saturated, there are exceptions.

Fish and tropical oils are two of these exceptions. Although fish are of animal origin, they are primarily unsaturated. On the other hand, tropical oils including coconut, palm, and palm kernel are of plant origin but naturally high in saturated fat.

HYDROGENATED OILS

Unsaturated fats can also become more saturated by hydrogenation. In this process, liquid plant oils are converted to more solid forms, for example, hydrogenated vegetable oil or shortening. As the hardness of the oil increases, saturation does too. This explains why the softest margarines or the liquid margarines sold in squeeze containers provide less saturated fat than tub margarines, which provide less than the firmer stick margarines.

Another key to a margarine's level of saturation is its list of ingredients. Those margarines that list the first ingredient as liquid vegetable oil such as corn, safflower, or soybean are richer in polyunsaturated fats than those that list partially hydrogenated or hardened oil first.

EXAMPLE

Calculating Trans Fat

Nutrition Facts
Total fat = 14 grams
Saturated fat = 2 grams
Polyunsaturated fat = 4 grams
Monounsaturated fat = 6 grams

14 g total fat − (2 g *saturated* + 4 g *poly- and 6 g monounsaturated fats*) = 2 g trans fat

Trans fat = 2 grams

TRANS FAT

When vegetable oils are converted into solid margarine and shortening by hydrogenation, two things happen. Some of the oils' unsaturated fats become saturated and others become trans fats or change their spatial configuration. Excessive heating of fats in frying can also create trans fats. It is now known that the unsaturated trans fats, like saturated fats, raise cholesterol. Some experts estimate the cholesterol-raising effect of trans fat may be nearly equal to that of saturated fat. The question then is why do companies continue to make and use hydrogenated fat. It performs valuable functions in food. For a start, it prevents oil from becoming rancid and increases its deep-frying life, makes baked goods tender and flaky, and helps margarines to spread more easily.

Of course, trans fat is found in solid margarine and shortening, as well as in most of the deep-fried foods served in restaurants, crackers, potato chips, and many other processed foods. Unfortunately, while the new food labels list saturated fat, they are not required to list trans fat. The new labels do provide some information about a product's trans fat content. When a food's unsaturated fat content is voluntarily listed, it cannot include the item's trans fat content even though the trans fat is unsaturated. Thus, the amount of trans fat can be calculated in products voluntarily listing their unsaturated fat content by subtracting the item's saturated, mono-, and polyunsaturated fats from its total fat. See the example on this page.

Second, if a food's label states it is "saturated-fat-free," the food must contain less than half a gram of trans fat. Therefore, if a product is labeled "saturated-fat-free," it is also low in trans fat.

OMEGA-3 FATTY ACIDS

There are also special kinds of polyunsaturated fatty acids called omega-3's. They are found in deep-water fish, especially fatty varieties such as albacore, herring, shad, salmon, mackerel, sardines, anchovies, and bluefin tuna; leafy vegetables; and some seeds and oils. They are noted for their benefits in the fight against heart attacks and strokes. Recent studies suggest that they play roles in protecting against cancer and combatting rheumatoid arthritis, psoriasis, and other common disorders too. Eating fish about two times per week is recommended.

SIGNIFICANCE OF FAT SATURATION LEVEL

Whether a fat is saturated or unsaturated is significant because saturated fats increase and unsaturated fats decrease blood cholesterol levels. High blood cholesterol levels put an individual at greater risk for cardiovascular disease which causes heart attacks and strokes, the number one killer in the United States.

Fat Requirement

RECOMMENDED DIETARY ALLOWANCES (RDAS) FOR FAT
Currently, no RDAs have been established for fat or what percentage should be saturated and unsaturated, but many health experts suggest 30% of calories or less should be derived from fat and no more than 10% of these should be saturated, 10% or less polyunsaturated, and the remaining 10% monounsaturated fats. See Table 1.1 for maximum recommended daily total and saturated fat intake levels based on 1600- to 2800-calorie diets.

Cholesterol in the Body and in Food

Cholesterol, like saturated fats, is a dietary risk factor for heart disease.

Sources of Cholesterol

Cholesterol is derived from two sources. First, it is made by the body. Second, it is found in foods of animal origin (see Table 1.2). It appears in dairy products such as butter, cream, ice cream, and cheeses like blue, camembert, cheddar, cream, and Swiss. Egg whites are of no concern, but yolks are concentrated sources. Meat, fish, and poultry all contain cholesterol; organ meats contain a particularly high amount. For example, a large egg provides about 213 milligrams of cholesterol while a 3-½-ounce portion of beef brains (head cheese) yields around ten times this amount, and a 3-½-ounce portion of beef kidneys more than four times the cholesterol in a similar portion of beef prime rib.

Since cholesterol comes only from foods of animal origin, plant foods do not contain cholesterol. These include vegetables and the oils made from them; fruits—even those high in fat like avocados; legumes; grains; and seeds and nuts, which are also high in fat. Thus, products like potato chips, corn oil margarine, peanut butter, and olive oil may be cholesterol free, but still very high in fat.

Cholesterol Functions

Cholesterol performs valuable functions in the body. It is involved in the production of hormones and vitamin D. Since the body

---

TABLE 1.1

Maximum Recommended Daily Total and Saturated Fat Intake Levels

Daily calorie intake	1600	1800	2000	2400	2800
Fat (grams) (30% of calories)	53	60	67	80	93
Saturated fat (grams) (10% of calories)	18	20	22	27	31

Calculating RDAs for Fat

To determine the maximum grams of total fat and saturated fat recommended for individuals whose caloric intakes are outside of these ranges, a few simple calculations can be made.

Fill in the blanks below to calculate the recommended maximum total fat grams (30% of calories) for specific calorie levels:

Total calories per day = _____.
Multiplied by 0.3 = _____.
Divided by 9 = _____.

Example:

2200 daily caloric intake × 0.3 = 660
660/9 = 73 grams of fat

To calculate the recommended maximum saturated fat grams (10% of calories) for specific calorie levels:

Total calories per day = _____.
Multiplied by 0.1 = _____.
Divided by 9 = _____.

Example:

2200 daily caloric intake × 0.1 = 220
220/9 = 24 grams of saturated fat

Quick Calculation of Recommended Fat Intake

In order to estimate the number of grams of fat an active adult can eat per day and not exceed the maximum 30% level of calories from fat, divide ideal weight by 2. To determine ideal weight, see page 231.

Example:

The maximum daily intake of fat grams for a 128-pound female is 64 and for a 160-pound male, 80.

> 128-pound female/2 = 64 grams fat
> and
> 160-pound male/2 = 80 grams fat

TABLE 1.2

Fat and Cholesterol Content of Common Foods

Item	Portion Size	Cholesterol (mg)	Fat (g)
Angel food cake	1 slice	0	0.1
American cheese, processed	1 ounce	27	8.9
Apple, raw	1 medium	0	0.5
Avocado	1 medium	0	30.0
Bacon, pork, broiled	3 medium slices	16	9.4
Beef, prime rib, roasted	3.5 ounces	85	33.9
Beef, brain, simmered	3.5 ounces	2054	12.5
Beef, kidney, simmered	3.5 ounces	387	3.4
Bread, whole wheat	1 slice	0	1.6
Butter	1 tablespoon	33	12.2
Chicken, dark meat with skin, roasted	3.5 ounces	91	15.8
Egg	1 large	213	5.0
Frank, beef	2 ounces	35	16.3
Lard	1 tablespoon	12	12.8

continued

produces cholesterol, however, it is not necessary to include it in the diet.

Cholesterol Requirements

Currently, the American Heart Association recommends that cholesterol intake be limited to 100 milligrams per 1,000 calories with a maximum intake of 300 milligrams per day. It is easy to exceed this number when the diet is rich in dairy products and meat. For example, one ham, egg, and cheese sandwich with about 245 milligrams of cholesterol will nearly meet the quota for a day, while one large beef, cheese, and chili pepper burrito yielding around 170 milligrams of cholesterol provides more than half of the maximum recommended amount.

Strategies to Reduce Total and/or Saturated Fat and/or Cholesterol in Menu Selections

In restaurants, diners often request items low in total fat, saturated fat, and/or cholesterol. Steps can be taken to help diners meet these concerns.

Lean Meat, Fish, and Poultry Selections Compared

Meat is a major source of fat in the American diet. The preferred choices are generally lean fish, chicken, turkey, and veal selections. Lean selections of beef, pork, and lamb usually contain more fat than the preferred choices, but red meats are slimmer now and lean ones in moderation are perfectly acceptable.

FAT AND CHOLESTEROL CONTENT OF MEAT, FISH, AND POULTRY
A lean fish selection is preferred over one of poultry or meat and a lean poultry selection is still generally better than one of lean meat. In comparison, a low-fat fish like haddock is nearly fat free, while skinless chicken breast meat yields a bit more fat, and lean beef like sirloin contains a substantial amount more. The amount of cholesterol in the three items is not much different, but again fish contains the least, chicken a bit more, and beef the most (see Table 1.3).

Seafood

Most fish and shellfish contain relatively little cholesterol and the small amount of fat most yield is primarily unsaturated (see Table

1.4). Those fish with the least amount of fat or those in the low-fat category include blue, cod, haddock, pike, snapper, sea bass, and whiting. Those with a bit more fat or in the medium-fat fish category include catfish, swordfish, and rainbow trout.

Some fish do derive more than 30% of their calories per serving from fat but at the same time are high in omega-3 fatty acids. They include albacore, anchovies, bluefin tuna, herring, shad, salmon, and mackerel. They should be prepared using techniques which require little or no additional fat.

Previously, shellfish was believed to be high in cholesterol. New analysis by the Food and Drug Administration shows this is not true of most types. The cholesterol in oysters, clams, mussels, and scallops is around 30–50 milligrams per 3 ounces. In comparison, 3 ounces of cod or haddock, low-fat fish, contains about the same amount, and an equal portion of lean beef or skinless chicken breast meat contains almost double the cholesterol. The 213 milligrams of cholesterol in an egg yolk far exceeds the quantity in these shellfish. Lobster contains a bit more cholesterol than oysters, clams, mussels, and scallops—75–85 milligrams per 3 ounces—and shrimp the most—130 milligrams per 3-ounce portion. For this reason, the American Heart Association recommends diners limit their intake to one 3-ounce portion of cooked shrimp or lobster per week.

Imitation crab meat, also known as "surimi," is formed from minced and washed white-fleshed fish like pollock or whiting which is mixed with carbohydrates, salt, and additives. Then it's cooked, flavored, and colored to resemble more expensive crab, lobster, or scallops. Like the whitefish it is made from, it contains

TABLE 1.2 (Continued)

Item	Portion Size	Cholesterol (mg)	Fat (g)
Margarine, corn	1 tablespoon	0	11.4
Milk, skim	8 ounces	4	0.4
Milk, whole	8 ounces	33	8.2
Olives, ripe	6 small	0	1.8
Olive oil	1 tablespoon	0	13.5
Peanuts, dry roasted	1 ounce	0	14.0
Peanut butter	1 tablespoon	0	8.5
Potato chips	1 ounce	0	9.8
Shortening, soybean + cottonseed	1 tablespoon	0	12.8
Sour cream, cultured	1 tablespoon	5	2.5
Thousand island dressing	1 tablespoon	2	1.6
Tuna, light, canned in water	3 ounces	25	0.7
Turkey breast tenderloins, cooked	3.5 ounces	66	2.0

Source: Data from J.A.T. Pennington (1994). *Bowes & Church's Food Values of Portions Commonly Used.* Philadelphia: J. B. Lippincott Co.

TABLE 1.3

Fat and Cholesterol in 3.5 Ounces of Lean Meat, Fish, and Poultry

Item	Calories	Fat (g)	Percentage of Fat Calories	Cholesterol (mg)
Haddock, cooked by dry heat	111	.9	7	73
Chicken light meat, skinless, roasted	173	4.5	23	85
Beef sirloin, select, 0 fat trim, broiled	195	7.6	35	89

Source: Data from J.A.T. Pennington (1994). *Bowes & Church's Food Values of Portions Commonly Used.* Philadelphia: J. B. Lippincott Co.

TABLE 1.4

Fat and Cholesterol Content of Seafood

Item	Portion Size	Calories	Fat (g)	Percentage of Fat Calories	Cholesterol (mg)	Unsaturated Fat (g)
Anchovy, raw	3 ounces	111	4.1	33	-	2.4
Bluefish	3 ounces	74	0.9	11	66	2.4
Catfish, channel	3 ounces	99	3.6	33	49	2.3
Clam	4 large	63	0.8	11	29	0.3
Cod, Pacific	3 ounces	70	0.5	6	31	0.3
Crab, Alaskan king	3 ounces	71	0.5	6	35	-
Crab, imitation from "surimi"	3 ounces	87	1.1	11	17	-
Haddock	3 ounces	74	0.6	7	49	0.3
Herring, Pacific	3 ounces	166	11.8	64	65	7.9
Lobster, northern	3 ounces	77	0.8	9	81	-
Mackerel, Pacific and Jack	3 ounces	133	6.7	45	40	3.9
Mussels, blue	3 ounces	73	1.9	23	24	0.9
Oysters, eastern	6 medium	58	2.1	33	46	0.8
Pike, northern	3 ounces	75	0.6	7	33	0.3
Salmon, coho	3 ounces	124	5.1	37	33	3.3
Scallops, mixed species	6 large	75	0.6	7	28	0.2
Sea Bass	3 ounces	82	1.7	19	35	1.0
Shad, American	3 ounces	167	11.7	63	-	-
Shrimp	12 large	90	1.5	15	130	0.8
Snapper	3 ounces	85	1.1	12	31	0.6
Swordfish	3 ounces	103	3.4	30	33	2.1
Trout, rainbow	3 ounces	100	2.9	26	48	1.9
Tuna, bluefin	3 ounces	122	4.2	31	32	2.6
Whiting	3 ounces	77	1.1	13	57	0.6

Source: Data from J.A.T. Pennington (1994). *Bowes & Church's Food Values of Portions Commonly Used.* Philadelphia: J. B. Lippincott Co.

little fat or saturated fat, and because of the added carbohydrates, has only 20–30 milligrams of cholesterol per 3-ounce portion.

HANDLING SEAFOOD

Seafood is a wholesome, high-protein, nutrient-rich food, well deserved of its healthy reputation. The FDA estimates less than one-quarter of 1% of all food-borne illness is attributed to seafood

(P. Parker, "Seafood Service" 1994. A supplement to *Restaurant Business* Inc. Publications, p. 10). The following tips will help food service professionals ensure that the quality of the seafood they serve is top notch.

1. Purchase fish from a reputable purveyor. The core temperature of fresh whole fish or portions should be 30–32° F ($-1°$ C), and frozen fish, 0° F ($-18°$ C) or less. Frozen fish with excessive frost or ice in its package or white, cottony blotches (freezer burn) should be refused. These are indicators that the fish has been thawed and refrozen.

2. Store unfrozen whole or filleted fish at 30–32° F ($-1°$ C) and thaw frozen fish in the refrigerator. In some cases, seafood (small portions) can be cooked from the frozen state.

3. Check fresh mollusks (oysters, mussels, and clams) for identification tags certifying that they were harvested in clean water and retain these tags for 90 days.

4. Avoid cross-contamination of raw and cooked fish by sanitizing equipment between uses, especially knives and cutting boards.

5. Keep in mind that fish are naturally tender. Overcooking will cause them to become dry and tough. Fish is done when (a) the fish is just beginning to flake, not falling apart, (b) the flesh has turned from translucent to opaque (generally white), and (c) if there is a bone present, it is no longer pink.

SEAFOOD SAFETY

It is true that some species of fish can cause diners to become sick. For those who are concerned about the safety of the fish they eat, the Center for Science in the Public Interest (which can be reached at 202-332-9110) recommends these precautions. In addition to being heart-healthy, lean fish are recommended because they do not contain the chemicals that accumulate in higher fat fish. Cooked shellfish are also generally acceptable, but raw forms like oysters, clams, and mussels can cause hepatitis or gastroenteritis. High-risk individuals or those with AIDS; chronic alcohol abuse; liver, stomach, or blood disorders; cancer; diabetes; and kidney disease are advised to eat their mollusks cooked.

Because of its mercury content, swordfish, shark, and fresh tuna steaks are recommended no more than once a week, and in the case of pregnant women, no more than once a month. Canned tuna contains lower levels of mercury than the tuna made into

TABLE 1.5

Fat Content of Chicken

Item	Percentage Fat Calories
Chicken breast, skinless	20
Chicken thigh, skinless	47
Chicken breast, with skin	35
Chicken thigh, with skin	56

Source: Data from J.A.T. Pennington (1994). *Bowes & Church's Food Values of Portions Commonly Used.* Philadelphia: J. B. Lippincott Co.

steaks and sushi; therefore, a maximum of about two medium-sized cans per week is generally okay. Species of fish from the tropical areas can also cause food-borne illness. Grouper, snapper, amberjack, moray eel, and barracuda may be contaminated with ciguatoxin, but hogfish, tropical mackerels, and certain trigger fish may also be dangerous.

Ciguatera poisoning can produce symptoms including diarrhea along with abdominal pain, nausea, and possibly vomiting followed by aches throughout the body and sensations that hot foods like steaming chicken broth taste cold and cold foods like ice water taste hot. Bluefish are more likely to contain PCBs. They, along with lake trout and other freshwater fish caught in inland lakes may contain the carcinogen dioxin. Finally, when bonito, fresh tuna, swordfish, bluefish, and mahi mahi are allowed to decompose through time and temperature abuse, they can produce scomboid poisoning.

Again, as discussed, some seafood may be contaminated, but the number is small. Most seafood is very low in fat and much of it is loaded with B vitamins and minerals (iron, zinc, selenium, and copper). Diners like the taste of seafood and like eating it when dining out. Food service professionals can select from over 250 species of seafood available commercially. It should not be overlooked by chefs for the range of heart-healthy textures and tastes it can add to the menu.

Poultry

The fat content of poultry may be more than fish or shellfish, but it's lower than red meat and both its taste and price are popular with customers. Chicken and turkey, two of the most popular forms of poultry, are both low in fat. Of the two, turkey tends to be the leanest.

DARK VERSUS WHITE MEAT POULTRY

Dark chicken and turkey thigh and leg meat are typically cheaper and more moist and flavorful than their white breast meat, but are also higher in fat.

The fat content of dark versus white meat can be illustrated with chicken (see Table 1.5). The percentage of fat in skinless chicken thigh meat is more than double that in skinless breast meat. Also, the percentage of fat calories in skinless chicken breast meat is substantially less than the 30% recommended, while the percentage of fat calories in skinless chicken thigh meat exceeds the recommended level.

POULTRY PARTS

In the case of packaged poultry products, if one of the ingredients on the food label is a poultry part such as a breast, leg, or wing, it means that the item contains both poultry meat and the fatty skin. When the list says breast meat, leg meat, or wing meat, on the other hand, the meat alone is in the product.

CHICKEN'S SKIN COLOR

With regard to the color of the chicken's skin, it is not an indication of its fat content or taste. The color of the skin depends on the breed and the chicken's diet. When chickens are fed diets rich in carotene (present in marigolds, etc.), their skins and egg yolks become more yellow or orange.

FREE-RANGE CHICKEN

While free-range chickens sound like healthy alternatives to regular chickens, likely they aren't, and further, are double to triple the price of traditionally raised birds. It is generally believed that free-range chickens, which are allowed to roam freely and forage for food, get more exercise than those confined to chicken coops, and, thus, accumulate less fat. Current studies do not support this belief or claims that free-range chickens are better sources of vitamins and minerals than regular chickens.

It is also commonly believed that free-range chickens subsist on more "natural" foods or ones free of antibiotics, pesticides, and other chemicals. This may not be the case either. Since there is no legal definition or certification for the term free-range chicken, there's no guarantee that free-range chickens are raised in any special manner.

With regard to unique flavors often attributed to free-range chickens, blind taste tests do not support this contention either.

Moreover, one study (Staff. 1994, January. "Free-Range Chickens: Not Necessarily a Better Bird." *Environmental Nutrition*, p. 7) revealed free-range chickens are almost twice as likely to be contaminated with salmonella bacteria as conventionally raised birds. It only makes sense because free-range chickens spend more time outside and, thus, are exposed to more potential sources of salmonella bacteria—soil, insects, and fecal matter dropping from birds flying overhead.

The fact that chickens are labeled "organically grown" is no assurance the birds are more nutritious than those raised by traditional methods either. See discussion of organic foods in Chapter 5.

KOSHER POULTRY

Likewise, kosher poultry is no more nutritious than regular poultry. It contains the same amount of fat and cholesterol and often more sodium than its nonkosher counterparts. Kosher poultry is regulated by a set of dietary laws which require it be salted after slaughtering to draw out its blood. In terms of amount, one study (S. Margen and the editors of the University of California at Berkeley *Wellness Letter*, 1992. *The Wellness Encyclopedia of Food and Nutrition*, p. 390. New York: Random House) revealed that the sodium in 8 ounces of kosher meat was 500 milligrams versus 150 milligrams in nonkosher. On the other hand, some producers claim they wash their birds to remove the excess sodium. Like regular poultry, kosher poultry is mechanically eviscerated and processed.

FAT UNDER POULTRY SKIN

The fat that lies under chicken, turkey, and other poultry's skin is a concern when cooking healthy. It even places white breast meat in the over-30%-calories-from-fat food category. Removing the skin before cooking may cut its fat by as much as one-third but at the same time, the poultry often becomes dry when cooked without its outer protective covering.

There is good news. A study published in the *New England Journal of Medicine* (September 13, 1990, p. 759) showed that if chicken is cooked with its skin on and removed before serving, it will be equivalent to serving a piece of chicken cooked without its skin. The study showed that very little fat is absorbed from the chicken's skin to its meat during cooking. The catch is that the chicken's skin must be removed before serving.

FLAVORING POULTRY TO BE SERVED SKINLESS

With this information in hand, a variety of low-fat chicken and other poultry dishes can be created which are moist and juicy. One method to add flavor to poultry items without fat or salt is to stuff blends of herbs, spices, and other seasoning ingredients under the skin of poultry selections; grill, bake, or roast the birds with their skins on; and then remove them before serving. Some examples of flavoring agents which might be tried are an Italian-style chunky tomato mixture hinting of freshly minced basil and garlic; a spicy hot south-of-the-border blend from finely chopped tomatoes, cilantro, and chili peppers; a Polynesian concoction made by seasoning an onion puree with coconut (extract), freshly minced ginger and garlic and orange zest; or a Moroccan-style creation of freshly grated ginger spiced with freshly ground cinnamon bark and clove berries.

To prevent skinless poultry products from drying when cooking with dry heat, their flesh can be protected with coatings made from bread, cracker, or cereal crumbs or mashed or shredded vegetables like potatoes. Taste can be added to skinless poultry products without fat by rubbing with freshly ground spices or freshly minced herbs, marinating with flavorful mixtures, glazing with clear, sweet, or starch-thickened savory sauces, or napping with heartier ones of fruits or vegetables.

For example, skinless cornish game hens are low in fat and still delicious when broiled brushed with a glaze made from an orange marmalade-like spread, balsamic vinegar, and freshly minced tarragon, and tandoori-style chicken drumsticks (see page 80) are equally good when skinless legs are rubbed with sweet red paprika and marinated at least 24 hours in a spicy yogurt mixture before grilling.

When cooking skinless poultry products by moist methods like steaming, poaching, simmering, braising, stewing, or making into fricassees or blanquettes, concerns about drying are eliminated. As far as taste, poultry will absorb the flavors of the cooking juices. They can be thickened into low-fat sauces and served with the poultry selections if desired. Cooking broths can be made from a variety of low-fat ingredients including rich stock, wine, beer, vegetables and fruits and their juices, herbs, spices, and condiments like low-sodium soy sauce.

GROUND TURKEY

Ground turkey and chicken may serve as low-fat options for all or part of the ground beef or pork in dishes. Ground turkey is relatively inexpensive; ground chicken generally costs a bit more. Both ground forms are difficult to distinguish from ground beef or pork when seasoned. Because both are low in fat, however, drying can be a problem. This can be prevented by using moist methods of cooking or cooking without liquid or fat only until no longer pink and combining with moisture-holding ingredients.

For example, juicy, spicy, pan-broiled, apple turkey burgers might be produced by blending ground turkey with coarsely shredded apples and rye bread crumbs and seasoning with a splash of brandy and sprinkle of freshly ground spices. Similarly, light, moist, mini turkey balls with lots of taste might be created by combining ground turkey, mashed potatoes, and minced onions, seasoning with freshly ground allspice, shaping into small balls, and braising in a starch-thickened, creamy chicken gravy.

When turkey and chicken are ground in-house or by a butcher from fresh white meat such as breast cutlets or tenderloins, chefs

TABLE 1.6

Lean Beef Cuts*

Beef Cut	Total Fat (g)	Saturated Fatty Acids (g)	Calories	Choles- terol (mg)
Eye of round	5.5	2.1	155	59
Top round	5.3	1.8	162	72
Tenderloin	7.9	3.1	174	72
Round tip	6.4	2.3	162	69
Top loin	7.6	3.0	172	65
Sirloin	7.4	3.0	177	76

Source: USDA (1981). Nutritive Value of Foods, Agriculture Handbooks 8-1 to 8-13. Washington, DC: U.S. Government Printing Office.
*The nutritional information listed is for 3 ounces of meat, cooked and trimmed of visible fat.

can be confident that the meat is very lean. Some processors sell ground poultry only from breast meat too. A product's label will provide this information.

Even if turkey or chicken is processed from higher fat dark meat rather than white, it is still likely lower in fat than ground beef or pork. Ground chicken usually comes from dark meat only and contains about 3 grams of fat and 50 calories per ounce. Ground turkey is generally a combination of white and dark meat and runs about 2 grams of fat and 40 calories per ounce. Chicken and turkey both lose a few calories during cooking. This brings their fat and calorie count to less than even extra-lean beef. Because of their higher fat and cholesterol content, both chicken and turkey ground with their skins and added fat are undesirable for use in the healthy kitchen.

WHOLE TURKEYS

When buying whole turkeys, the self-basting type are not recommended. They contain commercial basting solutions which are high in fat.

As a side note, there is no need to be concerned when turkey roasted in a gas oven develops a pink area beneath its surface. It can form when carbon monoxide reacts with nitric oxide from the gas. Nitric oxide can also come from bacon or root vegetables cooked in the same oven. The outcome is a slight nitrite cure like the one that gives ham its pink color.

Lean Meat

Beef, lamb, and pork generally contain more fat then fish, chicken, turkey, or veal, but they are slimmer now and lean red meat in moderation is perfectly acceptable.

BEEF

Through improved breeding techniques and animal nutrition, muscle has replaced much of the fat in today's beef animals. As a result, lean cuts of beef have become popular menu choices with health-conscious diners.

Lean beef cuts. The beef industry has identified six of its "skinniest" cuts or those lowest in fat, cholesterol, and calories (see Table 1.6). They are eye of round, round tip, top round, top loin, sirloin, and tenderloin. Each of these cuts has less than 8 grams of fat and 180 calories per 3-ounce cooked portion.

Restaurants offer lean cuts of beef under many names:

Eye of Round	*Round Tip*	*Top Loin*
Roast or Steak	Kabob	New York, Club, Delmonico, or Strip Steak
Tenderloin	*Sirloin*	*Top Round*
Filet Mignon	Sirloin Steak	London Broil
Filet Steak	London Broil	
Medallions	Kabob	
Tips as Kabob		

Lean beef cuts can be made into an enormous variety of healthy selections. For starters, beef sirloin steak might be sauteed in a nonstick pan, sliced thin and napped with a spicy red pepper tomato sauce; or beef top round can be marinated in a broth flavored with red wine, herbs, spices and vegetables, simmered until fork tender, and topped with its cooking juices thickened with gingersnap crumbs.

Beef quality grades. When purchasing beef, lower grade cuts contain less fat than higher grade ones. For example, beef is graded from highest to lowest in the following order: prime, choice, select (previously good), standard, commercial, utility, cutter, canner. By serving select or standard grades rather than choice, the beef will yield on the average 25% or less fat. The four lowest grades of beef (commercial, utility, cutter, and canner) are normally not sold directly to the public.

One drawback is that lower grade beef is less tender. This can be rectified by breaking down the meat's connective tissues mechanically by pounding, grinding, cubing, or slicing across the grain; by marinating in low-fat mixtures; or by cooking with a moist method like stewing, pot roasting, or braising.

Very lean beef products. Special lines of very lean beef are also available. For example, Vermillion Valley (Covington Ranch) in Yankton, South Dakota markets a variety of lean beef cuts and products, including roasts, rib eyes, tenderloins, and ground beef, all with significantly reduced amounts of fat, calories, and cholesterol. It comes from a breed of Piedmontese cattle which was imported from the Italian Alps. This particular brand was developed through a selective breeding and feeding program. It is produced without fillers or preservatives. A typical 3-ounce serving of Covington Ranch beef tenderloin has less than 2 grams of fat, 47 milligrams of cholesterol, and 84 calories. For additional information, Vermillion Valley can be reached by phone at (800) 365-2333.

Other new lean beef products include Brae, zebu, beefalo, and Chianina Lite. They contain 25–85% less fat and 32–79% fewer calories than traditional forms of beef. Beefalo is a cross between Black Angus and bison, and the other three are produced from cattle which are fed special diets. The tastes and textures of the leaner beefs are quite unique.

Ground beef selections. Dishes containing ground beef continue to be popular menu items. For low-fat ground beef dishes, extra-lean ground beef is preferred, and ground round is even better. According to the United States Department of Agriculture (USDA) regulations, lean and extra-lean ground beef contain no more than 22.5% fat as compared to up to 30% in regular ground beef or regular hamburger.

Ground beef is often labeled by the percentage of lean beef that it contains, for example, 85% lean ground beef or not less than 73% lean. A good rule is to look for products with less than 10% fat by raw weight. The primal-cut origin of the meat can also provide a clue to the product's leanness. Ground round is the leanest and ground chuck the highest in fat. Ground sirloin falls in between but because it comes from the loin-sirloin area, it is usually the most expensive.

After crumbled ground beef and other meats are cooked and drained of fat, any fat remaining in the meats can be pressed from them by placing in a wire strainer.

When preparing shaped ground beef dishes like meatballs, meat loaf, and even patties, fat and cholesterol can be reduced by replacing part of the meat with other ingredients. They might be grains, preferably whole ones like brown rice or cracked wheat; whole grain bread, cereal, or low-fat cracker crumbs; dried legumes like kidney or garbanzo beans; or grated or minced vegetables like onions, carrots, tomatoes, or bell peppers. For example, an Italian-style meat loaf might be created by extending ground round with diced tomatoes and bell peppers, minced onions and garlic, and flavoring with Italian seasonings.

Similarly, to cut the fat in the meatballs of a hearty Mexican-style stew, extra-lean ground beef might be mixed with whole wheat bread crumbs. When paired with a rich broth, lots of tomatoes, red beans and corn, and for spice, of course, some green chilies, a smaller portion of meat will go unnoticed. It might be offered as a homestyle lunch or dinner main course selection.

Low-fat ground beef replacements. In the past few years, burgers and ground beef products that range from 7.5%–9% fat by weight have become available. Part of the fat in many of these items is replaced with water and a small amount of carrageenan, a powdery white vegetable gum derived from seaweed. The carrageenan binds with water to retain the meat's natural moisture, resulting in a juicier burger.

Other ground beef products are prepared by blending ground beef with fat substitutes. One is prepared with a substance called Leanesse, a fat substitute derived from oat flour. Upon heating, Leanesse changes into a gel that mimics the texture and mouthfeel of fat. But, while fat supplies 9 calories per gram, Leanesse gel contains less than 1 calorie.

Many of the low-fat ground beef products are expensive and some are very high in sodium. Most of the products cook more quickly than regular ground beef and become overcooked and dry easily because of their reduced fat content.

Low-fat and cholesterol blends of ground beef may be appropriate for some food service operations. Like all the reduced fat and cholesterol products available, it is important for an operation to try them to determine if they meet its standards.

Reducing fat in ground beef by the extraction method. Cooking techniques have also been proposed by researchers which substantially reduce both the saturated fat and cholesterol in cooked, crumbled ground meat. In one method, some of the saturated fat and cholesterol was extracted from raw ground meat by cooking the meat in vegetable oil at 175° F (80° C), followed by rinsing with boiling water (D. M. Small, C. Oliva, and A. Tercyak, 1991. "Chemistry in the Kitchen—Making Ground Meat More Healthful." *New England Journal of Medicine 324*, 73–77).

In comparison with meat which was stir-fried and rinsed with boiling water, about 10% more fat was reduced in the extraction method than in the stir-fry method. The unique feature of this extraction system is that the fat remaining in the meat had a significantly lower level of saturated fatty acids than the stir-fried meat. The saturated fatty acids seem to have been extracted from the meat by the vegetable oil and partially replaced by unsaturated fatty acids found in the oil.

Cholesterol levels were reduced significantly in the meat using the extraction method (43.2%) versus the stir-fry (15.6%) method too.

While recipes using meat prepared by the extraction method will be lower in fat and cholesterol than the same dishes prepared by stir-frying meat, this study dealt only with crumbled ground meat products. Such meat would be suitable for use in recipes calling for crumbled ground meat like tacos, chili, and spaghetti sauce rather than whole meat products, such as steak, or formed ones such as hamburger patties. Whole and formed meat products will behave differently using these two methods, because of their decreased surface areas.

PORK

Historically, hogs were prized for their lean meat as well as their fat, which was converted to lard. In the 1940s, when plant oils became more economical than lard, leaner, meatier hogs were produced using breeding techniques. Today, it is estimated that pork is 23% leaner than previously.

The pork industry, not to be outdone by the beef industry, has identified eight fresh pork cuts that contain less than 9 grams of fat and 190 calories per 3-ounce cooked portion (see Table 1.7). These cuts come from the loin or pork leg. They are the tenderloin, boneless sirloin chop, rib chop, center loin chop, boneless

TABLE 1.7

Lean Pork Cuts*

Pork Cut	Total Fat (g)	Saturated Fatty Acids (g)	Calories	Cholesterol (mg)
Tenderloin	4.1	1.4	139	67
Boneless Sirloin Chop	5.7	1.9	164	78
Rib Chop	8.3	2.9	186	69
Center Loin Chop	6.9	2.5	172	70
Boneless Loin Roast	6.1	2.2	165	66
Boneless Top Loin Chop	6.6	2.3	173	68
Sirloin Roast	8.7	3.1	184	73
Boneless Rib Roast	8.6	3.0	182	71

Source: USDA, HNIS. *Composition of Foods, Agricultural Handbook 8-5 (1979) and 8-10 (1991).* Washington, DC: U.S. Government Printing Office.
*The nutritional information listed is for 3 ounces, cooked and trimmed of visible fat.

loin roast, boneless top loin chop, sirloin roast, and boneless rib roast.

When ham is on the menu, diners eating healthfully can be accommodated by serving those with less than 10% fat by weight, including both water-added and dry-cured ham.

LAMB

More restaurants are offering lamb on the menu than ever before. For low-fat dishes, the National Live Stock and Meat Board has identified six of lamb's leanest cuts or ones with less than 200 calories per 3-ounce trimmed, cooked portion. They are shank half leg roast, sirloin roast, loin chops, blade chops, foreshank, and rack (back). For example, broiled herb marinated leg of lamb might make a healthy, mouth-watering main course selection but be equally tasty and nutritious layered between slices of whole grain bread or tossed with fresh pasta.

VEAL

Veal is the meat from calves three months or younger in age. Because veal comes from such young animals, most of its cuts are low in fat. Those cuts identified by the National Live Stock and Meat Board which are particularly lean or contain less than 200 calories per 3-ounce trimmed, cooked portion are veal cutlet, arm steak, blade steak, sirloin chop, loin chop, and rib roast.

Veal may be a smart meat choice for diners monitoring their fat intake. However, some are opposed to its inclusion on the menu. They consider the manner in which milk-fed veal is produced to be cruel, and, as a result, advocate a "no veal this meal" policy.

GAME MEAT AND BIRDS

Farm-raised game, ranging from squab and rabbit to buffalo and venison, is appearing on more restaurants' menus. Nutritionally, game meat looks good (see Table 1.8). Many types are low in fat, cholesterol, and calories. An added benefit is that the animals are often raised free range without growth hormones or antibiotics.

In comparison to skinless breast of chicken, the fat content of antelope, bison, boar, deer, skinless guinea hen, and skinless breast of pheasant is similar. For a change from chicken and turkey, for example, guinea hen might be offered roasted, infused with madeira. Its impressive nutritional attributes along with its pleasantly gamey flavor will likely be appreciated by health-conscious diners.

Another meat which has received recent publicity for its low

TABLE 1.8

Fat and Cholesterol Content in a 3.5-Ounce Portion of Game Birds and Meats and Other Meats

Item	Calories	Fat (g)	Percentage of Fat Calories	Cholesterol (mg)
Antelope, roasted	150	2.7	16	126
Beefalo, roasted	188	6.3	30	58
Bison, roasted	143	2.4	15	82
Boar, wild, roasted	160	4.4	25	-
Deer, roasted	158	3.2	18	112
Duck, without skin, roasted	201	11.2	50	89
Goat, roasted	143	3.0	19	75
Guinea Hen, without skin, raw	110	2.5	20	63
Pheasant, without skin, raw	133	3.6	24	-
Quail, without skin, raw	134	4.5	30	-
Rabbit, roasted, domesticated	197	8.1	37	82
Rabbit, wild, stewed	173	3.5	18	123
Squab, without skin, raw	142	7.5	47	90

Source: Data from J.A.T. Pennington, 1994. *Bowes & Church's Food Values of Portions Commonly Used.* Philadelphia: J. B. Lippincott Co.

fat content is goat. Again, it is comparable in fat to skinless chicken breast.

Because game meat is lean and tender, for best results, with the exception of perhaps wild boar, it should be served rare to medium-rare. Tender cuts of buffalo and venison, in particular, are juicy and succulent when served rare. For example, when paired with sauteed wild mushrooms and napped with a red wine sauce, thin slices of venison roasted rare make a good healthy selection.

The low fat content of rabbit makes it another excellent choice for health-conscious diners. Similar to chicken, the mild flavored and tender young animals can be cooked in many ways. For a moist and faintly spicy dish, rabbit might be marinated in a mixture of cider, mustard, and thyme, roasted and garnished with buttery tasting apple slices; or for a healthy variation on a Spanish dish called conejo (rabbit) a la navarra, it might be braised in a Mediterranean-style chunky tomato sauce, flavored with white wine, and seasoned with fresh rosemary.

Quail is another relatively good choice. A whole bird contains only 134 calories and yields 30% of its calories from fat. It makes an elegant appetizer course served pan roasted, topped with a light parsley sauce, and presented on a bed of onion and red bell pepper compote.

Squab and duck are higher in fat than skinless chicken breast, but this can be partially remedied by removing their skins before cooking or serving. For example, skinless, boneless duck breasts might be briefly marinated in a dry spice mixture, seared in a hot pan until rare to medium-rare, and thinly sliced. Accompanied by a cool fruit sauce like mango salsa and crunchy wild rice, pan-broiled duck makes a healthy gourmet meal.

VARIETY MEATS

Variety meats such as livers, brains, sweetbreads, and kidneys are prohibitively high in fat and/or cholesterol. Diners watching their fat and/or cholesterol intakes are advised to limit their consumption of such meats and those dishes made from them to one or two servings per month. For example, health-conscious diners will likely be delighted when freshly baked, whole grain bread is served with a low cholesterol and fat lentil spread or roast garlic rather than head cheese or paté.

FRANKFURTERS

Fortunately, for those concerned about all the fat in wieners, things have changed a great deal in the last few years. Today, franks can be purchased with just 1 gram of fat or a mere 9 calories of fat per dog. They are produced by allowing some of the beef and pork traditionally found in hot dogs to remain and altering their water content and such ingredients as milk and vegetable proteins. The proteins bind to the water and meat and create a taste and mouthfeel that simulates the taste and mouthfeel of the higher fat counterparts.

There are also a number of hot dogs which appear to be low fat but aren't. The claims can be misleading because they simply refer to the fact that fat makes up a small percentage of the frank's weight. This is relatively meaningless in terms of nutritional health. The relevant fact is that each frank may contain substantial grams of fat, and in turn, the fat contributes to a high percentage of the frank's calories. For example, a frank with as much as 11 grams of fat or 73% of its calories from fat might be promoted as 90% fat free. Yet the fat in this single hot dog would account for about one-sixth of the maximum amount recommended daily in a 2,000 calorie diet.

It's a similar story for turkey and chicken franks. While poultry often contains less fat than beef or pork, this is generally not true for hot dogs. Even poultry franks labeled 50% less fat can have as much as 10 grams of fat per wiener or obtain as much as 70% of their calories from fat. If a diner consuming 2,000 calories daily were to eat two hot dogs, as many do, these would equate to nearly a third of recommended daily fat intake.

When looking for low-fat hot dogs, select ones with less than 3 grams fat per ounce or those promoted as less than 10% fat by weight.

COLD CUTS

Cold cuts, other lunchtime sandwich favorites, are high in fat and cholesterol too. Freshly roasted, baked, broiled, or grilled lean meats and poultry are healthier choices. For example, a low-fat and easy to eat chicken sandwich might be prepared by combining cubed, roasted, skinless, chicken breast meat with shredded carrots, and diced celery, coating with nonfat yogurt and reduced fat Italian dressing, and serving in a whole wheat pita. This zesty garden chicken pocket is appealing yet healthy.

PERCENTAGE OF FAT IN MEAT PRODUCTS BY WEIGHT

The percentage of fat by weight is stated on the labels of many meat products. This is not to be confused with the percentage of calories from fat. While the percentage of fat in a meat product might be small by weight, the amount of fat might calculate to a substantial percentage in terms of calories.

Again, a good rule is to select lean meats with less than 10% fat content by raw weight or less than 3 grams fat per ounce.

Preparing Meat, Seafood, and Poultry

Fat, cholesterol, and calories can be reduced by trimming meat, seafood, and poultry of any visible fat. Whether the fat is removed from some types of meat before or after cooking, at least in the case of cholesterol, may not be significant. A study reported that cooking beef steaks and pork chops with or without the external fat did not affect the total amount of cholesterol in the lean meat, while lamb chops cooked with external fat had more fat in their lean meat than those chops cooked with their external fat trimmed (S. S. Swize, K. B. Harris, J. W. Savel, and H. R. Cross, June 1992.

"Cholesterol Content of Lean and Fat from Beef, Pork, and Lamb Cuts." *Journal of Food Composition and Analysis 5*, 160–67). Recall though, regardless of whether the external fat is trimmed from meat before or after cooking, there is still invisible fat in the meat in the form of marbling.

Reducing Meat, Seafood, and Poultry Portion Sizes

Reducing portion size or eliminating meat, seafood, or poultry from the menu is another way to cut calories, cholesterol, and/or fat from main course selections. Current dietary guidelines recommend two 3-ounce cooked portions per day. Visually, this amount equates to a portion about the size of a deck of cards or a cassette tape.

Three techniques can make this an easy task.

♦ **Step One**   Offer more combination dishes made from small amounts of meat, seafood, and poultry cut into small pieces or thin slices and larger ones of grains, vegetables, and/or fruits. The following are a few examples.

MAIN COURSE SALADS

For example, Chinese duck salad might be featured as a glamorous, yet relatively low fat offering when prepared with 3 ounces of thinly sliced, broiled, skinless, duck breast meat layered on a bed of shredded lettuce and garnished with crispy, baked wonton strips. Or, for a hearty, homestyle, low-fat main course salad, hot potato, sausage, and broccoli salad might be suggested—a 3-ounce portion of mouth-watering, lean ground pork sausage balls complemented by steamed, brilliant green broccoli spears and new, red-skinned potatoes, all gently tossed in a freshly squeezed lime and vegetable-thickened dressing.

PASTAS

Pasta primavera has the light and fresh appeal of a summer special. Three ounces of grilled, skinless, chicken breast meat seems substantial when cut into julienne strips and combined with extra vegetables and cholesterol- and saturated fat free noodles made without egg yolks.

Note: Whether flavored or plain, if eggs are an ingredient in pasta, a standard, 2-ounce, dried serving will yield an additional 2 to 3 grams of fat and about 55 milligrams of cholesterol. While flavored pastas might have more appeal than everyday wheat pastas, their nutrients and calories are comparable. On the other hand, their price often isn't. They can be as much as six times higher.

RAGOUTS AND STEWS

Likewise, it is hard to tell there's only 3 ounces of lean, tender beef cubes in a country ragout when simmered in a rich brown stock with lots of sliced and cubed, flavorful, winter vegetables. It is also hard to tell that there's a mere 3 ounces of lean lamb cubes in a spicy lamb stew when it is combined with fresh, tender leaves of spinach and baby new potatoes in a well-seasoned, tomato-flavored broth.

STIR-FRIES

A veal and asparagus stir-fry may look like a lot of food and be a humongous portion too. Yet, likely, because of all the vegetables in this dish, there's no need for more than 3 ounces of the delicate-flavored and fine-textured cooked meat.

♦ **Step Two** Maximize the presence of small amounts of meat, seafood, and poultry.

AMERICAN-STYLE OFFERINGS

When meat, seafood, and poultry selections are served in the traditional American mode along with a vegetable and starch, a reduction in portion size might be minimized by cutting these items into small pieces or slicing them thin, fanning them out on the plate, and complementing them with larger portions of low-fat, high-carbohydrate vegetable and starch side dishes.

Smaller portions of meat, seafood, and poultry will stand out less if stuffed, mixed, layered, topped with or placed on beds of low-fat vegetables, fruits, or grains. For example, to reduce the serving size of a beef top round steak, it might be stuffed with a mixture of sauteed spinach, onions, and garlic and seasoned with fresh marjoram. In the case of a pork tenderloin roast, a smaller portion of meat can be made to look large by forming a ribbon of colorful vegetables through its center. To create the ribbon, the meat is rolled with a filling of diced zucchini, carrots, and freshly minced basil and thyme and after roasting, sliced into circular rounds.

Similarly, a 3-ounce portion of Asian-style steamed squid might be made to appear bountiful by mounding over a bed of shredded iceberg lettuce; likewise for a grilled, skinless, half chicken breast on a toasted, whole wheat bun by topping with lots of shredded cabbage, thinly sliced cucumbers and tomatoes and sprouts.

MAKING HIGH-FAT OR CHOLESTEROL-RICH MEATS, SEAFOOD, AND POULTRY VISIBLE

In some recipes, the amount of high-fat or cholesterol-rich meat, seafood, or poultry can be reduced greatly by placing a small quantity in a prominent place where it will be observed and appreciated. For example, a small amount of minced, crisp bacon can add lots of flavor to a dish of mild, creamy cannellini beans and, at the same time, be perceived as more by sprinkling on top.

- ◆ **Step Three** Best yet, offer fewer or no items from the meat, seafood, and poultry group in menu selections. When evaluating the fat content of an item, many dishes will work with less or no fatty or high-cholesterol meat, seafood, or poultry.

MEAT AND POULTRY ANALOGS

When a meat- or poultry-free dish is desired with the flavor and texture of meat or poultry, meat and poultry analogs are an option. Their fat content generally exceeds the 30% recommended level, but they are cholesterol-free. In addition to ground beef, the flavors and textures of any number of meat and poultry products, ranging from fried chicken, bacon, and ham to hot dogs and sausage, have been simulated primarily from textured vegetable (soy) protein. Canned, dried, frozen and freeze-dried forms are available alone and in combination with other ingredients.

DRIED BEANS, PEAS, AND LENTILS

In lieu of meat, poultry, or seafood, many diners are taking a second look at selections prepared with high-protein, low-fat, cholesterol-free dried beans, peas, and lentils. Dishes might be created to promote the attributes of a single bean, such as southern Louisiana-style red beans and rice, or several types of legumes, such as Indian-inspired three-bean, lentil, and pea stew.

Legumes are suitable substitutes for part or all of the ground meat in many meat-based recipes too. Chili con carne (no beans) is a good example. Some or all of the ground beef in the common Americanized version of this hearty dish might be replaced with more kidney beans or other legumes. The outcome is a lower fat and cholesterol selection and a dish that can still garner rave reviews.

Each pound of ground meat omitted in a recipe can be replaced with approximately 1 cup of dried beans or 2 cups of cooked or canned beans.

MEATY VEGETABLE SUBSTITUTES

Vegetables like eggplant and wild mushrooms cooked with low-sodium soy sauce make good meaty substitutes. Another meaty vegetable option is a few smoky-flavored, sun-dried tomatoes. For example, a rich and hearty, meatless, spicy black bean chili might be enriched with sun-dried tomatoes. The lack of meat will go unnoticed.

TABLE 1.9

Dry Heat Cooking Methods

Bake/Roast
To cook food surrounded by hot dry air.

Broil
To cook food with radiant heat from above.

Deep-fry
To cook food submerged in hot fat.

Grill
To cook food on an open grid over a heat source.

Pan broil
To cook food uncovered in a skillet or saute pan without fat and remove fat as it accumulates.

Pan fry
To cook in a moderate amount of fat in a pan over moderate heat.

Saute
To cook quickly in a small amount of fat.

Source: W. Gisslen (1995). *Professional Cooking.* New York: John Wiley & Sons.

Low-Fat Cooking Methods

DRY COOKING METHODS

When cooking healthy, the preferred methods are those that don't add fat, or that remove excess fat. Dry cooking methods (see Table 1.9) which allow fat within items to melt and drip away during cooking include baking, roasting, broiling, and grilling. Of course, it's essential to place items on a rack when baking or roasting. The grid on the broiler or grill provides a built-in rack when broiling and grilling. For every tablespoon of fat that drips away, 100 plus calories are being lost from fat.

Pan broiling is another healthy method of dry cooking. In this technique, products are cooked without adding fat and drippings are drained off as they form.

Unlike the preferred, dry cooking methods, sauteing and pan and deep frying, not only don't remove fat from dishes, they add it. These are methods which should be avoided if possible. When using dry cooking methods, best results will be achieved if foods are cooked only until done. Overcooking causes items to lose their natural juices and become dry.

Even pork does not need to be cooked to 185° F (85° C) or the stage of being dry and overcooked to eliminate the danger of trichinosis, as once believed. The parasite which causes food-borne illness is killed at 137° F (58° C). Therefore, pork cooked to the medium to medium well done stage or 150–155° F (65–68° C) is safe to eat. Even if cooked slightly more than this to 160–170° F (71–77° C), as most people prefer, pork will still be moist and juicy.

When cooking chicken, the flesh should be white in color and the juices should run clear. If a small area of the bone and flesh next to it retain a deep red hue, this is not an indication that the chicken is undercooked and not safe to eat. Today, chickens are sold younger than previously, an average of 7 to 9 weeks. As a result, the bones in such young birds are porous. During cooking, the bones can draw red pigment through them from the bone marrow. This causes the bones, and possibly a portion of the flesh next to them, to become stained. It is not harmful, and in fact, younger chickens with more porous bones tend to be more tender.

Baking in the healthy kitchen. Crispy crusted fish and chicken are Americans' favorites. There is no need for health-conscious diners to avoid them. To achieve a crispy crust without added fat, these selections can be coated with a cereal or cracker breading like crushed, oat cereal flakes or reduced-fat, whole wheat cracker crumbs and baked in the oven. To help the crumbs adhere to the items, they can be dipped in egg whites, nonfat yogurt, or skim milk rather than the traditional flour and whole-egg wash technique, and extra cholesterol and calories will be avoided.

For example, a healthy simulation of fried chicken might be prepared by coating skinless thighs with egg whites, dredging in cinnamon-flavored bran flake crumbs, and baking (see page 127). A healthy version of the fish part of fish n' chips can be achieved by baking sole fillets coated with corn flake crumbs, seasoned with orange zest and garlic and onion powders.

Meat loaf, another traditional favorite, can add unwanted fat and cholesterol to the menu. There's no need. Begin with lean ground meat like extra lean ground beef, veal, or ground skinless chicken or turkey white meat. Extend and flavor the meat with a grain or grain product like rolled oats, seasoning vegetables like garlic, onion, and bell peppers, dried fruits like currants if desired, and herbs and spices. Some chopped parsley, salt, and pepper would do but for some charm, try ground allspice, ginger, and cinnamon. Bind the meat loaf with egg whites rather than whole eggs, add a splash of hot pepper sauce for zip, and fruit or vegetable puree like tomato or peach for moisture. Bake it in a perforated loaf or perforated counter pan over another pan so that the excess fat drips off the loaf. It can be served hot but is almost better cold in sandwiches with a chutney.

Roasting in the healthy kitchen. Rather than pan- or deep-fried fish, roasted fish might be offered. For example, roasted, whole sea trout is equally as succulent and flavorful as fried or sauteed fillets but without any added fat and calories from oil or butter. For an interesting touch, roasted fish might be served to diners right from its baking dish.

While baking, roasting, broiling, and grilling are generally considered cooking methods reserved for meat, fish, and poultry items, sauteing and deep fat and pan frying can add lots of fat to vegetables too. They also are equally delicious baked, roasted, broiled and grilled.

For example, French fries and potato chips are high-fat, high-calorie vegetable favorites. Both can be replaced with low-fat, low-calorie flavorful roasted potatoes. Oven roasted potato wedges with rosemary might be offered hot out of the oven splashed with malt vinegar in lieu of French fries, and roasted slices of paper-thin, skin-on, Idaho potatoes, plain or seasoned with Cajun spices can substitute for potato chips.

When roasting large cuts of meat, cooking continuously at lower temperatures of 200–325° F (95–165° C) produces superior results. The outcomes are more juicy, flavorful, and tender meats. They are easier to carve and done more evenly from outside to in. Depending on an operation's production schedule, generally, the larger the cut of meat, the lower the temperature recommended for even cooking throughout. The disadvantage of low-temperature roasting is less surface browning and thus, less flavor. There is also the potential for bacterial growth due to the very low cooking temperature.

Grilling. Previously, if vegetables weren't coated in butter or a rich sauce, likely they were pan- or deep-fried. A healthy method to add a delicate, smoky flavor to vegetables and other foods without fat is grilling. For example, slices of eggplant might be grilled for a toasty flavor and then topped with an oil free marinara sauce; or summer vegetables, including yellow summer squash, bell peppers, corn on the cob, and zucchini can be served grilled and sprinkled with balsamic-rice vinegar dressing.

Many believe eating food cooked on the grill increases the risk of cancer. When using any cooking method in which high temperatures are reached, it is possible for potentially hazardous chemicals or ones carcinogenic for humans to be produced. High-temperature cooking methods include frying, broiling, roasting, baking, as well as grilling. Additionally, in grilling, smoke containing another group of carcinogens results when fat drips from the food into the heating element. As the smoke rises, it covers the food with the hazardous substance.

However, the risk of eating grilled food is small in comparison to the many other risks Americans indulge in routinely (smoking, high-fat diet). Several professional organizations, including the National Cancer Institute, the American Cancer Society, the American Institute for Cancer Research, and the U.S. Department of Agriculture do not think Americans should stop eating all foods which have been grilled, broiled, fried, roasted, or baked.

These organizations recommend that food service operations employ the following steps to make grilling as safe as possible.

1. Serve meat cooked to the medium stage rather than well done. The longer the food is kept over the heat, the greater the likelihood harmful chemicals will develop.

2. Grill foods as far away from the heat as possible. The black, charred spots which form when the flames strike the food are sites most concentrated in carcinogens.

3. Select lean cuts of meat, trim excess fat, and remove skin from poultry before grilling to prevent the fat from dripping onto the heating element and producing the carcinogen-containing smoke.

4. Partially cook food by relatively low-temperature (300° F (150° C) or less) cooking methods like poaching, simmering, or microwaving, and finish on the grill for the desired aroma and taste. Low-temperature cooking methods account for negligible formation of potential carcinogens. If not precooking meats, make sure they are completely thawed before grilling. This will reduce cooking time and prevent charring.

5. Grill meat on skewers. This method requires smaller pieces of meat to be used so cooking time will be reduced.

6. Use low-fat marinades on meat and other items to be grilled. This prevents fat from dripping into the source of heat and also reduces the total fat intake.

7. If grilling with charcoal, use regular charcoal made from hard wood. Soft woods burn at higher temperatures.

Broiling in the healthy kitchen. The term broiled has a very healthy connotation with diners, as does fish. Fish higher in fat such as salmon, swordfish, and shark are ideal cooked by this method. Served with low-fat fruit or vegetable salsas, they exude a fresh, light feeling. For example, shark steaks might be lightly marinated in a lemony garlic mixture, broiled, and presented garnished with a spicy papaya mango salsa.

Pan broiling in the healthy kitchen. In broiling, items are cooked with radiant heat from above. As its name suggests, in pan broiling, items are cooked in a saute pan or skillet uncovered without liquid, removing fat as it forms. This technique works well in operations without a grill or broiler. For example, rather than grilling or broiling extra-lean ground beef burgers seasoned with onions, bell peppers, and low-sodium worcestershire, they might be pan broiled.

My instructor explained the pan broiling technique to me some years ago using a pork chop as an example. These were her directions. First, trim the fat from the chop. Next, rub the trimmed fat over the bottom of the pan to prevent the meat from sticking. This was in the days before nonstick pans and vegetable cooking sprays were available. Finally, cook the chops in a pan on the range, removing fat as it accumulates until the chops are no longer

TABLE 1.10

Moist Heat Cooking Methods

Braise
To cook covered in a small amount of liquid with or without preliminary browning.

Boil
To cook in rapidly bubbling water or other liquid (212° F or 100° C).

Poach
To cook in hot water or other liquid (160–180° F or 71–82° C).

Simmer
To cook in gently bubbling liquid or water (185–205° F or 85–96° C).

Steam
To cook by direct contact with steam.

Source: W. Gisslen (1995). Professional Cooking. New York: John Wiley & Sons.

pink in the center but still moist and juicy and brown on the exterior.

With this in mind, a recipe for citrus-flavored pan-broiled pork chops was created. Pan-broiled, juicy, tender loin pork chops, seasoned with mustard powder, salt and pepper are lightly coated with a sauce made from freshly squeezed orange and lemon juices enhanced with freshly minced herbs.

MOIST COOKING METHODS

Moist methods of cooking (see Table 1.10) include steaming, poaching, simmering, boiling, and braising (pot roasts, swiss steaks, stews, fricassees, or blanquettes). They can be performed without fat or with only small amounts. It can be skimmed away in the cooking liquid along with any fat accumulating during the cooking process.

Steaming in the healthy kitchen. Steaming is a low-fat cooking method which works well with delicate items like fish and vegetables. It requires no fat either. For example, rather than fried egg rolls, steamed dumplings filled with vegetables, rice, tofu, or chicken might be offered. For a crisp texture without much fat, they can be sauteed in a lightly oiled pan a minute or two until golden.

For an elegant touch, steaming can be done en papillote (in parchment). When dishes like jumbo shrimp topped with pesto sauce or sliced potatoes seasoned with Italian herbs and spices are served this style, guests will likely say "simply divine." To release the tempting aromas inside the parchment packages, it is best to cut them open tableside.

Steaming in lettuce, banana, grape, and cabbage leaves or corn husks is an equally charming and healthy method of cookery. Fruits and vegetables, as well as any type of light fish fillet like red snapper or sea bass, are suited to cooking by this technique. For a tropical flavor, fillets might be marinated in a reduced sodium soy-flavored broth, seasoned with cilantro, wrapped in banana leaves, baked (steamed) and finished with pineapple salsa. Garnished with a cocktail pineapple they make a truly memorable meal.

Poaching in the healthy kitchen. While fruits, fish, and eggs are commonly poached, some fowl can be too. For example, turkey breast, whether served during the holidays or at another time of year, can be delicious poached. Sliced thin and napped with its cooking broth, thickened with pureed vegetables, and popping with ruby red cranberries (see page 76), it's a treat to both the eyes and palate.

Awesome results can be achieved with seafood by wrapping it along with flavoring agents in plastic and poaching in plain water. For example, shrimp might be poached enveloped in plastic along with an aromatic blend of fresh thyme, rosemary, and savory, minced garlic and shallots, slivered sun-dried tomatoes, and a splash of white wine and extra-virgin olive oil or sea scallops mixed with freshly grated ginger, minced green chilies, and lemon grass, sliced green onions, freshly squeezed lemon juice, light soy sauce, cracked pepper and aniseeds. In effect, when seafood is poached enclosed in plastic, it cooks in its own juices. Further, this low-fat, simple and flavorful method of poaching in a packet is quicker than poaching in the traditional style.

Simmering or boiling in the healthy kitchen. There's no need to add fat when simmering or boiling ingredients. While recipes often call for added butter or oil when boiling grains and their products like rice and pasta, there's no need. Tender, fluffy grains of boiled, long-grain white rice can be produced by washing the rice first and simmering one part of rice in two parts of water, covered, without stirring for 20 minutes. Since washing the rice increases the loss of soluble nutrients, this step is not necessary if the rice is to be sauteed in fat prior to simmering or when it is not important that the cooked rice grains stay completely separate. Similarly, separate strands of al dente pasta can be produced by boiling pasta in ample water or 1 gallon for each pound until "to the bite," stirring occasionally.

Braising in the healthy kitchen. When less tender or low-fat tender cuts of meat and poultry are to be cooked, braising or cooking in a small amount of liquid, covered on the range or in the oven, usually after browning, is an appropriate cooking method. For example, lean cubes of lamb stew meat can be transformed into tender, moist, and juicy pieces by simmering in a tomato-flavored spicy broth. Of course, fat needs to be skimmed from the surface as it accumulates. Combined with simmered garbanzo beans, zucchini and carrot slices and presented on a bed of couscous, the result is a hearty, tasty, nutritious African-style stew.

MICROWAVE COOKING
Microwave ovens cook with high-frequency radio waves that cause food molecules to vibrate. This creates friction that heats and cooks food. While microwave ovens traditionally have been used in most food service operations to reheat food, they can be used to cook healthy foods too. Because foods cook quickly with

little or no liquid in microwaves, this method of cooking helps foods retain their color, texture, flavor, and nutrients. At the same time, microwave cooking requires little or no fat.

Those items best suited for microwave cooking are ones with high water contents like fruits, vegetables, fish, soups, sauces, and beverages and those generally prepared by moist cooking methods. Of course, there are exceptions. Popcorn is an example. Traditionally, the hard, dried corn was transformed into snowy white, fluffy kernels by heating in oil. In the microwave, popcorn can be popped with no added fat. A special container sold for this purpose should always be used. Plain paper bags may catch on fire. To dress up the air-popped snack without butter or salt, the hot popcorn might be lightly misted with water and sprinkled with freshly ground cinnamon and sugar, Hungarian paprika, or grated skim milk parmesan cheese, or tossed with maple syrup, dried apricot bits, and pumpkin pie spice.

SAUTEING WITH NO OR LESS FAT

Many traditional recipes require that the meat, fowl, or seasoning vegetables be sauteed prior to using one of the preferred cooking methods.

Pan selection. The amount of fat used in sauteing can be reduced by selecting a pan appropriate for the task. Nonstick pans are effective in minimizing the amount of fat required. However, because their surfaces are easily destroyed by metal spoons, spatulas, and pot scrubbers, their life in the commercial kitchen is often limited.

In the event that the coating is scraped off into the food, experts have indicated that it presents no safety risk. The coatings are made from fluorocarbon resins—mixtures of carbon and fluorine that are nontoxic and simply pass through the body without being digested.

When cooking with nonstick pans, low to medium heat is preferred when possible. Exposure to long periods of high heat is more likely to cause fluorocarbon resins to break down. Obviously, nonabrasive cooking utensils (plastic) and cleaning materials work best with nonstick pans.

Calphalon pans are another excellent option. While more expensive than nonstick, they are more durable and require little or no fat for cooking. They are made from hard anodized aluminum with cast iron handles and nickel chrome plating. Calphalon also has a professional nonstick line available. For more information about Calphalon, they can be reached at (419) 666-8700.

Oil for sauteing. Next, the amount of fat should be limited to the minimum needed for items to brown without sticking. This means when the pan is turned upside down, no oil should drain out. The surface of pans can be coated lightly by brushing with oil or spraying with vegetable cooking sprays.

The advantage of vegetable cooking sprays is they are easier to use. Like other oils, they provide fat and calories. A light, 1–2-second spray adds about 2 calories, less than a gram of fat, and no cholesterol or sodium. Most of them are made from polyunsaturated vegetable oils, like corn or soybean, with lecithin added, but canola oil sprays are also available. It is important to read labels before purchasing. Some include water on their ingredient lists. Cooking sprays are commonly sold in natural, butter, and olive flavor but you can choose from a variety of other flavors too. They include Oriental, mesquite, garlic, and Italian.

As in traditional recipes, when browning ingredients in reduced-fat recipes, they should be added to a pan coated with oil only after it is hot. They will sear faster and absorb less fat.

Braise-deglazing. When recipes call for browning seasoning ingredients like garlic, ginger, onions, mushrooms, and bell peppers by sauteing in oil or clarified butter prior to combining with other ingredients, a rich flavor can be achieved without fat by using a procedure called braise-deglazing.

To braise-deglaze:

1. The seasoning ingredients are placed in a nonstick skillet and

2. Covered with a fat-free liquid. It should be selected to complement the finished product. Unsweetened fruit or vegetable juices, broth, dry wine, vinegar or water are possibilities.

3. The mixture is placed over moderately high heat and cooked until the ingredients begin to brown and stick to the pan.

4. At this point, more liquid is added, a small amount at a time while

5. The ingredients are stirred to release them and the browned bits from the pan.

6. This reduction and deglazing process is repeated until the color of the ingredients is rich and appealing. It is essential to monitor ingredients closely to prevent burning.

Sweating without fat. If it isn't necessary to brown the seasoning ingredients, they can be simmered in a small amount of fat-free liquid. Again, the liquid should be selected to complement the finished dish. When sweating larger quantities of seasoning ingredients or ones naturally higher in moisture like tomatoes and mushrooms, no liquid may be required. The vegetables will provide enough moisture to prevent them from sticking to the pan.

FLAVORING LEAN MEAT, SEAFOOD, AND POULTRY SELECTIONS
One of the concerns often expressed by diners eating healthfully is that low-fat meat, seafood, and poultry dishes will be tasteless.

Marinating. Marinating is one technique which can enhance the flavor of items without adding lots of fat. Marinades prepared from combinations of stock, minced vegetables and fruits, or their dried ground powders or juices; wine; beer; nonfat, plain yogurt or buttermilk; low-sodium soy or reduced-sodium worcestershire sauces; prepared mustard; vinegars; and herbs and spices along with little or no oil are some possible choices.

It is important to be careful when marinating selections in mixtures with a low pH (high acidity level). Besides adding flavor, they break down connective tissues in meat, fish, and poultry items and tenderize them. More than 24 hours in a low pH marinade can make them mushy. Since fish is marinated solely for flavor, it requires only short marinating periods. It is naturally tender. Basting with marinades while cooking items can improve their flavor too.

Dry rubs. Dry rubs—mixtures of herbs, spices, and other seasonings—are one of the hottest new techniques (really only new name for traditional technique) being employed to infuse meat, fish, and poultry and other items with low-fat and cholesterol-free flavor. While the term dry rub suggests a mixture of only dry ingredients, moist ones such as orange zests and minced garlic can also be included. The taste sensations that can be created with dry rubs are as vast as one's imagination. These are a few combinations suggested by the Beef Industry Council.

Aztec Rub: Crushed cumin seeds, garlic, liquid smoke, coarse salt, cayenne pepper, olive oil
Country Rub: Crushed bacon bits, minced parsley, tomato paste, cracked black pepper, paprika
Dry BBQ Rub: Mesquite, hickory or smoky dry seasoning, dried chopped garlic, whole mustard seeds, cracked black pepper
Mustard Pack: Dijon-style mustard, minced parsley, dried orange or lemon peel, dried crushed rosemary leaves, cracked pepper

Dry rubs should be rubbed evenly over the surface of selections and then allowed to stand, refrigerated if high in protein, a few hours, if small in size like half chicken breasts, and for several hours or longer on larger items like roasts. The seasoning mixtures may be scraped off before cooking or left on depending on the level of flavor desired and cooking temperature to be used. Dry rubs are usually scraped off smaller items cooked at high temperatures to prevent the seasoning agents from masking items' natural flavors and/or burning. To enhance the penetration of dry rubs throughout items, they may be scored (see grilled chicken drumsticks, tandoori-style on page 80). Omit salt in dry rubs when sodium is of concern too.

Ground, dried fruit and vegetable pulps. Low-fat flavoring agents might also be created to enhance the taste of meat, seafood, and poultry selections by drying and grinding the pulp from fruits and vegetables after their juice has been extracted. The ground, dried vegetable and fruit pulps might augment or reduce the use of traditional herbs and seasonings.

For example, dried, ground red pepper, onion, and pineapple pulp might serve as a complement for grilled prawns, while dried, ground apple, onion, gingerroot, and garlic pulp might season roasted chicken.

Sauces and Gravies

The sauces and gravies served with meat, fish, and poultry dishes can add flavor to low-fat and low-cholesterol dishes but at the same time be rich in fat and cholesterol.

TRADITIONAL THICKENING AGENTS

Historically, many sauces were thickened with roux, a cooked mixture of equal parts by weight of clarified butter and flour; beurre manie, equal parts of softened butter kneaded with flour to form a smooth paste; or liaisons, a mixture of one part egg yolks with two to three parts of cream.

THICKENING AGENTS IN THE HEALTHY COOKING KITCHEN

More nutritious, flavorful approaches can be used to thicken sauces. The following are a few options.

Vegetable purees. Flavorful purees of cooked vegetables can achieve excellent results. For example, to make chicken gravy, a reduction of rich white chicken stock might be thickened with a puree of cooked carrots, onions, and tomatoes and finished with evaporated skim milk. Depending on the flavors and colors desired in sauces, the types and combinations of vegetables selected will vary. High-starch vegetables with mild or sweet flavors work best. Parsnips, potatoes, sweet potatoes, yams, winter squash, pumpkin, corn, and peas are some possibilities.

Cooked vegetable purees are appropriate thickening agents for soups, stews, and other dishes as well. For example, a puree of cooked butternut squash might be used to thicken and enrich a harvest vegetable bisque without added fat.

Reduction. Another low-fat method to thicken cooking liquids and at the same time concentrate flavors is reducing the cooking juices of meat, seafood, and poultry by boiling. The end result is a rich and flavorful sauce. Of course, any fat needs to be skimmed from the cooking juices. This process can be facilitated by chilling broths first. The fat will harden on top, allowing for easy removal.

If there isn't time to chill the broth, a few ice cubes can be added to the hot liquid after skimming off as much fat as possible. The fat will cling to the ice cubes, which can be removed and discarded.

Special fat-off ladles are useful for removing fat from cooking juices, stocks, broths, soups, gravies, sauces, stews, and more. When a fat-off ladle is dipped in a fatty liquid, the fat rises to the top and flows through small slots around its raised rim. The fat collects in its bowl and is ready to be discarded. Bulb basters are not new to the kitchen. Updated models with more than one tip are other tools that can help chefs remove the fat from their soups, sauces, and other cooking liquids. If not available locally, the Williams-Sonoma Catalog at (800) 541-2233 offers a dishwasher-safe bulb baster with two interchangeable tips. The basters come with the regular round tip, as well as a flat wide-mouthed tip. The flat tip allows chefs to remove fatty pan juices from meat, seafood, and poultry selections, discard the fat, and baste with the remaining flavorful juices. Similarly, defatting pitchers make it easy for chefs to lose the fat but keep the flavor in their liquid-based dishes. To use a defatting pitcher, pour in the fatty liquid. Watch the fat quickly rise to the top. Now, simply pour off the rich juices through a spout at the bottom of the pitcher, leaving the grease behind.

Starch thickeners. If cooking juices require further thickening with a starch after reduction, the broth can be thickened with a slurry. A slurry is a smooth paste made by mixing a starch such as flour, cornstarch, arrowroot, or potato starch with a cold liquid like water or stock. Slurries contain no added fat, unlike rouxs and beurre manies.

Flour might be used to thicken sauces made from milk or poultry or fish broth such as white sauce (bechamel) or veloute (white stock thickened with roux). One tablespoon will thicken about 1½ to 2 cups of liquid. To prevent the flour from lumping, mix it with two parts of cold water or liquid until it forms a smooth paste. Stir the paste into the hot sauce liquid. To thicken the sauce and reduce the starchy taste, heat the sauce to a boil; reduce the heat and simmer at least 5 minutes.

In sauces traditionally calling for a brown roux, such as beef gravy, brown or bordelaise sauce, a slurry might be made with browned flour. To brown the flour, cook it on the range in a non-stick skillet or bake on a sheet pan in the oven, stirring occasionally until it is dark brown and produces a nutty aroma.

For example, a healthy version of marchand de vin sauce (red wine sauce similar to bordelaise, flavored with chopped parsley, shallots, and butter) might be prepared by reducing a hearty beef stock, blending with a browned flour and water slurry and garlic puree, and finishing with a red wine reduction.

Cornstarch is a good thickening agent to choose when a more translucent sauce such as a dark cherry sauce for roasted quail is desired. One tablespoon of cornstarch will thicken about 1½ to 2 cups of liquid. To add, mix the cornstarch with a small amount of cold liquid; stir into the hot liquid and simmer until the sauce is clear and thickened. For best results, cornstarch should be added to sauces near the end of cooking. Cornstarch-thickened sauces do not hold up well with extended cooking or for long periods on a steam table.

Arrowroot is more expensive than cornstarch but produces a clearer sauce and does not need to be cooked to remove a starchy taste. This neutral-flavored starch also thickens at a lower temperature than flour or cornstarch. This makes it ideal for thickening sauces which should not be boiled, such as those containing liaisons of egg and cream or simply eggs, reduced amounts, of course. Two and one-half teaspoons of arrowroot will thicken about 1 cup of liquid.

Potato starch, like cornstarch, yields a translucent sauce and does not hold well with long periods of heating. It should be added to mixtures near the end of cooking. One tablespoon of potato starch will thicken about 1 cup of liquid.

Crumbs from breads, cakes, and cookies are another agent

traditionally used to thicken sauces. They make excellent low-fat and cholesterol choices when the smoothness of the sauce is not a factor. For example, the cooking liquids of a marinated, spicy pot roast might be thickened with gingersnap crumbs. Since the starch in crumbs is already cooked, sauces thicken instantly with this method and require no further cooking.

The flavors of the thickening crumbs should be compatible with the flavors in dishes. For example, pumpernickel bread crumbs are a suitable thickening agent for beef cubes braised in mustard beer sauce (see page 73), while wild rice oatmeal bread crumbs might make an excellent thickener for a rabbit or venison stew.

Finishing sauces thickened by low-fat methods with butter. When thickening sauces without fat, a bit of butter or polyunsaturated margarine might be added at the end of cooking for gloss and taste. If the amount is small, it won't raise the total or saturated fat or cholesterol of the sauce substantially and may be well worth the additional flavor it gives to the sauce.

FRUIT AND VEGETABLE SAUCES

Finally, as far as sauces, fruit and vegetable sauces—chutneys, coulis, relishes, and salsas—are excellent choices. Many can be prepared with no or minimal fat.

The term salsa is often associated with the spicy tomato sauce served in Mexican restaurants with tortilla chips. Likewise, the connotation of the word relish is likely the sweet pickle condiment put on hot dogs and sausages. These shouldn't be eliminated from the healthy menu but supplemented with other salsas, relishes, coulis, and chutneys.

Considering the combination of ingredients that can be mixed in fruit and vegetable sauces, the list could be endless. It might include a papaya peach salsa, a green apple or a lemony tart sorrel salsa. A sweet and sour corn relish might be offered with a turkey burger, a cranberry pineapple relish (see page 84) with a sliced roast beef sandwich, or a fresh mint and cilantro chutney (see page 82) with grilled tuna on toasted sourdough bread, while a combination of diced mango and apple, minced ginger, and freshly ground allspice is delicious with roast beef, grilled pork, or broiled poultry, as is a fat-free pear and pomegranate coulis.

Fruit and vegetable sauces can be made from many fruits or vegetables, as well as from just one. For example, a ruby red, pureed berry sauce, relying primarily on the natural sweet, tart flavors of

the raspberry, is a heavenly sauce to nap over roast lamb tenderloin.

On delicate items, a more flavorful sauce may be appropriate.
For example, in the case of mild-flavored, creamy lime green broccoli timbales, a red tomato coulis seasoned with basil might yield
a nice contrast.

On spicier items, like grilled Caribbean grouper, a mellower
sauce like a mango avocado salsa will be more desirable. While avocados are high in fat, when combined with fat-free, red bell peppers, mango, and onions, the fat in the end product is minimal.

Dairy Products

Dairy products including milk, butter, cheese, cream, and ice
cream are a concern of diners monitoring their fat, cholesterol,
and calorie intakes. Widely accepted low-fat and nonfat forms of
many dairy products are now available.

MILK

Low-fat and nonfat forms of milk are in common use. Both are nutritionally better choices than whole milk. While whole milk contains 3.3% fat or about 2 teaspoons butter per cup, the fat content
of low-fat milk is 1% or 2% as specified on the label, and nonfat
or skim milk contains less than 0.5%. As a result, the calories drop
from 150 to 85 for a cup of whole versus nonfat milk and fall some-
where in between for low-fat milk. While nonfat milk may be the
form of milk lowest in fat, the flavor and mouthfeel may not be acceptable to some health-conscious diners. Rather, they may prefer
the creamier, low-fat milk as a beverage and base for cream-style
dishes containing milk.

Since 2% low-fat milk obtains about 35% of its calories from
fat, a more healthy method for obtaining the taste of whole milk
than low-fat milk is fortifying nonfat milk with nonfat dry milk.
The milk powder gives the nonfat milk a richer color and texture
while adding protein and calcium. Similar results can be achieved
with nonfat buttermilk by enriching it with nonfat buttermilk
powder. If not available locally, it can be ordered through the King
Arthur Flour Bakers Catalogue, P.O. Box 876, Norwich, Vermont
05055, at (800) 827-6836. When making puddings and soups,
these are some other ideas to keep their fat counts low and flavor
ratings high.

Pudding. Traditionally, puddings were often made with whole
milk and thickened with egg yolks. A healthier approach is to

prepare creamy puddings from nonfat or low-fat milk and thicken with purees of cooked fruits or vegetables or starches. For example, sweet potato bread pudding might be produced by baking cubes of whole grain bread in a custard of pureed, cooked sweet potatoes blended with nonfat milk, brown sugar, sweet spices, and egg whites. Then add a sprinkle on top of brown sugar, sweetened, toasted bread crumbs, high-fiber granola, or graham cracker crumbs, and it's a dessert fit for any occasion.

Cream soups. Diners tend to love cream soups. Their rich taste and texture give them sensory appeal. To make velvety, luscious soups fit for fat- and calorie-conscious guests, whole milk, half and half, or heavy cream might be replaced with nonfat or low-fat milk or buttermilk, evaporated skim milk or nonfat, plain yogurt. Rather than thickening with a roux, a slurry or puree of vegetables might be used. A small amount of rice, oatmeal, or potato might be cooked with the vegetables for additional fat-free thickening before pureeing. Bread or low-fat cracker crumbs or nonfat, plain yogurt blended with cornstarch are other options. Finished with a splash of wine such as sherry, or liqueur such as anise-flavored Pernod or anisette, low-fat cream soups can be sensational offerings.

Low-fat cream soup alternatives. While low-fat cream soups can be pleasing, clear vegetable and fruit soups are naturally low in fat and don't contain cholesterol. Other very low-fat soups are clear soups filled with yolk-free noodles, rice, barley, and other grains, and lean meats, seafood, and poultry. For example, a thick cup of vegetarian minestrone soup filled with vitamin- and mineral-rich, tender, garden-fresh, diced vegetables might be offered as a low-fat appetizer course or along with a sandwich as a main course.

Those who are watching their fat and cholesterol intake, as well as calorie-conscious and vegetarian guests, will appreciate low-fat and cholesterol-free dried bean, pea, and lentil soups. In a selection like protein-rich lentil and orzo (tiny rice-shaped pasta) soup, there is no need for this nutrient from higher fat and cholesterol meat, seafood, or poultry.

CREAM

In recipes calling for cream, evaporated skim milk works quite well. Because it is skim milk with 60% of its water removed, it adds creaminess without the fat and cholesterol of cream. It can be whipped and substituted for whipped cream or a creamy topping. For best beating results, it should be partially frozen and beaten at high speed with chilled beaters in a chilled bowl. A little unfla-vored gelatin can prevent it from deflating, about 3 tablespoons per pint. To do this, heat a small amount of the evaporated milk; stir in the gelatin until dissolved and then whip with the remain-ing chilled, evaporated milk.

Other options for whipped cream or creamy dessert toppings with less cholesterol and/or fat than cream are lightly sweetened, low-fat yogurt alone, or folded into whipped cream and nonfat ri-cotta cheese or tofu whipped with honey, vanilla, and a small amount of canola oil. To prevent separation, whipped ricotta or tofu topping should be stored in the freezer.

SOUR CREAM

Sour cream is a high-cholesterol, high-fat dairy product often used in sauces, fillings, and dips. Of course, a low-fat, low-cholesterol, commercial sour cream product is one option. Better yet, replace high-fat, high-cholesterol sour cream with a reduced-fat and cho-lesterol version. To do this, simply whip a small amount of fresh sour cream with evaporated skim or low or nonfat milk until the mixture is quite runny, and then refrigerate to cure for a day or two. The mixture will thicken into wonderful sour cream without the preservatives and additives of commercial forms. Other substitutes for sour cream are cheeses like low-fat or nonfat cottage, skim-milk ricotta, or low-fat white cheeses made on premise from low-fat milk or low-fat yogurt blended smooth with nonfat milk, about 3 tablespoons per cup.

YOGURT

Of all the sour cream substitutes nonfat, plain yogurt is likely the most popular. It contains almost no fat and cholesterol and about one-fourth the calories of sour cream.

Yogurt labels. The label can be a valuable source of informa-tion when selecting a low-fat, plain yogurt, if calories and fat are a concern. Some low-fat, plain yogurts provide more calories than whole milk yogurts. They are not higher in fat but rather nonfat milk solids (powdered nonfat milk) have likely been added to strengthen their texture and taste.

Cooking with yogurt. While yogurt makes a thick, creamy ad-dition to soups and sauces, it curdles easily when added to hot liq-uids. To prevent this from occurring, 1 cup of yogurt can be blend-ed with 2 tablespoons of flour or 1 tablespoon cornstarch before adding it to simmering liquids. Further, it should be tempered with a small amount of hot liquid and whipped in at the end of cooking. The mixture should not be boiled after it has been enriched with yogurt. For example, to lighten up a traditional Polish lemon soup, the rice-and-chicken-filled broth might be finished with nonfat, plain yogurt rather than sour cream. For added fiber, brown rice might replace the white; to cut the fat, skinless chicken breast meat can substitute for the dark meat; and to eliminate the need for thickening with a high-fat roux, a portion of the brown rice can be pureed with the broth.

Yogurt uses. Nonfat, plain yogurt has many other uses. It makes an easy low-fat dairy garnish when piped on soups or swirled in sauces. For example, a dollop on top is a nice complement to a hot, creamy soup like gingered carrot bisque or brandied pumpkin soup. When swirled in a bowl of chilled raspberry and strawberry soup, creamy yogurt provides a nice contrast to its sweet, tart flavor too.

Yogurt can enhance desserts as well. It combines well with fruit-based desserts in particular. For example, a dollop of low-fat lemon yogurt on blueberries makes a simple but refreshing light dessert.

The term sour cream is often associated with the topping on baked potatoes. Nonfat, plain yogurt can make a tasty alternative here when seasoned with a blend of herbs and spices or vegetables, maybe a sprinkle of green onions, freshly ground pepper, chives, and parsley.

This or similar yogurt-based mixtures can be offered as dips for vegetables or low-fat chips like roasted corn tortilla chips or roasted Idaho potato chips. Healthwise, they are certainly better than higher fat ones made with sour cream and/or cream cheese.

To glamorize the presentation of such low-fat dips, they might be served in the hollowed-out cavities of whole grain (preferably) bread loaves or buns or vegetables. When the choice is shiny red, yellow, or green bell peppers, sparkling, yellow summer squash, bright green cucumbers, or dark red cabbage, their color is another plus.

While creamy, dairy-based dips are popular with diners, the foundation for dips is not limited to dairy products. Low-fat and cholesterol-free salsas prepared from fruits and vegetables are tasty options, as are dips from high-protein, low-fat, and cholesterol-free dried beans, peas, and lentils or tofu-filtered, cooked, pureed soybeans.

For example, a tomato salsa with cilantro and chilies or can-

nellini bean dip with vegetables might be served with an assort-
ment of vegetables or toasted pita triangles.

CHEESE

Cheeses are often high in fat and cholesterol. Popular cheeses like
cheddar, colby, meunster, Swiss, and cream contain 8 or more
grams of fat per ounce. Most obtain about 70% of their calories
from fat (see Table 1.11) with cream cheese yielding about 90% of
its calories from fat.

   Low-fat cream cheese alternatives. In the case of cream cheese,
possible lower fat substitutes exist. Low-fat forms of cottage
cheese, the familiar dieter's delight, are readily available. Only
13% of its calories come from fat, a 77% reduction in fat over
cream cheese. While cottage cheese is usually salted, unsalted and
even lactose (milk sugar)-free versions of low-fat forms are being
marketed.
   Skim farmer cheese, also known as pot, hoop, or bakers' cheese,
is another healthy alternative to cream cheese. It is a mildly

TABLE 1.11

Fat Content of Common Cheeses

Type	Amount*	Fat (g)	Calories	Percentage of Fat Calories
American	1 ounce	7.0	93	68
Blue	1 ounce	8.2	100	74
Cheddar	1 ounce	9.4	114	74
Colby	1 ounce	9.1	112	73
Cottage, low-fat 1%	1 cup	2.3	164	13
Cream	1 ounce	9.9	99	90
Meunster	1 ounce	8.5	104	74
Monterey Jack	1 ounce	8.6	106	73
Mozzarella, part-skim	1 ounce	4.5	72	56
Neufchatel	1 ounce	6.6	74	80
Provolone	1 ounce	7.6	100	68
Ricotta, part-skim	1/2 cup	9.8	171	51
Swiss	1 ounce	7.8	107	66

Source: Data from J.A.T. Pennington (1994). *Bowes & Church's Food Values of Portions Commonly Used.*
Philadelphia: J. B. Lippincott Co.
*Usually one ounce of cheese is about the size of a pair of dice or an adult's thumb.

tart-flavored, very low-fat cheese with a firm but grainy texture. It can be sliced or crumbled and used in baking. It can also be transformed into a savory or sweet dipping or spreading cheese by blending with minced fresh herbs, freshly ground spices, honey or other sweetening agent, or diced or pureed vegetables or fruits or their juices.

Part-skim ricotta cheese with about 50% of its calories from fat, light or low-fat cream cheese with about 75% fat calories, and even neufchatel cheese, obtaining about 80% of its calories from fat, are lower fat cheeses than cream cheese but still very high in fat.

Fresh nonfat yogurt cheese is a soft cheese with a soft, creamy texture. It makes a good low-fat cream cheese substitute. The cheese can be made in house with little effort by draining the whey from yogurt.

Very similar to yogurt cheese and also a good replacement for cream cheese is paneer cheese. Again, it is a soft white, traditional East Indian cheese which can be made on premise by simmering low or nonfat milk with an acid—lemon juice or vinegar, until curds form, and then draining the whey from the curds.

Lower fat aged cheese. With the possible exception of sapsago, there are literally no aged cheeses which are low in fat. Sapsago is a very hard, green-colored Swiss product made from skim milk. It is flavored with a special type of clover.

For a lower fat and cholesterol cheese with a texture similar to an aged cheese like Swiss or provolone, part-skim mozzarella, an atypical fresh cheese, might be considered. Mozzarella's curds have been heated and stretched giving them elasticity when heated. Unlike the mozzarella cheese often made with part-skim milk in the United States, Italian mozzarella is commonly made with Italian buffalo whole milk.

"New" low fat cheeses. For diners who want their cheese but need to limit their fat and cholesterol intakes, lower fat, reduced fat, low-cholesterol, and cholesterol-free versions of many cheeses are now available. Flavors and styles have been created to replicate everything from cheddar and Swiss to mozzarella and blue cheeses.

Fat and cholesterol modified cheeses are made by replacing their whole milk or cream with nonfat or low-fat milk, sometimes water, and/or their butterfat with vegetable oil. Their quality varies. Most tend to be bland and rubbery. Further, many of them are high in sodium. Extra salt is added to compensate for the flavor lost with the fat, and sodium phosphate is often used as an emulsifying agent.

Soy cheeses are another cholesterol-free (unless dairy products are added) option. They are ideal for cholesterol-conscious diners who eat no foods of animal origin or are allergic to dairy products. Soy cheeses, however, are still high in fat and possibly sodium.

Prior to implementing any modified cheeses in an operation, it is important to evaluate the products' qualities and determine if they meet the operation's needs. A good rule when purchasing modified cheeses for low-fat recipes is 5 grams or less per ounce.

Smaller amounts of high-fat cheeses. Using smaller amounts of finely grated, stronger, sharper varieties of cheese like asiago, parmesan, romano, aged cheddar, or gruyere is another method to reduce the fat in dishes traditionally prepared with lots of high-fat cheese. The visual impact of their flavor can be maximized by sprinkling them sparingly on top of dishes rather than mixing with items. As is well known, diners eat with their eyes first.

For example, smaller amounts of skim-milk parmesan cheese will likely be noticed when freshly grated tableside over a colorful ziti medley boasting the flavors of fresh asparagus, red, yellow, and green bell peppers, and toasted pine nuts.

CREAMY FROZEN DESSERTS

Ice cream is a wonderful dairy treat, one of many food service operation's most popular desserts year round. The problem for healthy diners is a half-cup scoop provides around 7 grams fat (45% fat calories) and 140 calories. Some ice creams contain as much as 16 to 24 grams of fat per half-cup scoop and 270 to 310 calories.

Eating healthy doesn't mean never eating creamy frozen desserts. In fact, there's nothing wrong with diners eating them regularly when they are prepared with low-fat ingredients like pureed and chopped fruit, fruit juices, low or nonfat milk or yogurt, egg whites and/or gelatin rather than primarily cream and flavoring agents. For example, low-fat peach sherbet might be prepared from a puree of very ripe, sweet peaches, sweetened with concentrated fruit juices, thickened with gelatin, and made light and airy by folding with beaten egg whites.

Rather than preparing creamy frozen desserts on premise, low-fat frozen yogurts, sherbets, sorbets, and reduced-fat ice creams (ice milks) are available commercially too. A general recommendation is one with 5 or less grams per one-half cup.

High-fat and high-cholesterol ice cream shakes and malts are popular beverages too, especially with kids. More healthy and equally as tasty are fruit smoothies—fruits blended with nonfat milk or yogurt. For example, to prepare a berry smoothie, simply blend sweet, ripe strawberries or whatever berries are available with nonfat, plain yogurt, and sweeten with concentrated fruit juice, honey or barley, malt or rice syrup.

BUTTER, LARD, AND SHORTENING

Obviously, saturated fat and cholesterol-filled butter is not on healthy diners' preferred list. However, because of butter's flavor, modest usage may be appropriate in nutritional cooking. Lard and shortening are another story. These saturated fat and/or cholesterol-loaded ingredients are more easily replaced in healthy cooking and should not be considered for use in most cases.

Margarine. Margarine has come under recent scrutiny as well. While butter is harder on the heart than margarine, margarine is not completely innocent. As mentioned earlier, findings show that the unsaturated trans fat found in margarine and other products containing hydrogenated oils works the same way as saturated fat in raising cholesterol. The trans fat content of margarines ranges from about 30% in stick-type, hard margarines made from partially hydrogenated vegetable oil to less than 1% in some soft, diet margarines.

When offering margarine as an alternative to butter, its ingredient list is a valuable source of information about its nutritional quality. The best margarines are those that list liquid vegetable oils like safflower and corn as their first ingredient. Regarding diet or reduced-calorie margarines, though all their calories (about 45% by weight) are derived from fat, they are diluted with water, so they provide about half the fat and calories of regular margarine.

An economical fat- and/or cholesterol-reducing approach to butter or diet margarine is whipped butter or margarine. When whipped to double its volume, butter or margarine contains one-half the fat and cholesterol of its conventional form and all that has occurred is air has been incorporated into it.

To cut fat further, margarine or butter can be whipped and blended with fruit purees, jams, jellies, preserves, spreads, syrups, or honey. Whipped cranberry spread—whipped margarine blended with ground cranberries and orange zest and sweetened with powdered sugar—makes a lovely tasting and looking addition to the menu during the holiday season. It might be offered as a topping for whole grain pancakes, waffles, or muffins at breakfast or along with a basket of whole grain breads later in the day.

Another strategy to use less butter or margarine is to replace raw butter or margarine with a smaller amount of browned butter (buerre noisette—burr-nwah-zett) or margarine. Browning the fat can double its flavor. Smaller amounts of butter or margarine, once browned, can do wonders to the flavor of numerous dishes. For example, a small amount of browned margarine is all it takes to flavor a sweet oat topping on an apple and currant crisp.

Oil. Oils are cholesterol-free choices generally high in mono- and/or polyunsaturated fats that may be used in cooking or offered on savory preparations like meat, seafood, and poultry products, grains, pastas, breads, and vegetables in lieu of butter or margarine. When replacing butter or high-cholesterol and/or saturated fats with oil, those high in poly- and monounsaturated fats are preferred. This is how a few of the frequently used ones rank (see Table 1.12). From highest to lowest in polyunsaturated fatty acids or the good fats, they are safflower, sunflower, corn,

TABLE 1.12

Comparison of Fatty Acid Percentages in Fats and Oils

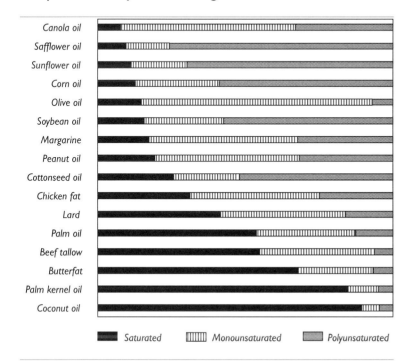

Source: USDA (1990). *Composition of Foods*, Agriculture Handbook 8-4. Washington, DC: USDA.

soybean, and cottonseed. Notice too that olive, peanut, and canola oil are high in monounsaturated fats, which also appear to be helpful in reducing the risk for heart disease.

Small amounts of the less common, more flavorful nut or seed oils like almond, sesame, or walnut, or a fruity extra-virgin olive oil, can provide a welcome change from butter or margarine. Flavored oils or those infused with flavors from fresh roots such as garlic, shallots, gingerroot, or horseradish; citrus zests; herbs; spices or other flavorful powders are other popular alternatives to butter and margarine. Because oil lends itself well to flavoring, the number of flavored oils that can be created is as vast as the chef's imagination. For starters, orange and ginger flavored safflower oil might be used to give everyday steamed baby carrots a new image, or to make simple roasted potatoes outstanding, try chervil scented canola oil.

Caution should be used when substituting oil for butter or margarine. Oils may contain less saturated fat than either butter or margarine and no cholesterol but they are 100% fat and concentrated sources of calories. One tablespoon of most contains 120 to 130 calories. For example, a diner can easily sop up large amounts of olive oil with a small chunk of bread.

Also keep in mind that while most vegetable oils are good replacements for butter and higher in poly- and monounsaturated fats than margarine, tropical oils including coconut, palm, palm kernel, and products containing these are high in saturated fats. The labels on packaged products should be examined for these saturated vegetable oils. For example, many of the cream substitutes sold for use in coffee contain tropical oils.

Butter-oil blends. Some chefs prefer to use a mixture of 50% whipped butter with 50% polyunsaturated fat oil like corn or safflower to replace butter. This mixture has a butter flavor, and at the same time, is lower in cholesterol and saturated fat than butter alone.

Low-fat alternatives to butter, margarine, or oil. For a fat- and cholesterol-free alternative to butter, margarine, or oil, roasted garlic might be served. The creamy, mellow spread is nice on bread, potatoes and other vegetables, pastas and grain dishes.

Other savory low-fat and cholesterol butter substitutes are herbed or garlic-flavored, low or nonfat, whipped ricotta cheese, a puree of seasoned stewed tomatoes or cooked dried beans, sauteed mushrooms, or roasted bell peppers.

Honey, syrups, marmalades, jams, jellies, and fruit spreads are sweet toppings which can replace butter without adding any fat or cholesterol. For example, rather than butter, cornmeal English muffins might be spread with a raspberry refrigerated jam prepared by cooking a mixture of fresh raspberries, unflavored gelatin, and fruit juice concentrate and chilling. On sandwiches, there's no need for butter or margarine either. Rather, the bread can be spread with a fat-free mustard or topped with a low-fat salsa, relish, chutney, or salad dressing.

Flavoring vegetables without butter, margarine, or oil. When serving vegetables, there are also many delicious and more healthful ways to prepare them than soaked in butter, margarine, or oil. For example, steamed green beans might be lightly sauteed Chinese-style with a splash of low-sodium soy sauce, a pinch of minced ginger, and garlic and a sprinkle of toasted sesame seeds.

Grilling, broiling, or roasting vegetables are other healthy preparation techniques. The browning process intensifies their flavors and gives them richness, eliminating the need for any additional fat. For example, broiling eggplant before peeling, pureeing, and seasoning with minced chilies and onions gives it a delicious smoky flavor.

Butter-flavored products. There are also commercial products which add butter flavor with little or no fat and cholesterol. They are spray-dried powders made from butter and other natural ingredients which can be sprinkled on hot foods such as baked potatoes and other vegetables or liquified by mixing the powder with hot water.

Margarine replacements. Products are appearing on the market to replace margarine too. For example, a dairy-free expeller-pressed canola spread made through a nonhydrogenation process is one such item which has been introduced.

Pastries Rich in Saturated Fat

Many pastries attain their flakiness from highly saturated or cholesterol-filled solid fats such as butter, shortening, or lard which have been rolled or kneaded into their doughs. Margarine is a cholesterol-free, solid fat which does not have all the flavor of butter but its taste has been widely accepted by many health-conscious diners. When making pastries, margarines high in water such as diet or light ones are unsuitable. The water will produce less tender products.

Polyunsaturated vegetable oils lack flavor and are liquid at room temperature. They are poor substitutes for the more saturated fats when making pastries.

Frozen vegetable oil mixed with a little flour is another option. While the mixture will not contribute the flavor of butter, it has the firm consistency of shortening without its level of saturated fats.

ONE-CRUST PIES

In the case of double-crust pies, a simple solution is to eliminate one of the crusts. Fat content will drop by as much as 50% and calories by around 150 depending on serving size. For example, in a cherry pie, the top crust might be eliminated by arranging a few decorative dough shapes on top of its fruit filling. The end result will be a low-fat pie with fewer calories per piece.

When there's only one crust on a pie, it can be placed on the bottom or top of the filling. For example, in a blueberry pie, the crust might cover the filling rather than serve as a base for it. By placing thin strips of dough in a lattice pattern, the amount of dough used can be reduced further and presentation enhanced at the same time.

In the case of fruit pies, their fillings might be covered with low-fat crumb toppings rather than serving between two high-fat crusts. For example, crunchy nuggets of wheat and barley cereal might be lightly coated with brown rice syrup and sprinkled over a plum filling or an apple and raisin filling topped with a crumbly mixture of rolled oats, whole wheat flour, melted polyunsaturated margarine, and brown sugar.

CRUSTLESS PIES

Some pies are delicious without a crust too. Cream pies, including pumpkin, lemon, and chiffon-type pies, might be served crustless. A crisp, low-fat cookie on the side like a gingersnap can compensate for the crunchy texture lost with the pie's crust.

BREAD DOUGH CRUSTS

Yeast bread dough is a good option for a low-fat crust on savory pies like ones filled with vegetables, lean meat, seafood, skinless poultry, and low-fat cheeses. For a low-fat pot pie or turnover, cubes of skinless, turkey breast meat and spring vegetables might be simmered in a starch-thickened chicken gravy and encased in a crust of high-fiber, whole wheat bread dough. The grainy, nutty flavor of the crust is a natural for this homestyle dish.

CRUMB CRUSTS

Crumbs from sweet crackers like grahams, cookies like vanilla and chocolate wafers, cereals like oat and wheat flakes, and cakes like angel food can often be made with less fat than pastry crusts. Typically, they are bound together with melted butter. It adds flavor but serves as a binding agent, helping the crumbs to form shells and maintain their shapes when sliced. Without a binder, each bite is more like a forkful of filling and a pile of crumbs.

To reduce the amount of fat in crumb crusts, yet produce flavorful shells that hold their shape, crumbs can be moistened with water and bound with a small amount of flavor-enriching melted butter or margarine along with egg whites. When crumb shells are not to be baked, the egg whites can be omitted and sweetened with concentrated fruit juice, honey or maple, rice or barley malt syrup rather than sugar.

For example, a chocolate wafer cookie crumb crust and creamy, coffee-flavored cappuccino mousse pie make a winning team, while the more familiar graham cracker crust pairs well with a light and airy whipped, creamy raspberry filling. Of course, both fillings should be prepared from a base of nonfat and low-fat ingredients.

PHYLLO PASTRY

Good low-fat pie shells might also be made by layering sheets of either refined or whole wheat phyllo pastry dough. In most recipes, the butter or margarine typically used to prepare the phyllo pastry shells can be reduced substantially. One tablespoon is enough to separate three sheets of phyllo.

Better yet, sheets of phyllo can be separated by spraying with butter-flavored cooking spray. Some chefs also recommend separating the dough sheets for the phyllo shells with a mixture of whipped egg whites and vegetable or nut oil, about 1 tablespoon per large egg white. The flavor of the oil should be selected to complement the flavor of the filling. To further separate the phyllo layers without fat, bread, cereal, or low-fat cracker or cookie crumbs might be sprinkled between sheets of the dough along with the egg white mixture.

For example, in a phyllo fruit ambrosia tart garnished with freshly flaked toasted coconut, thin-as-tissue-paper phyllo might be used to create a dramatic free-form shell for the fruit. When the pastry is cut, the thin sheets of pastry crumble, making a charming albeit rather messy effect.

Likewise, phyllo dough might be substituted for high-fat pastry doughs when preparing strudels. For example, an apple strudel might be prepared by tightly rolling a mixture of apple slices and currants sprinkled with brown sugar and cinnamon in phyllo pastry, baking, and slicing to serve. If refined or whole wheat phyllo dough is not available locally, it can be purchased through Athens Foods at (800) 837-5683.

MERINGUE CRUSTS

Finally, meringue pastry crusts can be made without any fat at all. These crisp sweet shells were favorites long before fat became an issue of concern. Because of their "heavenly" lightness, the term "angel" is often used to describe pies served in meringue shells. When a lemon orange chiffon, prepared from nonfat yogurt, flavored with fruit juice concentrate and thickened with gelatin is served in a meringue shell made from whipped egg whites and sugar, the results are delicious. As the name of this lemon orange chiffon angel pie suggests, it is a dessert fit to feed angels. The creamy textures of rich tasting chiffon fillings are ideal matches for crisp meringue shells but they work well with a variety of other low-fat and low-cholesterol fillings. For example, ripe sliced peaches and raspberries arranged in a meringue shell, topped with a small scoop of reduced-fat vanilla ice cream and drizzled with chilled raspberry sauce is divine. When fillings like chiffons are refrigerated in meringue shells, they are best prepared the day of service. While the pie shell tastes fine the next day, the shell loses its crispness over time.

Baked Goods

With few exceptions, sweet baked goods are generally not low in fat and cholesterol.

COATING BAKING PANS

To reduce the amount of fat in baked goods, baking pans and containers might be lightly coated with vegetable cooking spray or vegetable oil. Baking pans prepared in this fashion can be floured in the same manner as those coated with shortening and butter were traditionally.

DRIED PLUM PUREE AS A FAT REPLACEMENT

Fat can also be reduced in sweet baked products with a cake, bread, or chewy cookie texture by replacing butter, margarine, shortening, oil, or other fat with an equal volume of dried plum (prune) puree.

To make 1 tablespoon of dried plum puree, 1 ounce of dried, pitted plums (prunes) is pureed in a food processor or blender with

1 tablespoon of hot tap water. In other words, 1 pint of dried plum puree can be prepared by blending 1 pound of pitted prunes with 1 cup of hot water. This amount can take the place of 1 pint (1 pound) of butter in many cakes, bars, cookies, muffins, and sweet quick breads. Dried plum puree stores well refrigerated in a nonmetallic container if prepared in advance or left over.

Dried plum puree makes a particularly good replacement for fat in full-flavored baked goods. In lightly flavored products, the fruity tasting puree may dominate. Excellent results can be produced in hearty baked goods such as carrot date nut bars seasoned with a hint of freshly ground cinnamon; moist and chewy, fudgey brownies sprinkled with confectioners' sugar; pumpkin raisin quick bread; and low-fat oatmeal, chocolate chip cookies.

Dried plum puree works well as a fat substitute because prunes are high in pectin. Pectin forms the necessary structure to hold air molecules in baked goods, giving them volume. At the same time, pectin traps and enhances flavor.

Further, dried plums contain sorbitol, the mildly sweet alcohol sugar. Sorbitol is a caloric sweetening agent commonly found in sugar-free products. Most fruits are composed of 1% or less sorbitol, while dried plums yield 15%. Sorbitol, like butter, shortening, and other fats, keeps low-fat baked products moist and provides them with the mouthfeel typically associated with their higher fat counterparts. While sorbitol is a humectant or substance that attracts and binds moisture, fats keep baked products moist because they don't evaporate.

Nutritionally, for each pound of butter replaced with dried plum puree (1 pint), the fat drops from 362 grams to 2, calories from 3200 to 814, and cholesterol from 1056 milligrams to 0, not to mention the amount of fiber, vitamins, and minerals added by the dried plum puree. Another benefit for some, prunes contain diphenylesatin, a natural laxative.

OTHER FAT SUBSTITUTES FOR BAKED GOODS

The purees of many other fruits including dates, figs, raisins, cooked apples (applesauce), and very ripe or baked bananas might also be substituted for part or all of the fat in baked goods. For example, cranberry-orange flavored upside down cake not only tastes as good as it looks but nutritionally is a real gem when its fat is replaced with applesauce. Similarly, when a puree of very ripe bananas fills in for a good share of the fat in a whole wheat gingerbread cake, this aromatic, homestyle dessert is still irresistible but in a healthier form.

Professional bakers have reported success in replacing part or all the fat in baked goods with additional ingredients (S. G. Purdy, 1993. *Have Your Cake and Eat It Too*. New York: William Morrow & Co.). They include light and dark corn syrups and combinations of fruit purees and fruit butters with corn syrup and a small amount of oil.

FLAVOR WITHOUT FAT

In addition to its effect on texture and mouthfeel, another concern when cutting the fat partially or totally from baked goods is the flavor lost in the process. There are a variety of foods which might put taste back into baked goods with little or no fat or cholesterol. Fruits are an excellent resource. They might be mixed into baked goods, baked on their tops or bottoms, or blended into sauces and serve as a base or top for baked goods. Particularly good choices are dried fruits (currants) and their purees (dried apricot puree), concentrated fruit juices (frozen pineapple juice concentrate), fruit jams, jellies, marmalades and spreads (blueberry spread), and zests of citrus fruits (finely grated orange zest).

Other low-fat ingredients to consider for their flavors or the power they have on flavor include sweet herbs and spices (mint leaves, cardamom pods), liqueurs and wines (hazelnut liqueur, port wine), flavor extracts, granules and powders (almond extract, instant coffee granules, cocoa powder), some sweet and/or intensely flavored vegetables (yams, gingerroot), sweet and/or hearty syrups (honey, molasses), salt and dark sugars (brown sugar).

Whole grains and their flours (barley, buckwheat) and small amounts of some toasted high-fat ingredients (nuts like almonds; seeds like sesame) are other foods which can add pizazz to low-fat and low-cholesterol baked goods.

FROSTING

Frostings traditionally were often made with high-fat and/or high-cholesterol ingredients like butter, shortening or margarine, cream cheese, egg yolks, whole milk and/or cream. To cut fat and cholesterol, frostings, like seven-minute frosting, might be made from cooked and whipped egg whites, sugar, corn syrup, and/or marshmallows or icings prepared primarily from sugar like powdered sugar icing (powdered sugar blended with fruit juice or nonfat milk).

Jams, jellies, preserves, ripe, sweet fruit and their sauces, fat-free candies like peppermint chips, marshmallow creme, sweet syrups like maple, are other low-fat and cholesterol-free options to less healthy (higher fat) frostings. In lieu of frosting, these flavorful ingredients might also be baked on the top or bottom of cakes (pear-raisin upside down cake), incorporated into cakes (pineapple carrot cake), or serve as fillings for them (blueberry jelly roll).

Sugars like powdered, alone or blended with sweet ground spices like cinnamon, are other alternatives to high-fat and high-cholesterol frostings. When these are sprinkled over cakes in decorative patterns, the need for frosting disappears.

In some cases, a small scoop of a low-fat and low-cholesterol frozen dessert might replace a cake's frosting. For example, a scoop of vanilla nonfat yogurt and drizzle of raspberry sauce might be offered on a fudge cake or brownie instead of a dense, rich, chocolate frosting.

COCONUT

Coconut is commonly associated in the American kitchen, first, with the dried flaked form and second, with desserts. But coconut, whether fresh, dried, or its milk, works well in highly spiced savory dishes too. Because coconut is of plant origin, it often is not suspected of being high in saturated fats. But it is. To avoid all fat and still obtain coconut flavor, coconut extract might be used in the healthy cooking kitchen. Smaller amounts of freshly grated toasted coconut might also be sprinkled on top of dishes rather than incorporating large amounts of dried coconut into them. The superior flavor and texture of the fresh coconut will make a little seem like a lot, and because it's visible, be more appreciated.

Chocolate

Both baking and dark sweet chocolate are other ingredients from plant sources that are high in saturated fats. Baking chocolate is the highest of the two in total fat, calories, and saturated fat. To put this into perspective, the number of grams of fat that individuals eating 1800 calories per day can consume and still maintain their fat level at 30% is 60. Thus, three and one-half ounces of dark, sweet chocolate with 53 grams of fat would nearly meet their fat quota for an entire day.

COCOA POWDER

As for a chocolate replacement, there's cocoa powder. While both chocolate and cocoa powder come from cocoa beans, cocoa powder is what remains when most of the cocoa butter is pressed from unsweetened chocolate. It can give cakes, baked goods, and other desserts a chocolate flavor, yet is much lower in saturated and total fat than solid chocolate. Cocoa powders should be selected that are 10–12% fat. Some gourmet cocoa varieties have twice this amount. When replacing chocolate with cocoa powder, 3 tablespoons of cocoa powder along with a tablespoon of polyunsaturated margarine can be substituted for each square or ounce of chocolate required.

For example, to serve strawberries dipped in a chocolate-flavored coating without the saturated fat of chocolate, a luscious, creamy, chocolate sauce can be prepared by blending neufchatel cheese, nonfat yogurt, and powdered sugar with cocoa powder. The cocoa will provide a great chocolate taste without the fat of milk chocolate.

Or for rave reviews on a dessert, bananas might be served on a pool of dark, rich, bittersweet chocolate prepared from cocoa powder, brown sugar, and nonfat milk. Because of its intense flavor, only a small amount of sauce will be plenty.

CAROB POWDER

Carob powder has a sweet flavor that is somewhat similar to chocolate. Because it is naturally sweet, lower in fat and calories than cocoa powder, and unlike chocolate contains no caffeine, carob powder may also be used as an alternative to chocolate.

However, carob and chocolate candies, available commercially, are often similar nutritionally, with about 135 calories per ounce, and about 35–45% of those calories come from fat. Fat, often the saturated palm, palm kernel, and coconut oils, and sugar are added to carob to make the chocolate-flavored candy.

Eggs

There could hardly be a discussion about healthy cooking without mentioning eggs.

EGG YOLKS

On the bright side, egg yolks have less cholesterol than previously thought. The yolk of a large egg contains only 213 milligrams of cholesterol rather than the 275 still listed in some references. The bad news—this is still a significant amount, given that current recommendations suggest cholesterol consumption be limited to 300 milligrams per day.

The yolk of the egg is also the source of all an egg's fat and most of its calories. In a large egg, the yolk provides 59 calories, while the white contains only 17. For these reasons, many health-conscious diners are still eliminating from their diets dishes that contain egg yolks.

WHOLE EGGS

Generally there is no need for healthy diners to completely remove whole eggs from the diet. While they are high in cholesterol, they are not high in saturated fat and are inexpensive sources of high-quality protein. Most nutritionists agree that the three to four whole eggs which the average American eats each week, fat, cholesterol and all, fit well within the bounds of a healthy diet.

EGG SUBSTITUTES

Today there is a whole range of liquid egg products that have been formulated as substitutes for real eggs. These products contain varying levels of fat and cholesterol. Most of them are made from egg whites and other ingredients that simulate the yolk's color, flavor, texture, nutritional value, and mouthfeel, including oils, milk products, tofu, artificial color, vitamins, minerals, emulsifiers, and antioxidants. There are also egg substitutes which contain blends of whole eggs and whites, and even products that contain a small amount of egg yolk from which the cholesterol has been extracted.

EGG WHITES

In many dishes, including omelets, scrambled eggs, quiches, and baked goods like muffins and cakes, two egg whites can be substituted for one whole egg or a combination of two egg whites and one whole egg for every two whole eggs required. For dishes like scrambled eggs and omelets, adding one teaspoon of polyunsaturated vegetable oil to every four egg whites will help prevent sticking in the pan and add some flavor. The oil will increase the calories and total fat in the dish but the fat is polyunsaturated.

Adding color to egg whites. When a yellow color is important in egg white dishes, a tad of yellow food color or saffron can be added. Other ingredients which can give egg white dishes a yellow to orange color are turmeric, curry powder, and orange juice concentrate. The drawback of each of these ingredients is their intense flavor.

While purees of yellow and orange fruits and vegetables such as cooked winter squash, pumpkin, sweet potatoes and carrots, roasted yellow bell peppers, peaches, and apricots appear to be good candidates for adding a natural egg yolk-like color to egg whites, they are not particularly effective either.

Mixing bright green, freshly minced herbs or brightly colored, diced vegetables with egg white dishes like omelets before cooking doesn't produce the natural color of whole egg dishes, but it can spark up their bland color. At the same time, the herbs and vegetables add flavor, replacing that lost when the high-fat yolks are eliminated.

Egg white desserts. Traditionally, many desserts were made from egg whites only. They make a nice ending to a meal for cholesterol- and fat-conscious diners. There are lots of possibilities.

Angel food cake, Americans' favorite birthday cake, is naturally cholesterol free. It's primarily whipped egg whites blended with flour and sugar. It can be served plain or lavished with a puree or chunks of fruit, or a scoop of frozen, nonfat yogurt. Flavored angel cakes are fun and a nice change too. Their options are numerous—an orange angel cake might be created by adding orange juice concentrate and finely grated orange zest or orange extract, a licorice-flavored angel cake by blending in anise seeds or anise extract, or a chocolate one by flavoring with cocoa powder or chocolate extract.

It's hard to imagine anyone who doesn't like baked Alaska, the cake and ice cream coated egg white meringue dessert. A low-fat, and low-cholesterol version can be created by replacing the ice cream with a low-fat, frozen dessert like frozen, nonfat yogurt, sherbet, reduced-fat ice cream (ice milk), granita or sorbet, and the sponge cake with angel cake. The meringue is naturally cholesterol free. Again, the flavor combinations and permutations of angel cakes; frozen, low-fat desserts; and meringues are endless. One of a kind baked Alaskas could be featured on the menu every day of the year. It might be vanilla angel cake with cherry, nonfat frozen yogurt and chocolate-flavored meringue on Washington's birthday, while for Christmas, licorice-flavored angel cake and meringue with smooth cranberry sherbet might be promoted.

For another great low-fat, low-cholesterol alternative to traditional baked Alaska, an orange Alaska might be offered, a scalloped orange shell with its pulp removed, filled with orange sherbet and topped with lightly browned egg white meringue.

The list of popular desserts prepared from egg whites doesn't end here. A healthy version of the crisp-crusted, Australian pavlova might be prepared from a swirl of meringue, covered with sweet, vanilla-flavored, nonfat yogurt and bordered by circular patterns of sweet, ripe, peach slices and thin kiwi rounds. On all counts, it makes a luscious, standout dessert.

For a totally decadent, low-fat dessert, a roulade might be filled and coated with egg white meringue. One such variation might be a raspberry roulade, prepared by rolling a light, raspberry sponge cake over a luxurious, chocolate-flavored meringue and icing with more meringue.

Floating islands are sweetened, poached mounds of meringue. Served in a passion fruit sauce in stemmed goblets, garnished with fresh mint sprigs, they take on a formal touch.

A cholesterol-free crisp egg white meringue topping on a chewy bar is a nice change from a high-fat frosting. For example, a sweet crunchy vanilla meringue might complement a moist lemon bar.

PASTEURIZED EGGS

Following the salmonella scare, some restaurants began using pasteurized eggs in their blended egg dishes. The pasteurized egg options include dried, frozen, and liquid eggs. Dried eggs are inferior to frozen and liquid products and generally are not recommended for restaurant use.

Frozen eggs are created by a combination of pasteurization and blast freezing. Once thawed, frozen eggs can be used in recipes calling for beaten eggs such as scrambled eggs, omelets, cakes, and muffins.

Liquid eggs have been pasteurized but not frozen. Likewise, they can be substituted for beaten eggs in dishes. Their drawback previously was their 7–10 day shelf life. Extended-life liquid eggs are now available which can be stored at 40° F (5° C) or less for up to 8 weeks.

HANDLING EGGS

Whatever type of egg is selected, the following sanitary handling procedures* can reduce the possibility of contamination.

1. Refrigerate eggs and egg-containing dishes under 40° F (5° C) or keep hot over 140° F (60° C) at all times.

2. Cook eggs to 140° F (60° C) and hold for 3 minutes or heat the egg material to 160° F (70° C) to make it bacteria-free. As a general rule, egg whites are coagulated and no longer translucent and the yolk thickened but not runny when these conditions are met.

3. Keep dishes with raw or lightly cooked eggs refrigerated or prepare them for immediate consumption. Rather than serve dishes containing raw eggs, select recipes using light precooking techniques which increase the temperature to pasteurization levels or incorporate acidifiers, such as lemon juice,

*California Egg Commission, 1150 North Mountain Avenue, Suite 114, Upland, California 91786 at (909) 981-4923/FAX (909) 946-5563.

which lower the pH sufficiently to remove the risk of bacteria growth.

4. Replace fresh eggs in dishes with pasteurized ones.

Salads

Salads are potential sources of fat, cholesterol, and calories.

FRUIT SALADS

Fruits are a good choice for low-fat, low-cholesterol salads since fruits don't contain cholesterol and most are low in fat. In addition, some need no dressing at all while others simply call for a low-fat and/or low-cholesterol dressing. For example, when a medley of ripe, juicy fruits is tossed together, their own naturally sweet juices can provide all the flavor required. Or, as the Mexicans do, the crunchy Mexican root vegetable, jicama, and other favorite fruits might be served lightly sprinkled with chili powder. Likely, diners won't even notice there's no dressing when served an eye-catching platter of fruits and vegetables contrasted deliciously by the spice.

In the case of a salad filled with tropical fruits, a creamy peach poppy seed dressing might be served on the side in a large section of orange peel. Not only does presentation look good, but it gives diners the option to use as much or little of the dressing as they choose. Because it is made by blending peaches with nonfat, plain yogurt, honey and poppy seeds, even health-conscious diners who want seconds can do so freely.

VEGETABLE SALADS

It is true, raw vegetables contain minimal calories, no cholesterol, and generally little or no fat. For example, a diner could eat a quart of fat-free shredded iceberg lettuce for only 28 calories, but as soon as the lettuce is tossed with 4 tablespoons of French dressing, the classic one part vinegar to three parts oil combination, the fat count shoots up by 42 grams and the calories by 360. The 3 tablespoons of oil in the dressing provide all the fat and all but 2 of the 362 total calories in the dressing.

GRAIN AND LEGUME SALADS

Grains and legumes contain no cholesterol and are low in fat. Salads prepared from them need very little oil. Dried beans like kidney or garbanzo are especially nice marinated in low-fat vinaigrettes because they hold their shapes and textures. In the case of delicate grains and legumes like amaranth and lentils, it is important not to overdress them or they lose their light textures.

SALAD DRESSING

It's acceptable to serve fat- and cholesterol-conscious diners all the salad greens, vegetables, fruits, legumes or grains they can eat, but enhanced with small amounts of high-fat, high-cholesterol dressings or larger portions of reduced fat and cholesterol ones.

Flavorful oils in salad dressings. More acceptable salad dressings are those with 1 to 2 tablespoons of oil per cup of dressing. This goal can be achieved without sacrificing flavor by selecting oils with taste. It might be a nut oil, nice olive or flavored oil. For example, a mere splash of the subtle yet distinctively flavored macadamia nut oil can add a rich oil taste to a low-fat dressing. At the same time, this oil is high in monounsaturated fats and as healthful as it is good. For more information or to purchase macadamia nut oil, contact the Hawaiian Macadamia Nut Oil Co., P.O. Box 685, Wailua, HI 96791.

When selecting an olive oil, the lower the acidity the better the flavor, so the higher the grade. While only a taste test will tell how good an olive oil's flavor is, generally ones labeled extra virgin will yield the best flavor. Other terms which might be used to define quality are virgin, pure, 100%, olive pomace oil, and light (see Table 1.13).

Vinegars. To produce balanced salad dressings, hearty oils like extra-virgin olive need to be paired with assertive vinegars. Red and white wine vinegars are good choices, or better yet, balsamic vinegar, the priciest of all the vinegars. This dark brown, pungent, sweet smooth vinegar is produced from unfermented grape juice which has been aged in wooden barrels. The well-rounded mellow flavor of sherry vinegar makes it a good substitute for balsamic when costs need to be cut.

Infused vinegars might be produced in house or purchased commercially. When combined with herbs, fruits and spices, vinegars take on intense flavors that can wake up salads, as well as soups and side dishes. Again, the possibilities are enormous, perhaps an herb vinegar, like rosemary, thyme, white wine vinegar, or a berry vinegar. Raspberry- and blueberry-infused white wine vinegars are two favorites.

Delicate, mild-flavored vinegars can dress salads blended with almost no oil. For example, a dressing of rice vinegar seasoned with a tad of concentrated fruit juice, low-sodium soy sauce, and a small

---

TABLE 1.13
Olive Oil Terms

Term	Definition
Extra virgin	Obtained from the mechanical pressing of the olives, using no chemical solvents, under controlled temperature conditions. The most expensive form with a maximum of 1% acidity and the highest quality flavor. Because it loses some flavor when heated, it should be used at room temperature.
Virgin	Made in the same manner as extra virgin with an acidity of more than 1% and less than 3% and high flavor. Rarely sold alone in the United States, but used to add flavor to refined olive oil.
Olive oil	Formerly known as pure olive oil. A blend of refined and virgin olive oil with the terms pure or 100% pure often listed on the label. Has an acidity of less than 1.5%.
Olive pomace oil	Extracted from the olive pomace with solvents and then blended with virgin. Relatively low in cost and most suited for use in cooking.
Light	Bland or lighter in taste, not lower in calories or fat.

Source: International Olive Oil Council, P.O. Box 2197, J.A.F. Station, New York, NY 10116.
For additional information about olive oil, call the International Olive Oil Hotline at (800) 232-6548.

amount of sesame oil, gently tossed with grilled chicken strips and pineapple cubes, makes an excellent salad.

Other salad dressing ingredients. In addition to vinegar, other good low-fat and/or low-cholesterol salad dressing extenders are fat-free meat, poultry, and vegetable broths; pureed and diced vegetables and fruits and their dried pulps; vegetable juices such as tomato or carrot; soft tofu (high-fat but cholesterol-free); naturally sweet fruit juices and their concentrates including apple, pineapple, white grape, and orange; nonfat, plain yogurt; nonfat buttermilk and milk; liqueurs; wines; sugars; syrups like honey; and fresh, low-fat cheeses like cottage, paneer, and yogurt cheeses (see page 44).

While mashed olives, both ripe and green, olive juice, fish pastes like anchovies, fermented black beans, ground nuts, peanut and other nut butters, and tahini (ground sesame seeds) are high in fat and/or sodium, they are rich in flavor. A tad of one of these ingredients can do wonders to a low-fat salad dressing. In some cases, one of these ingredients can eliminate the need for additional oil in a dressing.

LOW-FAT AND/OR LOW-CHOLESTEROL SALADS

With a bit of ingenuity, a whole array of low-fat and/or low-cholesterol dressings can be created to embellish low-fat and/or low-cholesterol fruit, vegetable, legume, grain, pasta, and main course salads. Like their higher fat and/or cholesterol counterparts, healthy dressings should supply the sharp flavors needed to accent the subtle characteristics of salads. At the same time, healthy dressings should blend with and not mask their salads' ingredients.

For example, a curry-flavored yogurt dressing—a mixture of low-fat yogurt with a tad of honey, curry powder, and lemon juice—is excellent on an apple, grape, and celery salad, while a buttermilk herb dressing—low-fat buttermilk blended with low-fat ricotta cheese, onions, garlic, and freshly minced herbs— makes a tasty, creamy slaw dressing. Additionally, a spicy tomato dressing, from gelatin-thickened freshly prepared spicy tomato juice (see page 248) blended with low-sodium catsup, mustard, and lots of seasoning vegetables, herbs, and spices, yields a lively topping for mixed salad greens or thinly sliced avocado, while a light peach dressing, prepared by thickening naturally sweet peach juices with liquid fruit pectin and steeping with whole spices, is great over melon balls.

Salsas also make charming, low-fat and low-cholesterol salad dressings. For example, a warm fajita salad might be topped with tomato bell pepper salsa (see page 197). The outcome is a satisfying main course selection without excessive fat or calories.

Sweet syrups may be high in sugar but they are fat- and cholesterol-free. Dressings produced from them marry especially well with the flavors of fruit and vegetable salads. For example, a honey and chive dressing thinned with white wine vinegar might enhance the garden-fresh appeal of a carrot salad tossed with green onions and red and green bell peppers.

One of the readily available flavorful commercial, low-fat and low-cholesterol salad dressings is always another option. Higher fat commercial dressings or ones prepared on premise can be thinned with juices or water and vinegar to create versions that are lower in fat and sodium without significant loss of flavor. Additional seasonings can be added if desired.

COATING SALADS WITH DRESSING

When ladled over the top of salads, a small portion of dressing may appear skimpy and inadequate. The key to creating good looking and tasting salads coated with smaller amounts of dressing is to lightly toss the dressing with the greens right before service. Spray bottles make this an easy task. One or two squirts and a salad is covered. The dressing is spread evenly among the greens, allowing a small amount to cling to each leaf.

Squirter bottles are gems with thin creamy dressings and plain vinaigrette-style ones. They are not recommended for dressings containing minced herbs and flavoring ingredients such as garlic, onions, and ginger, because they can clog the spray nozzle.

Mayonnaise

Mayonnaise, with 176 grams of fat, 816 milligrams of cholesterol, and 1600 calories per cup, should be used sparingly in salads and other dishes.

MAYONNAISE SUBSTITUTES

It can be replaced in dressings and dips with lower fat and/or cholesterol and calorie options like tofu; part-skim ricotta cheese; blended, low-fat cottage cheese; low or nonfat, plain yogurt and low-fat, commercial mayonnaise or salad dressing. For example, a cup of nonfat plain yogurt provides less than 1 gram of fat, 4 milligrams of cholesterol, and 127 calories, or less than one-tenth of the calories in mayonnaise.

A creamy, low-fat or cholesterol-free mayonnaise-style dressing might also be prepared in house. For example, a low-fat dressing might be created by thickening nonfat milk with starch, enriching with egg yolks, and lightening by folding into stiffly beaten egg whites, and a cholesterol-free dressing can be made by blending tofu with Dijon mustard and lemon juice.

Flavoring mayonnaise substitutes. When low-fat mayonnaise alternatives are being served as salad dressings or sandwich spreads, they can be spiced up with additional flavoring ingredients. One or more of the following might be tried: minced garlic, green onions, gingerroot, lemongrass, horseradish, chilies, chives or fresh herbs; freshly ground spices; purees of roasted bell peppers; tomato paste or sun-dried tomatoes; dried cherries, apricots, raisins, or other dried fruits; mustard; or low-sodium soy or worcestershire sauces.

For example, curry powder and dried cranberries might be mixed with one of the low-fat mayonnaise alternatives. When spread on pumpernickel bread and topped with grilled slices of skinless turkey breast, low-fat Swiss cheese, crisp lettuce, this open-face sandwich is one to remember.

MUSTARDS

Prepared and flavored mustards served alone or blended with low-fat mayonnaise alternatives are other creamy, low-fat and/or low-cholesterol mayonnaise replacements. There are many prepared mustards on the market, ranging from mild to strong in flavor. Dijon is an example of a popular, strong mustard, while whole grain mustard is a common, mild type.

Flavored mustards are prepared mustards fortified with herbs, spices, or other seasoning ingredients. They might be enhanced with delicate herbs such as basil or mint; with spicier ingredients, perhaps chilies or horseradish; or with fruits, maybe orange or strawberry. For example, moutarde aux quatre fruits, a French mustard, is flavored with four summer fruits and beets. It is delicious when mixed with nonfat, plain yogurt and served as an accompaniment for poached fish.

GARLIC PUREE SAUCES

Some chefs prefer to replace mayonnaise with a blend of equal parts simmered garlic puree and extra-virgin olive oil seasoned with lemon juice, mustard, salt and pepper. While higher in fat than other "light mayonnaise" choices, this cold garlic sauce contains no cholesterol and is still lower in fat and calories than classical mayonnaise.

Some diners might consider the garlic sauce to be healthful not because it is cholesterol free but because it's rich in garlic. Garlic has been touted as an antidote for everything from toothaches to high blood pressure. Until recently, most believed the claims to be old wives' tales, but this may not be so.

A growing body of scientific evidence suggests that garlic, or many of the 200 active compounds it contains, combats bacterial infections, stimulates the immune system, and protects against blood clotting pollutants. Moreover, it might help prevent and possibly treat heart disease and some types of cancer. Nobody seems to know whether cooking destroys or reduces any medicinal powers garlic may have.

The Fresh Garlic Association, based in California (where more than 90% of all garlic in the U.S. is grown), recommends these methods to alleviate or eliminate the not so subtle scent that emanates from the mouth long after one savors the taste of a dish flavored with garlic.

1. Eat fresh parsley. The chlorophyll it contains supposedly masks the garlic smell.

2. Chew on a coffee bean.

3. Drink some lemon juice.

4. Eat a bowl of lime sherbet for dessert.

To remove the scent from the skin which lingers on the hands long after chopping fresh garlic, the Association suggests rubbing the fingers with the bowl of a stainless steel spoon under running water. The metal reportedly neutralizes the garlic's odor. Then wash with soap and water. Another option they suggest is to rub the hands with lemon, then with salt, rinse and wash with warm soapy water.

One caution when cooking with garlic: Storing fresh garlic in oil, especially if not refrigerated, can breed botulism. Commercial garlic-and-oil products containing an antibacterial agent such as citric or phosphoric acid are preferred.

Nuts and Seeds

Nuts and seeds are high-fat ingredients. Because of their fat content, a few tablespoons can add several grams of fat and a substantial amount of calories to a recipe. They should be used sparingly. For example, 15 pecan halves will add 18 grams of fat and 187 calories to a recipe, and 10–12 macadamia nuts will add 21 grams of fat and 200 calories. Likewise, while toasted almonds may add a crisp, flavorful contrast to a delicate trout, sauteed in a non-stick skillet, 1 ounce will increase the fat by 15 grams and 167 calories.

If nuts and seeds are toasted, their flavor is intensified and dishes can be prepared with less of them. In some cases, a flavoring agent like almond extract might replace part or all of the nuts in a dish too.

For texture and as toppings, granola or nugget-style cereals, water chestnuts, roasted garbanzo beans or pumpkin seeds all make possible lower fat options than nuts. For example, a baked peach half might be stuffed with part chopped walnuts and part ready-to-eat wheat and barley nugget cereal (see page 79), and still achieve the crunchy effect of nuts.

Low-Fat and Low-Cholesterol Commercial Products

There are a variety of reduced fat and cholesterol products available commercially. They range from low-fat and low-cholesterol cream cheese, sour cream, milk, salad dressing, and mayonnaise to commercially prepared cookies and desserts. When considering low-fat and low-cholesterol products for implementation in a food service operation, caution should be used. Some of them are quite good, but many lack taste and are not recommended. All need to be evaluated with the standards of the operation and needs of the clientele in mind.

Peanut butter is an example. Parents might be delighted to see that their six-year-old can order a sandwich made with reduced-fat peanut butter. However, if Mom or Dad decides to finish their child's half-eaten sandwich, they may discover why their child refused to eat it. Some commercial brands are reducing the fat in regular peanut butter by using fewer peanuts in the butter. To compensate for their loss, corn syrup or maltodextrin (sweeteners that for all practical purposes are nutritionally identical to sugar) and soybean protein are added.

A better strategy might be to offer a sandwich made with less peanut butter but combined with jelly, jam, or sliced ripe fruit like bananas. The outcome is a reduced-fat peanut butter sandwich with a sweet, fruit flavor both kids and adults love.

When ordering low-fat, low-cholesterol products like salad dressing and diet margarine, many health-conscious diners prefer them served in their original container or listed by brand name on the menu. This assures them that the product promoted as low in fat and cholesterol does meet these criteria and, further, allows diners to determine the exact values of those nutrients of interest.

Nutrition Labeling Claims

New nutrition labeling and nutrient content descriptors on food labels went into effect on May 8, 1994. The updated labels reveal sizable information about products' fat and cholesterol content. The new labels list the grams of total and saturated fat, milligrams of cholesterol, and number of calories derived from fat per standardized serving. The new labels also contain the percentage of saturated and total fat and cholesterol provided per one serving based on the recommendations of less than 65 grams of total fat, less than 20 grams of saturated fat, and less than 300 milligrams of cholesterol daily for a 2,000-calorie diet.

The following are the new definitions of the standards which must be met in order for a product to make claims about its fat and cholesterol content.*

Reduced cholesterol, saturated fat or fat—contains at least 25% less of the specified nutrient than the regular product. If the "regular" product already meets the requirements for low in the specified nutrient, a reduced claim for the specified nutrient cannot be given on the product. For example, whipped butter spread contains 30% less cholesterol than butter.

Cholesterol, saturated fat or fat free—contains none or only trivial amounts of the component.

Extra lean—for specific seafood, poultry, meat, and game meat products, as packaged, which contain less than 5 grams of total fat, less than 2 grams of saturated fat, and less than 95 milligrams of cholesterol per standardized serving and per 100 grams.

Lean—for specific seafood, poultry, meat, and game meat products, as packaged, which contain less than 10 grams of total fat, less than 4 grams of saturated fat, and less than 95 milligrams of cholesterol per standardized serving and per 100 grams.

Light or lite—has several meanings. (1) If a food originally derives less than 50% of its calories from fat, it must contain one-third fewer calories or half the fat per standardized serving of

*Collier, Shannon, Rill, and Scott, 1993. *1993 Nutrition Labeling Regulations*. Washington, DC: Collier, Shannon, Rill & Scott.

the regular food, or if a food originally derives 50% or more of its calories from fat, the food must contain one-half less fat per standardized serving of the regular food; and (2) a low-calorie and low-fat food has 50% less sodium per standardized serving than the regular food. (3) The term "light/lite in sodium" may indicate the food meets the low-sodium definition. (4) "Light" may still be used to describe such properties as texture and color as long as the label explains the intent; for example, "light brown sugar" and "light and fluffy."

Low fat—3 grams or less per standardized serving.

Low saturated fat—1 gram or less per standardized serving and 15% or less of calories from saturated fatty acids.

Low cholesterol—20 milligrams or less, and 2 grams or less of saturated fat per standardized serving. When fat exceeds 13 grams per serving, both for the standardized serving and for 50 grams, the same requirements as those for foods bearing "cholesterol free" claims must be met.

Percent fat free—must be a low-fat or a fat-free product and the claim must accurately reflect the amount of fat present in 100 grams of the food. For example, if a food contains 2.5 grams of fat per 50 grams, the claim would be "95% fat free." Note, 95% fat free doesn't meant the product necessarily derives 5% of its calories from fat. For example, assume the food contains 100 calories. The 2.5 grams of fat supply 22.5 (2.5 grams × 9 grams/fat) of them and as a result, 22.5% of the 100 total calories.

Creating Low-Fat Dishes

When creating low-fat and/or low-cholesterol dishes, as a general rule, fat should be limited to 10 grams per entree, 6 grams per vegetable salad, and 5 grams per dessert. If a main course recipe exceeds the 30% limit, it should be served with lower fat items like fruits, vegetables, and grains to bring the meal's fat content to the 30% or less level. If the total fat of a recipe is low, and poly- and monounsaturated fats are emphasized, its cholesterol content is likely within the recommended levels as well.

Finally, even health-conscious diners need some fat in their diets to stay healthy. In other words, the object when creating low-fat dishes is not to completely remove the fat but to reduce the amount to less than 30% of the calories. Thus, sharing a portion of a high-fat item like a rich and gooey cake may be nutritionally acceptable for diners who have closely monitored their fat intake during previous meals.

Summary—Reducing Total and/or Saturated Fat and/or Cholesterol in the Menu

Many techniques have been discussed to reduce the total and/or saturated fat and/or cholesterol in selections. In brief, the following recommendations are key strategies which can be employed to meet diners' demand for tasty menu fare with less total and/or saturated fat and/or cholesterol.

1. Offer lean cuts of meat, seafood, and poultry on the menu.

2. Serve the white versus dark meat of poultry with its skin removed.

3. Replace regular ground beef and pork in dishes with extra lean ground beef, ground round or ground, skinless chicken or skinless turkey (white meat only preferred).

4. Prepare beef selections with lean cuts containing less than 8 grams of fat and 180 calories per 3-ounce portion, like eye of round, round tip, top round, top loin, sirloin, and tenderloin.

5. Prepare pork dishes with cuts containing less than 9 grams of fat and 190 calories per 3-ounce portion from the loin or leg.

6. Add dishes to the menu containing lean lamb, goat, veal, and game like venison, rabbit, antelope, pheasant, and guinea hen.

7. Replace organ meats, hot dogs, and cold cuts or dishes made from them with freshly roasted, baked, broiled, or grilled lean meats.

8. Select lower grade cuts of meat like choice and select versus prime.

9. Make smaller portions of lean meat, seafood, and poultry, trimmed of their visible fat look large by cutting them into thin slices or small pieces, fanning them out across the plate, and combining with larger quantities of pasta, grains, fruits, and vegetables.

10. Replace meat, seafood, and poultry with dried beans, peas, and lentils and "meaty" vegetables like mushrooms.

11. Choose cooking methods that don't add fat and remove excess fat, like baking, roasting, grilling, broiling, pan broiling, poaching, simmering, steaming, and braising.

12. Reduce oil in sauteing by using a nonstick pan, lightly coating the pan with oil, or braise-deglazing or sweating in fat-free liquids.

13. Add flavor to meat, seafood, and poultry dishes by marinating in low-fat mixtures or coating with dry seasoning rubs.

14. Replace high-fat sauces with ones thickened with vegetable purees, slurries, or crumbs or by reduction or prepared from fruits or vegetables like salsas, chutneys, relishes, or coulis.

15. Substitute nonfat and low-fat milk or evaporated, skim milk in recipes for whole milk and cream.

16. Substitute nonfat, plain yogurt for sour cream and mayonnaise in selections.

17. Reduce the amount of high-fat, aged and fresh cheese in dishes by replacing with lower fat products commercially available or ones made in house from reduced fat milks or yogurts.

18. Rather than ice cream, serve nonfat frozen yogurt, sherbet, sorbet, granita, or reduced-fat ice cream (ice milk).

19. Serve whipped margarine; oil; roasted or sauteed vegetables or their purees; mustards; seasoned, whipped, low-fat fresh cheeses; jams; jellies; marmalades; fruit spreads or honey in lieu of butter on breads.

20. Flavor cooked vegetables by browning or seasoning with herbs, spices, low-fat condiments, or a commercial butter flavoring agent.

21. Serve pastries with one or no crusts or crusts prepared from crumbs, meringue or phyllo or their shortening, lard or butter replaced with polyunsaturated margarine or frozen oil.

22. Replace fats highly saturated and rich in cholesterol with ones high in poly- or monounsaturated fats like safflower, sunflower, corn, soybean, cottonseed, canola, olive, or peanut.

23. Add chocolate flavor to items with cocoa or carob powder, and add coconut flavor with coconut extract or small amounts of freshly grated coconut.

24. Substitute 4 egg whites or 2 egg whites and 1 whole egg for 2 whole eggs.

25. Offer desserts on the menu prepared from egg whites like angel cakes and meringues.

26. Reduce the amount of fat in salad dressings by preparing them with high-quality oils, flavorful vinegars, broths, pureed and diced vegetables and fruits, their juices and dried pulps, low-fat condiments and reduced fat yogurts, buttermilks and cheeses.

27. Use low-fat and low-cholesterol commercial products if suitable to the operation and acceptable to customers.

Fat Activities

1. Identify items from the list below which are low in fat and/or cholesterol. Describe how the fat and/or cholesterol content of the other items on the list could be reduced. See Appendix 5 for a sample of correct answers.

A. Roasted Chicken with Bread Stuffing Laced with Ground Pork and Seasoning Vegetables

B. Whole Wheat Pizza Crust Topped with Shrimp, Bell Peppers, Onions, and Melted Mozzarella Cheese

C. Cream of Tomato Soup Sprinkled with Basil-Seasoned Croutons

D. Spaghetti Tossed with Olive Oil, Bacon Bits, and Parmesan Cheese

E. Old Fashioned Potato Salad

F. Marinara-Coated Meatball Sandwich on Whole Wheat Bun Topped with Vinegar, Ripe Olives, Shredded Lettuce, and Mozzarella Cheese

G. Beets Glazed in Sweet and Sour Sauce

H. Freshly Prepared Peach Crisp Topped with a Scoop of Low-Fat Vanilla Frozen Yogurt

I. Baked Potato Topped with Sour Cream and Chives

J. Deep-Fried, Batter-Coated Cod Fillet Topped with Tartar Sauce

K. Fresh Fruit Coated in Lemony Whipped Cream

L. Macaroni and Cheese Dotted with Cubes of Ham and Topped with Buttered Bread Crumbs

M. Vegetable Beef Soup

N. Lamb Stew with Vegetables

O. Banana Nut Cake with Cream Cheese Frosting

P. Pork Fried Rice with Vegetables

DIRECTIONS

Complete the following activities with a specific operation in mind, ideally one you are currently involved with. See instructor to check your responses.

2. List items on your menu high in saturated fat or cholesterol.

3. List items on your menu other than those listed above which are high in total fat.

4. Identify selections on your menu low in total fat and/or cholesterol and saturated fat.

5. Identify new, low-fat and low-cholesterol selections you might add to your menu or how you might modify existing items to cut their fat and/or cholesterol content.

Beef Cubes Braised in Mustard Beer Sauce

This specialty beef dish of Flemish origin was too good to remain exclusive to Belgium. Like its traditional counterpart, in this modified version, the beef's braising broth is thickened with pumpernickel bread. The dark rye crumbs add flavor without fat.

Servings: 24
Serving Size: 3 ounces meat coated with sauce
Yield: 4½ pounds meat and sauce

Vegetable cooking spray
Onions, thin slices   2 pounds
Garlic, minced   2 teaspoons
Beef, stew cubes, lean, trimmed of fat, patted dry   6 pounds
Beer, dark   2½ quarts
Rich Brown Veal Stock (see page 74) or beef stock   2 quarts
Vinegar, red wine   ¼ cup
Fruit or apple juice concentrate, unsweetened   ¼ cup
Parsley, minced   ¼ cup + 2 tablespoons
Bay leaves   2
Thyme, dried   2 teaspoons
Pepper, freshly ground   to taste or 2 teaspoons
Pumpernickel bread, crusts removed   8 ounces
Mustard, Dijon-style   2 tablespoons
Salt   To taste

1. Coat a brazier with cooking spray. Place over medium heat until hot. Add the onions and garlic; cook until tender or about 4 minutes. Remove from the pan; set aside.
2. Increase the heat to medium-high. Add the beef cubes; saute until dark brown or about 5 minutes. Add the beer, veal stock, vinegar, fruit juice concentrate, parsley, bay leaves, thyme, pepper, and onion-garlic mixture. Heat to a boil; reduce the heat to very low and cover. Simmer until the beef is partially cooked, or about 1 hour.
3. Spread the bread with the mustard. Cut into cubes. Add to the braising liquid. Cover and cook another hour or until the beef is very tender and the bread has disintegrated and thickened the sauce. Stir occasionally to break the bread.
4. To thicken the sauce further, reduce it; to thin it, add water or stock. Remove the bay leaves. Season with salt to taste and additional pepper as desired. Serve with boiled, baby new potatoes.

Servings	Calories	Protein (g/%)	Fat (g/%)	Cholesterol (mg)	Carbohydrates (g/%)	Fiber (g)	Sodium (mg)
1	251	28 g/45%	5.8 g/21%	58.7	14.4 g/23%	2.5	164

73

Rich Brown Veal Stock

Veal bones are preferred for this recipe. They are high in connective tissue called collagen. It breaks down to form gelatin when simmered in water. Gelatin gives body to the stock. The bones should be cut in 3-inch pieces for maximum extraction of nutrients and flavor. When compared to a standard brown stock recipe, the quantity of bones, vegetables, and seasonings in Rich Brown Veal Stock is high in relation to the amount of water. Since the object is to create a stock that is full bodied, tastes and smells good, and will contribute complex and well-rounded flavor without fat to sauces and soups, the higher proportions of flavoring ingredients are recommended.

Use this stock as a base for soups such as mushroom beef and barley, sauces like brown sauce thickened with pureed, roasted vegetables, stews such as homestyle beef stew garnished with winter vegetables, and braised dishes, such as beef round roast braised in red wine broth topped with onion puree and as a cooking medium for grains like cracked wheat pilaf and vegetables like braised tomatoes and bell peppers seasoned with fresh herbs.

Servings: 24
Serving Size: 6 ounces
Yield: 1 ⅛ gallons

Veal bones, cut into 3-inch pieces   12 pounds
Water, cold   1 ¾ gallons
Onions, peeled, cut into 1-inch pieces   1 pound
Carrots, washed, trimmed, cut into 1-inch pieces   8 ounces
Celery, washed, trimmed, cut into 1-inch pieces   8 ounces
Tomatoes, coarsely chopped   1 pound
Sachet:
    Bay leaf   1
    Thyme, sprigs or dried   4 or ¼ teaspoon
    Peppercorns   ¼ teaspoon
    Parsley stems   8
    Cloves, whole   2

1. Place the bones in a roasting pan. Roast in a 400° F (205° C) oven, turning occasionally until well browned, or about 1 hour.
2. Place the bones in a stock pot. Cover with the cold water. Heat to a boil. Reduce the heat to low; simmer for 8 hours, skimming the froth as required.
3. Drain the fat from the roasting pan; reserve. Place the roasting

pan over moderate heat. Add about 1 cup of the cooking stock to the pan; stirring, scrape the browned bits of food from the bottom. Add to the stock pot.

4. Lightly coat the bottom of the roasting pan with the reserved fat. Since the fat will be skimmed before using, it is not a concern. Add the onions, carrots, and celery. Return to the 400° F (205° C) oven. Cook, turning occasionally, until well browned, or about 45 minutes.

5. Add the browned vegetables, tomatoes, and sachet to the stock pot halfway through cooking.

6. Continue simmering, skimming as required. Strain through a china cap lined with several layers of cheesecloth. Discard the solids.

7. Cool, vented in a cold water bath. Cover and refrigerate for up to 2 days. Prior to using, skim any fat from the stock's surface.

Note: It was not possible to calculate the nutritional value of this recipe. It is nearly free of all fat because the fat is skimmed from the stock before using and contains only the sodium in the water and that absorbed from the bones, vegetables, herbs, and spices simmered in it. Calories are negligible.

Sliced Moist Turkey Breast Napped with Creamy Cranberry-Enriched Sauce

Turkey and cranberries are made for each other. For a fresh approach, in this recipe, low-fat skinless turkey breast meat is poached in flavorful chicken stock. To complement the tender, juicy turkey white meat, its cooking broth is thickened with a puree of vegetables and flavored with concentrated fruit juices and balsamic vinegar. For the finishing touch, fresh, ruby red cranberries are simmered in the sauce with a tad of creme de cassis (black currant liqueur). In one word, the moist slices of thinly sliced turkey lightly coated with the creamy, tangy cranberry sauce might be described as "heavenly."

Servings: 24
Serving Size: 3 ounces turkey with 6 tablespoons sauce
Yield: 4½ pounds turkey with 2¼ quarts sauce

Turkey breast, bone in, skinless   7 pounds
Onions, chopped roughly   1¼ pounds
Carrots, washed, chopped roughly   8 ounces
Sachet:
  Parsley sprigs   6
  Bay leaves   2
  Peppercorns   8
  Cloves, whole   4
Rich White Chicken Stock (see page 78)   3½ quarts
Balsamic vinegar   ¾ cup
Fruit or apple juice concentrate, unsweetened   ¾ cup
Orange juice concentrate, unsweetened   3 tablespoons
Cranberries, fresh or frozen   12 ounces
Creme de cassis   ¼ cup + 2 tablespoons
Salt   To taste
Pepper, freshly ground   To taste
Watercress, sprigs   1 ounce (24)

1. Place the turkey breast in a brazier, breast side up. Surround with the onions, carrots, and sachet.
2. Combine the chicken stock, vinegar, and juice concentrates. Pour over the turkey breast. It should barely cover. Add stock or water if needed to cover initially and during cooking.
3. Cover the turkey with a round of parchment or wax paper. Place the brazier over low heat. Simmer until the turkey's internal temperature registers 160° F (71° C), or about 1½ hours.

4. Remove the pan from the heat. Let the turkey finish cooking in its hot broth for about 20 minutes. Remove the breast from the broth to a warm place; cover.
5. Remove the sachet. Skim any fat from the broth. Place over high heat; reduce the liquid to 2 quarts.
6. Puree the poaching broth and vegetables in a food processor or blender until smooth. Return to the pan. Heat to a boil. Add the cranberries and creme de cassis.
7. Reduce the heat to low; simmer until the cranberries have popped, or about 5 minutes.* Add stock or water to thin the sauce or reduce to thicken. Season with salt and pepper to taste.
8. To slice the turkey, carefully remove each side of the breast from the carcass in one piece.
9. Cut the meat at a slant, crosswise against the grain, into thin slices.
10. Overlap two turkey slices on each heated plate. Nap with sauce. Garnish with a watercress sprig.

*For a smoother sauce but one lower in fiber, strain out the cranberry skins.

Servings	Calories	Protein (g/%)	Fat (g/%)	Cholesterol (mg)	Carbo-hydrates (g/%)	Fiber (g)	Sodium (mg)
1	196	29 g/61%	1.9 g/9%	72.9	12 g/25%	1.3	96.8

Rich White Chicken Stock

Some chefs blanch the chicken bones prior to using them for stock to eliminate the blood and some of the other impurities that may cause the stock to become cloudy. In this recipe, the chicken bones are not blanched prior to using. This enhances retention of valuable flavors in the bones that might be lost in the blanching process.

Use this stock as a base for soups such as black mushroom and pearl barley, or butternut squash bisque, sauces, braised dishes such as chicken breast cubes in creamy coconut sauce, stews like chicken cubes simmered in chunky tomato sauce with carrots, corn, zucchini, and bell peppers, and as a cooking medium for grains such as barley risotto with mushrooms and spinach, and vegetables such as sliced potatoes layered with onions simmered in chicken broth.

Servings: 24
Serving Size: 6 ounces
Yield: 1 ⅛ gallons

Chicken bones, trimmed of fat and skin, cut into 3-inch pieces
    12 pounds
Water, cold   1 gallon + 1 quart
Onions, peeled, cut into 1-inch pieces   1 pound
Carrots, trimmed, washed, cut into 1-inch pieces   8 ounces
Celery, washed, trimmed, cut into 1-inch pieces   8 ounces
Sachet:
    Bay leaf   1
    Thyme, sprigs or dried   4 or ¼ teaspoon
    Peppercorns   ¼ teaspoon
    Parsley stems   8
    Cloves, whole   2

1. Place the bones in a stock pot. Cover with the cold water. Heat to a boil. Reduce the heat to low; simmer for 4 hours, skimming the froth as needed. Add water if necessary to keep the bones covered.
2. After simmering 2 hours, add the vegetables and sachet. Simmer for another 2 hours, skimming as required.
3. Strain through a china cap lined with several layers of cheese cloth. Discard the solids.
4. Cool vented in a cold-water bath. Cover and refrigerate for up to 2 days. Prior to using, skim any fat from the stock's surface.

Note: It was not possible to calculate the nutritional value of this recipe. It is nearly free of all fat because the fat is skimmed from the stock before using and contains only the sodium in the water and that absorbed from the bones, vegetables, herbs and spices simmered in it. Calories are negligible.

Baked Peaches Stuffed with Grape Nuts and Walnuts

These baked peaches look good, taste good, and are good for you too. To create a crunchy filling for the peaches without all the fat of simply nuts, walnuts are mixed with Grape Nuts cereal and bound with egg whites. Glazed in a light brown sugar syrup, commonplace peaches are transformed into gourmet fare.

Servings: 24
Serving Size: ½ stuffed peach
Yield: 24 stuffed peach halves

Peaches, medium-sized, ripe   12
Sugar, brown (divided)   4 ounces
Walnuts, chopped   3½ ounces
Grape Nuts cereal   3½ ounces
Egg whites   1¼ ounce (1)
Water   1½ pint

1. Peel* each peach; cut in half; remove the pit; discard. Scoop out a bit more of the center to make a cavity. Cut a small slice off each peach's rounded edge so it sets flat. Place the peaches in a counter pan.
2. Finely chop the remaining peach. In a bowl, mix the chopped peaches and all but about 2 tablespoons of the brown sugar with the walnuts, grape nuts, and egg whites. Spoon the nut mixture into the peach cavities.
3. In a bowl, mix the remaining brown sugar and water; pour over the peaches. Bake in a 400° F (205° C) oven until the peaches are tender, or about 20 minutes. Spoon the sauce over the peaches' tops to glaze. Serve hot or chilled in decorative dessert dishes placed on plates lined with doilies.

* To peel the peaches, blanch in boiling water for 10 to 20 seconds. Drain. Refresh in ice water. Drain. The skins should slip off easily.

Servings	Calories	Protein (g/%)	Fat (g/%)	Cholesterol (mg)	Carbo-hydrates (g/%)	Fiber (g)	Sodium (mg)
1	98	1.8 g/7%	3 g/26%	0	17.8 g/67%	1.9	30.1

Grilled Chicken Drumsticks, Tandoori Style

Restaurateurs are responding to a marked change in the American palate by adding more ethnic selections to their menus. Rather than American-style barbecue chicken, one way to diversify the menu is by offering these grilled chicken legs, an adaptation of a traditionally light Indian favorite. While normally cooked in a tandoor (clay oven that blasts meat with very intense heat), similar results can be produced on a regular grill.

Servings: 24
Serving Size: 2 drumsticks
Yield: 48 drumsticks

Paprika, Hungarian, sweet   3 tablespoons
Salt   To taste
Cardamom pods, skins removed   6
Cloves, whole   6
Cinnamon bark, ¼-inch chips   3
Peppercorns   9
Cumin seeds   ¼ teaspoon
Coriander seeds   ¼ teaspoon
Gingerroot, peeled, coarsely chopped   1 ounce
Garlic cloves, peeled   1 ounce
Yogurt, nonfat, plain   1½ pints
Lemon juice, freshly squeezed   3 tablespoons
Coriander, freshly ground   3 tablespoons
Cumin, freshly ground   2 tablespoons
Chicken drumsticks, skinless   8 pounds (48)*
Limes, cut into eighths   1 pound (6)

1. In a small bowl, mix the paprika and salt to taste. Set aside.
2. In a nonstick skillet, saute the cardamom and next 5 spices over medium high heat until lightly browned without popping. Grind the spices to a powder in a spice grinder, mini food processor, or blender.
3. Blend the ginger and garlic in a food processor or blender until it forms a paste. Mix in a small amount of the yogurt if necessary to blend. Mix in the remaining yogurt, lemon juice, ground coriander, cumin, and browned spice mixture until well blended.
4. Score the chicken legs at 1-inch intervals, cutting through the meat. Rub the legs with the paprika mixture until well coated and inserted into the cuts.

5. Rub the yogurt paste on the legs, inserting into the cuts. Cover and marinate refrigerated for 24 hours.
6. Remove the excess paste from the legs; discard. Place the legs on an oiled grill rack. Grill at moderately low heat until the chicken is half cooked.
7. Turn the chicken over using tongs. Continue grilling until the chicken is cooked through, turning as needed. Remove from the grill. Serve the legs garnished with the limes. Accompany with fresh mint and cilantro chutney (see page 82).

Note: This recipe is equally good prepared with chicken thighs, breasts, or wings and other types of poultry like turkey, cornish game hen, pheasant, squab, or quail.

Servings	Calories	Protein (g/%)	Fat (g/%)	Cholesterol (mg)	Carbo-hydrates (g/%)	Fiber (g)	Sodium (mg)
1	145	22.4 g/64%	2.9 g/28%	70.5	2.9 g/8%	0.5	84.2

Fresh Mint and Cilantro Chutney

I fell in love with this chutney while living in India. There, it is used as a condiment the way ketchup and mustard are used in the United States. Offer it here in a similar fashion with grilled or roasted meat, seafood, and poultry selections, as a dip with low-fat chips and vegetables, or on sandwiches. One of my favorite ways to enjoy this chutney is as an alternative to butter along with whole grain flat breads, hot out of the oven.

Servings: 24
Serving Size: 2 tablespoons
Yield: 3 cups

Gingerroot, peeled, sliced   1 ounce
Garlic cloves, medium-sized, peeled   2
Onion, coarsely chopped   4 ounces
Yogurt, nonfat, plain   1 ½ cup
Lemon juice, freshly squeezed   2 teaspoons
Cilantro, washed, stems removed   4 ounces
Mint, washed, stems removed   2 ounces
Red pepper, ground   To taste or ¼ teaspoon
Salt   To taste
Pepper, freshly ground   To taste

1. In a blender or food processor, puree the ginger, garlic, and onions with a small amount of the yogurt until smooth.
2. Add all the remaining ingredients; blend until smooth.
3. Refrigerate until chilled and the flavors are mellowed. Serve as a condiment with meat, seafood, and poultry selections such as grilled chicken drumsticks Tandoori style (see page 80), or offer with bread in lieu of butter or in sandwiches filled with vegetables like sliced cucumbers, tomatoes, radishes, and red onions.

Servings	Calories	Protein (g/%)	Fat (g/%)	Cholesterol (mg)	Carbo-hydrates (g/%)	Fiber (g)	Sodium (mg)
1	13	1.1 g/33%	0.1 g/6%	0.3	2.1 g/61%	0.2	14.2

Indian-Inspired Spice Blend

This seasoning agent is a blend of several aromatic spices with a peppery bite. It is a variation of the Indian seasoning mixture called garam masala. Commercial blends are available but often contain unnecessary ingredients, are stale and prepared from spices that have not been roasted. For best results, prepare your own. Indian-Inspired Spice Blend will keep fresh up to 3 months stored in an airtight container in a dark, cool, dry place.

This can be used to season meat, fish, poultry, dried bean and lentil dishes, such as pink lentils seasoned with cumin, cardamom and coriander or vegetable selections such as green peas and fresh cheese in tomato sauce.

Servings: 144
Serving Size: 1 teaspoon
Yield: 3 cups or 7⅔ ounces

Cinnamon, 3-inch sticks   ¼ ounce (6)
Cardamom pods   ½ ounce (¼ cup)
Coriander seeds   1⅓ ounce (1 cup)
Cumin seeds   4 ounces (1 cup)
Peppercorns   1⅓ ounce (½ cup)
Cloves, whole   ¼ ounce (2 tablespoons)

1. Break the cinnamon sticks into small pieces with a kitchen mallet or rolling pin.
2. Break open the cardamom pods. Remove the seeds; discard the skins.
3. Add all the spices to a nonstick or heavy skillet. Roast over high heat, stirring until the spices begin to burst.
4. In a coffee grinder, mini food processor, spice mill, or blender, grind the spices to a fine powder. Store in an airtight, covered container in a cool, dry, dark place for up to 3 months.

Servings	Calories	Protein (g/%)	Fat (g/%)	Cholesterol (mg)	Carbo-hydrates (g/%)	Fiber (g)	Sodium (mg)
1	6	0.2 g/12%	0.3 g/30%	0	1.1 g/58%	0.6	1.6

Cranberry Pineapple Relish

Keep your menu up to date with accompaniments beyond ketchup and mustard, like this Cranberry Pineapple Relish. Everyone profits, both diners and the bottom line.

Servings: 24
Serving Size: ¼ cup
Yield: 3 pints

Cranberries, fresh or frozen, unsweetened   12 ounces
Pineapple juice concentrate, unsweetened   ½ cup
Orange juice concentrate, unsweetened   ¼ cup
Pineapple, small dice, fresh or canned without sugar, drained
    1 ½ pounds
Carrot, washed, coarsely grated   6 ounces

1. Heat the cranberries and juices to a boil in a saucepan. Cook until most of the berries have popped, or about 5 minutes.
2. Remove the cranberries from the heat. Stir in the pineapple and carrots. Refrigerate until chilled. Serve as a condiment with poultry selections such as roasted turkey or grilled chicken breasts.

Servings	Calories	Protein (g/%)	Fat (g/%)	Cholesterol (mg)	Carbohydrates (g/%)	Fiber (g)	Sodium (mg)
1	39	0.4 g/4%	0.2 g/4%	0	9.8 g/93%	1.2	3.2

2

The Truth about Complex Carbohydrates

One nutrient Americans are being encouraged to eat more of is carbohydrates, primarily complex carbohydrates. Complex carbohydrates consist of starch and fiber. Both are found in grains and their products, cereals, fruits, vegetables, and legumes.

The only form of carbohydrates Americans are being told to eat less of is the simple carbohydrate, sugar—sugar in its concentrated form, as in honey, corn syrup, and the sugar in the sugar bowl, not the sugar in milk and other dairy products, fruits, and some vegetables (Chapter 3 discusses sugar).

Sources of Starch

Starch comes from foods of plant origin. It is found in grains and their products. Some types of grains (see Table 2.4) include wheat, corn, rye, millet, barley, buckwheat, amaranth, triticale, quinoa, rice, and oats. Some products made from these grains and their flours are breads, cakes, cookies, cereals, pilafs, stuffings, and pastas.

Legumes (dried beans and peas) are another important source of starch (see Table 5.2). Some examples of legumes are kidney, navy, pinto, pink, white, lima, garbanzo, adzuki, black, anasazi, fava, and cranberry beans, lentils, and black-eyed and pigeon peas.

Starch is also found in vegetables, in particular, root vegetables and tubers like yams and potatoes and some fruits. For example,

TABLE 2.1

Average Fiber Content of Foods

Food	Fiber (g)
Milk, meat	0
Fruits (1 serving)	2
Vegetables (nonstarchy)	
Cooked (½–¾ cup)	2
Raw (1–2 cups)	2
Vegetables, starchy (½ cup)	3
Brown rice, barley (⅓ cup)	3
Beans, lentils (½ cup)	4–5
Whole grain breads, crackers (1 serving)	2
Shredded wheat, bran flakes (½–¾ cup)	3–4
Other whole grain cereals (½–¾ cup)	2
Concentrated bran cereals (⅓–½ cup)	8–9
Nuts, seeds (1 ounce)	3

Source: Excerpted from M. M. Eischleman (1991). Introductory Nutrition and Diet Therapy. Philadelphia: J. B. Lippincott Co.

green bananas are high in starch but as they ripen, their starch is converted to sugar and the bananas become sweeter.

Sources of Fiber

Fiber comes only from foods of plant origin. Good sources of fiber are the skins of plant foods (apples, grapes, potatoes), seeds (raspberries, sesame, green beans), stems (asparagus, rhubarb, celery), leaves (spinach, parsley, lettuce), outer grain coverings (brown rice, whole wheat flour, rye berries), and hulls (peanuts, dark buckwheat flour, popcorn). Fiber is not provided by foods of animal origin such as meat, seafood, poultry, dairy products, or eggs. See Table 2.1 for a listing of the average fiber content of foods by category and Table 2.6 for a listing of the dietary fiber content of selected common foods.

Carbohydrates—Fattening Foods?

Many diners believe foods high in starch are fattening and should be eaten in moderation. Undoubtedly, high-starch foods do not deserve their bad reputation. This mistake is often made, however, because these items are frequently eaten with high-fat foods—bread with butter or margarine, potatoes with butter, gravy, and/or sour cream, and pasta with rich cream or cheese or heavy meat sauces.

The truth is, diners watching their waistlines couldn't do better than to eat a variety of low-fat, high-starch foods daily. Gram for gram, carbohydrates (4 calories per gram) yield less than one-half the calories of fat (9 calories per gram).

The fiber form of carbohydrates is an exception. Because humans, unlike cows, rabbits, and horses, lack the enzymes necessary to break fiber down, most passes through the gastrointestinal tract without being absorbed and is eliminated in the feces. This means negligible calories derive from fiber.

In addition, recent studies suggest that when an equal number of calories is eaten from carbohydrates and fat, the carbohydrates contribute less to body fat than does the dietary fat.

Functions of Carbohydrates

Carbohydrates perform valuable functions in the body. First, they are its preferred form of energy. Only two other nutrients, protein and fat, can provide fuel for the body. Protein-rich foods like meat and cheese are generally expensive and high in fat. They offer no advantages over carbohydrates as energy sources. High-fat foods like butter and oil cannot be used efficiently by the brain and central nervous system, and high-fat diets are likely to be hazardous to health. It only makes sense that carbohydrates are the body's first choice for energy.

Second, if carbohydrate intake is not adequate to meet the body's energy needs, either fat or protein can be converted to fuel for the body. When fat is used for energy without carbohydrates, potentially toxic substances called ketone bodies are produced. An excessive level of ketone bodies can lead to ketosis. Ketosis can cause dehydration and if not reversed, can be fatal. Carbohydrates are important in the regulation of fat metabolism.

Carbohydrates also serve a protein sparing function in the body. When carbohydrate intake is not adequate, protein will be used to provide energy. In fact, protein will even be sacrificed from lean body tissues like muscles to provide energy for the brain and nerve functions and body metabolic processes. This is a waste of valuable proteins which can better be used to build and repair the body.

About 100 grams of carbohydrate (2½ cups of cooked dried beans) is needed daily to provide energy for the brain and nervous system, prevent ketosis, and spare protein from being used for energy. This amount is the minimum needed. It is much less than the recommended amount. A fourth function of carbohydrates is to provide fiber or roughage in the diet.

Benefits of Fiber

Parents may know what they are talking about when they tell their children an apple a day will keep the doctor away. While a review of the nutritional content of an apple reveals it contains minimal amounts of vitamins and minerals and is basically empty calories, it does provide fiber.

Food manufacturers, health associations, and the Surgeon General's Report all suggest that the right kind and amount of fiber in the diet can reduce the chance of colon cancer and high blood cholesterol, an important risk factor for heart disease, and alleviate the symptoms of diverticulosis (the intestinal wall becomes weak and bulges out in places in response to pressure needed to excrete waste when bulk is inadequate).

Increasing the consumption of high-fiber foods might even help people lose weight. It is necessary to chew high-fiber foods

longer than those lower in fiber. In turn, digestive juices are se-
creted in the mouth and stomach, creating a sense of fullness. Furthermore, while fiber-rich foods pass through the gastrointestinal
tract more quickly than ones low in fiber, high-fiber foods remain
in the stomach longer and their bulk fills the intestines, leaving
diners feeling satisfied longer.

In addition to improving Americans healthwise, whole grains
and bran increase absorption and retention of moisture in baked
goods. This increases their shelf lives.

Recommended Intake of Complex Carbohydrates

Current dietary recommendations suggest more than 55% of total
calories come from carbohydrates, primarily complex carbohydrates. To help diners meet these recommendations, the
USDA and the U.S. Department of Health and Human Services
(DHHS) developed the Food Guide Pyramid (see Figure 2.1).
It advises Americans to eat 5–9 servings daily of fruits and
vegetables and 6–11 servings of a combination of bread, cereal,
rice, and pasta. At the same time, it recommends only 2–3
servings from the dairy group and 2–3 servings from the meat,
poultry, fish, and alternatives group per day and to use fats, oils,
and sweets sparingly. The fruit and vegetable and bread, cereal,
rice, and pasta groups are emphasized because it is known that a
diet rich in foods containing complex carbohydrates and low in
pure sugars is likely to be low in fat and calories and high in fiber,
vitamins, and minerals. Many health benefits might be expected
to follow.

Recommended Intake of Fiber

While there are no RDAs for fiber, nutritionists suggest Americans consume 20–30 grams of dietary fiber daily. Most aren't consuming anywhere near the recommended amount, rather only
about 11 grams of fiber per day. Table 2.2 illustrates how easy it is
to meet the fiber recommendations over the course of a day by eating according to the Pyramid guidelines.

Since there is some concern that too much fiber may interfere
with mineral absorption and displace consumption of nutrient-
dense foods, an upper limit of 35 grams each day, depending on
body size, is suggested.

Food Guide Pyramid
A Guide to Daily Food Choices

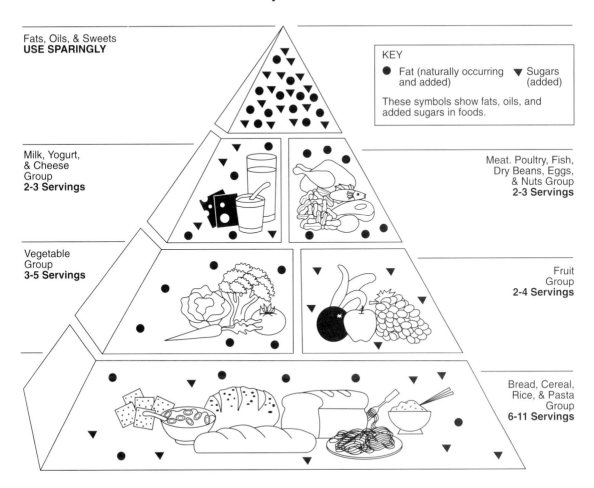

Fats, Oils, & Sweets
USE SPARINGLY

KEY
● Fat (naturally occurring and added)   ▼ Sugars (added)

These symbols show fats, oils, and added sugars in foods.

Milk, Yogurt, & Cheese Group
2-3 Servings

Meat. Poultry, Fish, Dry Beans, Eggs, & Nuts Group
2-3 Servings

Vegetable Group
3-5 Servings

Fruit Group
2-4 Servings

Bread, Cereal, Rice, & Pasta Group
6-11 Servings

Food Guide Pyramid Serving Size

Bread, Cereal, Rice, and Pasta Group

- 1 slice of bread
- 3 to 4 crackers
- 1 ounce of ready-to-eat cereal
- 1/2 cup of cooked cereal, pasta, or rice

Vegetable Group

- 1 cup of raw leafy vegetables
- 3/4 cup of vegetable juice
- 1/2 cup of other vegetables, cooked or chopped raw

Fruit Group

- 1 medium apple, banana, or orange
- 3/4 cup of fruit juice
- 1/2 cup of chopped, cooked, or canned fruit

Milk, Yogurt, and Cheese Group

- 1 1/2 ounces of natural cheese
- 2 ounces of process cheese
- 1 cup milk or yogurt

Meat, Poultry, Fish, Dry Beans, Eggs, and Nuts Group

- 2 to 3 ounces of cooked lean meat, poultry, or fish
- 1/2 cup of cooked dry beans, 1 egg, 1/4 cup egg alternative, 1/3 cup nuts, or 2 tablespoons of peanut butter count as 1 ounce of lean meat

Source: USDA

FIGURE 2.1

TABLE 2.2

Sample Daily Diet Plan: Meeting Fiber and USDA Food Guide Pyramid Recommendations

Menu	Servings	Food Group	Fiber (g)
Breakfast			
½ cup raisin bran	1	Bread, Cereal, Rice, Pasta	3
1 cup low-fat milk	1	Milk, Yogurt, Cheese	0
1 peeled orange	1	Fruit	2
Lunch			
2 slices whole wheat bread	2	Bread, Cereal, Rice, Pasta	4
3 ounces sliced roasted turkey	1	Meat, Poultry, Fish, Alternatives	0
½ cup shredded vegetables	1	Vegetable	1
1 cup bean soup (½ cup cooked dried beans)	1	Meat, Poultry, Fish, Alternatives	4
4 whole grain crackers	1	Bread, Cereal, Rice, Pasta	2
1 tablespoon mustard	-	Fats, Oils, Sweets	0
1 tablespoon mayonnaise	-	Fats, Oils, Sweets	0
Snack			
1 medium banana	1	Fruit	2
Dinner			
½ cup raw vegetable salad	1	Vegetable	1
3 tablespoon light vinaigrette	-	Fats, Oils, Sweets	0
3 ounces grilled fish	1	Meat, Poultry, Fish, Alternatives	0
¼ cup fruit chutney	½	Fruit	1
½ cup brown rice pilaf	1	Bread, Cereal, Rice, Pasta	3
½ cup glazed carrots	1	Vegetable	2
1 square apple crisp	1	Fruit	1
with oat topping	½	Bread, Cereal, Rice, Pasta	1
1 cup low-fat milk	1	Milk, Yogurt, Cheese	0
Snack			
2 cups popped popcorn	2	Bread, Cereal, Rice, Pasta	5
Total Fiber			*32 grams*

Food Groups	Sample Diet Plan Servings	Pyramid Recommended Servings
Bread, Cereal, Rice, Pasta	7½	6–11
Vegetable	3	3–5
Fruit	3½	2–4
Milk, Yogurt, Cheese	2	2–3
Meat, Poultry, Fish, Dry Beans, Nuts	3	2–3
Fats, Oils, Sweets	use sparingly	use sparingly

Types of Fiber

There are two types of fiber, insoluble and soluble. Each has different health benefits, so both are needed in the diet.

SOLUBLE FIBER

Soluble fiber is believed to assist with normal functioning of the digestive tract. Diets rich in soluble fiber have been found to reduce blood cholesterol levels. Sources include oat bran, oatmeal, fruits, vegetables, legumes, and psyllium (description follows).

PSYLLIUM

Psyllium is obtained from the seed husks of a plant grown primarily in India and the Mediterranean. It contains 60–70% soluble fiber by weight, eight times the amount in oat bran. It is found in ready-to-eat cereals along with oat bran and other fibers.

INSOLUBLE FIBER

Insoluble fiber is commonly referred to as "roughage." It is the chewy outer parts of seeds or fruit such as the skins, husks, and peels. Wheat bran; breads, pastas, cereals and other products made from whole grains; fruits and vegetables with their skins; and legumes are good sources of insoluble fibers. In addition to reducing the risk of constipation and other digestive disorders, diets high in insoluble fibers may be protective against colorectal cancer. Intestinal transit time is decreased when insoluble fiber is added to the diet, and this reduces the time that carcinogens in the feces may be in contact with the intestinal wall. Rice and corn bran appear to lower cholesterol too. But since they are primarily insoluble fiber, it is not certain whether their fiber is what gives them their cholesterol lowering clout.

Strategies to Increase Selections Rich in Starch and/or Fiber on the Menu

Many Americans are well aware of the benefits of increasing their consumption of foods rich in the complex carbohydrates. Some are asking for choices high in fiber and/or starch when dining out. Steps can be taken to meet these requests.

High-Starch Cereals Rich in Fiber

Breakfast cereals are particularly popular with middle-aged singles and working couples when dining out. Both cooked and ready-to-

TABLE 2.3

Fiber-Rich Cereals

Cereal	Amount (1 ounce)	Dietary Fiber (g)
All-Bran with extra fiber, Kellogg's	½ cup	14.0
Fiber One, General Mills	½ cup	13.0
All-Bran, Kellogg's	⅓ cup	10.0
Bran Chex, Ralston Purina	⅔ cup	6.1
Heartwise, Kellogg's	⅔ cup	6.0
Corn Bran, Quaker	⅔ cup	5.4
Wheat Chex, Ralston Purina	⅔ cup	3.7
Wheaties, General Mills	1 cup	3.0
Grape Nut Flakes, Post	⅞ cup	2.8
Oatmeal, instant, cooked, Quaker	¾ cup	2.8
Cheerios, General Mills	1¼ cup	2.0
Crispy Wheats & Raisins, General Mills	¾ cup	2.0

Source: J.A.T. Pennington (1994) *Bowes & Church's Food Values of Portions Commonly Used.* Philadelphia: J. B. Lippincott Co.

eat cereal choices might be offered on the breakfast menu (see Table 2.3) to accommodate these and other cereal eaters. Cereals with bran and oats are generally rich in both starch and fiber. Some companies are adding extra fiber to their cereals. A single serving of some of these cereals, like Kellogg's All Bran with extra fiber, can put more fiber (14 grams/ounce) in a diner's diet than most Americans are consuming in an entire day.

An unusual cooked cereal option might be a bowl of fruit and bulgur—a wholesome, hot cereal of molasses-flavored bulgur (cracked wheat) and rolled oats, speckled with bits of dried mixed fruit and topped with toasted wheat bran.

Another nutritious, warming way to start the day might be with a selection of starch- and fiber-filled cinnamon apple oatmeal—rolled oats simmered in water and apple juice with currants and cinnamon and garnished with diced apple and a sprinkle of brown sugar.

Granola, made with a couple of high-starch and fiber cereals and fiber-rich, dried fruits and seeds (small amount) is a big seller with all age groups. It can be offered at breakfast or later in the day as a snack, and may also serve as an ingredient in other dishes. For added flavor, texture, and interest, granola might be sprinkled over a cup of sliced, fresh fruit or a scoop of nonfat, frozen yogurt. It might even function as a topping for a fruit-filled crisp. In the case of bananas, granola can transform an everyday fruit into a healthy candy. It's as simple as coating its thick, ripe slices in the sweet crunchy cereal and freezing.

Starch- and fiber-filled healthy bars and cookies can be made from cereals and fruits too, perhaps raspberry and oatmeal bars or a carbohydrate-rich fruit-granola bar. Both can be offered as nutritious hand-held breakfasts for diners who prefer to eat on the run.

Whole grain cereals can add fiber and starch to high-protein meat, seafood, and poultry dishes too. They might serve as delicious, low-fat coatings, toppings, and extenders on these otherwise low-fiber, low-starch main course selections. For example, chicken thighs might be rolled in crushed bran cereal flakes, seasoned with cinnamon and pepper and baked (see page 127) for a delicious, low-fat, crispy crusted alternative to fried chicken.

Starch-Filled Breads with Fiber

While a serving of whole grain bread only contains around 2 grams of fiber, when two or three slices are served at every meal, the grams of fiber add up over the course of a day. Because this high starch food is so popular with Americans, a couple of servings of whole grain bread at every meal is a good way to compensate for the lack of fiber in the diet. As far as being high in calories, one slice of whole grain bread provides only about 70 calories. However, spread on a tablespoon of butter or margarine and the calories increase another 100 or so.

There is no doubt that a healthy way to start the day is with breakfast. This is an ideal occasion to serve up fiber-rich, high-starch yeast or quick breads too. It might be a sit-down meal of whole grain, fruit-filled or topped pancakes, crepes, French toast, or waffles and a glass of low-fat milk, or a meal on the go of a multi-grain muffin, a piece of fruit, and small container of low-fat yogurt. While bran muffins may be old hat, new and improved versions like vitamin- and mineral-rich oat bran, pumpkin muffins studded with raisins or miniature whole wheat (germ and all) mango muffins can make a leisurely or quick first meal of the day a real treat. Of course, starch- and fiber-filled muffins are equally good served in bread baskets most any time of the day.

Whole grain bread selections, toasted or fresh out of the oven, might be offered as tasty, high-fiber, high-starch companions along with egg dishes on breakfast as well as lunch, supper, or late-night menus. Imagine eggs any way you like them, hot off the grill (egg white omelets included) with a choice of whole grain bread from a list like buttermilk bulgur bagels; triticale and caraway English muffins; whole wheat and onion sage biscuits; or freshly baked, toasted, granola oat bread.

High-fiber choices might be enjoyed with midday soups and salads too. For example, kasha (roasted, hulled buckwheat kernels) cornsticks might accompany a tropical chicken salad, or barley flatbread may be served with a bowl of steaming, clear, chunky vegetable and turkey soup.

Bread can be more than an accompaniment to a soup or salad too. It can be a primary ingredient of soups and salads. For example, as the Italians do, a baguette of day-old bread might be transformed into a bread salad. For a healthy version of this salad, toss cubes of grilled multigrain bread with broccoli florets, juicy diced tomatoes, sliced red onions, ripe olives, a handfull of fresh basil, a splash of olive oil and balsamic vinegar and present on a bed of salad greens. In the case of a soup, diners will be assured of getting bread with their broth when it's offered inside a crusty bread bowl. For example, a robust loaf of walnut oat bread, cut in half with its center pulled out, is wonderful filled with a chowder, perhaps a tomato-based Manhattan clam chowder or a vegetarian-style corn and potato chowder.

Sandwiches can take on a new dimension when prepared with

whole grain breads. For example, to create a high-fiber, low-fat, knockout grilled sandwich, 2 ounces of Canadian bacon, 1 ounce of low-fat cheese, and a few tomato slices might be layered between pieces of pumpernickel bread coated with honey mustard spread and browned in a waffle iron.

Or, for a California sandwich that might be promoted with a carbohydrate, fiber, and calorie count included, layer homestyle, seven-grain bread lightly coated with jalapeno jelly with thinly sliced, skinless turkey breast, low-fat yogurt cheese, and lots of alfalfa sprouts.

Rather than layering sandwich fillings between slices of bread, high-protein fillings can also be wrapped in breads. As the Chinese frequently do, buns filled with flavorful fillings like spicy barbecued pork might be offered steamed along with an appropriate low-fat condiment. In the case of steamed pork buns, hot Chinese mustard is a must.

Whole grain breads can do more than increase the carbohydrate and fiber count at each meal. They can lure diners to an establishment on their merits alone. Examples of high-fiber breads that might capture diners' attention include specialties such as bran molasses bread bursting with chopped apples; oatmeal drop biscuits laden with dried cherries; picnic basket yeast bread filled with all kinds of goodies—rolled oats, pumpernickel flour, wheat germ and cornmeal; or triticale biscuit bites. Traditional favorites like Boston brown bread made with rye flour and raisins, squares of warm cornmeal bread topped with warm maple syrup, and stoneground, whole wheat cloverleaf rolls hot out of the oven are always nice too.

In lieu of a bread basket filled with a variety of breads, an operation might become recognized for a single novelty bread. Buckwheat popovers are excellent candidates. The distinct buckwheat flavor and crisp-on-the-outside, crepe-like-on-the-inside textures of these delicacies give them one-of-a-kind charm. When they're a day old, they can be sliced, toasted, and served on appetizer plates.

In some cases, it is difficult to recognize high-fiber breads on the basis of their appearance, taste, and texture. It is generally assumed that high-fiber breads will be coarse and grainy. This is not always so. They can be soft and free of whole grain flecks just like those made with refined flours. Some varieties of whole wheat bread are deliberately made soft with the addition of dough conditioners such as mono- and diglycerides and sodium stearoyl lactate. These additions may sound scary but they are safe.

A bread's name is not always evidence of its fiber content either. Breads flaunting whole-grainy sounding names such as ten-grain bread or bran and nutty grain bread can be made primarily from white refined flour. One way to avoid this deceptive practice is to look for the word whole wheat in the bread's name. The Food and Drug Administration (FDA) requires that all the flour in breads, rolls, or buns using the term whole wheat in their names be whole wheat. Note that other products such as pancakes, pretzels, and cookies are not required to abide by this rule.

Finally, when adding bread to the menu, don't overlook its potential as a dessert. While bread is typically not considered an item reserved for the last course of the meal, there's no reason why not. Once diners try choices like Italian angel food bread, they'll wonder why they waited so long to make bread their dessert. With only a tad of cake's sugar, light and airy angel food cake bread is the perfect ending for a healthy meal. It might be served plain alongside a bowl of fresh fruit in season or sliced thin and used as a base for a frozen, low-fat yogurt-topped strawberry shortcake.

If kids are regular diners, a lightly sweetened yeast bread dough enriched with graham flour might be shaped into a delicious dessert creature, maybe a turtle, crocodile, or elephant. If a teddy bear is on the menu, all it takes is 9 flattened dough balls (1 5-inch, 1 3-inch, 4 2-inch, and 3 1-inch balls), a few raisins, and a brightly colored ribbon. Use the 5-inch dough ball for the body; attach the 3-inch flattened dough ball on top for the head. Tuck the 4 2-inch flattened dough balls around the outside of the bear's body for the legs. Add ears on each side of the head with the 2 1-inch flattened balls, and form a muzzle by placing the remaining 1-inch flattened dough ball in the middle of the head. Push two raisins in the head for eyes and 1 in the body for a belly button. Once baked, tie a red ribbon around the bear's neck and it's ready to be eaten.

While the kids are enjoying their animal breads with a glass of nonfat milk, recommend that their adult chaperones try a slice of citrus-flavored dessert bread or a piece of braided dried purple plum (prune) bread along with a cup of freshly brewed coffee.

High-Fiber, Starch-Filled Crackers

Crackers are almost expected with soups and salads. For convenience, high-fiber commercial crackers like rye krisps, Scandinavian flat bread, whole wheat melba toast, or other varieties made with whole grain flours might be offered, or more unique ones may be made on premise like crispy, whole wheat cheese wafers, if time and skill allow.

High-fiber crackers (like high-fiber breads and cakes) can be incorporated into endless dishes too. The crumbs of savory ones might serve as toppings, stuffings, coatings, or extenders for meat, seafood, poultry, and vegetable dishes. For example, they might be blended with extra lean ground beef in Mexican-style meat loaf, mixed with leftover, roasted, skinless turkey breast and vegetables in croquets, or paired with smoky eggplant puree seasoned with fresh chilies in the vegetable of the day. They might form a crispy crust on baked, low-fat sole or spicy crab cakes garnished with horseradish yogurt sauce, or serve as a binder in a stuffing for organically grown, ripe, baked tomatoes seasoned with Italian herbs.

Sweet whole grain crackers can increase the fiber count of dishes too. Their crumbs might be made into crusts or toppings for fruit or other low-fat fillings. For example, graham crackers are easy to make into crusts and are popular with diners too. One might serve as a base for a tart featuring a medley of summer fruits—strawberries, blueberries, peaches, and kiwi—or as the foundation for a creamy pie filled with a low-fat, apricot yogurt custard.

Complex Carbohydrate-Rich Flours Used in Baked Goods

NONWHEAT FLOURS

Nonwheat flours from other grains, vegetables, and legumes like amaranth, barley, brown rice, buckwheat, chickpea, corn, millet, oat, potato, pumpernickel, soy, soya, triticale, rye, and white rice can be substituted for part or all of the refined flour in baked goods, including bars, breads, cakes, cookies, muffins, pie crusts, and pastries. The result is a diet high in both starch and fiber. Descriptions of nonwheat flours follow.

Amaranth flour and the tiny grains it comes from has only recently become available commercially. When this high-protein flour is mixed with corn or wheat, higher fiber whole wheat preferably, the outcome is a balance of protein equal to that in milk.

Barley flour comes from finely ground hulled barley. Its slightly sweet taste and the improved keeping qualities it imparts to baked goods make it a welcome addition to cakes, cookies, breads, and muffins.

Buckwheat flour comes in two forms. Dark buckwheat flour, ground from the unhulled groat, is grayish in color with little black flecks. Buckwheat flour's light form is ground after the hull is removed. Both flours have a strong earthy taste, dark flour the strongest. This low-gluten flour is a well-known ingredient in blini, Russian yeasted buckwheat pancakes, and the Japanese buckwheat noodles called soba.

Cornmeal (yellow and white) is made from finely ground, dried, white and yellow corn. Commercially, it is generally ground from the corn kernel with the hull and germ removed. The higher fiber unbolted cornmeal, which retains its bran and germ, is available at some health food stores. The rich-tasting yellow cornmeal contains a bit more beta-carotene than white cornmeal. It is wonderful in everything from cornsticks to polenta (hot cornmeal mush), and white cornmeal is a must for the flat griddle "johnnycakes."

Blue cornmeal comes from the dried blue kernels of a special variety of field corn. It is available in some specialty food markets or by mail order. One consideration when substituting blue cornmeal for yellow is the bluish gray tinge it gives baked goods. Blue cornmeal is a common ingredient in tortillas but can also provide a nice change from yellow or white cornmeal in breads, pancakes, muffins, chips, puddings, and breakfast porridge.

Corn flour, available in yellow, white, or blue forms, is like cornmeal from ground dried corn but more finely ground than cornmeal.

Millet flour adds a nutty, somewhat sweet flavor to baked goods.

Oat flour, which retains much of its bran, is ground from whole oat groats. Oat flour's delicate, sweet flavor and ability to keep baked goods fresh make it a welcome addition to baked goods. Besides being rich in vitamins and minerals, oat flour is rich in soluble fiber, the compound recognized for its cholesterol-lowering effects.

Another form of oat flour, *hydrolyzed oat flour* or simply oat flour that has been treated with water to break down its starch into individual sugar components, recently began appearing on the ingredient lists of low-fat foods. In addition to mimicking fat's texture and mouthfeel, hydrolyzed oat flour is rich in cholesterol-lowering soluble fiber. To determine if this wonder ingredient is in a product, check its list of ingredients. Reduced-fat cookies, cheese, bologna, and franks are some possibilities.

Potato skin flour is a new high-fiber flour processed from potato skins that may soon be another option. It is estimated to provide three times the dietary fiber of oatmeal. The brown flour is currently being used in processed cookies, cereals, and muffins. In the meantime, the more common stark white and very fine *potato flour* makes a suitable alternative to wheat flour when creating wheat-free baked goods like vanilla-flavored sponge cake. Also known as potato starch, potato flour is made from steamed, ground and dried potatoes. While some diners may be allergic to the gluten formed from the proteins in wheat, other diners may omit wheat from their diets during certain religious holidays such as Jewish Passover.

Rice flour, available in white or brown forms, has a silky texture. Brown rice flour, ground from the bran, endosperm, and germ, gives baked goods a nutty rich flavor, while white rice flour imparts a slightly sweet flavor to products. To prevent brown rice flour from becoming rancid, it should be stored refrigerated.

Rye flour is available as light or white, medium, dark, and pumpernickel. Light rye flour is ground from the rye berry with most or all of the bran removed, while pumpernickel flour comes from the entire rye berry. All forms of rye add a strong taste to baked goods with the flavor being most pronounced in the pumpernickel flour and least in the light rye flour.

Soy, soya, and chickpea flours are high in protein, calcium, and other minerals. Soy flour is ground from raw soybeans while soya flour comes from lightly toasted soybeans. Both soy and soya flours improve the keeping quality of baked goods and impart a slightly sweet but pleasantly musty flavor to them. Chickpea flour, a staple of African and East Indian cooking, is also known as gram or besan.

Triticale flour is ground from the triticale grain, a man-made hybrid of rye and wheat. Flavorwise, it has the slightly bitter taste of rye along with the sweetness of wheat, and nutritionally, because it combines the protein of both grains, yields a better balance of amino acids than either rye or wheat alone.

Because nonwheat flours have very little of the proteins that form gluten when mixed with water, they must be combined with wheat flour to make yeast breads with an acceptable texture. Without a high gluten flour, the result will be very heavy and dense loaves. The California Culinary Academy (*Cooking A to Z* (1988). San Ramon, CA: Chevron Chemical Co., p. 236) recommends these proportions of nonwheat to wheat flour to produce satisfactory yeast breads.

If nonwheat flours cannot be found locally, these three sources may be able to either provide them by mail order or indicate local outlets that carry them.

Arrowhead Mills
Box 2059
Hereford, TX 79045-2059
(806) 364-0730

Flour	Proportions of Nonwheat/Wheat Flour
Barley	1/5
Brown Rice	1/4
Buckwheat	1/4
Corn	1/4
Millet	1/4
Oat	1/3
Rye (medium)	2/1
Rye (dark)	1/1
Soy and Soya	1/4
Triticale	1/1
White Rice	1/4

King Arthur's Flour
(The Baker's Catalogue)
Rural Route 2, Box 56
Norwich, VT 05055
(800) 827-6836

Morgan's Mills
Rural Route 2, Box 4602
Union, ME 04862
(207) 785-4900

WHEAT FLOURS

Flour that is milled from grains, wheat most commonly, is the primary ingredient in baked goods. There are many kinds of wheat flour available. Those milled from wheat varieties with less protein are softer and are preferred for making cakes and pastries. Those flours milled from higher protein varieties have more strength and thus, are good choices for yeast breads. They can provide the support needed for the expansion of gases during leavening and baking.

Whole wheat flour (graham flour) is a coarse-textured flour ground from the entire wheat kernel. It contains the fiber-rich, B vitamin-rich, and trace mineral rich outer head, bran portion of the berry along with the protein-rich fatty germ or embryo of the kernel and the starch-filled endosperm. The endosperm is the part of the wheat kernel that yields white flour and provides the gluten necessary to make bread rise.

All-purpose flour is made from the ground endosperm of the kernel from a combination of both hard and soft wheat. It can be used to produce acceptable baked products in all categories including yeast breads, cakes, cookies, and pastries.

Bread flour like all-purpose flour is ground from only the endosperm of the wheat kernel but because it is milled from a hard wheat, it is higher in gluten than all-purpose flour. It is the preferred choice for yeast breads.

Cake flour, milled from the endosperm of soft wheat kernels is low in protein and gluten, and thus is especially suitable for making cakes, cookies, and crackers.

Pastry flour, as its name implies, is desirable for preparing pastries. It is milled from the endosperm of soft, low-gluten wheat and has a protein level similar to cake flour but contains less starch.

Gluten flour contains much more protein than bread flour and can be used with refined and whole grain, low-protein or non-wheat flours to compensate for their lack of gluten. For example, flours such as potato, soy, rye, whole wheat pastry, and others lacking gluten-forming proteins can be combined with gluten flour in order to obtain a well-piled loaf with a fine grain and texture.

Unbleached, unbromonated and/or enriched wheat flours or ones labeled with these terms indicate that they are not high in fiber. Unbleached or unbromonated wheat flour is refined flour that has been bleached by oxygen in the air. Bleached flour has been treated with various agents that lighten its color and/or improve its baking quality. Nutritionally, unbleached and bleached flours are equivalent. Enriched wheat flour is refined flour which has been enriched with the B vitamins—thiamin, riboflavin, niacin—and the mineral iron. Each of these flours is low in fiber, containing no more fiber than refined white (wheat) flour.

Whole wheat pastry flour. In pastry making or baking powder risen breads, such as muffins, cookies, or cakes, gluten is not necessary and in fact not desired. While toughness may be an asset when making yeast breads, this is not the case in quick breads and cakes. Whole wheat pastry flour has a nutty taste and more minerals and fiber than white cake or pastry flour. It produces excellent results in pastry making and baking powder breads. If not available locally, whole wheat pastry flour can be ordered by mail from The Baker's Catalogue, P.O. Box 876, Norwich, VT 05055; (800) 827-6836. When purchased in bulk, whole wheat and other whole grain flours' freshness can be preserved by freezing. Half whole wheat and half all-purpose flour can be substituted for whole wheat pastry flour, but care should be used not to overmix. Because both whole wheat and all-purpose flours are high in gluten, tough elastic strands will form when mixed vigorously with liquids. The result will be less tender baked goods.

Whole white wheat flour, a whole wheat flour with the fiber and extra nutrients of whole wheat flour, along with a taste and appearance similar to refined flour, is now available. It is tan with flecks of gold rather than the darker brown ones found in regular whole wheat, thus it looks lighter. Because it contains none of the bitter-tasting substances called phenolic compounds found in regular whole wheat, it is also milder and sweeter-tasting than its counterpart. Another attribute of the new whole wheat flour is that it performs more like the refined all-purpose flour presently used in most baked goods. It mixes and rolls out more easily, yielding lighter and fluffier final products.

If whole white wheat flour is not available in the area, it can be purchased from these two mail order sources: (1) King Arthur Flour (800) 827-6836 or (2) American White Wheat Producers Association (913) 367-4422; P.O. Box 326, Atchison, KS 66002.

High-Fiber, Starch-Rich Cookies, Bars, Cakes, and Pastries

Many diners consider desserts to be off limits when eating healthfully. There's no need to refuse dessert when cookies, bars, cakes, and pastries are prepared with whole grain flours, supplemented with whole grains (see Table 2.4) or enriched with dried fruits, and small amounts of nuts and seeds. They will have unique flavors and be more nutritious than those prepared with refined flours alone. For example, molasses ginger cookies prepared from a mixture of whole wheat and unbleached flours and oat bran make charming, nutritious snacks with a glass of nonfat milk. They can also serve as crusts for dynamite fruit and cookie pizzas. Likewise, the list of bars might include apple, rum raisin bars brushed with reduced sugar, orange marmalade or quinoa and yogurt bars laced with dried apricot bits and toasted pine nuts. Such high-fiber treats will please diners who want more than fat and sugar for desert.

Although cakes are usually made with cake flour, ones with more body like banana, gingerbread, and farmer-style apple cakes can be made successfully with whole grain flours and enriched with whole grains, fruits, and nuts as well.

Pastry crusts and toppings for fruit and other low-fat fillings can add fiber to the dessert menu too. For low-fat and high-fiber desserts, fillings of favorite berries like blueberries, blackberries, raspberries, and strawberries might be covered with a high-fiber pastry top, perhaps an oat lattice prepared with oat flour and whole wheat pastry flours.

Pastries are found in more than sweet baked goods. They are components of savory dishes too. For example, the crusts of whole wheat calzones might be prepared with equal parts of whole wheat pastry and unbleached flours. Served packed with garden fresh vegetables and part-skim mozzarella cheese, whole wheat calzones are likely to be popular with health-conscious diners, as well as those not so concerned about what they eat.

At the mention of savory pastries, pot pies are sure to come to mind. For a contemporary version of this old-fashioned favorite, baby winter vegetables and cubes of chicken breast meat can be coated in a light ginger gravy and presented in a flaky whole wheat phyllo shell. Of course, to keep fat and calories in line, the phyllo basket is made by separating layers of the dough with butter-flavored vegetable spray and a sprinkle of crushed bran flakes.

The definition of what a pizza is varies greatly among Americans depending on what part of the country they live in. But whether its complex carbohydrate-rich crust is thin and crisp or thick and chewy, like a sandwich, a slice of pizza makes a splendid

TABLE 2.4

Grains

Amaranth	tiny, pale yellow, whole grains about the size of poppy seeds with a pronounced earthy sweet flavor and a gelatinous texture when cooked
Barley	
Hulled	brown grains removed of their inedible hull but not their bran with a mild nutty flavor and chewy texture
Job's Tears (Hato Mugi Barley, Juno's Tears or River Grain)	like over-sized pearl barley with a brown indented stripe down one side; has the chewiness of barley but a slight stickiness
Pearl	ivory-colored grains missing their hull, bran, and most of their germ
Pot or Scotch	less refined form than pearl barley with part of its bran layer remaining
Buckwheat	
Groats	whole white (unroasted) kernels with a fairly mild flavor or brown (roasted) kernels with a more assertive flavor; really a fruit and not a grain
Grits	finely ground, unroasted groats sold as buckwheat cereal or cream of buckwheat; develops a soft and creamy texture
Kasha	roasted, hulled buckwheat kernels with a toasty flavor; available cracked into coarse, medium, and fine granules
Kamut (Egyptian Wheat)	an ancient buttery tasting golden grain about 3 times larger than wheat berries with a pleasant chewiness that can be better tolerated by some diners sensitive to wheat
Millet	tiny, pale yellow or reddish orange beads with a delicate, bland flavor sold pearled for human consumption

(continued)

TABLE 2.4

Continued

Oats

Bran	*the outer layer of oat groats with a finer texture and lighter color than the wheat bran sold as a packaged cereal*
Groats	*whole kernels with their bran and germ*
Rolled (old-fashioned)	*groats that have been heated and pressed flat with steel rollers to shorten their cooking time*
Instant	*oats that have been precooked, dried, and pressed very thin*
Quinoa (keen-wa)	*a pale yellow seed slightly larger than mustard seed with a sweet flavor and soft texture*

Rice

Brown	*rice with only its outer husk removed in milling and a nutty flavor and chewy texture*
White	*rice completely removed of its husk, bran, and most of its germ*
Wild	*dark brown-colored slender grains even longer than long-grain rice with a nutty, earthy flavor; really the seed of an aquatic grass; available in giant (long), extra-fancy (medium), and select (short)*

Rye

Berries	*similar in shape to wheat with a bluish gray color and strong distinctive flavor; also called whole kernels or groats*
Cracked	*whole berries that have been cracked to shorten their cooking time*
Flakes	*berries that have been heated and then pressed with steel rollers*
Spelt	*ancient grain with a taste and texture similar to wheat but because it is slightly different genetically, diners*

(continued)

hand-held meal for diners on the go as well as for those choosing to enjoy a relaxed meal with friends or family members. Start with a whole wheat crust and offer a choice of toppings. To keep it low in fat and high in fiber, go heavy on the tomato-based pizza sauce and vegetables and light on the meat and cheese. For adventurous diners or as Californians do, fruit cubes might even be added to the list of topping choices.

High-Fiber, Carbohydrate-Rich Pastas

Pastas are well-known sources of starch. More than 75% of their calories come from these complex carbohydrates. Further, pasta adds protein, is low in fat, and if made from whole grain flours or refined flours that have been enriched, contains B vitamins and iron. Whole grain pastas provide another bonus. They contribute over 6 grams of fiber per cooked cup. Thus, a salad featuring whole grain pasta tossed with fiber-rich vegetables and fiber-filled nuts can easily supply a fourth of the 20–30 fiber grams recommended daily.

Besides being right in line with today's health-conscious trend, pasta is a versatile ingredient, available in an infinite variety of sizes, flavors, and shapes. Further, it is easy to prepare, is a very profitable menu item, and is compatible with endless flavors and shapes of ingredients. It is no wonder pasta's popularity is at an all-time high.

Traditional favorites like macaroni and cheese, and spaghetti with meatballs, are still favorites, but the possibilities go far beyond. Pasta can be boiled, baked, stir-fried, combined with ingredients of all types, served hot or cold, featured as an appetizer, entree, or side course, added to soups, made into salads, mixed into omelets, and can even be the primary ingredient in desserts.

Pastas are made from flour, usually wheat flour. It is combined with liquid, kneaded to make a dough, rolled out, and cut into the desired pasta shape. While Italian-style pasta dishes are the most familiar in the United States, many other cuisines use noodles too.

ITALIAN-STYLE PASTA

The finest Italian-style commercial dried pastas are made from a dough of semolina flour. This high-protein wheat flour gives pasta a deep yellow color, mellow flavor, and sturdy texture. Some manufacturers use farina and other wheat flours. When cooked, these pastas become soft and do not hold their shapes well. Some shapes of dried pasta, among the many, are the large hollow manicotti tubes, long hollow ziti rods, corkscrew fusilli, thin delicate angel hair or capellini strands, long, rodlike spaghetti, short elbow-shaped hollow macaroni, ridged hollow rigatoni tubes, ricelike orzo, wagon wheel ruote, and flat butterfly farfalle.

Fresh pastas are also commonly made from wheat flour but with eggs, water, and often oil and salt. Fresh pastas are used primarily for flat noodles such as fettuccine and lasagne or stuffed dumplings like ravioli squares, tortellini rings, and agnolotti crescents.

Besides whole and refined wheat, commercial dried and fresh pastas are available made from many other flours including amaranth, corn, quinoa, Jerusalem artichoke, and spelt, singly or in combination with wheat flour. Pastas may be made entirely from a nonwheat flour but most contain both wheat and nonwheat flours. Their nutritional value will depend on the type and amount of nonwheat flour added. For example, pasta made from corn flour contains less protein than wheat pasta, but otherwise is nutritiously comparable, while pasta made from a combination of amaranth and wheat flours is similar to wheat pasta but higher in fiber.

A really different pasta to recently join the ranks is made from lupin bean and semolina flours. Lupin pasta is a nutritional star on many counts. It serves up nearly quadruple the fiber, double the protein, and more B vitamins and calcium than wheat pasta, all for 25% fewer calories. Lupin pasta is available in health food stores or by the case from Lupini Foods, Saint Paul, Minnesota at (800) 203-4343.

Both fresh and dried pastas can be flavored and colored with one or a variety of ingredients. They include beets, tomatoes, red peppers, carrots, spinach, garlic, basil, parsley, squid ink, ground pepper, chocolate, and saffron. Manufacturers are offering choices such as lemon pepper angel hair, tomato pesto liguini, and tricolored rotini—mixtures of tomato, spinach, and wheat spiral-shaped pastas. Care is required to match flavored pastas with compatible toppings, fillings, and garnishes. No other special handling is necessary. For example, thin long strands of red bell pepper and basil, whole wheat linguine might be made into a light main course dish by topping with chopped tomatoes sauteed in a bit of olive oil seasoned with freshly minced garlic and Italian spices and sprinkled with freshly grated, part-skim parmesan cheese. Once diners have tried a dish as wonderful as this, they will probably always be asking for whole grain flavored pastas.

ASIAN NOODLES

While most Americans think rice is the Asian starch of choice, noodles have long been important ingredients in the cuisines of

TABLE 2.4

Continued

	with an intolerance to wheat may be able to digest it better
Teff	a very tiny seed (150 seeds equals the weight of about 1 wheat grain) of Ethiopian origin with a slight molasses taste and gelatinous texture, available in white, red, and brown
Triticale (trit-i-kay-lee)	
Berries	a hybrid of wheat and rye about twice the size of wheat berries with a nutlike flavor; contain their bran and germ
Cracked	whole berries that have been cracked to shorten their cooking time
Flakes	berries that have been steamed and flattened
Wheat	
Berries or groats	unprocessed whole wheat kernels with a hearty, nutty flavor and chewy texture
Bran	high-fiber, rough outer grain covering of wheat
Bulgur	whole wheat kernels that have been steamed, dried, and then cracked into coarse, medium, and fine granules
Cracked	wheat berries that have been cracked into coarse, medium, and fine granules for faster cooking
Germ	embryo of the wheat berry; must be refrigerated since contains oils that will become rancid if stored at room temperature

Sources: S.T. Herbst. 1990. *Food Lover's Companion.* Hauppauge, New York: Barron's Educational Series. California Culinary Academy. 1988. *Cooking A to Z.* San Ramon, CA: Chevron Chemical Co. pp. 268–78. P. Dowell and A. Bailey. 1980. *Cook's Ingredients.* New York: William Morrow and Co., pp. 122–23, 256–57. S. and M. London. 1992. *The Versatile Grain and the Elegant Bean.* New York: Simon and Schuster. K. Mayes and S. Gottfried. 1992. *Boutique Bean Pot.* Santa Barbara, CA: Woodbridge Press. S. Margen and the Editors of the University of California at Berkeley "Wellness Letter." 1992. *The Wellness Encyclopedia of Food and Nutrition.* New York: Random House. L. J. Sass. 1992. *Recipes from an Ecological Kitchen.* New York: William Morrow and Co. B. Greene. 1988. *The Grains Cookbook.* New York: Workman Publishing. J. Saltzman. 1990. *Amazing Grains.* New York: H. J. Kramer.

China, Japan, Korea, Vietnam, and other Asian countries. Unlike Italian-style pastas, Asian noodles do not come in hundreds of sizes and shapes and they are not typically flavored or colored with vegetable purees, herbs, spices, and other ingredients. Virtually all Asian noodles are flat wrappers and ribbon shapes of varying lengths and widths. Also, unlike Italian-style pastas, Asian noodles may contain wheat, but equally common are noodles made from other flours and starches including rice and buckwheat flours and vegetable starches such as yam, soybean, corn, and potato.

The following are a few of the best known Asian noodle types.

Bean thread vermicelli, also known as cellophane noodles, jelly noodles, and transparent vermicelli, are thin, semi-translucent noodles made from mung beans. They are almost pure starch with little protein. Bean thread vermicelli can be used in soups, braised dishes, hot pots, or softened in water and added to stir-fries. In some Asian countries, boiled cellophane noodles are added to sweet coconut milk-based drinks and desserts. When Japanese shirataki noodles are not available, cellophane noodles make a good substitute.

Egg noodles are made like their Italian-style counterparts with wheat flour and eggs. Thus, nutritionally they are comparable. These versatile noodles are typically added to soups, boiled and topped with meat, seafood, poultry, and/or vegetables, or served cold with a soy sauce-based dressing. In fresh form, egg noodles are made into wontons and egg rolls.

Rice vermicelli are very thin noodles made from a dough of rice flour and water. Like bean thread vermicelli, they are almost pure starch with little protein. When rice vermicelli are deep-fried, they puff 4–6 times their dry size into delicate, crisp, feather-light, white noodles. Because they are bland tasting and readily absorb flavors, rice vermicelli can be softened with water and added to both savory and sweet dishes. In this lower fat form, they can serve as primary ingredients in stir-fries, be added to soups, made into puddings, and incorporated into beverages.

Soba noodles are Japanese dark brownish-gray spaghetti-like noodles made from buckwheat flour or buckwheat flour in combination with wheat flour. These protein-rich noodles are commonly served hot in broth or cold with a soy dipping sauce. Both fresh and dried forms are available. An interesting green-tinted variation of soba noodles is also available. It is created by adding green matcha tea powder to the buckwheat-based dough.

Udon noodles are generally round but sometimes flat, Japanese noodles made from wheat flour and water. They are popular in Japan served in soups and simmered dishes and braised in soy-based sauces. Nutritionally, they are comparable to Italian-style dried pastas.

SERVING PASTAS

The healthy attributes of pastas of all types can be enhanced by offering them mixed, topped, baked, stir-fried, or prepared in a variety of other ways combined with legumes, lots of vegetables and their sauces, and small amounts of lean meat, poultry, seafood, nuts, seeds, and/or low-fat cheeses. Such pasta dishes are far superior nutritionally to those prepared by traditional methods loaded with high-calorie, high-cholesterol, and high-fat ingredients like butter, heavy cream, cheese, and/or meat.

Delicate pastas like angel hair and vermicelli work well with light, thin sauces, while thicker pasta shapes like fettucine are best matched with heavier sauces. Pasta shapes with holes or ridges like ziti and fusilli are good served with chunky sauces. For example, a pasta dish as tasty as it is nutritious might be created by tossing 2-inch, whole wheat, penne tubes with a chunky ratatouille sauce of garlic and herb-flavored eggplant, tomatoes, onions, and bell peppers, or stir-frying thin Chinese egg noodles with strips of chicken breast meat, sliced green onions, bean sprouts, white cabbage, pea pods, and broccoli florets and seasoning with low-sodium soy sauce, ginger, and garlic.

Fiber-Filled, High-Starch Potato Dishes

Potatoes are Americans' favorite vegetable. They eat them prepared in a variety of ways at every meal of the day and as snacks too. It's hard to imagine a burger without fries, an omelet minus the hash browns, roast chicken and no mashed potatoes, baked ham—skip the au gratins, or a potato-free beef stew.

Potatoes are cholesterol-free, low-fat sources of complex carbohydrates. When dishes are made from potatoes with their skins and all and no or small amounts of fat, they can be promoted as healthy menu choices. For example, steamed, new, red-skinned potatoes sprinkled with fresh herbs are always popular.

Even French fries will receive top marks from fiber advocates when prepared from strips of unpeeled potatoes, coated with a small amount of vegetable oil, a sprinkle of seasoning with garlic powder, and baked in the oven.

The skins are best retained in potato salads too, not only for the fiber they add but for their color, flavor, and texture. For example, an impressive, warm, main course salad can be created by combining steamed, red-skinned, baby potatoes with broccoli spears and lean sausage balls and coating in a light vinaigrette dressing.

VARIETIES OF POTATOES

In addition to the familiar red, round, waxy and brown, oblong, starchy types of potatoes, there are many other varieties available. For starters, *fingerlings*, small, flavorful, typically knobby potatoes with relatively low starch content and thin skins might be added to the menu. These firm, waxy potatoes work well steamed, roasted, or tossed in a light vinaigrette. They include the Banana, Ozette, Purple Peruvian, Rose Finn, and Ruby Crescent varieties. For example, Ozette fingerlings roasted with rosemary and garlic, sliced, and tossed warm with a tad of extra-virgin olive oil, shallot marmalade, and balsamic vinegar might be offered as an alternative to the typical mayonnaise-coated, red-skinned new potato salad.

Yellow-fleshed potato varieties with skins ranging in color from *peach to rose* make good choices when a potato with more flavor than that of the white potato is desired. Cherry Reds, Desirees, Red Clouds, Red Dales, and Rose Golds are varieties in this group. One typically associates home fries with bacon and eggs. For a lighter but substantial breakfast or lunch offering, a single baked egg might be served on a bed of roasted Rose Gold potato cubes, lightly brushed with olive oil, and tossed with grilled corn kernels, tomato cubes, and fresh herbs.

Potatoes with *golden to tan* colored skins and yellow fleshes come in both starchy and waxy forms. Varieties in this group are known for their exceptional flavor. They include Bintje, Carole, Yellow Finn, and Yukon Gold potatoes. As an alternative to deep-fried potato croquettes, Yukon Golds might be roasted and served warm soaking up a light Asian-style chili dressing seasoned with lemongrass and freshly minced cilantro.

Potatoes with *blue to purple* skins and fleshes ranging from white to deep purple can even be found. While their color may be unique, most potatoes in this group are bland in flavor and change color with cooking. Varieties included in this category are All-Blue, Caribe, and Kerry Blue potatoes. For a special kind of potato terrine, Kerry Blue potatoes might be layered with other varieties of potatoes like Cherry Reds and Yellow Fins.

There are also all kinds of potatoes that might be lumped together in the *novelty or heirloom* category. These less common potatoes can be found at farmer's markets and in mail order catalogs. They include the Australian Crawler, Charlotte, Cherries Jubilee, Early Rose, German Butterball, Kasaan, Mandel, Norwegian, Nosebag, Purple Viking, and Seneca Horn. How could diners resist when violet-skinned, white-fleshed potatoes like Seneca Horns are served transformed into crusty, browned, mashed potato cakes with garlic.

Complex Carbohydrate-Rich Grains

Grains can add interesting texture and rustic appeal to plates at only pennies per serving. Traditional favorites might be offered on the menu along with less familiar or recently rediscovered whole grains.

Some of the options to pick from are listed in Table 2.4.

COMPOSITION OF GRAINS

Most grains are actually the edible seed kernels of cereal plants. These seed kernels consist of four parts: an edible husk, a fiber-, B vitamin-, and mineral-rich protective bran coat, a starch-filled endosperm, and a protein- and oil-rich embryo referred to as the germ.

NUTRIENT CONTENT OF GRAINS

Nutritionally, all grains are low in fat, cholesterol-free, and if unrefined, a good source of fiber. Vitamins, minerals, and other nutrients vary from grain to grain. A half cup serving of grain will add about 100 calories to the diet. The following is a review of the nutritional attributes of popular ones (see Sources for Table 2.4).

Amaranth rates very high nutritionally, number two of all grains, by the *Nutrition Action Newsletter* (April 1993, p. 10). It is rich in vitamins, high in calcium, iron, copper, and other minerals, and contains lysine, an essential protein building block (amino acid) missing in most grains. As a result, when one part of amaranth is combined with wheat or corn, it forms a protein equal to that found in milk.

Barley may contain a cholesterol-inhibiting substance. It is a good source of protein, fiber, iron, and other nutrients even in its more refined (pearled) form.

Bulgur is nutritionally similar to wheat berries (see below)— their steamed, dried, and cracked form.

Buckwheat is closer to yielding complete proteins than other grains. It is also rich in iron, B vitamins, and minerals. It makes a good choice for diners who can't eat wheat because of allergies. *Nutrition Action Newsletter* (April 1993, p. 10) ranked it number 3 nutritionally of all the grains.

Kamut is similar nutritionally to wheat. It is rich in protein, and a good source of potassium, zinc, and magnesium.

Millet is rich in amino acids and a good source of phosphorous and B vitamins. It also provides more iron than most grains; only amaranth and quinoa rate higher.

Oats have excellent nutritional qualities. They are well endowed with protein, B vitamins, calcium, and fiber.

Quinoa comes in first nutritionally on many counts. It is an excellent source of magnesium and rich in iron, calcium, and copper. Further, it is a good source of protein and rich in lysine, the amino acid lacking in most grains.

Rice in its whole grain brown form is rich in fiber, B vitamins, and minerals including iron, zinc, phosphorous, copper, and manganese. Brown rice is also the only form of rice that provides vitamin E.

White rice is almost pure starch. Most of its vitamins, minerals, protein, and fiber are removed in the milling process.

Rye is a good source of fiber and B vitamins, and is high in minerals including potassium, phosphorous, and iron.

Spelt is nutritionally similar to wheat (see below).

Teff, like amaranth, is loaded with nutrients. It is endowed with calcium, iron, copper, and zinc.

Triticale is a good source of B vitamins and provides a better balance of protein than either of its two parent grains, wheat or rye.

Wheat berries, because they are whole grains, provide all the nutrients found in wheat bran and wheat germ (see below) along with a supply of starch from their endosperm.

Wheat bran is recognized primarily for its high fiber content but also adds B vitamins and protein to the diet.

Wheat germ contains protein and polyunsaturated fat and is a source of vitamin E, B vitamins including thiamin, riboflavin, and niacin, minerals including zinc, and fiber.

Wild rice is a better source of protein than other types of rice and adds fiber, zinc, magnesium, and B vitamins to the diet.

COOKING GRAINS

Some grains will be purchased in packages with cooking directions. More often, they will be purchased in bulk and contain none. Thus, Table 2.5 describes simple cooking procedures for 1 cup of grain. These directions are only a guide and cooking times and yields are only approximations. When cooking larger amounts of grains, modifications may be required in the recipe.

Whole grains should be rinsed prior to cooking. Most have not been cleaned and are dusty. Some, like quinoa, contain a natural coating that can leave a bitter taste. Some long-cooking grains such as oat groats and triticale will also benefit from presoaking.

TABLE 2.5

Grain Cooking Procedures

Grain (1 cup)	Water (cups)	Cooking Time (minutes)	Let Stand (minutes)	Yield (cups)
Amaranth	3	25	0	2½
Barley, hulled or pearl	3½	30–35	10	3¼
Buckwheat groats*	2	10–12	5	4
Bulgur**				
coarse	3	0	60	3
medium	2½	0	30	3
fine	2½	0	15	3
Job's Tears, soaked	3	40	10	2½
Kasha*				
coarse	2	10–15	5	4
medium	2	8–10	5	4
fine	2	5–6	5	4
Millet, toasted	2½	25–30	10	4
Oat				
groats, soaked	2¾	25	10	3
rolled***	2¾	0	10	2½
Quinoa, toasted	2	12–15	5	3½
Rice				
brown	2¼–2½	40–45	10	3¼
white	2	15–18	5	3¼
Rye				
berries	3¼	60	10	2
flakes	3	25–30	5	2⅔
Teff	3	15	0	3
Triticale, soaked	3	70	5	2½
Wheat				
berries, soaked	3½	50–60	10	3
cracked, toasted	2⅓	15	5	2¾
Wild rice				
long	4	50–60	10	3
medium or short	4	45–60	10	3

Directions: Heat water to a boil, stir in the grain, return to a boil, reduce the heat, cover, and simmer.
*Coat buckwheat groats and kasha with beaten whole eggs or egg whites and toast before proceeding with the directions above.
**Directions: Pour boiling water over the bulgur, and steep without heat. After standing, drain in a colander lined with cheesecloth. Twist the cheesecloth around the bulgur to squeeze out excess moisture.
***Directions: heat water to a boil, stir in the rolled oats, cover, and stand without heat.
Source: Adapted from S. and M. London (1992). The Versatile Grain and the Elegant Bean. New York: Simon and Schuster.

The best way to tell when grains are done is to taste them. Some diners will like their grains soft while others will prefer them tender but chewy. In all cases, the liquid should be completely absorbed. If there is excess water after the grains are tender, it can be drained off and the grains returned to the pan until heated through. If the grains are not cooked enough, some boiling water can be added and simmering continued, repeating as needed until the grains reach their desired degree of doneness. Some grains will require standing after cooking. To prevent moisture from accumulating between them and their lid, place a paper towel under their lid.

Many methods can be used to perk up the taste of grains without adding lots of fat. They can be toasted before cooking or simmered in a rich flavorful broth or water with added seasoning agents such as a few slices of ginger, garlic cloves, hot peppers or citrus zests; condiments such as reduced sodium soy or worcestershire sauces or flavored mustard; herbs such as bay leaves, sorrel, or mint; spices such as cardamom pods, whole cloves, or allspice berries; vegetables such as minced shallots, sun-dried tomatoes, or mushrooms braise-deglazed in red wine; or fruits such as apple slices, raisins, or dried wild blueberries. Some flavoring agents like strawberry essence and coconut extract lose flavor with heat. They should be added to grains at the end of cooking.

Salt can also enhance the taste of grains. Sodium-conscious diners may prefer their grains without salt but if it is to be used, some grains such as amaranth, wheat berries, and triticale should be salted only after cooking. Salt toughens their outer hull and prevents them from absorbing liquid properly.

GRAIN SERVING IDEAS

Whole grains might be served as main course accompaniments, and also may be incorporated into many other dishes on the menu. They might be added to soups, salads, stuffings, stews and braised dishes, puddings or blended into batters for cakes, cookies, yeast and quick breads. They are easy to prepare and because of their unique tastes, textures, and appearances, lend themselves well to creative menu development.

For example, a high-fiber barley pine nut casserole—barley simmered in stock and seasoned with pine nuts, some fresh parsley, and a grind of pepper—might replace fried potatoes as an accompaniment for skinless roasted squab glazed with black currant syrup.

In addition to tasting good solo, grains combine well with each other and can be flavored with a variety of herbs and spices.

For example, a flavorful, crunchy complement to poultry, pork, or lamb might be created by simmering barley and quinoa in flavorful, fat-free stock, seasoning with curry powder, onion, and garlic and at service, sprinkling with toasted, slivered almonds and finely chopped parsley.

Another possibility is barley and wheat berry pilaf, a combination of the two grains tossed with chopped prunes. It might complete a dinner comprised of lean, sliced, beef tenderloin topped with sauteed mushrooms, steamed baby carrots, and a fresh green salad.

For added color and texture, grains might be combined with vegetables, as in fried brown rice sprinkled with vegetables (see page 123). With the addition of dried beans, peas, or lentils, poultry or seafood, this dish might be converted into a main course selection.

Two of my favorite high-fiber breakfast grain dishes are wild rice waffles and blueberry bulgur pancakes. Both bulgur and wild rice are excellent in soups and salads too.

For example, cooked bulgur might be made into a great summer salad by tossing with diced cucumbers, red onions, yellow summer squash, plum tomatoes, and a light vinaigrette and garnishing with edible flowers.

The less familiar quinoa also is excellent as the primary ingredient in salads. For a salad in a league of its own, pineapple cubes, mandarin oranges, and sliced water chestnuts might be combined with quinoa and sprayed with a light orange-flavored dressing.

While the ancient grain, amaranth, only began to reappear on menus in the mid-1970s, it might be made into delicious, starch-filled, low-fat, high-fiber bars. It is as simple as popping the grains and coating them with a lemon-flavored syrup. Another dessert favorite, rice pudding, takes on new charm and its fiber content is raised by substituting brown rice for the standard white and studding with dried cherries rather than the more commonplace raisins.

Fiber- and Starch-Filled Dried Beans, Peas, and Lentils

Previously, dried beans, peas, and lentils rarely appeared on the menu. In comparison to many other foods, these high-protein, starch-filled foods are especially rich sources of fiber (see Table 2.6). For example, while a small apple yields almost 3 grams of dietary fiber, a half cup of dried, cooked navy beans provides more than double this amount. Similarly, the 6 grams of fiber in a half

TABLE 2.6

Fiber Content of Some Common Foods

Food	Amount	Total Dietary Fiber/Serving (g)	Soluble Fiber/Serving (g)
Navy beans, dried, cooked	½ cup	6.78	2.29
Pinto beans, dried, cooked	½ cup	5.90	1.84
Kidney beans, canned	½ cup	5.75	1.45
White beans, dried, cooked	½ cup	5.07	1.48
White beans, canned	½ cup	4.98	1.50
Pinto beans, canned	½ cup	4.34	1.01
Pork and beans, canned	½ cup	3.74	1.84
Blackeyed peas, canned	½ cup	3.21	0.35
Lima beans, canned	½ cup	3.02	0.79
Garbanzo beans, canned	⅓ cup	2.08	0.32
Oat bran	⅓ cup	4.03	2.01
Apple	1 small	2.76	0.97
Whole wheat flour	2 ½ tablespoons	2.80	0.35
Grapefruit	½ medium	1.46	0.90
Whole wheat bread	1 slice	1.53	0.34
Banana	½ small	1.09	0.32

Source: Data from J. W. Anderson (1988). "Dietary Fiber Content of Selected Foods." *American Journal of Clinical Nutrition 47*, 440–447.

cup of cooked pinto beans is over 3 times the amount in a slice of whole wheat bread.

Today, dried beans, peas, and lentils are becoming more common on menus (see Table 5.2). They can be included in every course.

Black bean patties topped with tomato and bell pepper salsa (see page 197) or herb-seasoned pita crisps with cannellini bean dip adorned with green onions, bell peppers and tomatoes might head off the appetizer list. A soup filled with legumes like split pea laced with spinach or fresh fava bean soup sprinkled with minced basil might be promoted as a first course, but can be combined with a sandwich or a salad for a light lunch or supper too.

There are many more options for salads than lettuce and dressing. Those featuring legumes can taste and look as good as they sound. The list might include a crunchy, green lentil salad dressed in a light tarragon vinaigrette, red kidney bean and corn salad coated with chili dressing, or a black and white bean salad on a bed of shredded romaine lettuce topped with chunky tomato salsa and lots of cilantro.

Many chefs are turning to dried beans, peas, and lentils as accompaniments for meat, fish, and poultry selections. For example, white beans with garlic might make a charming complement to marinated, roasted rack of lamb, thinly sliced and moistened with a fat-free au jus, while kidney beans simmered in spicy broth might be excellent with tender chunks of slowly braised, lean pork. Cannellini beans fresca and lima bean succotash are two other dishes highlighting legumes. Both are refreshing alternatives to more commonplace cooked vegetable accompaniments.

Legumes are economically good replacements for meat in stews and other braised dishes. At the same time, they can add color, flavor, and texture to these dishes, while cutting their fat and cholesterol and increasing their fiber content. For example, Mediterranean lamb stew garnished with northern beans or Moroccan stew filled with lentils and vegetables might be promoted as hearty and satisfying main course selections. To make the Middle Eastern stew into a truly ethnic experience, it might be offered with whole wheat flat bread, and diners encouraged to eat it with their hands.

Dishes featuring legumes flavored with small amounts of lean meat, seafood, and poultry are another option. Hoppin' John (black-eyed peas cooked with seasonings and served with cooked rice), a long-time favorite in many parts of the country, might be suggested as a nutritious alternative to a main-plate meat, seafood, or poultry item. For non-red-meat eaters, this traditional dish might be combined with diced turkey ham, and for additional fiber, be presented on a bed of steamed brown rice.

Dried beans, peas, and lentils work equally well as high-protein main course selections without any meat, seafood, or poultry. For example, Jamaican-style brown rice and kidney beans or three bean, lentil, and pea stew might be prepared with no ingredients of animal origin and promoted as vegetarian specials of the day.

Pasta is especially popular with diners these days. Legumes are nice compliments to pastas of all flavors, sizes, and shapes. For example, smaller portions of chili fettucine tossed with white beans and strips of skinless, grilled duck breast might be offered as a first course or larger portions as main course selections.

Even sandwiches might be filled with dried beans, peas, or lentils. For example, an open-face sandwich might be created by layering a smooth lentil spread seasoned with Asian spices, shredded lettuce, sliced tomatoes, and a sprinkle of freshly grated ginger on whole wheat bread, or for a hand-held sandwich, wrap whole wheat tortillas around simmered and seasoned pinto beans, low-fat cheddar cheese, and spicy tomato salsa.

High-Fiber, Complex Carbohydrate-Rich Vegetables

Vegetables are not only high in fiber and rich in vitamins and minerals, but are also low in calories and contain varying amounts of starch. Some chefs believe that it is necessary to remove the skins and seeds of vegetables before serving. In some cases, this may be desirable but it also reduces their fiber content. A good method to determine which diners prefer—skin on and seeds in or skin off and seeds out—is to ask them. After all, some diners may disapprove when the skins of vegetables like cucumbers or eggplants or the fibrous stems of ones like asparagus or broccoli are peeled or both the skins and seeds of vegetables like tomatoes are removed.

The bright colors, crisp textures, and fresh flavors of vegetables, preferably unpeeled, can be added to every course of the menu. One place they have commonly appeared on diners' plates is as main course accompaniments. Lightly seasoned, steamed, garden fresh vegetables bursting with color are always a treat, but the list of preparation techniques for vegetables only begins here. With a bit of imagination, varieties of innovative vegetable side dishes can be created. For example, zucchini boats might be filled with a colorful medley of tasty diced vegetables or fresh corn sauteed with onion and simmered in a few tablespoons of low-fat milk, lightly sweetened and flavored with maple and a dash of freshly ground cinnamon.

Traditional recipes for vegetables are popular with diners too. Tender cauliflower florets coated in a creamy, low-fat cheese sauce might be served topped with browned, whole wheat bread crumbs or bright orange, sliced carrots glazed in a citrus-flavored syrup and sprinkled with minced parsley.

Vegetables are equally delicious served in salads, soups, stews, stir-fries, and sandwiches, as toppings on pastas and pizzas, and can even add starch, fiber, flavor, and nutrients to desserts and breads. Vegetables hardly seem ingredients suitable for making cakes but gardeners with an over-abundance of produce blend them into their cakes all the time and create some of the best cakes. Following their direction, the menu might feature a carrot, raisin and pineapple cake (see page 124), chocolate potato, zucchini oat, or sweet potato apple nut cakes, but beets and winter squashes are other favorite vegetables waiting to be added to cakes. On a scale of 1 to 10, dense vegetable-based cakes rate 10 on all counts.

Thanksgiving wouldn't be complete without pumpkin pie. Along with beta carotene-rich sweet potatoes and yams, pumpkin is good in stews, soups, bars, buns, mousses, and puddings too. Further, these nutritious orange-colored vegetables work well in quick breads, as do many others. The menu might be rounded out with a sweet quick breadlike sunny carrot cornbread, zucchini raisin muffins, or pumpkin whole wheat pancakes (see page 126). On the savory side, diners might be tempted with vegetable-filled quick breads like red pepper scones, sun-dried tomato herb biscuits, or buckwheat, corn, and bell pepper waffles.

High-Fiber, Complex Carbohydrate-Rich Fruits

Fruits, like vegetables, can be good sources of both starch and fiber. They are readily available year round, fresh, frozen, dried, and canned. The fiber content of the menu might be raised by serving these naturally sweat treats fresh on fruit plates or cooked in sauces, puddings, pies, tarts, dumplings, and cobblers. Sliced fruit or its sauce might be served over cakes in lieu of frosting, replace high-fat toppings on frozen, low-fat yogurts, or substituted for a sugary syrup on whole grain pancakes or waffles. Fruits can also be incorporated into quick breads, cookies, cakes, bars, gelatins, and frozen desserts. For example, bananas might be blended into bran walnut muffins, replace a frosting on a gingerbread cake prepared with a combination of whole wheat and refined flours (see page 154), served sliced and frozen coated in crunchy whole grain cereal nuggets, or give a whole wheat cake with no added fat a new image (taste) by incorporating them in pureed form along with pureed apricots.

For additional fiber, fruits might be presented on pastry crusts made from whole grain flours or whole grain cookie, cracker, cake, or cereal crumbs or cooked coated, topped, or stuffed with one of these options along with high-fiber nuts, seeds, or dried fruits. For example, fresh, ripe, peach halves might be stuffed with a crunchy filling of sweetened, whole grain cereal nuggets and chopped walnuts (see page 79); sliced, sweetened apples sprinkled with raisins, topped with a crumbly oat mixture, and baked into a wonderful crisp; or raspberries blended into an airy light filling for a graham-cracker-crusted, raspberry snow tart garnished with mint leaves and yogurt honey topping.

Some fruit purees can even reduce the fat content of cakes

and other baked goods while increasing their fiber, vitamin, and mineral levels. Dried plum (prune) purees have been particularly successful as fat substitutes, but date and raisin purees (see page 125) work well too.

While frequently associated with desserts, fruits don't need to be limited to this section of the menu. They can be incorporated into dishes offered at every course. For example, high-fiber fresh blueberries might be paired with strips of grilled, skinless, chicken breast and pasta to produce a wonderful main course salad. Moistened with a flavorful low-fat yogurt and blueberry vinegar-based dressing, it makes a healthy offering all the way around. Blueberries are equally good when dried and combined with grains. For example, to present wild rice at its best, it might be tossed with dried blueberries and shiitake mushrooms.

Although apples aren't typically combined with chicken, they, like blueberries, make delicious complements. For example, poached chicken might be topped with a braised green apple and red onion sauce flavored with tarragon vinegar.

One doesn't normally think of eating cooked vegetables and fruits together either, but they make delightful combinations. Both cooked carrots and cabbage are good companions to apples.

The sky's the limit when conceiving dishes with high-fiber fruits. Selections can be created from scratch or classics modified. For example, a variation of the popular chef's salad might be created by preparing with fruit. Vitamin-rich kiwi, red bartlett pears, and crunchy carrots might be tossed with slivered, skinless, turkey breast and grated, low-fat mozzarella cheese and served on a bed of red leaf lettuce. There's little need for dressing but for those who ask, a sweet mustard dressing might be offered. Banana and peanut butter sandwiches are another well-known American favorite. For an upscale version of this sandwich, a light coat of macadamia nut butter and papaya slices might be layered between bite-size cutouts of whole grain bread.

Shrimp cocktail, one of those dishes most diners can't get enough of, is also a good candidate to enrich with fruit. The light tartness of sweet, peeled orange and grapefruit sections and buttery-flavored avocado slices are a perfect match for chilled, peeled, deveined shrimp.

Soups are another place one doesn't generally expect to find fruit. But, both chilled and warm, sweet fruit soups are a nice change as a first or last course in the meal. A chilled peach soup flavored with cinnamon and clove might be just right on a hot summer day, while when the weather turns cold, it's more likely to be a warm cherry soup finished with a dollop of low-fat yogurt.

High-Fiber Nuts and Seeds

Although nuts and seeds are high in fiber and protein and contain small amounts of starch, they are concentrated sources of fat, and thus, calories. To produce dishes with more fiber but moderate calories and fat, controlled amounts of nuts and seeds might be added. For example, a carbohydrate-rich, high-fiber, reduced-fat and calorie lasagne might be created vegetarian style by layering whole wheat noodles with chopped, blanched spinach, toasted, slivered almonds, low-fat cheeses, and Italian-style tomato sauce.

In many dishes, nuts or seeds can reduce the need for salt or butter. For example, in lieu of salt, stone ground whole wheat pretzels might be coated with caraway seeds, and rather than using butter or bacon drippings, sauteed greens might be flavored with freshly ground peanuts. When steamed green beans are sprinkled with toasted sesame seeds, there's no need for butter or salt.

Complex Carbohydrate-Rich Ethnic Dishes

When planning menu selections containing complex carbohydrates, many of the dishes from around the world have traditionally been good sources. Such selections might be added to menus in their authentic forms or adapted to accommodate the American palate. For example, the chef's specials for the day might include Middle Eastern tabbouleh—cracked wheat salad flavored with mint, parsley, olive oil, and lemon, South American-style corn pudding, or Spanish-inspired gazpacho—the spicy, cold, chunky tomato soup. Equally good might be ratatouille, a high-fiber vegetable stew of eggplants, tomatoes, green peppers, zucchini, onions and garlic, seasoned with herbs and a whisper of olive oil that originated in France.

Some say fassoulatha, a white bean soup, saved Greece during the Italian and German occupation of World War II. Dried beans were their only source of winter protein. Today, they are still a staple in poor households in Greece. For an economical but tasty fassoulatha-style soup, white beans might be simmered along with onions, celery, tomatoes, and carrots, and flavored with oregano.

When a restaurant breakfast diner asks for cereal, the choice is often a selection of brightly colored miniature boxes of mass-produced refined flakes and puffs, many of which are coated in sugar. Whole grains can give diners a new appreciation of what breakfast can be. Muesli, the multigrain cereal invention of a famous Swiss doctor near the end of the nineteenth century, might top the list. This popular Swiss/German grain mixture can include raw or toasted grains such as oats, wheat, and millet; dried fruits such as raisins, dates, and apricots; nuts like almonds, pecans, and walnuts; and wheat bran and germ. It is typically eaten raw after being soaked in milk or water overnight, but fruit juice works well too. Offer it topped with honey, brown sugar, or other sweetener and choice of milk, fruit juice, or yogurt. Add sliced fresh fruit if desired. The complexity of flavors and textures makes every bite of this healthful multigrain cereal a satisfying experience. It is a feel-good way to start the day.

Effect of Processing on Fiber Content

When planning high-fiber selections, ingredients rich in fiber can be cooked, canned, or frozen and it won't affect their fiber content. But refining or milling, peeling, or juicing ingredients reduces it. For example, while baking pears doesn't change their fiber content, removing their peels does. To create a high-fiber, totally delicious, light finish to a meal, pears might be served poached and chilled, "au natural" style with their peels on.

Likewise, if there are two identical oranges, one squeezed into juice and the other peeled and sliced, the sliced orange will provide more fiber than the glass of orange juice.

Ingredient Labels

Ingredient labels are sources of complex carbohydrate and fiber information too. Words on labels like whole grain, whole wheat, cracked wheat, rye, or no refined grains are indicators of fiber and complex carbohydrates. It is often assumed that if a baked good like bread is brown in color, it is high in fiber. This is not always true. It might simply mean molasses or caramel coloring has been added to darken the loaf. In fact, unless the ingredient list so specifies, the dark, starch-filled breads, crackers, and other baked goods like pumpernickel and rye bagels are not whole grain.

A term that may cause confusion about the fiber content of baked carbohydrate-rich goods is "light." In the case of light bread, it usually yields about half the calories of regular bread, either because it's sliced thinner or contains partially indigestible, and therefore, noncaloric, vegetable fiber. In the past, wood pulp appeared in "light" breads, but no longer.

The names of items can be misleading too. Oat bran muffins and oatmeal cookies may sound like they are rich in fiber but they probably aren't. Likely, they are prepared by combining a little oat bran or oatmeal with lots of refined wheat flour.

Other terms that might suggest that carbohydrate-rich baked goods have been prepared with whole grain flours but often are not are stone ground wheat, natural wheat, and whole ground goodness.

To be sure that items are good sources of complex carbohydrates and dietary fiber, this information can be found listed on the labels of packaged products. The FDA implemented guidelines in 1994 (Collier, Shannon, Rill, and Scott. 1993. *1993 Nutrition Labeling Regulations*. Washington, DC: Collier, Shannon, Rill & Scott) requiring that the grams of total carbohydrate, dietary fiber, and sugar be listed on labels per standardized serving. Also required is the percentage of the recommended fiber and the percentage of the total carbohydrate one standardized serving yields for an individual consuming a 2,000-calorie diet.

When a product is labeled a "good source of fiber," one standardized serving must contain 10–19% of the 25 grams of fiber recommended for an individual consuming 2,000 calories per day, and the term "high in fiber" can only be used when a standardized serving of an item contains 20% or more of the 25 grams of fiber recommended for an individual consuming 2,000 calories per day.

Summary—Increasing Complex Carbohydrates on the Menu

Many techniques have been discussed to increase the complex carbohydrates in selections. In brief, the following are key strategies which can be employed to meet diners' demand for tasty, high-starch, high-fiber dishes on the menu.

1. Offer a variety of cooked and ready-to-eat cereals on the menu, ideally prepared from whole grains.

2. Offer interesting crackers and breads with meals, ideally prepared from whole grain flours or enriched with whole grains.

3. Check the labels on products for words like whole grain, whole wheat, cracked wheat, rye, or no refined grains.

4. Substitute whole grain flours like whole wheat, barley, rye, and oat for part or all of the refined wheat flour in baked goods—breads, pastries, cakes, cookies, and bars.

5. Offer pastas combined with low-fat ingredients in soups, sal-

ads, desserts, and beverages, and as accompaniments and main course dishes.

6. Offer potatoes, preferably with their skins on prepared in many different ways.

7. Serve grains, preferably whole grains, as main course accompaniments, as well as incorporated into dishes throughout the menu.

8. Include dried beans, peas, and lentils in every course of the menu.

9. Offer fruits and vegetables, ideally unpeeled and with their seeds, on the menu prepared in a number of ways and in a variety of dishes.

10. Add small amounts of high-fiber nuts and seeds to dishes.

11. Offer one or more dishes filled with complex carbohydrate-rich grains, vegetables, dried beans, peas, or lentils or fruits inspired by cuisines from around the world.

12. Cook or freeze ingredients high in fiber or use canned ones, but don't refine, mill, peel, or juice them or their fiber content will decrease.

13. Evaluate ingredient labels on packaged foods for their complex carbohydrate and fiber content.

Complex Carbohydrate Activities

1. Select the items from the list below that are good sources of complex carbohydrates and/or fiber. Explain why. Describe how the complex carbohydrate and/or fiber content of other items on the list could be increased. See Appendix 6 for a sample of correct answers.

A. Turkey Hot Dogs with Ketchup and Mustard on Wheat Buns

B. Roasted Potato Chips Sprinkled with Herbs

C. Granola

D. Bran Muffins with Honey

E. Applesauce

F. Buckwheat Waffles Topped with a Dollop of Honey Orange Yogurt

G. Chicken Noodle Soup with Vegetables

H. Stuffed Baked Potatoes with Diced Roasted Bell Peppers

I. Corn on the Cob Coated with Margarine

J. Frozen Yogurt Topped with Fruit-Sweetened Strawberry Sauce

K. Spinach Fettuccine Coated in a Light Swiss Cheese Sauce

DIRECTIONS

Complete the following two activities with a specific operation in mind, ideally one you are currently involved with. See instructor to check your responses.

2. Identify dishes on your menu that are rich in complex carbohydrates and/or fiber.

3. List and describe complex carbohydrate and/or fiber-filled items that could be added to your menu. Consider factors such as the operation's theme, price range, clientele, method of service, equipment, and labor required to prepare them.

Sweet Chunky Corn Cake

This is a vitamin-rich, high-fiber cake. By preparing with a mixture of stone ground, yellow cornmeal, coarsely chopped corn kernels, and masa,* the end result is equally tasty as nutritious.

Servings: 36
Serving Size: 2¼ × 3-inch piece
Yield: 1 12 × 20 × 2-inch counter pan

Margarine, unsalted, corn oil   8½ ounces
Masa   1 pound + ½ ounce
Fruit or apple juice concentrate, unsweetened   2¼ cups
Corn, kernels, fresh, blanched, or frozen   4 pounds + 20 ounces
Cornmeal, yellow, stone-ground   6 ounces
Baking powder   1½ teaspoons
Salt   To taste or 1½ teaspoons
Milk, evaporated, skim   ¾ cup
Vegetable cooking spray, butter-flavored

1. Whip the margarine in a mixing bowl until fluffy and creamy.
2. Add the masa gradually, mixing until well blended.
3. Gradually mix in the fruit juice concentrate until well blended.
4. In a blender or food processor, coarsely chop the corn kernels.
5. In another mixing bowl, mix the cornmeal, baking powder, salt to taste, and evaporated milk. Add the masa-margarine mixture and the chopped corn; mix just until blended.
6. Pour into a 12 × 20 × 2-inch counter pan coated with cooking spray. Cover with foil; bake in a 350° F (175° C) oven until the cake is firm, or about 50 minutes. Stand in a warm place to set up for about 10 minutes. To serve, cut the cake 8 × 3 into 36 2¼ × 3-inch pieces, or portion with a scoop.

*Masa is made with sun- or fire-dried corn kernels that have been cooked in limewater. After they have been cooked, then soaked in the limewater overnight, the wet corn is ground into masa (masa harina). Masa is available at stores offering Mexican food ingredients.

Servings	Calories	Protein (g/%)	Fat (g/%)	Cholesterol (mg)	Carbo-hydrates (g/%)	Fiber (g)	Sodium (mg)
1	191	3.8 g/8%	6.8 g/30%	0.2	31.3 g/62%	3.9	38.5

Fried Brown Rice Sprinkled with Vegetables

Fried rice is a good way to use up almost any ingredients on hand, both leftover and fresh. When additional rice is boiled or steamed, a light vegetarian entree can be cooked in minutes.

Servings: 24

Serving Size: 1 cup

Yield: 1½ gallons

Brown rice,* long-grain, cooked without salt or fat,
*   chilled   4 pounds (1 pound + 2 ounces as purchased)*
Vegetable cooking spray
Green onions, white only, thin slices, reserve stems
*   for garnish   1 pound*
Gingerroot, minced   1⅓ ounces (¼ cup)
Garlic, minced   2 tablespoons
Cauliflower, florets   2 pounds
Carrots, washed, cut into thin diagonal slices   1¼ pounds
Broccoli, florets and thin diagonal slices of stem   2 pounds
Soy sauce, low-sodium   1 cup
Sherry, dry   ½ cup
Salt   To taste
Egg whites, large, lightly beaten   1¼ pounds (16)

1. Separate the rice grains.
2. Coat a wok or nonstick skillet with cooking spray. Place over medium heat until hot. Add the green onions, ginger, and garlic; stir-fry until tender, or about 5 minutes.
3. Add the cauliflower and carrots; stir-fry until crisp tender, or about 8 minutes.
4. Add the broccoli; stir-fry until crisp tender, or about 4 minutes. Add water if the mixture becomes too dry.
5. Add the rice, soy sauce, sherry, and salt to taste; stir-fry until heated through, or about 5 minutes.
6. Coat a large nonstick skillet with cooking spray. Place over heat until hot. Add the egg whites and cook as a flat omelet. Roll the omelet and cut into strips. Add the egg strips to the rice. Mix well. Serve the rice garnished with sliced green onion stems.

*Boiled Brown Rice—Place 1 pound 2 ounces long-grain brown rice in a saucepan with 1¼ quarts of water. Heat to a boil. Stir. Cover and cook over low heat until done or 40–45 minutes. Test and cook a few minutes longer if necessary. Let stand 10 minutes.

Servings	Calories	Protein (g/%)	Fat (g/%)	Cholesterol (mg)	Carbo-hydrates (g/%)	Fiber (g)	Sodium (mg)
1	146	7.7 g/21%	1 g/6%	0	27.4 g/73%	4.6	401

Carrot, Raisin, and Pineapple Whole Wheat Cake

When hearty cakes with more body, such as this one, are prepared, a combination of whole grain and cake or pastry flours can replace refined flours to produce nutritionally superior cakes, ones with more vitamins, trace minerals, and fiber.

Servings: 36
Serving Size: 1 wedge (⅑ 9-inch round)
Yield: 4 9-inch cake rounds

Flour, cake or pastry, sifted   14 ounces   3½ oz
Flour, whole wheat, pastry   6 ounces   1½ oz
Sugar, brown   8 ounces   2 oz
Baking soda   1 ounce   ¼ oz
Cinnamon, freshly ground   1 tablespoon (¼ ounce)   ¾ tea
Allspice, freshly ground   1½ teaspoon   ½ tea
Nutmeg, freshly ground   ½ teaspoon   pinch
Date puree (see page 125)   1 quart + 1½ cups
Egg whites, large   5 ounces (4)   1¼ oz
Eggs, large   4 ounces (2)   1 oz
Carrots, washed, shredded   1 pound + 6 ounces   5½ oz
Pineapple, crushed, packed without sugar, drained (reserve juice for frosting or other use)   1 pound
Raisins, seedless, or dried currants   5 ounces   1¼ oz
Vegetable cooking spray, butter-flavored

1. Mix the first 7 ingredients until well blended in a mixing bowl.
2. Add the date puree; mix to blend.
3. Add the egg whites and eggs; mix well.
4. Stir in the carrots, pineapple, and raisins. Pour the batter into 4 9-inch pans coated with cooking spray. Bake in a 350° F (175° C) oven until a wooden pick comes out clean, or about 40–45 minutes. Cover the cake tops with aluminum foil after 30 minutes to prevent over-browning. Set on a rack to cool. Cut each cake into 9 wedges. Serve sprinkled with powdered sugar.

Servings	Calories	Protein (g/%)	Fat (g/%)	Cholesterol (mg)	Carbo-hydrates (g/%)	Fiber (g)	Sodium (mg)
1	200	3.7 g/7%	0.9 g/4%	11.8	46.8 g/89%	5.0	239

124

Date Puree

Most dried fruits can be pureed and served as a substitute for part or all of the fat in cakes and other baked goods. Dates, dried plums (prunes), and raisins are the three types described in this recipe.

Servings: 24
Serving Size: 1 tablespoon + 1½ teaspoon
Yield: 1⅛ pt

Dates, pitted   14 ounces
Water   ¾ cup
Vanilla extract   1 tablespoon

1. Place the dates in a food processor or blender. Puree, adding the water and vanilla slowly, until smooth. Use as a replacement for fat and to add sweetness to baked goods such as carrot, raisin, and pineapple whole wheat cake (see page 124).

Note: For dried plum and raisin purees, substitute prunes and seedless raisins for the dates.

Servings	Calories	Protein (g/%)	Fat (g/%)	Cholesterol (mg)	Carbo-hydrates (g/%)	Fiber (g)	Sodium (mg)
1	47	0.3 g/3%	0.1 g/1%	0	12.3 g/96%	1.4	0.7

Pumpkin Whole Wheat Pancakes

For cholesterol- and fat-conscious diners who want to squeeze a variety of vitamins and minerals into breakfast, pumpkin whole wheat pancakes are a great way to start the day. Top with melon ball scoops of maple syrup-flavored nonfat frozen vanilla yogurt and diners will wonder why they ever skipped breakfast.

Servings: 24
Serving Size: 4 3-inch pancakes
Yield: 72 pancakes

Flour, whole wheat, stone-ground   9 ounces
Flour, cake or all-purpose   6 ounces
Baking powder   2 tablespoons
Cinnamon, freshly ground   1½ teaspoons
Nutmeg, freshly ground   ½ teaspoon
Ginger, ground   ½ teaspoon
Cloves, freshly ground   ¼ teaspoon
Pumpkin, cooked without salt, cold, mashed,
*   or canned   12 ounces*
Milk, nonfat   1 quart
Egg whites, large, slightly beaten   15 ounces (12)
Fruit or apple juice concentrate, unsweetened   ¾ cup
Canola or vegetable oil   2 tablespoons
Vegetable cooking spray, butter-flavored,
*   2-second sprays   12*

1. In a mixing bowl, mix the whole wheat flour and next 6 ingredients.
2. In another bowl, mix the pumpkin, milk, egg whites, juice concentrate, and oil until smooth.
3. Mix the liquid ingredients into the dry ingredients until moistened; there may be some lumps. Stand loosely covered for 30 minutes.
4. Coat a nonstick skillet with cooking spray. Place over medium-high heat until hot. Cooking to order, gently pour ⅛-cup portions of the batter into the pan. Cook until bubbles appear on the surface of the pancakes and the bottoms are golden, or about 2 minutes. Turn and cook until the other sides are golden, or about 2 minutes. Repeat, using all the batter. Serve the pancakes with whipped honey margarine, warm maple syrup, or a dollop of frozen nonfat yogurt.

Servings	Calories	Protein (g/%)	Fat (g/%)	Cholesterol (mg)	Carbo-hydrates (g/%)	Fiber (g)	Sodium (mg)
1	114	5.5 g/19%	1.6 g/12%	0.7	20 g/69%	1.9	158

Chicken Thighs in Crispy Cinnamon Crust

Fried chicken is an all-American favorite. Give customers crispy crusted chicken without the fat in fried chicken by coating skinless chicken pieces in seasoned, crushed cereal flakes and baking in the oven. Once diners have tried this dish, they'll wonder why they ever sacrificed their health and wasted their calories on fried chicken. Serve with mashed buttermilk potatoes or grilled corn on the cob, choice of steamed vegetables, and a crisp green salad.

Servings: 24
Serving Size: 1 chicken thigh
Yield: 24 chicken thighs

Bran cereal, shredded, crumbs (All Bran)   12 ounces
Cinnamon, freshly ground   1½ teaspoons
Salt   To taste
Pepper, freshly ground   To taste or 1½ teaspoons
Chicken, thighs, skinless, fat removed   7½ pounds
   (24 5-ounce pieces)
Vegetable cooking spray, butter-flavored

1. In a shallow container, mix the first four ingredients. Dip the chicken thighs into the seasoned crumbs, turning to coat. Shake off the excess crumbs.
2. Coat a shallow baking pan with cooking spray. Add the chicken. Cook uncovered in a 350° F (175° C) oven, turning once, until evenly browned and cooked through, or about 50 minutes.

Servings	Calories	Protein (g/%)	Fat (g/%)	Cholesterol (mg)	Carbohydrates (g/%)	Fiber (g)	Sodium (mg)
1	137	18.8 g/50%	3.6 g/22%	70.6	10.6 g/28%	5	233

3

Get the Scoop on Sugar

More than one hundred sweetening agents are called sugars. Many have names that make them difficult to identify (see Table 3.1 and 3.8). The most common is refined table sugar, the pure white sucrose crystals from sugar cane or beets.

Current versus Recommended Intake of Sugar

According to data from the USDA (1991. "Food Consumption, Prices and Expenditures, 1968–1989." *Statistical Bulletin No. 825*, Washington, DC), the amount of daily added sugar (nutritive sweetener, i.e., corn sweeteners, honey, and edible syrups) Americans eat has increased 14% over the past 20 years. Intake of added sugar increased from 118 pounds in 1968 to 138 in 1990. This far exceeds the current recommendation of approximately 10–15% of calories. In the case of a 2,000 calorie diet, this equates to 200–300 calories daily from sugar. With an increase in daily caloric intake to 3,000, the suggested sugar intake jumps to 300 to 400 calories. The over 650 sugar calories or nearly 1 cup currently averaged daily by Americans far exceeds these amounts.

Benefits of Sugar

In the United States, losing weight is of more concern to most people than gaining it. But for those who need the calories, sugar is a delicious source of concentrated calories.

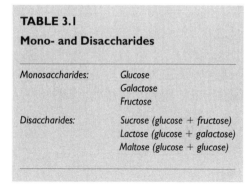

TABLE 3.1

Mono- and Disaccharides

Monosaccharides:	Glucose
	Galactose
	Fructose
Disaccharides:	Sucrose (glucose + fructose)
	Lactose (glucose + galactose)
	Maltose (glucose + glucose)

Sugar also performs valuable functions in cooking and baking. It adds flavor and sweetness to dishes but also crispness, tenderness, and color, and may serve as a preservative (jams and jellies) or act as an aid in fermentation (yeast breads and rolls).

Adverse Effects of Sugar

Problems may occur when large amounts of sugar are consumed. The calories become substantial, and they are empty calories with little nutritional value. Empty calories not only replace nutritious foods in the diet but contribute to obesity and tooth decay. For individuals consuming 1,200–1,800 calorie diets, it's easy to use up their allotted calories on sweets before an adequate amount of nutrient-dense foods are eaten. Moreover, humans really don't need simple sugars in the diet. Sugar does not cause diabetes, but diabetics are unable to properly metabolize carbohydrates. As a result, weight watchers and diabetics, as well as health-conscious diners, may seek alternatives to sugar-laden selections when dining outside the home.

Strategies to Reduce Sugar in Menu Selections

When attempting to reduce or eliminate sugar from recipes, it is important to recognize the functions it performs. With these in mind, generally sugar can be reduced in most traditional recipes by as much as one-third to one-half and still produce acceptable results.

Cutting Sugar in Baked Goods

As a rule of thumb, the sugar in recipes for most baked goods can be limited to one-fourth cup per cup of flour. For each cup of sugar eliminated, nearly 800 empty calories will be removed from the recipe.

For example, a healthy pound cake that is as delicious and tender as its traditional version can be made by replacing the butter with margarine, whole eggs with whites, sour cream with low-fat, plain yogurt, and cutting the amount of sugar in half. Some diners will appreciate it with no further embellishment and others think it's even better topped with a chunky fruit sauce.

Temperature of Foods

The sweet flavor of foods can be maximized by serving dishes warm or at room temperature rather than chilled. For example, a dense, low-fat hot fudge pudding cake (see page 249) presented with creamy chocolate topping appears to be sweeter when eaten warm versus chilled, yet the temperature of the cake is all that has changed.

Sweet Spices and Extracts

Another method to enhance the sweetness of reduced-sugar recipes is with the so-called sweet spices. These spices include cinnamon, cloves, nutmeg, allspice, ginger, cardamom, anise, fennel, and mint. Extracts like vanilla, maple, and almond have the same effect. This technique works well in recipes ranging from custards and puddings to muffins, fruit breads, and crisps. For example, it's amazing the difference a sprinkle of freshly ground cinnamon and crushed anise seeds can make to the perceived sweetness of a cornmeal cake, or freshly ground allspice, cinnamon, and nutmeg to a whole wheat applesauce cake.

In the case of a bread pudding with all the taste and texture but containing half the sugar of its traditional counterpart, its perceived sweetness might be strengthened by flavoring with freshly ground cinnamon and nutmeg and vanilla extract. Additional natural sweetness can be provided by baking ripe banana slices in the pudding. Similarly, coffee drinkers reducing their sugar consumption will find that flavored coffees like vanilla and cinnamon require less sweetening.

Types of Sugars and Sweetening Agents

Sweetening agents and sugars come in a variety of forms. Most are basically empty calories or provide 4 calories per gram along with few other nutrients. Yet, some health-conscious diners believe certain sweetening agents are better for them than others.

Nutritionally, sugars are classified as simple carbohydrates. Some are found as single sugar units (monosaccharides) and others as pairs of sugars linked together (disaccharides; see Table 3.1). Many sugars are combinations of mono- and disaccharides. While all simple carbohydrates are referred to as sugars, their level of sweetness varies. Therefore, all sugars do not serve as sweetening agents in cooking. These are some of sugar's forms:

MONOSACCHARIDES (SEE TABLE 3.1)

Glucose. The monosaccharide glucose, also called dextrose and sometimes known as blood sugar, is used in both plant and animal tissues for quick energy. It is also found naturally in grape juice, certain vegetables, and honey. Corn syrup is a form of glucose made from cornstarch. Because glucose doesn't crystallize easily, it is used to make commercial candies as well as baked goods and other processed foods.

Fructose. Fructose, also known as fruit sugar and levulose, is the monosaccharide that gives fruits and vegetables their natural sweetness. On the other hand, the fructose available commercially is produced from cornstarch in a process called isomerization. Commercial fructose is a free-flowing, granulated substance which looks and tastes similar to white sugar but is approximately 1.2 to 1.8 times sweeter.

Since fructose is sweeter than refined white sugar, it can be used in smaller amounts in recipes. As a result, fructose offers advantages in the preparation of low-calorie desserts and other sweets. It works best as a sweetening agent in cold and high acid foods like citrus drinks. Its disadvantage is its price. On a weight basis, fructose is about ten times more expensive than white sugar.

In recent years, fructose has been heavily promoted as a natural alternative to purified, refined white sugar. There is no obvious reason why. Refined white sugar is produced naturally from sugar cane or beets and occurs naturally in many fruits and vegetables.

Galactose. Galactose is also a monosaccharide but it does not occur singly in foods.

DISACCHARIDES (SEE TABLE 3.1)

Sucrose. The two monosaccharides glucose and fructose bind together to form the disaccharide sucrose, or white refined sugar. At about 45 empty calories per tablespoon, it is understandable why many health-conscious diners monitor their intake of table sugar.

Lactose. Lactose or milk sugar is composed of the two monosaccharides glucose and galactose. Milk is not considered sweet because lactose is not a particularly sweet sugar. About 80% of the world's population over the age of 5 or 6, including most Asians,

Africans, Native Americans, and Black Americans, lack the enzyme lactase, which digests lactose. After drinking milk or eating lactose-containing products, individuals with this condition (lactose intolerance) experience bloating, diarrhea, gas, and cramps.

Most lactose-intolerant individuals can consume small amounts of milk and milk products. Many can tolerate aged cheeses and cultured milk products such as yogurt because the lactose in these products has already been partially fermented. Lactase-treated milk and lactase drops and tablets are also available commercially. The lactose in the treated products is broken into single sugars which can then be digested by lactose-intolerant diners. Milk treated with lactase does taste sweeter than untreated milk.

Maltose. Another disaccharide found naturally in food is maltose or malt sugar. It is made from two glucose units and occurs in germinating seeds and arises during the digestion of starch in the human body.

RAW SUGAR

In addition to table sugar, other sweeteners are made from sugar beets and cane. They include raw, turbinado, and brown sugar and the sugar in molasses. Raw sugar is a coarsely granulated, tan to brown solid obtained before refining. It is banned for sale in the United States because it contains contaminants such as insect parts, dirt, and mold.

TURBINADO AND BROWN SUGARS

Turbinado and brown sugars are two sweeteners some think are more healthful because of their dark colors and distinct flavor. Turbinado sugar is partially refined to make it sanitary. Brown sugar is white sugar crystals coated with molasses. While these two sugars contain a few extra nutrients not found in table sugar, the quantity is so minuscule that for all practical purposes they are useless. However, since many health-conscious diners believe turbinado and brown sugar are better for them than white, chefs might consider them as alternatives to white sugar. For example, when high-fiber banana bran walnut muffins are prepared with brown rather than white sugar, some diners likely will consider these muffins more healthful than if prepared with white sugar. Furthermore, the brown sugar amplifies the flavors in the muffins and produces rich and moist tasting ones.

MOLASSES

Molasses is what is left behind after sugar has been refined. Colonists used to substitute it for the more costly sugar. Light molasses has only gone through the extraction process once. It has a fairly high sugar content. So-called dark molasses is a product of second boiling. Each time sugar is extracted, its sugar content decreases. Blackstrap molasses is third extraction molasses. It is a tarry looking, strong-tasting syrup, low in sugar, and a rich source of nutrients. Modest additions to puddings, cakes, cookies, and even meatballs can enhance the nutritional value of these items.

Molasses is responsible for the characteristic reddish brown color of gingerbread cake. When prepared with a combination of whole wheat pastry and cake flours, egg whites, molasses, and sweet spices, the end result is a high-fiber, vitamin- and mineral-rich, low-fat, moist and dense cake.

SORGHUM MOLASSES

This is a thick syrup produced by boiling down the sweet juice extracted from sorghum's (cereal grass) stalks. It is often used as a table syrup and to sweeten and flavor baked products. It is also referred to as sorghum syrup or simply sorghum. Nutritionally, it contains small amounts of vitamins and minerals not found in refined sugar.

HONEY

Honey, made by bees, varies in composition. It is comprised predominantly of fructose along with glucose, the two monosaccharides in sucrose, and about 18% water. Some believe honey is more nutritious than white sugar. After all, they say, "it is natural." It is true, honey does provide vitamins and minerals in very small amounts that white sugar doesn't, but basically both are empty calories.

To accommodate those diners who prefer honey to white sugar, selections might feature honey as the sweetening agent. For example, a low-fat topping for fruit or whole grain pancakes or waffles like almond-flavored yogurt topping might be sweetened with honey rather than table sugar. Likewise, small cruets of honey are a nice touch with coffee or tea in lieu of the expected, refined white sugar.

In some cases, honey can be served as a fat-free alternative to a high-fat and/or high-cholesterol spread. For example, there's no need for butter, margarine, or cream cheese with high-fiber breads like apricot bran scones or applesauce raisin bread when honey is an option.

One virtue of honey is its sweetening power. Because of its high fructose content, it tastes sweeter than sugar. One-half cup of honey provides about the sweetening power of one cup of sugar. For this reason, about half the amount is required when substituting honey for sugar in recipes. Because of the amount of water in honey, the amount of liquid should be reduced when replacing sugar with honey in recipes too, about ¼ cup for each 1½ cups of honey used.

Thus, if a recipe specifies 3 cups of sugar, it can be replaced with about 1½ cups of honey and the total liquid cut by about ¼ cup. Beware though, a tablespoon of honey contains 64 calories, or 19 more than the 45 calories in a tablespoon of sugar. Therefore, honey is not necessarily a better choice for calorie-conscious diners if equal amounts of honey are substituted for sugar.

The chemical and physical properties of honey make it an amazingly versatile ingredient. It blends well in fermented dairy products such as yogurt and, like sugar, supports fermentation in yeast-leavened breads. Because of its colloidal properties, honey reduces the crumbliness in baked goods, retains moisture, and extends shelf life. This can be a real plus in low-fat baked products.

Additionally, honey's intense flavor heightens fruit and spicy flavors. For example, to strengthen the flavors in dishes such as cherry nut or gingerbread cake, rhubarb-strawberry crisp, cranberry-orange bars, pumpkin-whole wheat waffles, or pineapple frozen low-fat yogurt, honey is a good choice of sweetening agent.

Another attribute of honey is that it mixes well with fat. For example, when whipped with margarine, a creamy spread is formed. It might be promoted with bread baskets as a delicious, cholesterol-free, reduced fat alternative to butter.

In some products, honey's low pH (high acidity level) is also considered advantageous. For example, it can sweeten salad dressings without altering their low pH. However, in others, this may not be the case. For example, in baked goods, it can cause over-browning. If using honey to sweeten baking powder or soda leavened baked goods, see the discussion under Leavening Fruit Sweetened Baked Goods (page 142).

Most of the honey used in food service operations is USDA Grade A quality. This certifies that the honey is practically free from suspended particles, has no off flavors and off aromas resulting from caramelization, smoke, fermentation, or chemicals, and is clear in appearance.

There are many types of honey, more than three hundred, each with its own unique flavor and appearance. Some of the finest

TABLE 3.2

Types of Honey

Honey	Characteristics
Alcahual	brownish colored, fine-flavored honey
Buckwheat	dark brown, strongly flavored honey, typically used for making honey cakes and Jewish honey wine
Chunk comb	a section of the honey comb is found in each jar of this golden, liquid honey
Clover	mild-flavored, thick, pale amber-colored, well suited for general cooking uses and likely the most popular and common honey in both Europe and America
Eucalyptus	an Australian honey with approximately 500 different varieties ranging in color from light amber to quite dark and in flavor from delicate to strong
Heather	a favorite of Europeans and Britons, this creamy honey liquifies when stirred
Hungarian acacia	mild-tasting, very pale honey that always remains liquid
Hymetus	considered one of the best in the world, a fragrant, dark, clear and slightly thick, Greek honey whose flavor hints of thyme, savory, and marjoram
Ilex	mild, light-colored honey derived from the holly tree
Lavender	amber-colored honey with a creamy, smooth texture and often greenish tinge
Manuka	dense, rich-tasting, dark honey, from the tea tree of New Zealand; makes a good choice for cooking
Orange blossom	light, delicate, citrus-flavored honey especially tasty in creamy desserts like puddings
Pohutakawa	rare, New Zealand honey that has an unusual salty flavor

(continued)

types of honey available are described in Table 3.2. Mild-flavored ones like clover are generally preferred for use in cooking or baking, while strongly flavored ones like buckwheat are better choices for making spreads or when a distinctive flavor is desired.

In the event that honey crystallizes, it can be reliquified by heating in a warm water bath or microwaving on high power for 2 or 3 minutes, stirring every 30 seconds.

MAPLE SYRUP

Maple syrup, a delicacy unique to North America, is the refined sap from the sugar maple tree. It is mostly sucrose. While maple syrup is made in Canada and every state in New England, as well as several other states, Vermont is the industry leader in terms of both production and quality control.

According to the strict standards set by the state, the syrup is graded on the basis of its color and density. From highest to lowest, "Vermont Fancy" is light amber-colored with a delicate flavor, "Grade A medium amber" is slightly darker with a mild taste, "Grade A darker amber," a bit darker yet with a slight caramel flavor, and "Grade B," the lowest in quality with a very dark color and pronounced caramel flavor.

The highest grades of maple syrup are ideal for toppings on waffles, pancakes, and French toast, while the more robust, caramel-tasting, lower grades can be used as sweetening agents in cooking.

Unopened maple syrup keeps indefinitely; once opened it should be refrigerated. Like honey and other syrups, in the event that maple syrup crystallizes, it can be reliquefied by heating in a warm water bath or microwaving for a few minutes, stirring occasionally. As with honey and other syrups too, when substituting maple syrup for white sugar, the liquid needs to be reduced in the recipe by about ¼ cup for each 1½ cups of syrup used.

For a true appreciation of maple syrup, a few facts about its production deserve consideration (S. Raichlen. February 10, 1994. "Darkness Edible: The Syrups of Winter." *Los Angeles Times*, p. H28.)

It takes 40 gallons of maple sap to make 1 gallon of the syrup.
It takes four maple trees 2 weeks to produce 1 gallon of the syrup.
It takes 40 years for a maple tree to reach the 10-inch diameter necessary for tapping the sap.

All said and done, one taste of this delicious sweetening agent and the enjoyment is well worth the effort. Some health-conscious diners favor its "natural" appeal over refined white sugar. While maple-flavored syrups are less expensive, they are usually a blend of maple syrup and another sweetener, often corn syrup.

BARLEY MALT SYRUP AND POWDER

Barley malt syrup is a thick, amber-colored sweetener extracted from sprouted roasted barley. Barley malt is about half as sweet as sugar with a flavor like a cross between honey and molasses. Not to be confused with barley malt syrup, barley malt powder is a much more concentrated sweetener.

RICE SYRUP (BROWN RICE SYRUP)

Rice syrup is a thick, amber-colored sweetener made by fermenting sprouted barley with cooked brown rice. During fermentation, the starch in the rice is converted to the disaccharide maltose and other sugars. Some products contain barley enzymes rather than sprouted barley.

Both barley malt and rice syrups are preferred by some health-conscious diners over refined white sugar; again, they consider them to be more "natural." While they do provide small amounts of vitamins and minerals not found in sugar, the amounts are not significant. Barley malt and rice syrups are available at health food stores. If not available locally, Great Eastern Sun is one distributor of both of these products. They can be reached at (800) 334-5809.

UNSWEETENED FRUIT JUICE CONCENTRATES

Other ingredients that are becoming increasingly popular as sweetening agents are unsweetened fruit juice concentrates. Many consumers consider them to be more natural and healthful than white sugar.

The flavors in which unsweetened, frozen fruit juice concentrate is readily available are apple, pineapple, purple grape, and orange. Frozen, unsweetened, white grape juice concentrate also can be found in some locations.

Blends of fruit juice concentrates can be purchased from specialty companies. Fruit Sweet, a combination of unsweetened peach and pear juices and pineapple syrup, is produced by Wax Orchards. This and Wax Orchards' unsweetened, white grape juice concentrate have been used extensively by this author with much success. They are available in pasteurized-refrigerated and bottled forms. For more information regarding these and other fruit-sweetened products produced by Wax Orchards, write them at 22744 Wax Orchards Rd., S.W., Vashon, WA 98070 or call (800) 634-6132. Unsweetened apple juice concentrate is

TABLE 3.2
Continued

Honey	Characteristics
Rosemary	thin, amber-colored, aromatic herb honey with an intense flavor
Sunflower	golden honey that loses its fragrance in cooking and has a thin consistency but whose quality is still rated good
Sweet basil	very light-colored, herbal-flavored honey, well liked in Europe
Tasmanian leatherwood	rich creamy, distinct-tasting honey from Australia which is rated one of the world's best
Tulip tree	dark brown-colored honey with a heavy yet delicate consistency and quincelike flavor

Sources: S. J. Herbst. 1990. Food Lover's Companion. Hauppauge, New York: Barron's Educational Series. E. Lambert Ortiz, 1992. The Encyclopedia of Herbs, Spices & Flavorings. New York: Dorling Kindersley, Inc., p. 199. California Culinary Academy. 1988. Cooking A to Z. San Ramon, CA: Chevron Chemical Co., pp. 304–5. J. Scarpa, December 10, 1992. "Honey." Restaurant Business, p. 115. P. Dowell and A. Bailey. 1980. Cooks' Ingredients. New York: William Morrow and Co., pp. 40–41, 226–27.

recommended as an alternative for Wax Orchards' Fruit Sweet or unsweetened, white grape juice concentrate if not available. It is readily obtainable in frozen form.

The color of frozen purple grape concentrate limits its use as a sweetening agent, while the flavor of frozen, unsweetened, pineapple juice concentrate overpowers the natural flavors in many sweet dishes. Both orange juice's color and flavor make it unacceptable as a sweetening agent in some dishes. The fruity flavor and clear color of frozen, pasteurized or bottled, unsweetened, white grape juice concentrate, the caramel color of frozen, unsweetened, apple juice concentrate, and rose-gold color of Fruit Sweet better complement the ingredients in many sweet dishes.

Replacing sugar with juice concentrates. Replacing sugar in recipes with juice concentrates generally requires extensive experimentation. Fruit juice concentrates add unique flavors unlike those of white sugar or honey.

In comparison to refined sugar at 45 calories per tablespoon, Wax Orchard's Fruit Sweet provides 39, and most of the frozen unsweetened juice concentrates, around 30.

In most cases, the sugar in a recipe can be replaced with an equal volume of unsweetened juice concentrate. Further, the volume of the recipe's other liquids needs to be reduced by about one-third the volume of juice concentrate added. In other words, for every cup of sugar listed in a formula, replace it with one cup of juice concentrate and reduce the liquid ingredients by about one-third cup. Since the calories in juice concentrates are less than an equal volume of refined sugar, calories will drop in products when sugar is replaced with an equal volume of juice concentrate.

Juice concentrates work especially well in liquid-based desserts like sweet sauces, sherbets, sorbets, frozen yogurts, puddings, and gelatins. For example, unsweetened fruit juice concentrate is the ideal sweetener for chunky fruit sauces, purees, and coulis. Compared with high-fat and/or white sugar laden frostings, syrups, and sauces, they make healthy toppings for low-fat cakes, high-fiber pancakes and waffles, nonfat frozen yogurts, and fresh fruit.

For example, a pureed red plum sauce (plums simmered in red port wine and unsweetened white or purple grape juice concentrate) might be napped over any one of these items. If the cake being offered is more specifically a low-fat chocolate cake (see page 156) or a vanilla angel cake, the plum puree would make a nice complement for either, as would a raspberry coulis sweetened with unsweetened fruit juice concentrate and flavored with a splash of raspberry liqueur (see page 157).

Frozen desserts are popular year round with diners of all ages. When the list includes ones prepared without table sugar from mixtures of nonfat milk or yogurt with diced or pureed fruits which are sweetened with fruit juice concentrates, diners will get both taste and nutrition. More specifically, the menu might include sherbets such as chunky pineapple or smooth, low-fat peach, sorbets, perhaps a tropical mango, strawberry, or kiwi, a frozen yogurt like nonfat apricot and for kids and adults feeling young maybe banana-papaya (see page 153) or raspberry-flavored popsicles.

Baked goods like cakes, cookies, and bars can be sweetened with unsweetened fruit juice concentrates too. In addition to their positive health connotations, baked goods sweetened with juice concentrates, like ones prepared with honey and other syrups, stay fresh longer and retain moisture better than those sweetened with white sugar.

For example, an innovative version of old-fashioned strawberry shortcake, a fruit juice sweetened fruit shortcake drizzled with a fruit juice sweetened strawberry sauce and topped with sliced nectarines, might be promoted as a dessert containing no white sugar.

Like honey, fruit juice concentrates also have a low pH (high acidity level). When preparing sweet milk-based sauces, with fruit juice concentrates and other acidic sweeteners, protein coagulation may be a problem. For example, brown sugar would be a better sweetening agent to choose than fruit juice concentrate for a low-fat, creamy, buttermilk-based, chocolate-flavored (cocoa) sauce.

Naturally Sweet Fruit

Fresh, cooked, canned, and dried fruits are healthy alternatives to white sugar laden desserts, and they reduce the amount or eliminate the need for sugar in dishes. In comparison to the empty calories in white sugar, fruits are good sources of fiber, vitamins, and minerals.

FRUIT DESSERTS

For example, a simple fruit salad might be promoted as a nice ending to almost any meal. But, for a lush, unforgettable one, a trio of kiwi, pineapple, and mango might be marinated in a sauce of naturally sweet fruit juice syrup and accented with vanilla, freshly ground cloves, freshly squeezed lemon and lime juices, and freshly minced mint and ginger.

Restaurants report tarts are one of their most popular desserts.

For one on the healthy side, sliced fruit like peaches or pears might be arranged attractively on a whole grain crust like an oat and graham crust and glazed with a fruit juice sweetened puree or spread like ginger apricot.

Berries also are rated high by most diners. For an innovative dessert, a combination of berries, perhaps raspberries and strawberries, might be coated in a fruit juice syrup and covered with sweet fruit juice soaked, thinly sliced, cholesterol-free angel cake. It's sure to please.

Whether diners are avoiding sugar or not, they are likely to be delighted when attractively displayed ripe and flavorful fruits are offered for dessert. A readily available and popular fruit like ripe bananas might be served warm, baked, coated in graham cracker crumbs and napped with a chilled, orange-pineapple, yogurt topping. For a striking presentation, this potassium and fiber-rich dessert might be arranged on a dark blue dessert plate lined with a lemon yellow base plate.

CANNED FRUIT

Canned fruit is also an option but preferably packed in its own natural juice or water. Light and heavy syrups have added sugar; heavy syrup has the most—about 4 teaspoons per half cup. Canned fruit might be selected when fresh isn't readily available or it is more convenient. For example, crushed pineapple packed in its own natural juices might be used in a whole wheat pineapple upside-down cake rather than freshly cut pineapple tidbits.

DRIED FRUIT

Dried fruits are delicious, nutritious chewy snacks and can add "natural" sweetness to baked goods, salads, vegetable or grain dishes, and entrees. For example, a whole wheat, date and almond quick bread might rely on dates and currants for a good deal of its sweetness. Similarly, because of all the natural sugar in dried figs, fig bars are another treat which require little additional sweetening. In terms of grains, dried peaches might provide just the right contrast in flavor and texture to rank a triticale (hybrid of wheat) pilaf in the outstanding category.

While generally raisins, or maybe apricots or prunes, are associated with the term dried fruit, there are a great variety of other dried fruits which are readily available or can be dried on premise. They range from dried apples, bananas, mangoes, currants, papayas, peaches, and pears to pineapples.

Nutritionally, dried fruits have many attributes. They contain no fat or cholesterol, are rich in fiber, and because their water content is reduced during drying, they are concentrated sources of minerals including iron, copper, potassium, and vitamins including the vitamin A precursor, beta carotene. Dried fruits do have drawbacks though. The drying process concentrates their sugar and calories and destroys vitamin C. For this reason, while the addition of ⅔ cup of raisins or 10 dried pitted prunes may provide one-fifth of an adult male's recommended daily requirement for iron, raisins contain about five times more calories than an equal portion by weight of grapes, and the same goes for prunes compared to plums.

Sulfites are another concern in some dried fruits. These preservatives prevent light-colored dried fruits like apples, pears, and golden raisins from turning brown but can also cause allergic reactions in some diners, and for some, such as asthmatics, it may cause severe reactions. Sulfite-free light-colored dried fruits can be purchased. If sulfites are a concern, it is best to check labels. Commercial packers are required to clearly list any preservatives used on the labels of their products.

FRUIT PUREES

In some recipes, the amount of white sugar, as well as fat, including margarine, butter, shortening, and oil, can be reduced or replaced with purees of fresh, cooked, canned, or dried fruits.

Very ripe bananas work particularly well. For those occasions when there isn't time to allow the bananas to ripen naturally, the softening and sweetening processes can be shortened by baking the bananas in their skins. Depending on their size and state of ripeness, baking in a 350° F (175° C) oven for around 10 minutes will turn their skins black, and their fruit will become soft and sweet. For example, pureed, very ripe bananas and strawberries might be responsible not only for the fresh, fruity flavor and body of a banana-strawberry frozen yogurt, but its natural sweetness too. Banana puree can reduce or replace sugar and fat in baked goods too. For example, there is no need for white sugar when a zucchini oat cake is sweetened with banana puree along with unsweetened, frozen apple juice concentrate. Topped with sliced, baked bananas, glazed with unsweetened fruit juice, this moist cake is a tribute to healthy dining.

Some cooks recommend sweetening dishes with baby food banana flakes. If used, proceed cautiously. I found them to lack body and their flavor to be bland. I do not recommend them. Further, the flakes cake easily in storage.

Applesauce is another fruit which can be substituted relatively successfully for some or all of the sugar and fat in baked goods. For example, to produce applesauce bran muffins that taste as good as they look, and yet contain no white sugar, they might be sweetened with applesauce and unsweetened, frozen apple juice concentrate. They will seem even sweeter when their batter is sprinkled with freshly ground cinnamon and cloves.

Some fruit purees, like pear, have limited use as fat and sugar substitutes due to their grainy texture. However, in whole grain products with coarse textures, like oatmeal-whole wheat pancakes, shredded pears blend in fine and their sweet, fruity flavor eliminates the need for much additional sweetening. Of course, rather than a concentrated sugar syrup, a naturally sweet fruit puree, spread, or compote might be suggested as a topping.

Purees of dried fruits can produce excellent results in lieu of part or all of the white sugar and fat in baked goods too. For example, a moist and aromatic four-spice cake might be created without any added fat or white sugar by replacing both with a puree of prunes (dried plums). Or in the case of a chocolate cake (see page 156), a date puree (see page 125) might be traded for its butter and sugar.

While baked goods prepared with less or no fat and white sugar obviously don't have the delicious decadence of their all-butter and sugar counterparts, they look similar, have good texture, are more moist, and have a fruity taste that's quite nice. Some excellent low-fat and white sugar free cakes, muffins, cookies, bars, and other baked goods can be developed using this method.

LEAVENING FRUIT-SWEETENED BAKED GOODS

When substituting fruit juice concentrates or purees for refined sugar in baked goods, adjustments are needed in the baking powder and soda. Baking powder is a chemical leavening agent composed of acid reacting materials and the alkaline ingredient, baking soda. Baking soda reacts much the same as baking powder when the necessary acid is provided from ingredients in items such as fruit purees, juices, and concentrates, honey, molasses, yogurt, cocoa (except Dutch-processed cocoa), buttermilk, and sour milk. To make 1 cup of fresh milk into sour milk, mix it with 1⅓ tablespoons of vinegar or 1½ tablespoons of lemon juice.

When using baking soda as a leavening agent, it is important to understand that the activation of baking soda is rapid. Therefore, mixes and doughs leavened with baking soda must be handled without much delay. If not, the release of gases might be almost complete before the product is placed in the oven. This will cause a loss of volume.

Baking soda should not be added to baked products unless required for leavening. Any substantial amount without acid can produce an unpleasant (soapy) taste and odor, result in products with a coarse texture and cause undesirable effects on crumb color. For example, white cake crumbs might turn yellow, chocolate cake crumbs a reddish hue and blueberries become green. Too much acid is equally undesirable. It can result in products that are heavy with dense crumbs.

The following substitution procedure provides a basis for adding baking soda when developing recipes with fruit purees, juices, concentrates or other ingredients which have a low pH. It is only a rough guide because several variables are involved. The acid in one cup of fruit juice, fruit pulp (mashed banana or date puree), moderately sour milk, yogurt, buttermilk or one-third cup unsweetened, frozen fruit juice concentrate can be neutralized by about one-half teaspoon of baking soda. This combination provides leavening equivalent to about 2 teaspoons of baking powder or 4 eggs. One and one-half teaspoons of baking powder will generally leaven 1½–2 cups of flour but the amount will vary depending on the composition of the batter and preparation method.

Reduced or Sugar-Free Beverages

Beverages are often a source of sugar on the menu. Consider soda pop. One-half can (1 cup) of many colas contains around 5 teaspoons of sugar.

TEA

There are many tasty beverage options available today with no sugar added. For starters, the beverage list might include hot or iced tea.

When prepared without sugar or cream, tea adds no calories. Most teas like Lipton and Earl Grey are black and readily available. The less popular green tea, the tea served in Japanese (not Chinese) restaurants, can be found in Asian food stores.

Tea, whether green or black, decaffeinated or regular, is believed to be healthy. Researchers (B. Liebman, November, 1994. "Tea for 250 Million?" *Nutrition Action*, pp. 4–5) have found that it may reduce the risk of cancer and possibly heart disease. This evidence does not apply to herbal teas. They differ chemically.

In fact, those herbal teas touted to aid in weight loss may even be dangerous. Mark Meskin, R.D., PhD (Staff. 1994. "Herbal Teas Touted for Weight Loss: 'Quick Fix' with Hidden Dangers." *Environmental Nutrition 17*(9), p. 8) has reported that weight-loss herbal teas may contain ingredients that can produce unwanted

TABLE 3.3

Five Steps to Brewing Tea

1. Heat fresh cold water, preferably letting the tap run a while first to maximize the oxygen content. This enhances tea's flavor.

2. As the water is heating, swirl some hot water into the teapot to warm it, then pour the water out.

3. Add the tea leaves. An acceptable measure is one teaspoon per cup, plus one for the pot.

4. As soon as the water reaches a rolling boil, pour it over the tea leaves and cover the pot. Overboiling, Twining says, will release too much oxygen and result in flat tea; water that hasn't boiled won't draw out its full flavor.

5. Allow small-leaf tea to brew about 3 minutes; large-leaf tea for 5 to 6 minutes. Stir gently and pour into cups, using a strainer if desired.

If tea bags are being used, the tea should be brewed for only a minute or two. They contain broken leaves which release flavor more quickly than loose tea. When a strong cup of tea is desired, it's better to use more tea than to brew longer. Overbrewing releases tannins which produce bitter tea.

Source: Excerpted from "Tips on Tea Brewing." (July, 1988). Restaurant Management, p. 76.

side effects. For example, ma huang, one of the most popular herbs used in these teas, can raise blood pressure and stimulate the heart. It is also common for herbal weight-loss teas to contain laxatives and cathartics (agents that cause water loss and bowel movement).

Samuel Twining, regarded by some as the world's foremost authority on tea, offers a five-step recipe to bring out the most in tea (see Table 3.3).

COFFEE

Hot and chilled coffees, skip the sugar and cream, are also calorie-free beverages. Decaffeinated or regular, flavored coffees like vanilla or Irish cream are particularly popular with dieters. One might be recommended in lieu of a rich dessert or as an accompaniment to a lighter dessert.

With the craze over coffees and the drinks made from them, an iced orange cappuccino, prepared with nonfat milk and sweetened with honey rather than refined white sugar, might be featured on the breakfast or brunch beverage menu or suggested as the first or last course of a light and healthy meal later in the day.

Starbucks Coffee recommends these easy steps for brewing good coffee every time.

1. Begin with freshly roasted beans and fresh, cold tap water. A filter or bottled water may be considered if tap water has a distinct flavor or is hard. It can contribute an undesirable flavor to coffee.

2. For the most flavorful coffee, use water that has just boiled or a coffeemaker that heats water to 195–205° F (90–96° C).

3. Use the correct grind for the coffeemaker.

4. Use 2 rounded tablespoons of ground coffee for each 6 fluid ounces of water.

5. Use an airpot or thermal carafe to keep coffee hot and delicious. If held over a burner, the taste of coffee begins to deteriorate in 20 minutes.

6. Coffee should not be reheated. It should be made fresh each time it is to be served. Coffee holds best at 185° F (85° C).

Caffeine withdrawal. For those among the three out of every four caffeine-consuming adults in the United States who choose to cut down or eliminate caffeine or coffee from their diet, a gradual approach is advised to avoid the symptoms of caffeine withdrawal. While caffeine might cause stomach upset, nervousness, sleeplessness, irritability, headaches, and diarrhea and its diuretic effect be potentially hazardous for exercisers in a hot environment, abrupt removal from the diet might cause unpleasant symptoms too. They range from headaches, fatigue, depression, and anxiety to, in some cases, nausea, vomiting, muscle pain, and stiffness. Previously, it was believed that these symptoms occurred only when heavy coffee drinkers quit the habit abruptly. It now appears that those who consume only a daily cup or two of coffee can, without their usual "dose," suffer withdrawal effects so severe that they may think they need to see a doctor.

Caffeine in foods. While most people hear the word caffeine and think coffee, it is present in other foods too (see Table 3.4).

WATER

Water, which has no calories, sugar, artificial sweeteners, or caffeine, remains the healthiest beverage choice. There are many bottled forms to pick from. In the United States alone, there are hundreds of brand name waters bottled. Many more are imported from around the world.

However, what is in a bottle of water is not always clear. For example, currently there is no legal definition of "mineral water" or "natural water." The International Bottled Water Association (see Table 3.5) has established standards which are very close to those under consideration by the FDA for implementation.

A variety of bottled waters might be included on the menu. Many diners are opting for them instead of alcoholic and sugary soft drinks in casual to fine dining establishments.

FRUIT OR VEGETABLE JUICES

Unsweetened fruit or vegetable juices are other healthy beverage options. Freshly squeezed juices are popular with diners of all age groups. They make nutritious, refreshing drinks any time of day. In addition to the standard freshly squeezed orange and grapefruit juices, juice extractors allow chefs to add a wide range of delicious fresh juices to the beverage menu. It might feature single or combinations of fruit and vegetable juices. For vegetable juices, the choices might include a simple carrot juice or a more complex blend of carrot-apple-ginger and parsley juices. On the fruit juice list, apple-cranberry-grape juice might be featured during cranberry season, while for an island touch, a freshly squeezed pineapple, papaya, nectarine, and passion fruit juice might be promoted.

Even without a juice extractor, but with a food processor and

TABLE 3.4

Caffeine Content of Foods

Food	Caffeine (mg)
Brewed coffee (6 fluid ounces)	103
Instant coffee (6 fluid ounces)	57
Instant decaffeinated coffee (6 fluid ounces)	2
Brewed black tea (6 fluid ounces)	36
Instant tea powder (1 teaspoon)	31
Coca-Cola (12 fluid ounces)	46
Diet Pepsi (12 fluid ounces)	36
Unsweetened baking chocolate (1-ounce square)	58
Cocoa mix powder (1-ounce packet)	5
Duncan Hines chocolate chip cookies (2)	3
Hershey's Kit Kat wafer (1.65-ounce bar)	15

Source: Data from J.A.T. Pennington (1994). *Bowes & Church's Food Values of Portions Commonly Used*. Philadelphia: J. B. Lippincott Co.

TABLE 3.5

Bottled Waters

Bottled water: water that is placed in a sealed container or package which may contain added carbonation and be prepared with added flavors, extracts, and/or essences derived from a spice or fruit which comprises less than 1% by weight of the final product. These products contain no sweeteners, acidulants, or additives other than these flavors, extracts, or essences. When containing carbon dioxide other than that naturally occurring in the source of the product, the bottled water shall be labeled with the words "carbonated," "carbonation added," or "sparkling" when the carbonation is obtained from a natural or manufactured source.

continued

TABLE 3.5
Continued

Carbonated or sparkling water	bottled water containing carbon dioxide.
Mineral water	bottled water coming from an approved source tapped at one or more boreholes or natural springs, originating from a geologically and physically protected underground water source. The mineral and trace element content of the product will distinguish it from other types of water and be stated in milligrams per liter on the label of the bottle. Bottled water to which minerals are added shall be labeled to reveal that minerals have been added and may not be labeled "natural mineral water."
Natural water	bottled spring, mineral, or well water which is derived from an underground formation and is not derived from a municipal system or public water supply.
Spring water or natural spring water	derived from an underground formation from which water flows naturally to the surface of the earth and which meets the requirements of "natural water."
Well or natural well water	water from a hole bored, drilled, or otherwise constructed in the ground which taps the water of an aquifer and which meets the requirements of "natural water."
Club sodas, seltzers, or new age waters	flavored and/or sweetened products, not recognized as bottled waters but soft drinks.

Source: Excerpted from the International Bottled Water Association. (January 23, 1993). *Model Bottled Water Regulation.*

a bit more effort, a variety of tasty vegetable and fruit juices can be created. A couple of guidelines will help chefs to create enjoyable, fresh fruit and vegetable juices (J. Kordich, 1992. *The Juiceman's Power of Juicing.* New York: William Morrow & Co.). First, juices prepared from most green vegetables such as spinach, broccoli, kale, lettuce, and parsley may cause temporary gastric discomfort. Celery and cucumber juices are exceptions. To prevent this problem from occurring, no more than one-fourth part juice from a green vegetable should be combined with carrot or apple juice and sometimes celery juice.

Second, do not serve juices containing more than one-half cup of beet or wheatgrass juice per serving. Similarly, in larger amounts, they may cause temporary gastric discomfort. Third, do not combine fruit and vegetable juices, with two exceptions—carrots and apples. They typically don't mix well.

Finally, prepare fresh juices to serve. They are not meant to be stored. Their nutritional value and taste are at their best when consumed immediately. Keep in mind though, that generally it doesn't matter whether freshly squeezed, pasteurized, or frozen concentrated juices are served. Nutritionally, they are not significantly different. For example, while freshly squeezed orange juice may be perceived as more nutritious, all forms are good sources of vitamin C. To obtain the most vitamin C from orange juice and other fruit or vegetable juices, they should be chilled and kept refrigerated. Once the container is opened, it begins losing its vitamin C. If it remains chilled, it will retain 90% of its vitamin C up to one week.

MILK

Low-fat and nonfat milks are well known for their nutritional attributes. A nice, cold glass along with a piece of warm dried cherry, pear, and currant cake with brandy (contains no refined sugar) might be recommended as a healthy way to end a meal or as a delicious mid-day snack. But, low-fat and nonfat milks are good choices in lieu of sugar-filled sodas with or without food any time of the day.

HEALTHY DRINK COMBINATIONS

A rainbow of delicious, refined sugar-free drinks might be created by combining unsweetened fruit and vegetable juices, bottled waters, teas, coffees, nonfat milk and yogurt, pureed fruits, and naturally sweet essences and flavorings. Some possible options might be a citrus spritzer prepared from a mixture of unsweetened orange and white grape juices and mineral water; a blueberry sipper combining fresh juices extracted from blueberries, honeydew melon and green grapes; orange iced tea created by steeping black tea leaves in water with cinnamon chips, whole cloves, allspice berries, and mint leaves and finishing with orange, lemon, and apple juices; or a strawberry, banana, and kiwi orange shake in which strawberries, cubes of kiwi, and banana are blended with orange juice and ice cubes.

Diners looking for a nonalcoholic cocktail will appreciate sugar-free beverage options too. For example, one of my father's favorite alternatives to a beer is freshly prepared spicy tomato juice (see page 248) served in a frosted, stemmed glass, garnished with a crisp rib of celery.

PRESENTING HEALTHY BEVERAGES

Several techniques can be employed to make healthy beverages more enticing. They might be presented in special glasses, for example, a crystal goblet for a sophisticated touch, or for a fun tone, green cactus stemmed ones. Diners of all ages like straws with their beverages. Disposable ones with colorful pictures, messages, or designs compatible with the operation's theme can be excellent conversation pieces. They are a simple method to help healthy beverages stand out. Unusual low-calorie and sugar-free garnishes are other options to give beverages spark. Fruit is a good choice. It might be as simple as a strawberry fan or fresh pineapple wedge. Uniquely shaped, flavored, and/or colored ice cubes can add charm to beverages too, maybe animal cubes for kids' drinks or bright red and blue, fruit juice sweetened strawberry and blueberry ones to celebrate the Fourth of July. Freezing ice cubes with ingredients like herbs or flowers in their centers is another innovative way to add excitement to waters and other healthy beverages without sugar.

Sugar-Free Breakfast Foods

Sugar is generally not considered to be a concern at breakfast, yet a cup of many cold cereals can add from 0 to 9 teaspoons to the daily count (see Table 3.6). For example, a cereal like Granola with Almonds sounds very healthy, yet it contains 9 teaspoons per cup. Likewise, Bran Buds, while a high-fiber (24 grams/cup) cereal, yields 5½ teaspoons of sugar per cup.

For those diners watching their sugar consumption, both cooked and ready-to-eat unsweetened cereals can be included on the menu. Oatmeal is a good, sugar-free, cooked wintertime favorite, while ready-to-eat cereals like Fiber One and Shredded

TABLE 3.6
Sugar in Cereals

Cereal	Sugar (teaspoons/cup)*
Granola with Almonds, Sun Country	9
Honey Bran Oatbake, Kellogg's	6
Milk Chocolate Instant Oatmeal, Oatmeal Swirlers	5½
Bran Buds, Kellogg's	5½
Lucky Charms, General Mills	4½
All-Bran, Kellog's	4
Golden Graham, General Mills	3
Almond Delight, Ralston Purina	2½
Heartwise, Kellogg's	2
Rice Krispies, Kellogg's	1
Corn Chex, Ralston Purina	1
Post Toasties Corn Flakes, Post	½
Oatmeal, quick, Total	0
Fiber One, General Mills	0

Source: Data from J.A.T. Pennington. (1994). *Bowes & Church's Food Values of Portions Commonly Used.* Philadelphia: J. B. Lippincott Co.
*Serving sizes have been standardized to 1 cup. Four grams of sugar equal 1 level teaspoon. Values have been rounded to the nearest ½ teaspoon.

Wheat are more convenient sugar-free options. A good rule is to limit choices to cereals with no more than 1½ teaspoons (7 grams) sugar per serving and those containing dried fruit to no more than 3 teaspoons (12 grams) sugar per serving

Vitamin-, mineral-, and fiber-rich, ripe fresh fruits such as sliced bananas and strawberries and dried fruits like currants and peaches can reduce the need for sugar on cereal while adding interesting textures and fruity flavors. For example, when bran and rye flakes, rolled oats, sunflower seeds, and almonds in triple grain granola are tossed with sweet dried apricots and raisins, the need for additional sweetening is minimized. The cereal might be offered moistened with nonfat milk or fruit juice but can be munched dry for a snack or breakfast on the run too. Granolas made on premise with large amounts of grains and small amounts of seeds, nuts and dried fruits certainly beat the many high-fat, high-sugar commercial granolas being distributed.

Another place where excess sugar often shows up at breakfast is in the jellies, jams, and marmalades served with muffins, bagels, and toast. For a fresh fruit flavor without the excess refined sugar of their counterparts, sliced fresh fruit, fruit juice sweetened fruit sauces, low-sugar jams or jellies, and fruit spreads might be made available.

While these fruit-sweetened or low-sugar products might contain less white sugar, they are not necessarily lower in calories. For example, fruit spreads sweetened with unsweetened fruit juices generally provide around the same number of calories, about 14 per teaspoon, as refined sugar sweetened jams and jellies. Fruit-sweetened jam, jelly, and marmaladelike spreads can be purchased commercially or made from scratch. Low-sugar toppings can also be created by blending nonfat yogurt cheese or other low-fat cheeses with an all fruit spread or pureed fruit. For example, a creamy spread of pureed strawberries and yogurt cheese might be offered as a tasty topping for breakfast breads.

When serving pancakes and waffles, syrups can be a source of refined sugar. Many are basically sugar and water with added flavoring agents. Natural maple or fruit syrups might be perceived as more healthy options by some diners, but most syrups are a source of empty calories and contain about 50 calories per tablespoon. Fruit sauces sweetened with naturally sweet fruit juices might be offered as refined sugar-free toppings for pancakes and waffles. For example, a chunky pear sauce is a great match over gingerbread pancakes, while rhubarb and orange sauce is heavenly over whole wheat, cholesterol-free French toast.

Hidden Sugar Sources

While sugar is an obvious ingredient in many foods, such as cakes, cookies, and candies, it is also found in unsuspected ones such as ketchup, canned corn, peanut butter, and salad dressing (see Table 3.7).

Since May 1994, the grams of sugar per serving have been listed on products unless they contain an insignificant amount or an amount that could be rounded to zero. For each 4 grams listed per serving under sugar, the product contains 1 teaspoon of sugar per serving. Thus, if one serving of a product contains 8 grams of sugar, each serving would provide 2 teaspoons of sugar.

While the new food labels do indicate the amount of sugar in products, the labels do not distinguish natural sugar from added sugar. The grams of sugar listed on a product include all sources of sugar—refined sugar (sucrose), milk sugar (lactose), molasses, honey, high-fructose syrup, and fruit juice concentrate. For example, apricot frozen yogurt might contain no refined white sugar yet its label lists sugar content as 10 grams per ½ cup. The 10 grams of sugar could come from the ingredients used to make the frozen yogurt—lactose in the yogurt and glucose and fructose in the dried apricots and orange juice and white grape juice concentrates.

The ingredient list also will give a little more information about the type of sugar in a food. Each added sugar must be listed here individually. Since ingredients are listed on labels in the order of greatest weight, products to watch out for are those that list sugar or one of its forms as one of the first three ingredients, or products containing several sources of sugar.

There are many terms that might indicate some form of sugar has been added to a product (see Table 3.8). Many might not be familiar and go unrecognized.

Sugar-Free Commercial Products

There are also a variety of sugar-free products available commercially. These range from beverages to desserts. Their quality varies. They should be used only if they meet the operation's standards.

Products labeled "sugar-free" must contain less than 0.5 grams of white sugar per standardized serving as defined by the FDA but can be sweetened with alcohol sugars—xylitol, sorbitol, maltitol, or mannitol. The alcohol sugars provide the same number of calories per gram as sugar.

"Sugar-free" products must also meet the definitions of reduced- or low-calorie foods, bear a claim of special dietary use,

TABLE 3.7

Sugar in Food

Food	Teaspoons
Zante currants, Sun Maid (¼ cup)	7½
Apple juice, 100% juice, Tree Top (8 ounces)	6½
Nonfat yogurt, key lime, Mountain High (6 ounces)	5½
Spaghetti sauce, 100% natural, Prego (½ cup)	3½
Barbecue sauce, fat free, Heinz (2 tablespoons)	2
Katalina fat-free dressing, Kraft (2 tablespoons)	2
Corn, canned, Del Monte (½ cup)	2
Thousand island dressing, Kraft (2 tablespoons)	1½
Peanut butter, creamy, Jif (2 tablespoons)	1
Sweet pickle relish, Vlasic (1 tablespoon)	1
Ketchup, Heinz (2 tablespoons)	1
Tomato paste, Hunt's (2 tablespoons)	1
Green beans, blue lake, canned, Del Monte (½ cup)	½
Vegetable thins, Nabisco (14 crackers)	½
Corn flake crumbs, Kellogg's (¼ cup)	½
American process cheese spread, Nabisco (2 tablespoons)	½
Potato chips, barbecue flavor, Lay's (1 ounce)	½
Beef bouillon, low sodium, Steero (2 teaspoons)	½

Source: Product labels, November 1994.
*Four grams of sugar equal 1 level teaspoon. Values have been rounded up to the nearest ½ teaspoon.

EXAMPLE

Calculation of Calories from Sugar

To determine the number of calories per serving from sugar in a product, (1) the number of grams of sugar per serving is multiplied by 4 or the number of calories per gram, and (2) to calculate the percentage of calories derived from sugar, the sugar calories per serving are divided by the calories per serving and multiplied by 100. Thus, if one serving of a product contains 32 grams of sucrose and 256 calories, 128 of the product's calories per serving are from sugar.

Example:

32 g sucrose × 4 cal/g = 128 sucrose cal per serving

128 sucrose cal/256 cal per serving = 0.5 of the cal from sucrose/1 cal
0.5 × 100 = 50% calories from sucrose

or state that the product does not meet these standards on the label.

Nonnutritive Sweeteners

Nonnutritive sweeteners which provide sweetness without calories do not contain sugar but rather other compounds with sweet flavors. The two most commonly used in foods are saccharin and aspartame. They might be placed on tables as alternatives to white sugar and other calorie concentrated-sweeteners. In some food service operations, they might be considered acceptable sweetening agents for dishes. Nonnutritive sweeteners are not used in the recipes in this text. While nonnutritive sweeteners contain no calories, they do have drawbacks. Saccharine has an aftertaste, aspartame loses flavor with cooking, and some diners have negative perceptions of foods prepared with nonnutritive sweeteners.

Summary—Reducing White Sugar in the Menu

Many techniques have been discussed to reduce table sugar in selections. In brief, the following are key strategies which can be employed to meet diners' requests for tasty menu fare with less white refined sugar.

1. Generally, reduce sugar in most traditional recipes by as much as one-third to one-half or as a rule of thumb, limit sugar in most baked goods to one-fourth cup per cup of flour.

2. Use sweet spices like cinnamon, clove, nutmeg, allspice, ginger, fennel, mint, anise, and cardamom and extracts like vanilla, almond, and maple to enhance the perceived sweetness of products reduced in sugar.

3. Replace sugar in recipes with fructose, turbinado or brown sugars, honey, or maple, rice, barley, or malt syrups if diners believe these sweeteners to be healthier than white refined sugar. Remember, nutritionally they are all comparable.

4. Add small amounts of blackstrap molasses to enhance the nutritional value and flavor of reduced sugar dishes ranging from puddings, cakes, and cookies to meatballs.

5. Replace white sugar in recipes with one-half the amount of the sweeter honey and reduce the liquid ¼ cup for every 1½ cups of honey used.

6. Sweeten dishes with unsweetened fruit juice concentrates such as apple, pineapple, white and purple grape, and orange,

and concentrated fruit blends like "Fruit Sweet" rather than sugar.

7. Replace white sugar with an equivalent volume of unsweetened fruit juice concentrate in recipes and reduce the liquid by one-third of the volume of fruit sweetener added.

8. In fruit-sweetened baked goods, substitute ½ teaspoon baking soda with ⅓ cup fruit juice concentrate or 1 cup fruit juice or pulp for 2 teaspoons baking powder.

9. Offer naturally sweet, fresh, dried, pureed, cooked, or canned fruits packed in their own juice or water for dessert or use as ingredients in them.

10. Replace part or all of the white sugar and fat in recipes with fruit purees from very ripe, sweet fresh; cooked; canned; or dried fruits.

11. Offer alternatives to beverages sweetened with refined sugars such as teas, coffees, bottled waters, fruit and vegetable juices, nonfat milk or combinations of these mixed or blended with nonfat plain yogurt, nonfat frozen yogurt, pureed fruits, and/or unsweetened flavoring agents to beverages sweetened with refined sugars.

12. Offer unsweetened breakfast cereals or ones sweetened with fruits or their juices and breakfast breads like waffles and pancakes with naturally sweet or fruit-sweetened fruit toppings.

13. Watch out for hidden sugar in foods by examining ingredient lists on labels for words like glucose, fructose, maltose, dextrose, sucrose, and syrup.

14. Substitute sugar-free, sugarless, or no sugar products for those containing sugar only if they provide the qualities desired.

15. Avoid products labeled sugar-free, sugarless, or no sugar which contain the alcohol sugars xylitol, sorbitol, mannitol, or maltitol.

16. Offer nonnutritive sweeteners such as saccharine and aspartame as table sweeteners, but be aware that some diners perceive them negatively and have reported them to produce off flavors in foods.

Sugar Activities

Complete the following activities with a specific operation in mind, ideally one you are currently involved with. See instructor to check your responses.

TABLE 3.8

Names of Sugar (Nutritive Sweeteners) Added to Food

Brown sugar

Confectioners' sugar (powdered sugar)

Corn syrup

Dextrose

Fructose

Fruit juice concentrates

Glucose

High-fructose corn syrup

Honey

Invert sugar

Lactose

Levulose

Maltodextrin

Maltose

Mannitol

Maple syrup

Molasses

Powdered sugar

Raw sugar

Sorbitol

Sorghum syrup

Sucrose

Sugar

Xylitol

1. Identify choices on your dessert menu prepared with little or no white, refined sugar. How are they sweetened?

2. Describe desserts that might be added to your menu containing little or no white, refined sugar. They should be compatible with your operation's theme, price range, clientele, method of service, equipment, and personnel's skill level.

3. List the items on your menu other than desserts that provide refined, white sugar or one of its other forms. What alternatives could be offered with less refined sugar or made with one of its other forms?

Banana-Papaya Popsicles

These vitamin- and mineral-rich frozen fruit treats are "lickin' good." They are a combination of frozen papaya and banana purees and concentrated fruit juices.

Servings: 24
Serving Size: 1 popsicle
Yield: 24 popsicles

Papaya, ripe, pureed   3½ pounds
Banana, very ripe, pureed*   1¾ pounds
Orange juice, freshly squeezed   ¾ cup + 2 tablespoons
Fruit or apple juice concentrate, unsweetened   ¾ cup + 2
*   tablespoons*
Paper cups, 4-ounce   24
Popsicle sticks or plastic spoons   24

1. In a mixing bowl, mix the papaya and next 3 ingredients until well blended.
2. Pour into 24 4-ounce paper cups. Cover with plastic wrap; freeze.
3. When partially frozen, place a stick or plastic spoon into each cup to form a handle. Freeze until hard. Unmold to serve.

*To oven-ripen bananas, place in a 350° F (175° C) oven until their skins turn black and their fruit becomes soft and sweet, or about 10 minutes.

Servings	Calories	Protein (g/%)	Fat (g/%)	Cholesterol (mg)	Carbo-hydrates (g/%)	Fiber (g)	Sodium (mg)
1	87	1.0 g/4%	0.3 g/3%	0	21.8 g/93%	2.3	5

Gingerbread Cake Topped with Bananas

While gingerbread is often topped with whipped cream or a rich lemon sauce, this whole wheat homestyle cake flavored with molasses, ginger, and other sweet spices is topped with sliced bananas glazed in fruit syrup. It's delicious served warm or at room temperature.

Servings: 24
Serving Size: 3 × 3⅓-inch piece
Yield: 1 12 × 20 × 2-inch counter pan

Apple juice concentrate, unsweetened (divided)   1½ pints
Vanilla extract   2 teaspoons
Vegetable cooking spray, butter-flavored
Bananas, ripe, peeled, cut into ¼ inch slices   2 pounds
Molasses, light   ½ cup
Margarine, unsalted, corn oil   4 ounces
Flour, whole wheat, pastry   12 ounces
Flour, unbleached, cake   8 ounces
Baking soda   1 tablespoon
Ginger, ground   1 tablespoon
Cinnamon, freshly ground   2 teaspoons
Cloves, freshly ground   ¼ teaspoon
Nutmeg, freshly ground   ¼ teaspoon
Egg whites, large, lightly beaten   10 ounces (8)

1. Blend ½ cup of the juice concentrate with the vanilla. Pour into a 12 × 20 × 2-inch counter pan coated with cooking spray.
2. Lay the banana slices evenly over the juice concentrate mixture. Set aside.
3. In a saucepan, heat the remaining 2½ cups of juice concentrate, molasses, and margarine to a boil, stirring constantly. Remove from the heat; transfer to a mixing bowl; set aside to cool.
4. Mix the whole wheat pastry flour and next 6 ingredients in another bowl until blended.
5. Alternately add the dry ingredients and egg whites to the juice concentrate mixture, beating after each addition. When smooth, pour the batter over the bananas.
6. Bake in a 350° F (175° C) oven until a wooden pick inserted in the center comes out clean, or about 30 minutes. Let stand 5 minutes.

7. Cut the cake 5 × 3 into 3⅓ × 3-inch pieces. Serve inverted.

Servings	Calories	Protein (g/%)	Fat (g/%)	Cholesterol (mg)	Carbo-hydrates (g/%)	Fiber (g)	Sodium (mg)
1	235	4.7 g/8%	4.5 g/17%	0	46.1 g/76%	3	134

Low-Fat and Low-Cholesterol Chocolate Cake

Promote "healthy meal deals" on your menu by offering a complementary dessert with selected entrees. When the dessert is one like this chocolate cake prepared without egg yolks or added fat (that's no butter, oil, shortening, or margarine), diners can literally "have their cake and eat it too."

Servings: 24
Serving Size: 1 wedge (one-eighth of 9-inch round)
Yield: 3 9-inch rounds

Flour, cake   9 ounces
Cornstarch   5 ounces
Cocoa powder   4 ounces
Baking powder   1 tablespoon
Baking soda   1 ½ teaspoons
Salt   To taste or ¾ teaspoon
Egg whites, large   7 ½ ounces (6)
Date puree (see page 125)   1 pint + ¼ cup
White grape or apple juice concentrate, unsweetened   1 ½ pints
Vanilla extract   2 teaspoons
Vegetable cooking spray, butter-flavored
Sugar, confectioners'   1 ½ ounces

1. In a bowl, sift together the first 6 ingredients; mix. In a mixing bowl, beat the egg whites with the date puree, juice concentrate, and vanilla. Add the dry mixture to the egg white mixture; mix together until blended.

2. Coat three 9-inch cake rounds with cooking spray. Divide the cake batter equally among the cake pans. Bake in a 350° F (175° C) oven until a wooden pick inserted in the center comes out clean, or 30–35 minutes. Cool on a rack.

3. To serve, sift confectioners' sugar on top; cut into wedges and garnish with fresh berries or other fruit in season. Another delicious option is to serve the cake laced with raspberry sauce. To prepare: cut each cake into two layers; coat the bottom layer with Naturally Sweetened Raspberry Sauce (recipe follows); cover with the top cake layer; cut into wedges; serve with the raspberry sauce napped over the center of each cake wedge.

Servings	Calories	Protein (g/%)	Fat (g/%)	Cholesterol (mg)	Carbo-hydrates (g/%)	Fiber (g)	Sodium (mg)
1	204	3.5 g/7%	1 g/4%	0	48.3 g/89%	3.7	130

Naturally Sweetened Raspberry Sauce

This puree of sweet, wine-tasting, ruby red raspberries looks and tastes elegant laced over a scoop of vanilla, nonfat frozen yogurt, soaking into whole wheat pancakes, or napped over rolled crepes filled with sauteed fruit.

Servings: 24
Serving Size: 3 tablespoons
Yield: 1⅛ quarts

Raspberries, fresh, washed or frozen without sugar   3 pounds
White grape or apple juice concentrate, unsweetened   1¾ cups
Raspberry liqueur   3 tablespoons (optional)

1. In a food processor or blender, puree all the ingredients until smooth. Strain through cheese cloth or a fine mesh strainer to remove the suds. Serve as a topping for nonfat frozen yogurt, low-fat cakes such as vanilla angel cake, or whole grain waffles or pancakes.

Servings	Calories	Protein (g/%)	Fat (g/%)	Cholesterol (mg)	Carbohydrates (g/%)	Fiber (g)	Sodium (mg)
1	62	0.6 g/4%	0.4 g/5%	0	14.9 g/91%	2.7	5.1

4

Say Goodbye to Sodium

Effect of Too Much Sodium

Like many things in life, too much sodium or salt (sodium chloride) may be harmful to health. While the cause of hypertension is unknown, sodium intake seems to be one of the factors. Obesity, heredity, lifestyle, kidney function, and the action of body hormones are other factors which can raise blood pressure and in turn lead to heart attacks, kidney disease, and strokes.

While only about 20% of Americans, 45% between the ages of 45 and 55, have hypertension, there is no way to tell who is sensitive to sodium and who isn't until the problems begin to appear. For all practical purposes, all Americans should consider themselves at risk.

Sodium Requirements/Recommendations

Although some sodium is necessary for the body to perform, most Americans consume far more than needed. The body requires only about 220 milligrams of sodium or one-tenth of a teaspoon of salt per day. One teaspoon of salt (40% sodium and 60% chloride) contains 2,300 milligrams of sodium. Yet, average intake in the United States is 4,000–5,000 milligrams of sodium. If Americans only obtained sodium from salt, this equals to 2 to 3 teaspoons (1 tablespoon) per day. Since few diets lack sodium, no RDAs have been established for this mineral.

The National Academy of Science (NAS) recommends a maximum of 2,400 milligrams of sodium per day, just a smidgen more than the 2,300 milligrams found in a teaspoon of salt. The American Heart Association recommends 3,000 milligrams of sodium per day, or again, about one and one-third teaspoons of salt a day if this is the only source of sodium in the diet.

Sources of Sodium in the Food Supply

About 75% of the sodium in the American food supply is added by food manufacturers, with another 15% coming from the salt added during cooking and eating. The other 10% occurs naturally in food and in some drinking water. Most Americans could get all the sodium they need from naturally occurring sources (see Table 4.1) even if salt was never added in processing or cooking food. Animal foods including milk, eggs, cheese, meat, seafood, and poultry are the major contributors of naturally occurring sodium. Fresh fruits and vegetables; unprocessed grains like rice and barley; sugar; oil and shortening contain minimal amounts.

Sources of Salt and Sodium in Recipes

Salt and sodium are easily recognizable in some foods, but in others, they are not. The following are both the obvious and less apparent sources of salt and sodium in foods.

Salt in the Kitchen

In the kitchen, salt is habitually added when cooking ingredients like pastas, cereals, eggs, grains, and vegetables in water. For most chefs, it is a natural reaction to sprinkle salt in the water before cooking items like poached eggs, boiled rice, or blanched green beans.

Some cooks (not chefs) attempt to enhance the flavor of dishes by simply adding salt too. Rather than elevating the more natural flavors of ingredients in dishes, some cooks take the easy route and overpower them with salt.

Salted Ingredients

Obviously, salted foods such as potato chips, pretzels, nuts, and crackers (see Table 4.7) are high in sodium. Besides serving as

TABLE 4.1

Sodium Content of Common Foods

Item	Amount	Sodium (mg)
Oil, corn	1 tablespoon	0
Shortening, Wesson	1 tablespoon	0
Butter	1 tablespoon	123
Eggs	1 large	63
Cheddar cheese	1 ounce	176
American processed cheese	1 ounce	406
Oatmeal, quick/old fashioned, Quaker	1/3 cup dry	1
Oatmeal crisp cereal, General Mills	1 ounce	180
Banana, raw	1 medium	1
Apple, raw	1 medium	1
Apple juice, canned	8 fluid ounces	7
Vegetable juice cocktail, canned	6 fluid ounces	664
White table wine	3½ ounces	5
Milk, skim	8 fluid ounces	126
Bass, fresh water, raw	3 ounces	59
Beef tenderloin, choice, broiled, 0 fat trim	3½ ounces	63
Turkey thigh, cooked	1 ounce	20
Salami, turkey	1 ounce slice	251
Ham, turkey	1 ounce slice	282
Summer sausage, turkey	1 ounce slice	324
Chicken, roasted, without skin	½ breast	63
Broccoli, raw	½ cup	12
Asparagus, fresh, boiled	½ cup	10
Asparagus, canned, Pillsbury	½ cup	376
Cream of asparagus soup, prepared with water	1 cup	981
Macaroni, whole wheat, cooked without salt	1 cup	4
Barley, cooked without salt	1 cup	5
Rice, cooked without salt	1 cup	4
Cornbread stuffing mix, Golden Grain	½ cup	870
Sugar	1 tablespoon	0
Corn syrup, light	1 tablespoon	24

Source: Data from J.A.T. Pennington (1994). *Bowes & Church's Food Values of Portions Commonly Used.* Philadelphia: J. B. Lippincott Co.

snacks, these high-sodium favorites can be found as toppings on vegetables, pastas, and a variety of other dishes. For example, salted cracker crumbs might top broiled tomatoes or stuffed bell peppers while crushed potato chips might be sprinkled over macaroni and cheese.

Salted crackers and chips might also be used as coatings on and extenders in selections including meat, seafood, poultry, and vegetables. In the midwest, where I grew up, fresh lake fish was commonly rolled in Saltine crumbs before pan frying. Also invariably, an ingredient in my Mom's tasty salmon patties and meat loaf was Saltine crackers. On the other hand, crushed potato chips were expected on tuna fish hot dish and often showed up on green bean casserole.

Yeast-Leavened Products

Yeast-leavened products like bread and rolls are sources of salt/sodium too. Because salt retards yeast's fermentation, it is a key player in the leavening process. While bread doesn't seem a likely candidate for sodium concern, it is. Because Americans eat so much bread, it contributes more sodium to the average person's diet than any other single food. Bread made on premise may yield one-third to one-half less sodium than commercially produced bread, but at around 100 milligrams per slice, the sodium can add up quickly when several slices are consumed. Commercially produced breads contain more sodium than "home-made" breads because they typically contain sodium-containing additives as well as salt. Thus, if diners eat two slices of commercially produced bread toasted for breakfast, a couple of hamburgers on commercially produced buns at lunch and two commercially produced rolls with dinner, they will have consumed more than half of the 2,300 milligrams of sodium recommended daily by the NAS.

Canned, Cured, Smoked, or Salty Meat, Seafoods, and Poultry

Other sodium no-no's are canned meat, seafood, and poultry like canned ham, anchovies, tuna, salmon, and chicken. For example, with the addition of five anchovies to a Caesar salad, its sodium content shoots up by 735 milligrams or more than one-fourth the amount recommended daily by the NAS.

While it might seem like saltwater fish will be high in sodium too, because it comes from the briny sea, this is not the case. Special cells in the gills and kidneys of fish eliminate excess sodium. As a result, the sodium content of fresh- and saltwater species is similar. For example, while a cooked 3-ounce portion of rainbow trout contains 29 milligrams of sodium, a 3-ounce portion of cooked bluefin tuna yields 43 milligrams, and an equal size portion of cooked pink salmon, 73 milligrams. But once canned, an equivalent portion of canned pink salmon increases to 458 milligrams and one of light tuna canned in spring water to 287 milligrams of sodium.

Cured, smoked, or salty meat, fish, and poultry like caviar, dried cod, smoked oysters, herring, sardines, smoked turkey, bacon, salt pork, dried or chipped beef, corned beef, and ham are also on the list of high-sodium ingredients. For example, Belgian endive spears topped with smoked salmon and goat cheese are wonderful tasting hors d'oeuvres, but they are high in sodium. How high? A mere ½ ounce of the smoked salmon (105 milligrams sodium) served with ½ ounce of the naturally high-sodium, high-fat goat cheese (75 milligrams sodium) on one spear of endive records a total of 181 milligrams of sodium. Recall, most diners need only 220 milligrams of sodium each day.

Poultry products that are cured or smoked can be deceptive. While items like ham, pastrami, and breakfast sausages made from turkey may be lower in fat and cholesterol than their traditional counterparts, they are still high in sodium. See Table 4.1. Imitation crab meat, also called "surimi," is another product which may appear to be low in sodium, but is not. Because it is formed by mixing minced, white-fleshed fish like pollock or whiting with carbohydrates, salt, and additives, a mere 4-ounce portion contains 900 milligrams of sodium, far more than the 150 milligrams in an equivalent portion of fresh pollock.

In fact, all luncheon meats, bolognas, sausages, hot dogs, and bratwursts are high in sodium. Again, just because frankfurters are made from chicken or turkey rather than beef or pork, this is no indication that they will be low in sodium (see Table 4.1).

Kosher Meat and Poultry

The term kosher was derived from the Hebrew word kasher meaning pure or proper. As such, meat and poultry labeled kosher are often overlooked as potential sources of sodium. This is a fallacy. Because kosher meat and poultry are salted after slaughter, they can contain twice as much sodium as nonkosher meat and poultry.

Pickled Foods

Of course, foods prepared in brines like olives, relishes, sauerkraut, and pickles, the condiments typically added to high-sodium hot dogs and sausages, are high in sodium. But, vegetables are not the only ingredients which are pickled and high in sodium. When I was growing up, it seemed two of my father's favorites, high-sodium pickled pig's feet and pickled beef heart, were always in the refrigerator. It might be of interest to also note that a 3½-ounce portion of pig's feet yields one-third of the maximum cholesterol recommended daily and is 71% fat, while a 3½-ounce portion of the heart has an acceptable level of fat (30%) but nearly two-thirds of the maximum 300 milligrams cholesterol advised daily.

Cheeses

Many cheeses, especially processed ones, are on the high-sodium list. Further, they are often combined with cured and smoked meats. For example, a sandwich made from sliced turkey ham, low-fat American processed cheese, and whole grain bread may sound like a healthful sandwich, but it is loaded with sodium. Similarly, an egg white omelet filled with lean veal sausage and cholesterol-free Swiss cheese has many nutritional attributes but is high in sodium.

Condiments

Many condiments tend to be high in sodium. Soy sauce is obviously high, but horseradish, catsup, mayonnaise, barbecue sauce, chili sauce, worcestershire sauce, and mustard are high in sodium as well.

For example, while both mild and hot and spicy mustards are great low-fat, low-calorie condiments for spreading on sandwiches, that isn't the case with sodium. One tablespoon of mustard contains almost 200 milligrams of sodium. Sodium in rye pretzels might be reduced by blending spices in the dough and coating with caraway seeds rather than salt, but a dip in stone ground mustard and their sodium shoots up.

Commercial salad dressings, both regular and lighter forms, generally fall in the high-sodium category too. For example, a tablespoon of commercially packed thousand island dressing raises the sodium content of a raw vegetable and lettuce salad by 110 milligrams. While commercially packed, low-calorie thousand island dressing may add fewer calories to the plate than its traditional form, its sodium content does not necessarily drop along with its calories.

Self-Rising Flour

Self-rising flour or all-purpose flour to which salt and baking powder have been added may be more convenient to use but contributes unnecessary sodium to recipes. For example, self-rising flour contains 1,349 milligrams of sodium per cup versus the 3 milligrams of sodium in a cup of all-purpose flour.

Commercial Tenderizers

Commercial tenderizers may be a method of breaking down connective tissues in less tender meat but are also high in sodium. One teaspoon contains 1,750 milligrams of sodium or more than two-thirds of the 2,400 milligrams recommended daily by the NAS.

Prepared Stocks, Soups, Sauces, and Gravies

Commercial bases for stocks, canned and dried broths, bouillons, soups, sauces, and gravies are high in sodium. For example, a cup of canned chicken noodle soup even after dilution with water contains 110 milligrams of sodium and all regular canned soups are similarly high in sodium.

Canned Vegetable Products and Juices

Canned tomato products, ranging from whole tomatoes and paste to tomato juice and tomato sauce, add sodium to the menu, as do most canned vegetables and vegetable juices. While a three-bean salad coated in a light vinaigrette may be appealing to calorie counters, if made from canned beans, its sodium content will be substantial.

Seasoning Blends

It is often believed that seasoning blends are sodium-free, but many are not. The clearly high sodium ones are seasoned salts like onion, garlic, and celery salt, but salt can also be added to seasoning blends like lemon pepper, BBQ seasoning, chili powder, and sometimes curry powder. Generally, salt isn't added to sweet spice blends like pumpkin or apple pie seasonings.

TABLE 4.2

Sodium Additives Commonly Found in Food

Anhydrous disodium phosphate

Calcium disodium

Dioctyl sodium sulfosuccinate

Disodium dihydrogen pyrophosphate

Disodium guanylate

Disodium inosinate

Disodium phosphate

Monosodium glutamate

Sodium acid pyrophosphate

Sodium alginate

Sodium aluminosilicate

Sodium aluminum

Sodium ascorbate

Sodium benzoate

Sodium bicarbonate

Sodium biphosphate

Sodium bisulfate

Sodium carboxymethyl cellulose

Sodium caseinate

Sodium chloride

Sodium citrate

Sodium erythorbate

Sodium ferrocyanide

Sodium gluconate

Sodium hexametaphosphate

Sodium hydroxide

Sodium iron pyrophosphate

Sodium metaphosphate

Sodium nitrate

Sodium nitrite

Sodium phosphate

Sodium propionate

Sodium saccharine

Sodium stearoly-2-lactylate

Sodium thiosulfate

Sodium triosulfate

Sodium tripolyphosphate

Trisodium citrate

Monosodium Glutamate

Monosodium glutamate (MSG) or Accent, the flavor enhancer often associated with Chinese food, is another source of sodium. For example, the recipe for Chinese hot and sour soup, the classic combination of spicy heat and vinegar, might be low in fat and cholesterol, but more than likely will contain MSG on its ingredient list. MSG is found in some unlikely foods too, for example, hydrolyzed vegetable protein and yeast extract. Further, sometimes they are unlabeled.

In addition to the sodium MSG adds to the diet, some diners report adverse reactions to MSG—the so-called Chinese restaurant syndrome—burning sensations, chest and facial flushing or pain, and throbbing headaches. At this point, there is much controversy about the effects of MSG. It has not been established whether MSG is the cause of these allergic reactions or not.

Processed Foods

Prepared foods that have gone through extensive processing at manufacturing plants are sources of sodium too. Prepared mixes for stuffings, rice dishes, and breadings are all high in sodium. Frozen entrees, including breaded meat, seafood, and poultry, also typically contain far more sodium than their fresh counterparts. Moreover, processed foods can be high in sodium without tasting salty. For example, one Hostess cherry snack pie or two Mrs. Paul's apple fritters provide more than three times the amount of sodium found in an ounce of most salted potato chips. Sodium-containing additives (see Table 4.2) are added to products to perform a variety of functions. They range from acting as preservatives, texturizers, neutralizers, emulsifiers, stabilizers, thickeners, and flavor enhancers to serving as leavening, glazing, and peeling agents.

Since ingredients on labels are listed in descending order by amount from largest to smallest, if salt or other sodium-containing ingredients appear at the top of the list or if several sodium compounds are on the list, the product likely contains a significant amount of sodium. Along with the words salt, sodium, and soda, the symbol Na indicates an ingredient is a source of sodium.

Soft Water

When softened, water may contribute appreciable amounts of sodium to items. In the water-softening process, sodium is exchanged for magnesium and calcium ions. As a result, the harder the water is initially, the more sodium the softened water will provide.

Strategies to Reduce Salt and Sodium in Recipes

Because of the detrimental effects high-sodium diets can have on health, it is likely some diners will request salt-free and low-sodium items when dining out. Many strategies can be employed to meet these needs.

Salt in the Kitchen

The first step to reduce sodium in dishes is to eliminate salt from recipes where possible. Rather, customers can be encouraged to add salt to dishes as they desire.

There's no need for the salt when cooking ingredients in water, for example, boiling grains like wild rice, cooked cereals like oatmeal, pastas like spinach linguine, and vegetables like baby red potatoes, braising meat or poultry selections like lean round steak, or skinless chicken legs, or poaching fish or poultry like salmon or skinless turkey breast. The quality of the products will not be affected.

The inherent flavors of many dishes will be more appreciated if not hidden with salt. For example, the flavor of a grilled beef and asparagus salad tossed in a light raspberry vinaigrette dressing splashed with macadamia nut oil is charming without added salt. Diners preferring a saltier taste can add their own.

When cutting salt in dishes, a gradual reduction over time seems to work best. Initially, the salt should be reduced in recipes by one-half and then as demand warrants. The preference for salt is learned. For those diners who have cut their salt intake, foods salted at traditional levels will likely taste too salty to them.

If a dish is unacceptable without salt, a small amount or about one-eighth teaspoon per serving might be added. Rather than blending the salt in during cooking, its effect will be maximized if sprinkled on selections right before service. The salt will be tasted immediately and satisfy diners' quest for the salty flavor.

Low-Sodium Marinades and Sauces

Low-sodium marinades and sauces made with vinegars, wines, beers, freshly extracted vegetable juices, fruit juices, freshly prepared stocks, and small amounts of oil along with herbs, spices and vegetables are another healthy method to add zest to meat, fish, poultry, and vegetable dishes without salt. Recall that dairy products like nonfat plain yogurt and skim buttermilk make excellent low-fat, low-cholesterol marinade bases, but they are naturally high in sodium. For tasty, salt-free entrees, skewers of lean, sirloin beef cubes, onion quarters, cherry tomatoes, mushroom and zucchini slices might be brushed with a sauce of freshly squeezed lemon juice, canola oil, dillweed, and paprika before and during grilling; or swordfish steaks can be marinated in a mixture of orange juice, sherry (not cooking sherry), minced garlic, and sesame oil prior to broiling. Both make nutritious, low-sodium, low-fat entrees. But the sky is the limit when creating salt-free flavor combinations.

Spirits

Drinking wines, beers, and spirits (see Table 4.3) are other low-sodium ingredients that can add pizzazz to dishes. On the other

TABLE 4.3

Cooking with Spirits

Product	Flavor	Menu Items
Benedictine	Medium-sweet honey/herbal, aromatic, combined flavors of 27 herbs and spices	Sauteed string beans dashed with benedictine; broiled swordfish with ginger and benedictine glaze; flapjacks with benedictine maple syrup
B & B liqueur	Slightly lighter and dryer than benedictine. Combines the flavor of French brandy with benedictine	Roasted quail with B&B and blood orange juice glaze; BBQ sauce accented with B&B; black bean soup with a hint of B&B; creamy, light, sweet butterscotch and B&B sauce
Carolans finest Irish cream liqueur	Creamy, honeyed Irish whiskey	Whole wheat bread pudding with a splash of Irish cream; low-sodium tofu cheesecake laced with Irish cream; low-fat brownies topped with creamy Irish cream icing; Irish cream marinated, raisin-studded coffee cake
Carolans light Irish cream liqueur	Light, creamy, honeyed Irish whiskey	Fruit tartlets glazed with fruity Irish cream sauce; honey-coated sweet potatoes with a touch of light Irish cream; light frozen raspberry souffle dashed with light Irish cream
Courvoisier cognac	Smooth, fruity with long robust aftertaste	Cassoulet of lean meats and vegetables flamed with cognac; low-fat and sodium Welsh rarebit finished with cognac; warm gingerbread pudding laced with cognac

(continued)

TABLE 4.3

Continued

Product	Flavor	Menu Items
Drambuie and Scotch whiskey	Heather honey, herbs	Drambuie shrimp Louis; warm low-sodium cheese dip flavored with Drambuie; candied yams with a touch of Drambuie; low-fat and sodium butterscotch topping finished with Drambuie
Harveys Bristol Cream	Sweet, nutty	She-crab soup spiked with Harveys Bristol Cream; Mulligatawny soup with essence of Harveys Bristol Cream; skewered chicken with bristol cream and walnut dipping sauce
Liqueurs	Armaretto-almond	Ginger almond shrimp with amaretto
	Triple sec-orange	Roasted turkey with triple sec and cranberry glaze
	Ginger schnapps-ginger	Pork loin with apple and ginger sauce accented with ginger schnapps
	Sloe gin-wild plum	Grilled squid with sloe gin salsa
Irish Mist liqueur	Combination of Irish whiskey, herbs with heather honey	Irish Mist glazed leeks; grilled salmon with Irish Mist mint chutney
Kahlua	Sweet, dark coffee	Light kahlua chocolate cake; Chile-kahlua marinated lean beef fajitas; kahlua and pumpkin marbled low-sodium tofu cheesecake; onion and ginger chutney sparked with kahlua
Bourbon	Mellow, nutty, woody when cooked	Bourbon-glazed country turkey legs; brown sugar and bourbon broiled pineapple; bourbon and sour cherry glazed, skinless duckling
Sambuca	Anise, elderberry, and a hint of lemon	Sambuca-accented biscotti; gazpacho seasoned with sambuca; grilled scallops basted with sambuca-spiked marinade; pound cake brushed with sambuca
Tuaca liqueur	Bittersweet orange with hints of vanilla and cocoa	Tuaca-laced one-crust apple pie; spicy jambalaya splashed with tuaca

Source: Adapted from *Cooking with Spirits* published by Hiram Walker in *Food Arts* (June 1993).

TABLE 4.4

Flavor Extracts

Almond

Anise

Banana

Brandy

Butter

Cherry

Chocolate

Coconut

Lemon

Maple

Orange

Peppermint

Pineapple

Rum

Strawberry

Vanilla

hand, cooking wines are generally of inferior quality and may be adulterated with salt.

Flavor Extracts

Imitation or pure flavor extracts can make dishes sparkle without sodium too (see Table 4.4). For example, vanilla may not be a flavor typically associated with fish but is excellent blended with chili peppers and thyme in a sauce and napped over pecan-crusted, roasted Coho salmon.

Herbs and Spices

Herbs and spices are good alternatives to salt, seasoned salts, MSG, and other high-sodium flavoring agents. While it is difficult to distinguish between herbs and spices in some cases, herbs are generally considered the fragrant leaves of plants with nonwoody stems like basil, thyme, and oregano and spices, the pungent or aromatic seasonings obtained from the bark, buds, fruits, roots, seeds, or stems of plants like cinnamon, cardamom, and nutmeg.

FRESH HERBS AND FRESHLY GROUND SPICES

If possible, freshly minced herbs and freshly ground spices are desirable. The fresh flavors and aromas of herbs are hard to replace with dried forms. Those herbs, in particular, that are best fresh are parsley, sorrel, and watercress. Dried, they taste little like their fresh forms and have lost much of their potency. The flavor in delicate herbs such as chervil, chives, cilantro, and dill also tends to diminish with drying.

ROBUST VERSUS MILD FLAVORED HERBS

D. Carolyn and S. Belanger (*Herbs in the Kitchen* (1992). Loveland, Colorado: Interweave Press) divide culinary herbs into two main categories, mild and robust. Mild herbs are those that become milder in flavor with cooking or combine well with most other herbs. Examples are basil, bay, chervil, dill, marjoram, and parsley. On the other hand, the flavors of robust herbs stand up well in cooking and generally form pleasing combinations with just a few other herbs. Examples include rosemary, sage, sorrel, tarragon, and thyme.

Chefs can be more creative when seasoning with herbs in the mild category, mixing more types and using larger quantities. When fresh, they produce good results in uncooked dishes like salsas and salads or dishes cooked briefly like eggs or pastas.

Robust herbs work better in dishes requiring long cooking such as sauces, stews, and braised dishes and grilled, basted lean meat, seafood, and poultry selections. Their flavors change subtly in cooking, sometimes mellowing and others intensifying.

SUBSTITUTING DRIED HERBS FOR FRESH
As a general rule, 1 teaspoon of dried herbs is equivalent to 3 tea-spoons (1 tablespoon) of fresh herbs. When seasoning with robust herbs, fresh forms may be replaced with smaller amounts of dried. Care is advised when adding. In the case of rosemary, savory, and thyme, for example, one-sixth of the dried herb may be all that's needed in place of its fresh form.

GRINDING WHOLE SPICES
In terms of spices, freshly ground spices are far more pungent than preground, and whole spices stay fresh much longer than ground forms. Whole spices can be ground with a mortar and pestle or in a pepper mill, clean coffee grinder, or electric miniprocessor. For some recipes, it may be desirable to toast whole spices before grinding. This helps bring out their flavors.

One example where roasting of the spices makes a big dif-ference in the outcome is a spice blend called garam masala. In this Indian seasoning agent, several aromatic spices, including cinnamon bark, clove berries, cardamom pods, and peppercorns are roasted whole and then ground together.

FLAVORING LIGHT DISHES WITH HERBS AND SPICES
Herbs and spices should be added to enhance the natural flavors of lighter dishes and make them more interesting and enjoyable to eat. They should not hide or mask the inherent flavors of their primary ingredients. Because fat is often reduced in healthier se-lections, it is easy to overpower them with herbs and spices. When flavoring such dishes, a good approach is to begin with small amounts of herbs and spices and add more as needed according to taste. If large amounts of herbs and spices are used initially and ap-pear to be too much, it's difficult to remove them.

The first step in replacing salt in recipes with herbs and spices is to become familiar with their flavors, aromas, and the effects they have on foods. Herb and spice charts are useful sources of in-formation (see Tables 4.5 and 4.6), but first-hand tasting and smelling of herbs and spices is better yet. With this information in mind and knowledge about the characteristics of the foods await-ing flavoring, experimentation can begin.

For starters, common herbs that work well with vegetables are

TABLE 4.5

Spice Reference Chart

Product	Description	Product Notes
Allspice (spice)	Dried, dark brown berries of an evergreen tree.	Clove-like flavor, but smoother, mellower; undertones of cinnamon, nutmeg, hence name; also called "pimento."
Anise Seed (herb seed)	Small, gray-brown seeds of plant of the parsley family.	Licorice-like flavor. Its oil is heavily used for licorice flavoring, though true licorice is from the roots of another plant.
Star Anise (spice)	Large, brown, star-shaped fruit of an evergreen tree. Each point contains a seed; whole fruit is used.	Anise-like flavor. Old-time pickling favorite; now available again since China trade embargo was lifted.
Basil (herb)	Bright green leaves of an herb of the mint family.	Special affinity for tomato flavored dishes; currently enjoying fastest popularity growth of an herb.
Bay Leaves (herb)	Large, olive-green leaves of the sweet-bay or laurel tree.	An imported product; only dried herb to come in original, whole leaf form. Also "laurel."
Caraway Seed (herb seed)	Hard, brown, scimiter-shaped seeds of an herb of the parsley family.	The seed of "seeded rye bread"; essential in the liqueur kummel; German sauerkraut favorite.
Cardamom Seed (spice)	Pod and dark brown seeds of a plant of the ginger family.	Scandinavian bakery goods; Indian foods; worldwide biggest use is in Middle East coffee.
Celery seed (herb seed)	Tiny brown seeds of the smal-lage, or wild celery plant.	Strong celery flavor; heavy use in salad dressings, sauces, vegetable cocktails.
Chervil (herb)	Lacy, fern-like leaves of a plant of the parsley family.	Much like parsley, but sweeter and more aromatic; anise-like fragrance with slight pepper flavor.
Chives (herb)	Tubular green leaves of a member of the onion family.	Normally freeze-dried to protect fragile quality and vibrant green color; product is tiny lengths of tubular shoots.
Cinnamon/ Cassia (spice)	Bark of various evergreen trees of the cinnamomum family.	Two main types: Zeylanicum (Ceylon) is tan colored, thin bark, mild, sweet flavor. Cassia is reddish brown, thicker bark, strong cinnamon flavor, most popular in U.S.

(continued)

TABLE 4.5
Continued

Product	Description	Product Notes
Cloves (spice)	Dried, unopened flower buds of an evergreen tree.	Intriguing, nail-like shape makes exotic garnish. Ground cloves very strong flavored.
Coriander leaves (herb)	Green leaves of a plant of the parsley family.	Most frequently called "cilantro." Strong, exotic flavor, associated with Mexican food.
Coriander Seed (herb seed)	Small, round, buff-colored seeds of the coriander plant.	Mild, delicately fragrant aroma with lemony/sage undertone.
Cumin Seed (herb seed)	Small, elongated, yellowish-brown seeds of a plant of the parsley family.	Also "comino." The aromatic flavor note in chili powder and essential in curries.
Dill Seed (herb seed)	Small, oval-shaped, tan seed of a member of the parsley family.	Principal flavor of dill pickles; also used in dips, sauces, sausages.
Dill Weed (herb)	Green, feathery leaves of the dill plant.	Dill weed is much used in sauces for fish, cheese dips, salads, dressings.
Fennel Seed (herb seed)	Small, yellowish-brown, watermelon-shaped seeds of a member of the parsley family.	Anise-like flavor. The distinctive note in Italian sausages (both sweet and hot).
Fenugreek Seed (herb seed)	Very small, reddish-brown seeds of a member of the pea family.	Pleasantly bitter flavor with curry-like aroma. Essential in curry powder; basis of imitation maple.
Ginger (spice)	Dried roots (rhizomes) of a member of the zingiber family.	Root pieces are called "hands." Smooth, straw-colored ones have been peeled, bleached.
Mace (spice)	Lacy, scarlet-colored aril (orange when dried) which surrounds the seed of the nutmeg fruit.	Flavor is stronger than nutmeg. Ground mace is often chosen for light-colored products, such as pound cake.
Marjoram (herb)	Grayish-green leaves of a member of the mint family	A cousin of oregano but with milder, sweeter flavor.
Mint Flakes (herb)	Dark green leaves of either the peppermint or spearmint plant.	Spearmint is the mint usually packed as mint flakes for retail and foodservice; peppermint is also available to industrial customers.
Mustard Seed (spice)	Tiny yellow or brownish seeds of a member of the cabbage family.	Yellow (or white) seeds have sharp bite, but no aromatic pungency. Brown (and oriental) seeds are aromatically pungent as well as biting (i.e., Chinese restaurant mustard).
Nutmeg (spice)	The brown seed of the fruit of an evergreen tree.	Of the two sources, Indonesian and West Indian compare favorably in aroma, but higher fixed oil in the W.I. restricts its use in some applications.

TABLE 4.5

Continued

Product	Description	Product Notes
Oregano (herb)	Light green leaves of members of the mint family.	Two distinct types: Mediterranean (Italian/Greek foods); Mexican (chili, Mexican, TexMex foods).
Paprika (spice)	Powder milled from the flesh of pods of certain capsicum plants.	Extractable color is principal evaluation of paprika. Flavor can range from sweet-mild to mildly pungent.
Parsley (herb)	Bright green leaves of the parsley plant.	About 12 pounds of de-stemmed parsley leaves are required to make one pound of parsley flakes.
Black Peppercorns (spice)	Dried, mature berries of a tropical vine.	The whole dried berry (peppercorn) is used for black pepper.
Chili Pepper (spice)	Large, mildly pungent pods of Anaheim (or "California-type") peppers and the newer "6-4" variety (New Mexican-type).	Spice industry reserves "chili peppers" for these mild pods; "chillies" for the hot little pods (see Red Pepper).
Green Peppercorns	Immature berries (dried or freeze-dried) of the pepper vine.	Pepper berries are picked while still green, resulting in somewhat milder flavor.
Pink Peppercorns	Dried, red berries of a shrub-like evergreen of the Anareardiacease.	No relation to black pepper. Proper label is Rose Baises (Red Berries).
Red Pepper (spice)	Dried fruit (pods) of various small, hot peppers. Whole pods are called "chillies."	"Red pepper" is today's industry designation for any ground hot pepper product. "Cayenne" is being phased out.
White Peppercorns	Light tan-colored seed of the pepper berry from which the dark outer husk has been removed.	White pepper has the heat but not the total bouquet of black. Often chosen for light colored soups, sauces.
Poppy Seed (herb seed)	Tiny, gray-blue seeds of the poppy plant.	The same plant produces opium and morphine, but the seeds have no drug significance.
Rosemary (herb)	Green, needle-like leaves of a shrub of the mint family.	Rosemary and lamb are closely associated, but it's also important in Italian herb blends, sauces and salad dressings. Has natural antioxidant properties.
Saffron (herb)	Dried flower stigmas of a member of the crocus family.	By the pound, our most expensive spice, but a pinch does so much flavoring and coloring that it is not prohibitive.

TABLE 4.5

Continued

Product	Description	Product Notes
Sage (herb)	Long, slender leaves (silver-gray when dried) of a member of the mint family.	Three types: "Cut" is used for end products where sage should show. "Rubbed" is minimally ground and coarsely sieved to a fluffy consistency. "Ground" is sieved to a fine degree.
Savory (herb)	Small, brownish-green (when dried) leaves of a summer savory—a member of the mint family.	So good with green beans, its German name translates to "bean herb." Also in poultry seasoning and other herb blends.
Sesame Seed (herb seed)	Small, oval, pearly white seeds of a member of the Pedaliacae family.	Also "benne." Needs toasting or high heat of baking to develop its nutty flavor.
Tarragon (herb)	Slender, dark green leaves of a member of the aster family.	Distinctive for its hint of anise flavor. Hallmark of sauce bearnaise, salad dressings, vinegars.
Thyme (herb)	Grayish green leaves of a member of the mint family.	One of the strongest herbs. Manhattan-style clam chowder and innumerable herb blends.
Turmeric (spice)	Orange colored roots (rhizomes) of a member of the ginger family.	Provides color for prepared mustards, curry powder, mayonnaise, sauces, pickles, relishes.

■ DEHYDRATED VEGETABLE SEASONINGS ■

Product	Description	Product Notes
Celery	Leaf and stalk material of vegetable celery.	Celery Flakes are the standard for foodservice but industrial buyers have a choice ranging from powdered and granules to minced to leaf and stalk flakes to diced stalks.
Garlic	Bulbs of a perennial plant, cousin to the onion and a member of the lily family.	Dehydrated garlic is milled to particle sizes ranging from powdered, granulated and ground to minced, chopped and sliced.
Onion	Bulbs of a biennial of the lily family.	Dehydrated onion is available as powdered or granulated (for flavor alone) and in such larger particle sizes as minced, chopped, diced and sliced (for use where texture and mouth feel are important). All sizes are also available in toasted form, for a sauteed-like flavor.
Sweet Pepper	Green and red sweet bell peppers.	For industrial use, dehydrated, sweet bell pepper is available as powder, granulated, minced, diced and sliced, including strips. And in green or red alone or mixed. For foodservice, "sweet pepper flakes" is the standard pack.

TABLE 4.5

Continued

■ *CLASSIC SPICE BLENDS* ■

As explained, large quantity spice buyers can obtain custom blends to satisfy any food prod-
uct formulation. However, following are the typical spice or spice/oleoresin blends offered in
most spice lines and therefore regularly available to foodservice operations which buy in small
units. Additionally, every company has other standard blends of its own. Note that some in-
gredient lists seem similar, but the proportions make the final product completely different.

Product	Description	Notes
Apple Pie Spice	Ground; predominantly cinnamon, but also cloves, nutmeg, allspice, ginger.	Also good for other fruit pies and pastries.
Barbecue Spice	Ground; paprika, salt, celery seed, chili pepper, cumin, coriander, garlic, cloves, black pepper, red pepper.	Good also in salad dress-ings, egg and cheese dishes.
Chili Powder	Ground; chili peppers, cumin, garlic, oregano, salt. Such spices as allspice, cloves, coriander and ginger may also be included.	Salt-free also available.
Crab Boil or Shrimp Spice	Whole; peppercorns, bay leaves, red peppers, celery seed, mustard seed, ginger and other spices in whole or cracked form.	Added to the water in which shellfish is boiled.
Curry Powder	Ground; cumin, coriander and fenugreek seeds, turmeric, black and red peppers and such others as cinnamon, ginger, cardamom, nutmeg, allspice, garlic, dill and celery seeds, etc.	May contain salt. Imported products often contain such other ingredients as flour, garlic, peanuts, asafetida and kari leaves.
Herb Seasoning	A blend of leaf herbs, i.e., marjoram, oregano, basil, chervil, etc.	For salads and salad dress-ings. May also contain salt.
Italian Seasoning	A blend of typical Italian herbs, such as thyme, oregano, basil, savory, marjoram, rosemary and sage.	The herbs are normally in leaf form and salt is not usually added.
Mixed Pickling Spice	Whole; typical formula consists of mustard seed, allspice, cassia (cinnamon), ginger, dill seed, celery seed, bay leaves, cloves, fennel seed, crushed red pepper, turmeric, black pepper, mace and cardamom seed.	Most items are in the com-pletely whole form, but cas-sia, ginger, bay leaves and turmeric are cracked into smaller pieces.
Mixed Vegetable Flakes	A blend which usually consists of dehy-drated flakes of onion, celery, red and green sweet bell peppers and carrots.	For seasoning soups, stews, sauces and stuffings. Usually softened before use by adding equal amount of water and letting stand 10 minutes.
Poultry Seasoning	A blend of such herbs as sage, marjoram, thyme, rosemary and oregano, plus spices such as pepper and ginger.	Always a ground product and usually without salt. Probably the first conve-nience blend.

TABLE 4.5

Continued

Product	Description	Notes
Pumpkin Pie Spice	Ginger predominant, with cinnamon, nutmeg and cloves typical.	Always ground. Good in a variety of sweet baked goods and with mashed root vegetables.
Seafood Seasoning	Ingredient make-up is similar to crab boil or shrimp spice.	This is a ground product which normally contains salt as well.
Seasoned or Flavor Salt	Blend varies widely, according to the manufacturer. Almost any spice or oleoresin can be used.	Basically, an all-purpose blend which goes under various names. Many companies also offer salt-free versions today.

Source: The American Spice Trade Association, Inc., P.O. Box 1267, Englewood Cliffs, NJ 07632

chives, tarragon, parsley, and basil. With meat dishes, thyme, oregano, sage, and rosemary are good choices. Generally, several herbs and spices can benefit the complex flavors of dishes like soups and stew, while two or three is adequate for most dishes. But, regardless of which or how many herbs or spices are selected, they should marry well with the flavors of the ingredients in their given dishes.

ADJUSTING HERBS AND SPICES WITH RECIPE QUANTITIES

When adjusting recipes for larger quantities, herbs and spices cannot always be increased in direct proportion to other ingredients. Tasting is the best method to determine if an item is seasoned properly, but the American Spice Trade Association offers a few guidelines that are helpful.

1. Tropical spices like black pepper, cinnamon, ginger, allspice, and cloves, and spice blends such as pizza spice, curry powder, and pumpkin pie spice, can usually be increased in proportion by weight to the other ingredients. Nutmeg, mace, and Italian seasoning are exceptions. Guideline number 2 is suggested for these flavoring agents.
2. Herbs such as basil, oregano, tarragon, and rosemary can be increased in proportion to the other ingredients when doubled. If the recipe is expanded further, for each multiple of the original recipe, half the amount of original herbs should be used.

TABLE 4.6
Your Spice Shelf Seasoning Chart

Spice	Appetizers	Soups	Pastas	Seafood & Poultry	Meats	Potatoes & Grains	Vegetables & Beans	Salads & Dressings	Desserts
Allspice	Liver Pate	Pepperpot	Middle-Eastern Tomato Sauce	Caribbean Chicken	Jamaican Pot Roast	Baked Rice	Honey Glazed Winter Squash	Creamy Fruit Salad Dressing	Baked Pears
Basil	Italian Tomato Toasts	Minestrone	Pesto Sauce	Shellfish Stew	Italian Beef Roll-Ups	Polenta	Stewed Tomatoes	Sliced Tomatoes & Onions	
Bay leaves	Marinated Mushrooms	Bean	Tomato-Meat Sauce	Marinades for Barbecuing	Skewered Grilled Lamb or Beef	Middle-Eastern Pilaf	Steamed Peas & Lettuce		
Caraway seeds	Liptauer Cheese Spread	Cabbage		Chicken Paprikash	Pork or Veal Stew	Roasted Potatoes	Sauerkraut	Potato Salad	Spice Cookes
Celery seeds	Tomato Juice Cocktail	Chicken Chowder		Chicken Salad	Meat Pies	Buttered Steamed Potatoes	Poached Celery Wedges	Cabbage & Carrot Slaw	
Chili powder	Bean Dips	Corn Chowder	Southwestern Chicken & Tomato Sauce	Oven-Fried Chicken	Corn Meal Topped Stews	Baked Stuffed Potatoes	Baked Beans	Sour Cream or Yogurt Dressing	
Cinnamon	Sugared Nuts	Pumpkin	Noodle Pudding	Moroccan Chicken Stew	Greek Lamb Stew	Couscous	Mashed Yams	Sugared Sliced Tomatoes	Fruit Pies, Cakes, Puddings
Cloves	Fruit Juices	Split Pea		Poached Fish	Beef Stew with Dumplings		Beets with Orange Sauce	Fruit Salad Dressing	Poached Apples
Coriander seeds		Lentil		Curried Chicken	Pork Kebabs	Indian Rice Pilaf	Coriander Butter for Winter Squash	Yogurt Dressing for Fruit	Coffee Cake
Cumin seeds	Guacamole Dip	Bean	Fettuccine Primavera	Mexican Seafood Stews	Chilis & Curries	Brown Rice	Black Beans	Vinaigrette	
Curry powder	Deviled Eggs	Mulligatawny	Tomato & Meat Sauces	Creamed Shellfish	Hamburgers	Rice Pilaf	Baked Winter Squash	Fruit Dressing	
Dill weed & seeds	Sour Cream & Yogurt Dips	Cream of Vegetable	Egg Noodles	Herbed Butters	Scandinavian Veal Meat Balls	Boiled New Potatoes	Green Beans	Marinated Cucumbers	
Fennel seeds	Pickled Shrimp	Pasta & Bean	Italian Tomato Sauces	Bouillabaisse	Beef Stew		Braised Celery	Seafood Salad	
Garlic	Cheese Dips	Vegetable	All Tomato-Based Sauces	Roast Chicken	Roast Lamb	Mashed Potatoes	Sauteed Spinach	Creamy Italian Dressing	
Ginger	Oriental Shrimp	Carrot	Lo Mein Noodles	Chinese Stir-Frys	Pot Roast	Chinese Fried Rice	Carrots	Sweet Potato & Apple Salad	Poached Winter Fruits

Spice	Spinach Quiche	Mushroom	All Tomato-Based Sauces	Fish Florentine	Italian Meatballs	Baked Sliced Potato & Onion Casserole	Grilled Vegetables	Italian Oil & Vinegar Dressings	
Italian seasoning									
Marjoram	Clam Dip	Split Pea	Seafood Sauce	Poultry Stuffings	Veal Stew	Roasted New Potatoes	Vegetable & Bean Stews	Vegetable Salads	
Mint	Pineapple Juice	Chilled Fruit			Roast Lamb	Greek Rice	Steamed Carrots	Creamy Fruit Dressing	Chilled Summer Fruits
Mustard	Pork Pate	Cheddar Cheese		Broiled Salmon	Baked Ham	Potatoes Au Gratin	Green Beans with Mustard Sauce	Vinaigrette Dressings	
Nutmeg	Chicken Kebabs	Cream of Onion	Delicate Cream Sauces	Creamy Seafood Sauces	Veal Meat Balls	Risotto	Creamed Spinach	Waldorf Salad	Apple Bread Pudding
Onion	Cream Cheese Spreads	Fish Chowder	Pasta with Artichokes	French Country Chicken with Herbs	Meat Loaf	Mashed Potatoes	Stewed Tomatoes	Marinated Beans	
Oregano	Vegetable Juices	Bean	Neapolitan Pizza Sauce	Broiled Fish	Greek Lamb Stews	Lemon Roasted Potatoes	Crumb-Topped Green Beans	Mixed Vegetable Salads	
Paprika	Baked Stuffed Clams	Potato-Onion	Baked Ziti with Ricotta	Crab Cakes	Beef Paprikash	Scalloped Potatoes	Corn Pudding	Macaroni Salad	
Red Pepper	Seafood Cocktail Sauce	Seafood Bisque	Southern Italian Tomato Sauce	Szechuan Stir-Frys	Hot Pepper Sauce for Lamb Chops	Rice Pilaf	Stewed Tomatoes	Tomato Salad Dressing	Lemon Ice
Rosemary	Marinated Artichokes	Lentil	Vegetable Lasagna	Chicken Saute with Olives	Lamb Kebabs	Sauteed Potatoes	Grilled Tomatoes	Warm Lamb & Bean Salad	Wine-Poached Fruits
Sage	Cheese Sticks	Bean	Browned Butter Sauce for Ravioli	Chestnut Stuffings	Sauteed Liver	Stuffed Peppers	Baked Lima Beans & Tomatoes		
Sesame seeds	Herbed Biscuits	Sprinkled over Carrot-Orange	Linguine Tossed with Sesame Oil	Red Snapper with Sesame Butter	Sesame Burgers	Coating for Potato Puffs	Topping for Vegetables	Toasted, over Fruit Salad	Baked Bananas
Tarragon	Marinated Mushrooms	Shrimp Gumbo	Tarragon Butter for Noodles	Chicken Breasts with Wine	Stuffed Veal Chops	Rice & Vegetable Casserole	Green Beans & Onions	Chicken & Vegetable Salad	Poached Pears
Thyme	Cheese-Stuffed Mushrooms	Vegetable Beef	Pork-Filled Cannelloni	Shrimp Creole	Boeuf Bourguignon	Wild Rice	Yellow & Red Pepper Saute	Tabouli	

About black pepper: So versatile is the flavor of our most important spice that it can be added to most dishes, including some desserts like spice cookies and cakes, strawberries and poached pears. Pepper can also be used as a seasoning corrector, just before serving.

Source: The American Spice Trade Association, P.O. Box 1267, Englewood, Cliffs, NJ 07633

For example, if a recipe for 25 calls for 1 ounce of herbs, the amount required for 100 portions will be 3 ounces of herbs, or another ounce for the first 25 portions and ½ ounce for the following two portions of 25.

3. Hot red peppers intensify in flavor even more than herbs. When the ingredients in a recipe are doubled, the red peppers can be doubled too. If the recipe is enlarged more, only one-fourth of the original amount should be added for each multiple of the original recipe.

For example, if a recipe for 25 calls for 1 ounce of hot red peppers, the amount needed for 100 portions would be 2½ ounces, or another ounce for the first 25 portions and ¼ ounce for each of the following two portions of 25.

STORING HERBS AND SPICES

To preserve the flavor of both dried herbs and spices, they should be stored in tightly covered opaque containers in cool (68° F or 20° C), dry (humidity less than 60%) environments, measured with dry utensils, and kept away from steam. Heat, light, and moisture cause them to lose flavor.

If possible, cold storage (32–45° F or 0–7° C) is recommended for capsicums (paprika, red pepper, chili powder) and herbs and spices where volatile oils and/or characteristic odors are important quality attributes, such as allspice, cloves, parsley flakes, dill, marjoram, and cumin.

Dried herbs and spices become stale over time too. No more than what will be used in 6 months should be purchased. While whole spices have longer shelf lives than ground, both forms lose substantial amounts of flavor after 6 months.

COOKING WITH HERBS AND SPICES

When flavoring liquids (stocks, sauces, soups, stews, or braised dishes) with whole herbs (parsley or thyme sprigs) and whole spices (peppercorns or cinnamon sticks), they can be tied in cheesecloth to form a sachet for easy removal.

Most herbs and spices need to be cooked to release their flavors. The length of time should be long enough to allow the flavors of the herbs and spices to blend in with those of the other ingredients in dishes, yet not be so long that their flavors are lost.

Whole spices need more cooking time than ground spices. Fresh herbs are an exception. They can be sprinkled in at the end of cooking. Depending on the length of time a dish is to be cooked, the type of seasoning agent, and method of cooking, herbs and spices might be mixed in at the beginning, middle, or end of cooking.

When dishes are not to be cooked, herbs and spices need several hours to release their flavors. Cases where herbs will ideally be allowed time to blend into dishes include cold soups, salsas, salads and their dressings, and dips.

It is much easier to overpower dishes with salt than season with herbs and spices. This requires skill and experience, but the creations can be gifts from heaven. For example, a touch of freshly ground cumin might awaken the sweet flavors of a garden fresh corn soup in a light creamy broth (see page 196) and reduce the need for salt, while a rolled leg of lamb layered with freshly minced, aromatic mint offers a nice change from salt and pepper. Or, as the Norwegians do, a pinch of ground ginger and cardamom might be blended with the meat in a hamburger patty for a lively but unusual burger.

Sour Ingredients

In soups, stews, sauces, and gravies, a few dashes of angostura bitters (description follows), vinegar, lemon juice, or other sour flavor can heighten the natural flavors in ingredients and reduce the need for salt, MSG, and other high-sodium ingredients. Angostura bitters are a bitter to bittersweet tasting liquid made from the distillation of aromatic herbs, barks, roots, and plants that is often used to flavor cocktails.

For this reason, sodium-conscious diners will likely be delighted when offered lemon wedges or half lemons (wrapped in cheese cloth and tied with colorful ribbons) to squeeze on their food. A splash of the tart juice on tender-crisp broccoli florets or asparagus spears is good competition for salt any day.

When all else fails, a zest of lemon, lime, or orange is an option. It can add spark to dishes and serve as a garnish at the same time.

Salt-Free Herb and Spice Blends

On dining tables or upon request, sodium-conscious guests might be offered an herb and/or spice blend to season their food when salt is off limits. It makes a welcome alternative. Commercially, there are products available, and some of them are quite nice. Restaurants can develop their own seasoning blends too. The possible combinations are endless. For example, a mixture of garlic powder, dried basil, and oregano, chili flakes and orange zest might be suggested to season savory dishes. Like salt, if spice blends are served in shakers, caking can be prevented by adding a few grains of rice to them.

Salt Substitutes

As far as salt substitutes, such as "half salt" and light salt products, potassium generally replaces all or some of the sodium. Salt substitutes contain no sodium and "half salt" and light salt have been reduced in sodium by 50% and 33% respectively. These products are not recommended for use in food preparation and should be offered to patrons only on special request. Some diners have found they leave a metallic taste, and potassium might build up in the bloodstream of customers suffering from kidney disease.

Flaked Salt and Other Forms of Salt

Flaked salt might appear to be lower in sodium than crystal salt but it isn't. Given two containers of equal size, flaked salt yields less sodium than crystal salt, but only because flat flakes of salt take up more space than crystals in a volume measure. As a result, less flaked salt is required to fill a container. But, by weight, the sodium content of crystal and flake forms of salt is the same.

Kosher salt is a coarse-grained salt that is free of additives and impurities and is about one-half as salty as table salt. It is a good choice for seasoning stocks, broths, consommés, and clear soups because it doesn't cloud them. Some chefs prefer its texture and flavor in uncooked dishes and salads too.

Sea salt, like table salt, is basically sodium chloride with small amounts of magnesium and calcium. Surprisingly, sea salt is not a good source of iodine. Iodine becomes a gas and escapes from the salt during the drying process. Nonetheless, since many believe it is more healthful than table salt, it might be offered instead.

Iodized salt is table salt with added iodine (sodium iodide). It is particularly important in areas of the United States in which the soil is poor in iodine (most notably the Great Plains states and Oregon's Willamette valley). Iodine deficiency may result in the formation of a goiter, the visible enlargement of the thyroid gland. People with this condition suffer sluggishness and weight gain, and in pregnant women, severe iodine deficiency may cause extreme and irreversible mental and physical retardation in the infant or the condition called cretinism.

Salted Ingredients

Many salted ingredients like chips, pretzels, popcorn, nuts, and crackers are available in unsalted forms. Salt-free versions can also be prepared in house. For example, onion bagel chips can be created by slicing refrigerated or day-old onion bagels into ¼-inch slices and baking in a 350° F (175° C) oven until crisp and light brown, or about 10 minutes.

Crispy wonton skins are another option to heavily salted crackers or chips. Tasty, low-fat, salt-free versions can easily be made too. Rather than deep frying and salting, they can be baked brushed with a mixture of seasonings such as ground ginger and onion powder along with water and just a tad of sesame oil. Skewers with raw fruit chunks or bite-sized vegetables along with a chunky fruit or vegetable dip are also welcome snacks to sodium-conscious diners. For example, the brilliant color of a beet dip flavored with mustard, tarragon and thyme and a splash of raspberry vinegar looks as appealing as it tastes along with broccoli and cauliflower florets, yellow summer squash slices, red bell pepper strips, carrot sticks, and mushroom caps.

Similarly, when creating dishes traditionally topped with salted cracker or chip crumbs, they might be covered with crumbs from unsalted snacks like salt-free sesame crackers, melba toast, or unsalted matzoh or pretzels instead. For example, a spinach casserole layered with low-fat, low-sodium cheeses might be topped with salt-free, low-fat, whole wheat cracker crumbs.

It might seem that the crumbs from ready-to-eat breakfast cereals and breads would be low-sodium alternatives for toppings made from salted ingredients, but this is not necessarily so. While they may not have salt on their surfaces, the sodium content of breads and ready-to-eat breakfast cereals is often comparable to those from salted ingredients. See Table 4.7. Nonetheless, most diners will perceive a chicken breast coated in salted potato chips to be higher in sodium than one with a crust of ready-to-eat cereal crumbs like wheat or bran flakes.

Unsalted chip or cracker crumbs also make good extenders in lieu of heavily salted forms. Other low-sodium extenders include the flakes of cooked cereals like cream of wheat, grains like amaranth or bulgur, and legumes and vegetables boiled without salt like pureed dried kidney beans or fresh corn.

For example, a salt-free turkey roll prepared from ground poultry meat could be extended with mashed potatoes (boiled without salt), sauteed minced onions, diced carrots, and bell peppers. The mashed potatoes give the roll its light texture, while the

TABLE 4.7

Sodium Content of Salted and Unsalted Foods

Item	Amount	Sodium Content (milligrams)
Peanuts, lightly salted, Eagle Snacks	1 ounce	90
Peanuts, unroasted	1 ounce	5
French bread	1 slice	163
Cracked wheat bread, Wonder	1 slice	180
Corn chips	1 ounce	218
Potato chips, natural	1 ounce	168
Potato chips, no salt, Cape Cod	1 ounce	0
Pretzels	1 ounce	486
Pretzels, unsalted, Estee	1 ounce	0
Cheerios, General Mills	1 ounce	290
Oat Bran Cereal, Common Sense	1 ounce	270
Product 19, Kellogg's	1 ounce	320
Raisin Bran, Kellogg's	1.4 ounces	230
Rice Chex, Ralston Purina	1 ounce	252
Rice Krispies, Kellogg's	1 ounce	290
Special K, Kellogg's	1 ounce	230
Wheaties, General Mills	1 ounce	200
Saltines	2 crackers	80
Triscuits, Nabisco	3 crackers	75
Triscuits, low-salt, Nabisco	3 crackers	35

Source: Data from J.A.T. Pennington (1994). *Bowes & Church's Food Values of Portions Commonly Used.* Philadelphia: J. B. Lippincott Co.

seasoning gives vegetables lots of taste with little sodium. In some cases, small amounts of salty or high-sodium ingredients might be added to dishes for their unique flavor. To maximize their effect, the ingredients should be cut into small pieces and distributed over dishes, since diners eat with their eyes first, and will appreciate them most if they are easily visible. For example, rather than hiding salted, whole cashews in a salad of tender greens, their presence will be more pronounced if sprinkled on top of the lettuce leaves. Similarly, rather than sauteing dandelion greens with diced Canadian bacon, the two ingredients might be sauteed separately, and at service, the greens can be garnished with the bacon bits.

Replacing Processed Foods with Whole Unprocessed Ones

Sodium can be eliminated from recipes by preparing dishes from whole, unprocessed foods versus processed ones. Recall that approximately 75% of the sodium in the American diet is from processed foods. Whole unprocessed foods contain only small amounts of sodium naturally.

Yeast-Leavened Products

In most recipes, the amount of salt can be reduced without altering the appearance, taste, or texture of dishes. One case where it shouldn't be omitted is in yeast-leavened items. To produce yeast-leavened bread, salt can be limited to 1 teaspoon per loaf without affecting the product's texture or appearance.

Canned, Cured, Smoked, or Salty Meat, Seafood, and Poultry

Rather than offering casseroles, stews, soups, and sandwiches with canned, cured, smoked, or salty meat, seafood, or poultry, dishes featuring these items cooked fresh on premise will yield less sodium. For example, a chicken salad sandwich might be prepared with poached or roasted chicken breast meat rather than canned. To produce salt-free meat, fish, poultry, and other ingredients with a pleasant smoky flavor, products can be smoke-roasted (see Table 4.8) without curing beforehand.

Foods smoked by traditional methods are typically cured with a mixture usually of salt or sodium-rich soy sauce and a sweetener such as sugar, honey, molasses, or maple syrup. This draws the moisture out of foods and prevents them from spoiling during the long smoking process. At the same time, the end products are high in sodium.

Because of the temperature used in smoke-roasting, products are safe without coating in high-sodium cures. Rather, smoke-roasted foods can be given plenty of taste with low-sodium and low-fat marinades, sprinkled with herbs, spices, and other seasoning ingredients or simply smoke-roasted with no additional flavoring agents. Even without high sodium cures, smoke-roasted foods absorb a mild but enjoyable smoke flavor and best of all, retain moisture better than if cooked by most other methods. Since smoke-roasting requires no added salt or fat, health-conscious diners can enjoy pan-smoked meat, seafood, and poultry selections such as pork tenderloin, skinless chicken breasts, or swordfish steaks without guilt.

TABLE 4.8
Smoke-Roasting Basics

Equipment:
  two counter pans reserved for smoking, two disposable aluminum pans or one pan and aluminum foil
  a wire rack
  fine hardwood flakes or coarse sawdust

Method:
Sprinkle wood flakes or sawdust over the inside of the pan. Set a lightly oiled rack in the pan. Position the food, trimmed, peeled, or prepared as it would be to roast on the rack. Place the pan over direct high heat on a burner or flattop. Cover tightly with a second pan or aluminum foil when wisps of smoke begin to rise. Reduce the heat to medium and smoke a few minutes or until items have a browned exterior and pleasing smoky flavor. Finish cooking thicker items in a hot oven. Continued smoke-roasting may overwhelm their natural flavor.

For example, the sodium in smoked salmon and potato cakes can be cut and still turn out a tasty dish by smoking the salmon in house, boiling the potatoes in unsalted water, and seasoning the cakes with freshly ground black pepper, fresh dill, and a tad of ground red pepper.

Pan smoking is a healthy cooking technique that can add pizzazz to foods typically not associated with smoking. For example, cubes of tofu might be smoked and tossed with penne pasta and fresh chopped tomato sauce for a low-sodium vegetarian offering. Vegetables, particularly peppers and tomatoes, are delectable when smoked. Smoke-roasted vegetables, like orange-flavored, smoke-roasted patty pan squash, might serve as side dishes or in some cases double both as garnishes and flavoring agents in selections, for example, smoke-roasted yellow, red, or green bell peppers on a chilled, chunky gazpacho-style soup or an egg white frittata.

Sausages are good just about any time. The problem is most commercial brands are high in not only sodium but fat and calories too. For example, a 2-ounce serving of canned, smoked beef sausage has 642 milligrams of sodium, 265 calories, and derives about 75% of its calories from fat.

By making them on premise, sausages can be created with reduced amounts of sodium and fat. For example, peppered turkey sausage links, veal-chicken sausage patties, and beef country sticks are three possible healthy sausages that might be promoted as chef's specials. The light bite of pepper can mask the need for salt in the turkey links, while salt will scarcely be missed when herbs and vegetables are added to the veal-chicken sausage patties. Similarly, in the beef country sticks, diced bell peppers and a variety of spices can be blended with the extra lean, ground beef and veal to create more healthful sausages.

Kosher Meat and Poultry

Some diners believe that kosher meat and poultry are cleaner and safer to eat than other meat and poultry because of the manner in which they are processed. This is a misnomer. Kosher meat and poultry provide no special health benefits for diners monitoring their sodium consumption. Some of the salt added during processing can be removed by washing them thoroughly and soaking them for an hour before cooking. Further, salt can be eliminated by removing the skin from kosher poultry and by simmering kosher beef in a generous amount of water and discarding the broth after cooking.

Pickled Foods

Relishes, pickles, and olives are mainstays of sandwiches. Raw vegetables like shredded iceberg lettuce, red cabbage and zucchini, sliced cucumbers, diced onions, chopped tomatoes, bell pepper strips, and sprouts have the same crunchiness without the sodium of these toppings. Sprinkled with an assertive vinegar and a dash of high-quality oil or topped with a freshly prepared salsa, this sandwich can skip the butter and mayonnaise too.

Cheeses

It's hard to imagine an end to dishes with cheese. And there's no need for sodium-conscious diners to do so. But, rather than using large amounts of blander, high-sodium processed cheeses, smaller amounts of aged ones are preferred. The flavor of aged cheese is far more intense and often contains less than half the sodium. Grated, firm tofu (soybean curd) might also be substituted for up to one-half of the high-sodium or processed cheese used in dishes. In comparison, 1 ounce of processed Swiss cheese provides 388 milligrams of sodium, while a half cup of firm tofu yields only 7 milligrams of sodium.

Condiments and Salad Dressings

High-sodium sauces are typically considered forbidden by those watching their sodium intake. This might not be justified. For example, the 460 milligrams of sodium per teaspoon of soy sauce is substantial, but less than the 2,300 milligrams in a teaspoon of salt. Thus, if the salt in a dish can be replaced with an equal volume of a high-sodium sauce, its sodium content might drop significantly.

Garden-fresh vegetables, raw or cooked, can give life to dishes in lieu of either salt or high-sodium condiments like steak sauce or soy sauce. For example, braise-deglazed, minced garlic or onions, diced green or red bell peppers or sliced mushrooms are possibilities. Hot pepper flakes, thinly sliced, raw green onions or grated gingerroot or horseradish also work nicely in some dishes.

When green leafy lettuce and vegetable salads are on the menu, sodium counts might be cut by preparing dressings in house. Rather than commercial versions, healthy ones might be prepared from fresh stocks, freshly extracted vegetable and fruit juices or their purees and dried powders, flavorful oils, ground unsalted nuts or vinegars and seasoned with diced seasoning vegetables, freshly ground spices and freshly minced herbs.

Salads from naturally sweet fruits, canned in their own juices, fresh or frozen, or from fruits glazed in unsweetened fruit juices, are low in sodium and refined sugar too. These vitamin- and mineral-rich medleys certainly deserve the attention given vegetable salads covered with high-sodium (and often fat) commercial dressings. Gelatin salad molds, made from unsweetened gelatin powder along with fruits, their juices, purees, and sweet juice concentrates or other sweetening agents, are low in sodium and can be prepared without refined sugar too. Gelatins produced from commercial mixes are generally higher in sodium, sources of artificial flavoring and coloring agents, and dominated by refined sugar.

Meat Tenderizers

If prepared properly, tougher cuts of meat can be just as tender as their more expensive tender counterparts and healthy choices for sodium-conscious diners too. Rather than using high-sodium tenderizers, tougher cuts of meat might be tenderized by marinating in low-sodium mixtures of freshly extracted vegetable juices, freshly squeezed fruit juices, assertive vinegars, dry to sweet wines, hearty to smooth beers, flavorful seed, nut, olive, or vegetable oils, freshly minced vegetables or herbs, and freshly ground spices; by mechanical means such as pounding, grinding, dicing, cubing, or slicing across the grain; and cooking using slow, moist methods such as braising, pot roasting, and stewing. Another benefit of tenderizing with low-sodium marinades is that there is no need for coating with sodium-laden sauces or gravies. They've already been infused with flavor.

Stocks, Soups, Sauces and Gravies

Stocks prepared from meat, fish or poultry bones, and/or vegetables simmered along with herbs and spices not only taste better than those from commercial bases, canned broths or bouillon cubes or granules, they are lower in sodium. Similarly, soups produced in house from fresh ingredients are generally more pleasing to the palate and lower in sodium than those purchased canned. For example, turkey chili prepared from ground turkey, dried kidney beans, fresh, chopped, peeled tomatoes, diced onions, chili powder and other seasonings, skip the salt of course, will be lower in sodium than a canned version or one prepared with canned tomatoes and kidney beans. Along with a basket of warm, whole wheat, lard-free tortillas, freshly prepared turkey chili might be featured as a Tex-Mex, hearty, low-sodium lunch or dinner offering.

Split pea soup prepared from dried peas simmered in fresh vegetable stock spotted with diced onions, carrots, and celery, seasoned with thyme, parsley, and freshly ground pepper, omit the ham and served with brown rice is another complete and filling, nutritious lunch or dinner selection. In addition to being low in sodium, it contains no foods of animal origin or cholesterol and is low in fat. These attributes make it appealing to a variety of health-conscious diners.

Sauces and gravies can awaken blander ingredients like meat, seafood, and poultry. In terms of sodium, ones made on premise are preferred over those that are canned or made from dry mixes. For example, rather than purchasing a commercial salsa, likely loaded with sodium, it might be made from fresh ingredients. It might be a black bean, traditional tomato, or tomatillo salsa. Not only are freshly prepared salsas good because they are reduced in sodium but can be prepared with less fat and calories too.

In some cases, high-sodium sauces and gravies can be replaced with toppings of sauteed, diced or sliced, flavor-packed vegetables. For example, rather than serving polenta, an Italian version of cornmeal mush with a traditional high-sodium and fat gravy, it might be topped with a wild mushroom ragout.

Canned Vegetable Products and Juices

Canned vegetables will not be selected by most diners when fresh or frozen ones are available. If cooked properly, fresh and frozen vegetables generally look and taste better than canned forms. For example, fresh corn is virtually sodium-free and so is the plain, frozen variety. But canned corn contains from 500 milligrams to more than 700 milligrams of sodium per cup. When the option is a canned vegetable or one frozen with a sauce or other additions, neither is a good choice. Both are laden with sodium.

In the case of pizza, rather than topping with a tomato sauce prepared from canned tomatoes, sodium can be reduced by embellishing with sliced, fresh tomatoes and seasoning with freshly minced Italian herbs.

Vegetable juices that are prepared by freshly extracting juices from vegetables, fruit juices, bottled waters, or ice tea are also low-sodium alternatives to canned vegetable juices. If appropriate, a glass of wine, beer, or a cocktail are low-sodium beverages. In the case of margaritas, they might be presented in herb-rimmed glasses in lieu of salted ones.

TABLE 4.9

Sodium-Free Baking Powder*

Ingredient	Weight
Potassium bicarbonate	79.5 grams (2¾ ounces)
Cornstarch	56 grams (2 ounces)
Tartaric acid	15 grams (½ ounce)
Potassium bitartrate	112 grams (4 ounces)

Source: C. M. Babigan (1982). "Low-sodium baking powder." In Good Housekeeping Special Diet Cookbook, p. 311. New York: Hearst Books.
*1½ teaspoon of sodium-free baking powder equals 1 teaspoon baking powder in recipes.

Processed Foods

Prepared dishes and packaged mixes are available for items ranging from stuffing, potatoes, and pasta to cakes, cookies, and puddings. They might be more convenient than cooking selections from fresh ingredients, but sodium comes with convenience. For example, when chocolate pudding is prepared from scratch versus a mix, the sodium content can drop by more than 700 milligrams per cup. But more important, when dishes are made in house from fresh ingredients, the quality tends to improve too. For example, low-sodium stuffing reminiscent of "grandma's" might be prepared by moistening cubes of dry bread with freshly prepared stock and seasoning with freshly minced herbs, freshly ground spices, diced vegetables, and dried fruit. There will be no need for salt.

In the case of commercial, high-sodium frozen entrees, lower-sodium main course dishes might be prepared on premise and frozen for use as needed. They'll be equally as convenient and likely taste better.

Baking Soda and Powder

Baking soda (sodium bicarbonate) and powder are two sodium-containing compounds found in certain baked goods whether purchased ready-to-eat, prepared from mixes, or made from scratch. Most cakes and quick breads like muffins, coffee cakes, and pancakes are high in sodium. For example, health-conscious diners may love buckwheat cornbread, but be wary of its high-sodium content.

The 1,000 milligrams of sodium per teaspoon of baking soda and 322 per teaspoon of baking powder is a sizable amount. The salt in products leavened with these agents first might be cut in their formulas by one-half or more. Further, low-sodium baking powder substitutes might be considered. They are available at health food stores or through distributors.

Sodium-free baking powder produced in house (see Table 4.9) is another option.

In the case of the cornbread, its sodium might be cut by preparing with sodium-free baking powder and flavoring with minced vegetables like onions, garlic, and bell peppers, and herbs, and spices like fresh chives and parsley, and ground red pepper in lieu of salt. Another advantage to this savory cornbread is it requires no margarine or butter. It is bursting with flavor already.

Eggs are well known for their leavening power. They do contain some sodium but only 63 milligrams per large egg with 56 milligrams of the sodium coming from the white. With regard to leavening action, egg whites perform the same function as whole eggs. Given one egg has the leavening power of about ½ teaspoon of baking powder, for each ½ teaspoon of baking powder replaced with an egg, the sodium content of a recipe will drop by about 100 milligrams. When quick breads like wild rice buckwheat waffles, sweet potato ginger pancakes, or crunchy four-grain muffins are made without salt and leavened with egg whites, sodium-conscious diners can indulge in these breakfast treats without concern.

Ingredient Labels

Ingredient labels are sources of salt and sodium information. The FDA implemented new guidelines in 1994 to make sodium claims on labels less confusing (see Table 4.10). In addition, unless specifically exempted, the new labels must list the milligrams of sodium per serving of food and what percentage this is of the less than 2,400 milligrams recommended daily for an individual consuming a 2,000-calorie diet.

Salt-Free and Reduced-Sodium Ingredients

There are also a variety of salt-free and reduced-sodium ingredients available commercially. They include everything from one-third less salt soups and no salt added tomato products to very low sodium worcestershire and reduced-sodium soy sauce. They should be substituted for higher sodium ingredients only if they have been tested and provide the outcomes desired.

Water

Hard water might cause problems in some areas of the restaurant but in terms of cooking, it will add less sodium than soft water.

Acceptable Levels of Sodium

As a general rule, when creating or modifying recipes for sodium-conscious diners, the sodium should be limited to less than 500 milligrams for entrees and 200 milligrams for side dishes. By meal period, a reasonable amount for breakfast is no more than 400 milligrams of sodium and for lunch and dinner, each 1,300 milligrams of sodium or less.

TABLE 4.10
Salt and Sodium Claims

Salt free—less than 5 milligrams per standardized serving

No salt added and unsalted—if (1) no salt is added during processing; (2) salt is normally added during processing; and (3) the statement "not a sodium-free food" is stated on the information panel.

Sodium free—less than 5 milligrams per standardized serving

Very low sodium—contains 35 milligrams or less per standardized serving

Low sodium—140 milligrams or less per standardized serving

Reduced or less sodium—contains 25% less sodium than the regular food. The claim cannot be made if the "regular" food already meets the requirement for a "low" claim.

Light or lite—140 milligrams or less per standardized serving or 50% less sodium per standardized serving as compared to the regular food if the food also meets the definition for "low" in calories and fat. In the event the sodium is reduced 50% in a food but is not low in fat and calories, the label must state "light in sodium."

Source: Collier, Shannon, Rill, and Scott. (1993). *1993 Nutrition labeling regulations.* Washington, DC: Collier, Shannon, Rill & Scott.

Summary—Reducing Salt and Sodium in Recipes

Many techniques have been discussed to reduce the salt and sodium in selections. In brief, the following are key strategies that can be employed to meet diners' requests for tasty menu fare with less salt or sodium.

1. Omit the salt in recipes if possible; reduce the salt in dishes gradually and over time as demand warrants.

2. In the kitchen, cook ingredients like pasta, grains, and vegetables in unsalted water.

3. If a dish is unacceptable without salt, sprinkle a small amount or about ⅛ teaspoon per serving over immediately before serving.

4. Add salt-free flavor to dishes with fruit juices, freshly prepared stocks, oils, wines, beers, spirits, flavor extracts, herbs and spices, or a combination of these ingredients in marinades and sauces.

5. Experiment with the effects of herbs and spices to learn which ones will replace salt best in recipes, but for a start, try chives, tarragon, parsley, or basil with vegetable selections and thyme, oregano, sage, or rosemary with meat dishes.

6. When substituting herbs and spices for salt in dishes, be careful not to overpower them. As a general rule, limit the total quantity of dried herbs and spices to 1 to 3 teaspoons per 24 portions.

7. Reduce the need for salt by heightening the natural flavors in dishes with sour ingredients like lemon juice, vinegar, angostura bitters, or citrus zests.

8. Offer diners salt-free spice blends and/or lemon wedges for flavoring selections in lieu of salt.

9. Offer salt substitutes, half salt, or light salt only on guests' special request. Do not use in food preparation.

10. Offer sea salt for guests who perceive it to be more healthy than table salt.

11. Replace salted foods like potato chips, crackers, pretzels, and nuts with unsalted forms when offering as snacks or using as coatings, toppings, and extenders for meat, fish, poultry and vegetable dishes. Keep in mind, items can be high in sodium without tasting salty.

12. When adding small amounts of salted or high-sodium ingredients like salted peanuts or bacon to dishes, make their flavor pronounced by cutting into small pieces and sprinkling over the tops of dishes.

13. In the case of yeast-leavened products where salt retards fermentation, include salt, but limit it to 1 teaspoon per loaf.

14. Prepare dishes from whole, unprocessed ingredients rather than processed ones with sodium-containing additives such as MSG. If the symbol Na or the words salt, sodium, or soda appear at the top of a product's ingredient list or are listed several times, it likely contains appreciable amounts of sodium.

15. Replace canned, cured, smoked, or salty meat, seafood, or poultry products with fresh, cooked, or uncured ones, smoked on premise and reduce the sodium in kosher meat and poultry by rinsing, soaking and simmering in water and discarding the liquid.

16. Avoid foods packed in brine; replace them with fresh forms of items.

17. Replace high-sodium, processed cheeses with smaller amounts of aged ones or in the case of grated, high-sodium cheeses, replace partially with grated firm tofu.

18. Replace high-sodium condiments and sauces like soy sauce, catsup, and mayonnaise with freshly prepared salsas or dressings prepared with low-sodium ingredients and/or tasty vegetables like minced garlic, onions or bell peppers, sliced mushrooms or scallions, grated gingerroot or horseradish, or hot pepper flakes.

19. If a choice needs to be made between equivalent amounts of salt and a high-sodium condiment or sauce like soy sauce, generally, select the high-sodium sauce.

20. Tenderize meat with low-sodium marinades; slow, moist methods of cookery; or break down connective tissues with mechanical methods.

21. Prepare stocks, soups, sauces, and gravies from meat, fish, poultry and their bones, fresh vegetables, grains, pastas, herbs and spices rather than dried or canned products.

22. Replace canned vegetables and their products with fresh or frozen ones. In the case of vegetable juices, substitute with a fruit juice, bottled water or tea, or cocktail, wine or beer if appropriate.

23. In lieu of packaged mixes or frozen entrees, prepare products in advance with whole, unprocessed ingredients and store for use as needed.

24. Reduce the salt in cakes and quick breads by at least one-half and replace their baking powder with eggs, a commercial low-sodium baking powder, or one prepared in house. Avoid self-rising flour; it contains salt and baking powder and therefore is high in sodium.

25. Examine food labels for nutrition claims such as "salt free" and "low sodium" and milligrams of sodium per serving.

26. Substitute salt-free and reduced-sodium forms of ingredients for higher sodium ones only if they provide the qualities desired.

27. Cook foods in hard rather than soft water.

28. As a general rule, when creating or modifying recipes for sodium-conscious diners, limit sodium to less than 500 milligrams for entrees, 200 milligrams for side dishes, and keep breakfast at 400 milligrams or less and lunch and dinner each at no more than 1,300 milligrams of sodium.

Salt/Sodium Activities

1. Identify the items on the list which appear to be low in sodium. Explain why. Describe how the sodium content of other items on the list could be reduced. See Appendix 7 for a sample of correct answers.

   A. Turkey Hot Dogs with Ketchup and Mustard on Wheat Buns

   B. Buckwheat Waffles (frozen) Topped with a Dollop of Honey Orange Yogurt

   C. Fresh Fettucine Coated with a Creamy Cheese Sauce (cream and melted butter and Gruyere and Parmesan cheeses)

   D. Freshly Roasted Potato Chips Sprinkled with Parmesan Cheese and Garlic Salt Accompanied by Low-Fat Sour Cream Dip

   E. Ham (low-fat) Sandwich with Low-Fat Cheddar Cheese and Low-Fat Mayonnaise Garnished with a Crisp Dill Pickle

   F. Bran Muffin Filled with Raisins Served with Margarine

G. Steamed Green Beans Sprinkled with Toasted Sesame Seeds, a Tad of Sesame Oil and Soy Sauce

H. Frozen Low-Fat Vanilla Yogurt (commercial) Topped with Strawberry Sauce (commercial)

I. Freshly Prepared Chicken Noodle Soup with Fresh Cooked Diced Vegetables (stock base used)

J. Tossed Green Salad Topped with Sliced Mushrooms and Cucumbers, Tomato and Boiled Egg Wedges, Garbanzo Beans (canned), Diced Turkey Salami, and Topped with Low-Fat Ranch House Dressing (commercial)

DIRECTIONS

Complete the following three activities with a specific operation in mind, ideally one you are currently involved with. See instructor to check your responses.

2. List items on your menu high in salt or sodium. Describe how they might be modified to reduce their high salt or sodium content or substitutions which might be offered to replace them.

3. Identify good choices on your menu for sodium-conscious diners.

4. List and describe good choices for sodium-conscious diners that could be added to your menu. Consider factors such as the operation's theme, price range, clientele, method of service, and equipment and labor required to prepare them.

Fresh Corn Soup in Light Creamy Broth Accented with Cumin

Offer a bowl of this soup along with a basket of hearty breads or a cup with a salad or half sandwich as a daily special. This healthy version is prepared by simmering fresh corn kernels, tomatoes, and onions in a rich chicken stock, seasoning with cumin, and finishing with evaporated skim milk and low-fat Monterey Jack cheese.

Servings: 24
Serving Size: 1 cup
Yield: 1 ½ gallons

Vegetable cooking spray, butter-flavored
Corn kernels, fresh* (divided)   4 pounds
Tomatoes, peeled, coarsely chopped   2 pounds
Onions, minced   12 ounces
Rich White Chicken Stock (see page 78) (divided)   3 ½ quarts
Cumin, freshly ground   1 teaspoon
Milk, evaporated, skim   1 pint
Monterey Jack cheese, shredded, low-fat, low-cholesterol, and
    low-sodium   4 ounces
Salt   To taste
Pepper, freshly ground   To taste

1. Coat a nonstick sauce pot with cooking spray. Place over medium-high heat until hot. Add 1 pound of the corn, the tomatoes, onions, and 1 cup of the stock or as needed; cook until tender.
2. In a blender or food processor, puree the vegetable mixture until smooth. Add more stock if needed to puree.
3. Return the pureed vegetables with the remaining corn, stock, and cumin to the sauce pot. Heat to a boil, reduce the heat to low; simmer until the corn is tender, or about 15 minutes.
4. Stir in the evaporated milk. To adjust the consistency, add water or stock to thin and reduce to thicken. Add the cheese; cook over low heat until melted; do not boil. Season with salt and pepper to taste. Serve in heated cups or bowls along with whole wheat tortillas prepared without lard.

*Use frozen corn to prepare this soup when fresh is not available. Delete the term "fresh" from its name.

Servings	Calories	Protein (g/%)	Fat (g/%)	Cholesterol (mg)	Carbo-hydrates (g/%)	Fiber (g)	Sodium (mg)
1	126	8.5 g/25%	2.3 g/15%	1.8	20.4 g/60%	3.2	82.8

Tomato Bell Pepper Salsa

The uses for this fat-free, cholesterol-free, fresh salsa are numerous. These are a few.

1. Offer with grilled vegetables, perhaps grilled zucchini, summer squash, or eggplant.
2. Use to dress cold pasta or vegetable salads such as ones prepared with short corkscrew pastas like rotelle.
3. Serve as an accompaniment to raw vegetables or chips such as roasted or baked corn or whole wheat tortillas.
4. Use to enhance tacos and burritos filled with lean meat, seafood, poultry, or simmered dried beans, low-fat cheeses, and shredded or chopped vegetables.

Servings: 24
Serving Size: ¼ cup
Yield: 1 ½ quarts

Tomatoes, ripe, very small dice   2 pounds
Onions, minced   6 ounces
Pepper, bell, green and yellow, very small dice   3 ounces each
Lemon juice, freshly squeezed   ¼ cup
Cilantro, minced   ¼ cup
Garlic, minced   1 tablespoon
Red pepper sauce   1 teaspoon or to taste
Salt   To taste
Pepper, freshly ground   To taste

1. Combine all the ingredients in a bowl; mix well. Refrigerate to mellow the flavors at least 4 hours.
2. Serve at room temperature or chilled as a dip or topping with items such as bean and cheese-filled whole wheat tortillas or roasted corn tortilla chips.

Servings	Calories	Protein (g/%)	Fat (g/%)	Cholesterol (mg)	Carbohydrates (g/%)	Fiber (g)	Sodium (mg)
1	14	0.5 g/13%	0.16 g/9%	0	3.2 g/79%	0.75	3.94

5

The Power of Protein

Protein Consumption

It was traditionally believed that to grow up big and strong, foods rich in high-quality protein—meat, seafood, poultry, eggs, and dairy products—had to be eaten. The more you consumed, the healthier you'd be.

It's now known that this is not necessarily true. There are drawbacks to eating too much protein. First, many good sources of protein, like red meat, eggs, and dairy products, are high in total fat, saturated fat, and cholesterol. The ramifications of eating too much of these are not good. They range from heart disease and obesity to gout and diabetes. In addition, eating too much protein imposes an extra burden on the kidneys to remove the waste products resulting from protein breakdown. Further, when more protein is eaten than the body needs, the extra is used for energy, a very expensive source of calories. Health authorities advise that the total daily protein intake not exceed twice the recommended amount (see Protein Requirement).

It is more likely that individuals who eat animal products (meat, seafood, poultry, eggs, and dairy products) will consume too much protein than those who eat a plant-based diet, because animal products contain abundant amounts of high-quality protein.

Functions of Proteins

While overconsumption of protein serves no purpose and may be hazardous to health, eating an adequate amount is necessary for good health. It performs many valuable functions in the body. Every cell contains protein and it works not only to build muscle, blood, and other tissues, but performs other functions as well. It is used to produce enzymes, hormones, and antibodies; maintain balance of fluids, electrolytes, and proper acid base balance. It is also required for tissue growth, repair, and maintenance, and provides energy.

Protein Requirement

Ideally, the amount of protein in the diet should be only 12–15% of the calories consumed. At the same time, recall 30% or less of the calories are recommended from fat and 55–60% from carbohydrates.

Many Americans far exceed the RDAs for protein. For example, consider the ever popular steak and baked potato. Make it an 8-ounce steak and alone it contributes 60 grams of protein to the diet, or more than the amount recommended for most men and women daily.

Animal Protein Sources

To achieve these recommendations, smaller portions of low fat, high quality protein foods like lean meats, poultry, and seafood, and low-fat dairy products and dishes prepared from egg whites rather than whole eggs should be offered (see Table 5.1). Visible fat should be removed from high-protein items and they should be cooked without additional fat. For many Americans conditioned to eating hearty portions of meat, seafood, and poultry, smaller portions will go unnoticed when presented cut into smaller pieces or thinner slices fanned out across the plate and accompanied by larger portions of grains and their products, vegetables, or fruits. Combination dishes like stews, stir-fries, main course salads, and pastas make this an easy task.

Unless the diet is composed primarily of fruits and certain vegetables, it is unlikely that a protein deficiency will occur. Fruits provide energy but most are low in protein. Even followers of a fruitarian diet include protein-rich nuts and seeds in their diets regularly.

Plant Protein Sources

Another option to achieve current dietary recommendations is to substitute low-fat and cholesterol-free plant foods which contain larger or moderate amounts of incomplete or low-quality protein for animal protein foods. These include legumes (dried beans, peas and lentils); grains and their products including rice, pasta, and bread; and vegetables (see Table 5.1). Nuts and seeds are good sources of low-quality protein and are cholesterol-free, but do contain high levels of fat.

Vegetarian Diets

While many Americans are reducing their consumption of meat and eating more grains and vegetables, some are abandoning meat totally and adopting a vegetarian diet. Vegetarians do not eat foods that require the death or injury of animals. Instead of eating meat selections, vegetarians opt for dishes emphasizing legumes, vegetables, and grains and their products.

Reasons for Following a Vegetarian Lifestyle

People follow vegetarian diets for various reasons. Some do it for health reasons: they hope to reduce their intake of the fat and cholesterol found in meat. Others avoid eating meat for ecological reasons: raising livestock and poultry requires more land, energy, water, and plant food than growing plants. Some, like Buddhists or Seventh Day Adventists, are vegetarians for philosophical or religious reasons, while others switch because of taste. Some choose to eat foods low on the food chain to avoid many of the accumulated contaminants in foods high on the chain, such as meat. Contaminants may include antibiotics, hormones, and other chemicals which are added to animal feed or drugs given directly to the animal. And many people become vegetarians out of economic necessity.

Types of Vegetarians

There are several types of vegetarians. Vegans, or total vegetarians, eat no foods of animal origin. For example, garlicky black beans and squash on a bed of brown rice is an item that might appeal to vegetarians who eat only plant foods, assuming that the garlic and other vegetables in the dish are sauteed in oil, not

TABLE 5.1

Protein Content of Some Common Foods

Item	Amount	Protein (g)
Apple, raw, with skin	1 medium	0.3
Barley, pearled, cooked	¼ cup	3.6
Beef, ground, extra lean, broiled	3½ ounces	25.4
Bread, whole wheat	1 slice	2.4
Broccoli, boiled	½ cup	2.3
Cheese, cheddar	1 ounce	7.1
Chicken, without skin, roasted	½ breast	26.7
Egg, whole	1 large	6.3
Egg, white	of 1 large	3.5
Halibut, cooked by dry heat	3 ounces	22.7
Macaroni, cooked	1 cup	6.7
Milk, nonfat	1 cup	8.4
Peanuts, dry roasted	1 ounce	6.6
Pinto beans, boiled	1 cup	14.0
Potato, baked with skin	1	4.7
Rice, white, cooked	1 cup	5.5
Sesame seeds, dried	¼ cup	1.6
Tuna, canned in water	3 ounces	21.7

Source: Data from J.A.T. Pennington (1994). *Bowes & Church's Food Values of Portions Commonly Used.* Philadelphia: J. B. Lippincott Co.

butter, and the black beans are simmered in vegetable stock, not the more common chicken or beef stock. For dishes offered on a bed of pasta instead of rice, vegans require eggless noodles.

LACTO VEGETARIANS

Lacto vegetarians eat no foods of animal origin except dairy products. For a main course selection, cheesy fettuccine topped with diced tomatoes on a choice of chile, curry, black or red pepper pasta might be suggested. Note, since lacto vegetarians eat no eggs, eggless pasta must be prepared for them too.

LACTO-OVO VEGETARIANS

Lacto-ovo vegetarians eat no foods of animal origin except dairy products and eggs. For a charming lacto-ovo selection, a vegetable hash baked in the skillet, filled with onions, carrots, potatoes, red bell peppers, shiitake mushrooms, and celery root, all bound by a puree of vegetables, egg whites, and nonfat yogurt and sprinkled with low-fat Swiss cheese might be offered. Since the vegetable hash contains both eggs and dairy products, it does not meet the dietary requirements of vegans, nor those of lacto vegetarians who eat dairy products but not eggs.

TYPES OF SEMI-VEGETARIANS

There are also semi vegetarians or those who eat fish—pesco vegetarians. Oven-steamed flounder—flounder briefly marinated in a low-sodium soy sauce, scallion, and ginger mixture and baked under foil—might be promoted to pesco vegetarian diners and other health-conscious diners. Black sea bass, sea snapper, walleye, and sole also make delicious pesco vegetarian selections prepared this way.

Others who sometimes call themselves vegetarians but consume poultry are pollo vegetarians. A skinless turkey breast stuffed with a shredded carrot and mushroom mixture might be offered as a main course to accommodate this group of diners. Or tortellini and chicken soup, a substantial combination of plump tortellini, hat-shaped dumplings filled with tender chunks of chicken, and chopped spinach floating in a clear chicken broth might be just what the pollo vegetarian yearns for. Even if the tortellini was filled with vegetables instead of chicken, the soup would not appeal to vegans, lacto-ovo, or lacto vegetarians unless it was prepared with a vegetable stock, and in the case of vegans and lacto vegetarians the tortellini made without eggs.

Finally, some diners abstain from meat but eat all other animal products. These diners can generally be accommodated by selections from the poultry or seafood section of the menu.

Many vegetarians restrict their intake of certain beverages, such as caffeinated and alcoholic ones, and specified foods, for example, highly processed ones containing pesticides and/or those that have not been grown organically.

Organic Foods

In general, the term organic means grown without pesticides or commercial fertilizers, free of synthetic additives, hormones, dyes, waxes, preservatives, and antibiotics. Organic food products include produce, meats, raw milk, and processed foods such as wines, flour, honey, potato chips, and baby food. While organically grown foods are no more nutritious than those not grown organically, diners of all types often believe they are. There are no federal regulations governing the use of the term organic; regulations are up to each state. Some have laws defining the term. For example, Texas certifies produce as organic only after it has been grown on a farm using organic methods for three years. Other states, such as California, mandate only one year.

Natural Foods

Foods labeled "natural" are generally preferred by vegetarians too. Currently, the definition of this term is vague. Two agencies, the USDA and FDA, oversee the labeling of food. The USDA monitors meat, poultry, and products containing significant portions of meat and poultry such as prepared entrees and many canned items. Under their policy, the term "natural" means a product generally must not contain artificial flavors, colors, preservatives, or synthetic ingredients. As a result, these items undergo minimal processing.

However, for all the remaining products regulated by the FDA, the meaning of the term "natural" is defined by the manufacturer. The term generally indicates that a product is free of intentional additives, but there are large discrepancies from product to product. For example, the term "natural" on grape juice might mean that it is pressed from grapes and on bran muffins that they are sweetened with honey. Aside from these inconsistencies, the term "natural" implies that foods are healthy. Yet, "natural peanut butter" might contain as much fat as the competition's peanut butter, "natural grape juice" may be as much a source of sugar as other brands, and "natural bran muffins" may be no richer in fiber, vitamins, and minerals or lower in calories and fat than other bran muffins.

The FDA does plan to establish a definition for "natural" but until this occurs, the contents of products bearing this label can be very misleading.

Label Ingredient Information

Ingredient information on products' labels can be a valuable source of information when creating recipes and planning menus to accommodate vegetarians, in particular vegans. Two labeling requirements were implemented quite recently (Federal Register, January 6, 1993) which will help identify products not suitable for use in vegetarian offerings.

First, any product which has a label that includes the statement "nondairy" and contains an ingredient derived from cow's milk (such as casein) will be required to declare in its ingredient list that casein is milk-derived.

Second, protein hydrolysates, which include proteins from plant and animal sources and yeast extracts, are used in foods to perform many functions, including acting as stabilizers, thickening agents, flavorings, and flavor enhancers. Previously, protein hydrolysates, including those derived from animal sources, were often listed on labels as "flavorings" or "natural flavors" so that it was not possible to identify the source of these ingredients. Now, protein hydrolysates must be listed and include the source, for example, beef, casein, soy and wheat gluten.

Planning a Plant-Based Diet

Although the protein in plant foods is lower in quality, a plant based diet can provide adequate protein when it is varied and balanced. Until recently, it was believed that animal foods containing rich sources of high-quality protein and/or plant foods containing high or moderate amounts of lower quality protein needed to be eaten together at the same meal to complement one another or to form the high-quality proteins needed for the body to function.

It is now known that for animal and/or vegetable proteins to complement each other, they do not need to be eaten at the same meal, but rather over the course of a day. In other words, a varied mixture of protein sources is needed on a daily basis but protein sources do not need to be complemented at every meal. Nonetheless, many vegetarians and diners eating less red meat will appreciate choices on the menu containing foods forming complementary protein relationships.

Complementary Protein Combinations

DAIRY FOODS WITH GRAINS

Complementary protein relationships can be formed by eating some animal protein (dairy like 2% milk, skim buttermilk, nonfat yogurt, or low-fat cheese and whole eggs or whites only) with vegetable protein (grains and products made from them like pasta, whole wheat bread, low-fat granola, oatmeal, and brown rice pilaf).

Sandwiches, pasta dishes, salads, and pizzas that can be designed to be healthy as well as combine complementary animal and vegetable proteins might include a grilled, low-fat, cheddar cheese sandwich on whole wheat bread; macaroni salad coated in a light vinaigrette dressing decorated with vegetables and low-fat Swiss cheese cubes; pasta primavera sprinkled with part-skim parmesan cheese; or whole wheat pizza crust topped with low-fat mozzarella cheese and vegetables.

An all-time vegetarian favorite, vegetable lasagne, is another example of animal and vegetable ingredients being combined to form a complementary protein relationship. When spinach and whole wheat noodles are layered with low-fat cheeses, baby whole zucchini, plum tomatoes, and thinly sliced summer squash, it can be promoted as a healthy main course vegetarian selection.

At breakfast, selections might be created with complementary protein relationships too. The incomplete vegetable protein in a toasted cornmeal-apple muffin wedge might be complemented by the animal protein in a maple, walnut, yogurt swirl; a whole wheat English muffin by an egg white omelet filled with exotic mushrooms, or simply a bowl of cold whole grain cereal like puffed brown rice with fruit and low-fat milk.

LEGUMES WITH GRAINS

Proteins can also be complemented by combining two vegetable proteins. It may be legumes (dried beans, peas, lentils, tofu) with grains (barley, buckwheat, rye, wheat) and their products. For example, garbanzo bean guacamole served with oven roasted, crisp pita chips or split pea soup with spinach and low-fat, whole wheat crackers are tasty, low-fat appetizers that combine ingredients with complementary vegetable proteins, while spicy lentil pie with a cornbread crust or red bean chili and corn pasta casserole are main course selections that might be promoted for their complementary grain and legume proteins.

Since peanuts are actually legumes, a grilled, homestyle chunky peanut butter and banana sandwich might be offered on whole grain bread as a nourishing and tasty sandwich special of the day. Diners of all ages will find this favorite hard to resist.

LEGUMES WITH NUTS OR SEEDS

Other complementary vegetable protein relationships exist between legumes (black-eyed peas, chickpeas, soybeans, split peas) and nuts or seeds (nuts—except cashews—like almonds and walnuts, and seeds—except pumpkin—like sesame (sesame seed paste—tahini), squash, and sunflower. Menu selections might include choices on the appetizer list like whole wheat sesame crackers with bell pepper spotted red bean dip or lentil salad in a light tahini and soy vinaigrette. For main course lunch or dinner items, the menu might feature grilled tofu and summer squash in spicy, sunflower seed sauce, lentil walnut patties on toasted whole wheat buns coated with honey mustard and topped with roasted bell pepper strips, or brown rice stir-fried with garbanzo beans, toasted almonds, and garden vegetables. Keep in mind when seasoning vegetarian dishes like these and others that some condiments contain meat, seafood, and poultry products. Worcestershire sauce, for example, is made with anchovies.

High-Protein Plant Foods

A variety of legumes, nuts, seeds, grains, and vegetables can be offered in selections at every meal to accommodate both diners eating less red meat and those eating only plant foods.

LEGUMES

While legumes have been food staples in many parts of the world for centuries, this has traditionally not been the case in the United States. Dishes containing dried beans, peas, or lentils were rarely consumed. The list of possibilities was short, maybe baked beans, split pea or navy bean soups, often with pork added, chili comprised primarily of high-fat ground beef, or possibly three-bean salad.

Types of legumes. There are many types of legumes to choose from (see Table 5.2); most are dried but some are available fresh, canned, and/or frozen. They can be incorporated into a variety of dishes.

Dried beans should be purchased which have been harvested within the last 12 months and used within 6 months. As beans

TABLE 5.2

Types of Legumes

Legume	Characteristics
Adzuki Beans *(Aduki Beans, Azuki Beans)*	small, sweet-flavored, brownish-red beans with slender white stripes, particularly popular in Japanese cuisine.
Anasazi Beans	maroon and white speckled beans about the size of pinto beans; pintos make good replacements for anasazis when not available.
Black Beans *(Black Turtle Beans)*	sturdy, black-skinned beans with cream-colored flesh and mildly sweet taste; delicious along with the spicy flavors of the cuisines of Mexico, Central and South America, and the Caribbean where they have long been popular.
Black-Eyed Peas *(Black-Eyed Beans, Cowpeas, Yellow-Eyed Peas)*	small, beige beans with black circular eyes, particularly popular in the South where they are a must in the traditional Hoppin' John; available fresh or dried; in the case of yellow-eyed peas, their eyes are yellow.
Cannellini Beans	large, white, Italian, oval-shaped beans with a creamy texture; they can be made into purees and spreads but are good in salads and soups too; available dried and canned.
Cranberry Beans *(Shell Beans, Shellouts)*	large, knobby, beige pods with pinkish red blotches and a delicious nutty flavor; unfortunately, they lose their bright color in cooking; available both fresh and dried.
Dried Peas	green or yellow peas dried from Field Peas (unlike common green peas); available whole and split; they are wonderful in soups and purees.
Fava Beans *(Faba Beans, Broad Beans, Horse Beans)*	similar in appearance to large lima beans with rust-tan skins and a narrow black stripe at one end; available fresh, dried, and canned; their earthy flavor and starchy texture is a good match for the Mediterranean and Middle Eastern dishes they are often associated with.
Flageolets	tiny, slender, pale green to creamy white-colored French beans most readily available dried and canned; their delicate flavor is conducive to simple preparation methods.
Garbanzo Beans *(Chick Peas, Ceci)*	mild, nutlike-flavored, round, creamy beige-colored beans with a firm texture; popular in Middle Eastern, Mediterranean, and Indian cuisines.
Kidney Beans	deep red skinned and cream-colored flesh beans with robust flavor which hold their shape well in cooking; most readily available canned and dried.
Lentils	a tiny lens-shaped legume available in many varieties; Brown Lentils are the most common with a mild peppery taste; olive green colored Green Lentils are a bit milder in taste; French or European Lentils are sold with their seed coats on and have a delicate sweetness; Red or Egyptian Lentils are smaller and rounder than brown lentils but unfortunately turn brown when cooked; Pink Masoor Dal and Yellow Toovar Dal are hulled varieties used in Indian cuisine; all types cook quickly without presoaking.

(continued)

TABLE 5.2

Types of Legumes

Legume	Characteristics
Lima Beans	two types are available, Fordhooks and Baby Limas. The fordhooks are larger with a fuller flavor than the smaller baby limas. They are available fresh, canned, frozen, and dried. Another variety of limas with deep red blotches called Calico or Speckled Butter Beans has recently become more available.
Mung Beans	tiny, pea-shaped beans with a green color which are popular in Chinese and Indian cuisines but more commonly in the U.S. used to grow bean sprouts; available split and hulled as well as whole.
Pigeon Peas (Congo Peas, No-Eyed Peas, Gandules)	tiny, roundish, brown beans native to Africa; popular in Southern and Caribbean cuisines; available fresh, frozen, canned, and dried.
Pink Beans	good replacements for pinto beans.
Pinto Beans (Red Mexican Beans)	beans with deep reddish brown streaks on a pale pink background; popular in the cuisines of Spanish-speaking countries; commonly used in refried beans and chili.
Soybeans	over 1,000 varieties available; most are not eaten alone because of their bland taste; Black Soybeans have a more interesting taste.
White Beans (Navy Beans, Marrow Beans, Pea Beans, Great Northern Beans)	a generic term referring to several kinds of white beans; they work well in salads, soups and commonly appear in baked beans.

Sources: S. T. Herbst. 1990. *Food Lover's Companion.* Hauppauge, New York: Barron's Educational Series. California Culinary Academy. 1988. *Cooking A to Z.* San Ramon, CA: Chevron Chemical Co., pp. 30–36. P. Dowell and A. Bailey. 1980. *Cooks' Ingredients.* New York: William Morrow and Co., pp. 92–95, 244–46. F. Levy. 1993. *International Vegetable Cookbook.* New York: Warner Books, pp. 64–65. S. and M. London. 1992. *The Versatile Grain and the Elegant Bean.* New York: Simon and Schuster. K. Mayes and S. Gottfried. 1992. *Boutique Bean Pot.* Santa Barbara, CA: Woodbridge Press. L. J. Sass. 1992. *Recipes from an Ecological Kitchen.* New York: William Morrow and Co. S. and M. Stone. 1988. *The Brilliant Bean.* New York: Bantam Books. P. Stapley. 1990. *The Little Bean Cookbook.* New York: Crown Publishing.

age, they lose flavor and become drier and harder, requiring more water and longer cooking to become tender. Beans maintain their fresh attributes longer if stored in a cool dark, dry place.

Two mail order sources of recently harvested beans are the Bean Bag, 818 Jefferson Street, Oakland, CA 94607; (800) 845-BEAN (2326); and Dean & Deluca, 560 Broadway, New York, NY 10012; (800) 221-7714.

Legume uses. Legumes are really quite versatile. They can be used in soups, stews, salads, and casseroles and served pureed as dips and sandwich spreads. For example, presented with water-crisped tortilla chips, a chunky, zesty, tomato and chili-flavored black-eyed pea dip makes a high-fiber, protein-rich vegetarian appetizer. It arouses the taste buds without bogging down the appetite.

As both snacks and main course selections, vegetarians and health-conscious diners will find spicy black bean tacos irresistible when offered with a selection of trimmings—chopped tomatoes; grated, low-fat cheese; shredded lettuce; strips of red bell pepper; thinly sliced, green onions; and nonfat, plain yogurt. They are ideal for eating out of the hand.

Nutritional value of legumes. In addition to being good sources of protein, legumes are rich in minerals, including calcium, phosphorous, iron, magnesium, zinc, several B vitamins, and fiber. Furthermore, legumes are economical.

Canned versus dried beans. Members of the legume family can be purchased most commonly in canned and dried forms. While canned forms are more convenient, they are higher in sodium and more costly than dried beans.

Presoaking legumes. Presoaking dried beans helps them to cook more evenly and shortens their cooking time. To presoak: place in 4 parts water, cover, and let stand 8 hours or overnight; drain and rinse.

When time is limited, the following quick method can be employed. Place washed beans in 4 parts water; heat to a boil; cook for 2 minutes; cover; turn the heat off; and let stand 1 hour; drain and rinse.

Some chefs advocate for the best-flavored beans to start cooking them in hot water without soaking. While many still believe that presoaking beans allows gas-producing sugars to dissolve in the soaking water and reduce the occurrence of flatulence, it's now known this is not true (R. Parsons, February 24, 1994. "Clearing the Air." *Los Angeles Times*, p. H10). Since the gas-producing sugars are part of what beans use for nourishment as they grow into plants, beans don't part with them easily. But even in cases where scientists have been able to rid beans of about 90% of their troublesome sugars, they found there wasn't a marked decrease in flatulence. The problem with beans is they are high in fiber which can also cause flatulence.

The best way to reduce flatulence from beans, it appears, is to eat them more frequently. It seems that the microflora which ferment the sugars causing gas adjust somewhat with increased consumption. This may explain why those cultures that eat beans routinely don't experience as many problems with flatulence as Americans who eat beans only occasionally.

Cooking legumes. When cooking legumes, a few simple rules are helpful.

1. Add acid ingredients such as tomatoes and wine to partially cooked dried beans or lentils. They harden their skins and interfere with proper cooking.

2. If salt is to be added, wait until the beans are nearly tender since it toughens bean skins and slows cooking. Beans with delicate skins such as black soybeans and limas are exceptions. Salt will help keep these beans' skins intact.

3. While baking soda can enhance the softening process, more than ⅛ teaspoon per cup of beans can destroy the B vitamin, thiamin, and cause mushiness and a bitter taste.

SOYBEANS AND SOY PRODUCTS

Soybeans, which contain the most protein of all the legumes, have been used to make a variety of products. They are available whole but more commonly are crushed to make soy milk, from which tofu, tempeh, and soy cheese and ice cream are made.

Soy milk. Soy milk is a milky liquid made by pressing ground, cooked soybeans. It is a nutritious beverage option for diners with milk allergies. It is about equivalent in calories to nonfat milk, low in sodium, cholesterol-free, high in protein, and rich in iron. In comparison to skim milk, however, it provides about ten times the fat (about 5 grams per cup) and is low in calcium. Often, soy milk is fortified with calcium. When combined with acid ingredients like lemon juice and vinegar, soy milk curdles easily.

Tofu. Tofu or bean curd is sold shaped in cakes of varying textures, packed in water. It is white in color and bland in taste. Because it readily picks up flavor, it is a good choice in combination dishes along with a variety of flavorful ingredients. For example, while alone tofu has virtually no taste, when seasoned with chilies and other familiar Chinese spices in a vegetable stir-fry, it's delicious.

Likewise, while curry spices are typically associated with meat and seafood dishes, tofu is equally good prepared in this style. The tofu mellows the hot spice of the seasonings and results in a rich blend of textures, colors and flavors. On a bed of steamed, brown rice, it makes a flavorful but inexpensive vegetarian selection.

Hard or medium-firm tofu holds its shape best in preparation and cooking. It can be sliced or crumbled in dishes or grilled, broiled, stir-fried, or baked. Thus, it can be used in casseroles and salads or substituted for ricotta cheese, for example, in vegetarian lasagne, as well as used in a variety of other dishes.

Hard tofu would be preferred in a dish like red cooked tofu with mushrooms. The red cooking process (cooked in red soy-based sauce) turns the tofu a deep reddish brown producing a rich, smoky-flavored dish. Filled with shiitake and button mushrooms, it is a delightful vegetarian main course when served over brown rice.

Soft tofu can be blended to make cream pies, spreads, dips, puddings, and cream soups. For example, soft tofu might serve as the primary ingredient in an orange cheesecake, as well as in a creamy lemon tofu salad dressing.

Reduced fat versions of tofu are now available too. If lower fat forms can't be found locally, Mori-Nu produces an aseptically packaged lite tofu with less than one-half the fat of regular tofu. Another advantage of the Mori-Nu product is that its packaging allows it to be stored without refrigeration. For more information about this product, call (800) NOW-TOFU.

Tempeh. Tempeh is a white cake made from fermenting soybeans. It is a pleasant-tasting, high-protein food that can be cooked quickly to make dishes such as barbecued tempeh, or cut into pieces and added to soups. Tempeh is cultured like cheese and yogurt, and therefore must be used when fresh or it will spoil.

Soy cheese. Imitation cheeses are available made from soy milk or tofu. While cholesterol-free (unless dairy products are added), they are still high in fat and possibly sodium.

Soy ice cream. Many brands of soy ice cream are available to food service operators that can be run through soft-serve machines. They might round out the dessert menu, served in cones or topped with fruit purees.

TVP and meat analogs. Other soy products that might be used in planning vegetarian selections are textured vegetable protein (TVP) and meat analogs. TVP is made of granules of isolated soy protein that must be rehydrated before using in recipes. It can replace up to one-quarter of the meat in a recipe without being unacceptable to most diners. It is a very concentrated source of protein and is almost fat-free. Like tofu, it is used most successfully in highly flavored dishes such as chili and curries.

Meat analogs are imitation meat products made from soy protein without any animal products. They therefore contain little or no saturated fat and no cholesterol but are often high in sodium. Some are fortified with vitamin B12, a nutrient found only in foods of animal origin and iron. They are offered in forms resembling meats such as hamburgers, hot dogs, bacon, ham, and chicken chunks. They can be expensive, and their acceptability is variable.

For example, cubes of hot dog analogs might be offered in an all American barbecue sauce; ham analog chunks in an egg white omelet along with sauteed garlic, onions, tomatoes, and basil; or chicken analog chunks in a pasta salad with lots of fresh vegetables and a spicy low-sodium soy sauce dressing.

When converting recipes to soy protein, these are a few tips. (1) Adjust the seasonings, adding up to double the amount typically used. Soybeans absorb flavors to a smaller degree than meat. (2) Modify sodium-containing seasonings depending on the soy product used. Soy foods vary greatly in sodium content.

More information about soy and soy products can be obtained by calling 1-800-TALK-SOY (1-800-825-5769). This service is sponsored by the United Soybean Board.

NUTS AND SEEDS

Nuts, including brazil nuts (actually seeds), almonds, macadamias, pecans, chestnuts, cashews, pistachios, pine nuts, coconut meat (actually fruit), black and English walnuts (actually fruit), peanuts (actually legumes), and hazelnuts (filberts), and seeds, including celery, coriander, poppy, soybean, sunflower, white and black sesame, and pumpkin or winter squash seed kernels, may be used as toppings on cooked vegetables and grains, in baked goods, salads, casseroles, vegetarian loaves, and stuffings. They can be made into butters such as walnut or almond and spread on vegetables, fruits, crackers, or served in sandwiches. Because of their high fat and relatively high cost, they should play a minor role when planning healthy vegetarian selections.

For example, a vegetable cabbage salad with yellow sweet peppers, snow peas, daikon radish, carrots, and red cabbage might be tossed in a low-sodium soy sauce and ginger dressing and garnished with toasted sesame seeds. Or chopped, unsalted, roasted cashews might be sprinkled on top of Hawaiian pineapple glazed carrots to enhance their tropical charm. To keep the glaze free of refined sugar, it might be sweetened with pineapple juice concentrate. If sweetened with honey, a product of animal origin, it would not be acceptable to some vegetarians.

In the case of peanuts, they may contain a mold called afla-toxin. If ingested in large amounts, it may contribute to liver can-cer. For this reason, peanuts that are discolored, shriveled, or moldy should be discarded. Likewise, if any mold appears on peanut butter, the entire container should be tossed.

Since the U.S. Department of Agriculture (USDA) inspects peanut shipments for signs of mold and most American food processors monitor the presence of aflatoxin, most commercially packaged, roasted and dry-roasted peanuts and peanut butters are safe. Many commercial peanut products contain added salt, which further helps to prevent the mold from forming. If freshly ground peanut butter is made on premise, it can be prepared without salt. It should be refrigerated to slow rancidity.

GRAINS

Cereal grains, preferably whole ones, make healthy additions to vegetarian selections (see Table 2.4). Some possibilities are ama-ranth, pearl barley, bulgur, cornmeal, white, brown, or wild rice, oat or buckwheat groats, triticale flakes, quinoa, wheat berries, cracked rye, and millet.

Dishes can be offered throughout the menu featuring one or more familiar, favorite, or fashionable new grains. For example, kasha, once a mainstay in the American diet, is reappearing on menus. Glazed with a light, fresh, orange juice dressing and stud-ded with dried apricots, mangoes, bananas, and apples, the roast-ed, hulled, buckwheat kernels provide plenty of nutrition and a nutty taste.

For a visual knockout, country-style brown rice pilaf, a savory blend of brown rice and a colorful medley of vegetables including bok choy, sweet red bell pepper, and scallions might be served gar-nished with a red bell pepper and scallion fan. Or bulgur (cracked wheat) can be transformed into a stylish salad by combining with asparagus and tossing with a light, basil-scented vinaigrette.

Ready-to-eat cereals are a quick and easy way for vegetarian diners to get their grains. The best choices are whole grain cereals like rolled oats or rolled whole wheat that are low in sugar and low in fat. Skip those cereals containing animal products (gelatin, whey, honey) and artificial colors or sweeteners. Some vegetarians may opt for a ready-to-eat cereal with added vitamins and miner-als. Others may prefer to obtain these nutrients from other sources.

Reed Mangels reported in the *Vegetarian Journal* (November/December, 1994, p. 20) that Nabisco, Ralston, and Post are a few cereal manufacturers who do not use vitamins and minerals from animal products. A bowl of Nabisco Spoon-Sized Shredded Wheat or Ralston Wheat Chex topped with sliced bananas or strawberries and soy milk are breakfasts that can be served within minutes.

VEGETABLES

A wide variety of vegetables can be used when developing vegetarian offerings. To retain their nutritional value, flavor, and color, generally they should be cooked only until al dente or tender to the bite without adding lots of fat (see page 239).

For example, as a main course dish, a meatless strudel of tender crisp broccoli, sweet corn kernels, and melted, low-fat cheeses encased in a golden brown, crispy, flaky phyllo pastry might be offered, or as the pasta of the day, manicotti tubes filled with spinach, mushrooms and low-fat cheeses and covered with tomato sauce.

As good as raw greens taste, a few roasted veggies can give a heartiness and substance usually supplied by meats and cheeses to salads. For example, roasted zucchini, yellow summer squash, red onion, and bell peppers seasoned with oregano, cumin, and a splash of sesame oil might be served tossed in a light, balsamic vinaigrette.

Existing Vegetarian Selections on the Menu

In many cases, there are main course items currently on the menu which might accommodate vegetarian and semi-vegetarian guests. For example, the list might include a stir-fry of colorful vegetables on a bed of rice with optional seafood or chicken, a burrito filled with refried beans, shredded lettuce, a spicy salsa, and optional cheese, or a make-your-own sandwich bar including the fixings to satisfy the desires of all types of diners.

For diners who are monitoring their fat intake and eating less red meat, selections might presently be offered which meet these needs, or with a few simple revisions, also be acceptable to diners eating healthy plant-based diets.

In addition to the entree list, selections might exist in other menu categories which can be suggested to vegetarian diners for their intended purposes or combined with each other to form main courses. For example, a plant-based meal might be created without making any changes to the menu by recommending that a first course be followed by a main course combining two items on the appetizer list, and of course, finished with a dessert made without eggs, honey, or dairy products.

APPETIZERS

The appetizer or first course list might include dishes prepared from egg-free pastas. These or pastas containing whole eggs or whites only might be topped with sauces prepared from vegetables, legumes, vegetable stocks, and/or low-fat milk or cheeses. For example, farfalle (butterfly-shaped pasta) with tomatoes, basil and optional freshly grated skim-milk parmesan cheese might be suggested as a starter course for a hearty vegetarian eater and as a lunch or dinner main course for a lighter vegetarian selection. Likewise, spaghetti tossed with cubes of roasted eggplant and spicy tomato sauce (optional skim-milk parmesan cheese) is a dish that might be promoted as low in fat and calories, cholesterol-free, and acceptable to any type of vegetarian as a first or main course.

Soups are other dishes on appetizer menus often prepared without red meat. A cup of a high-protein soup featuring dried beans, peas, or lentils like a brown lentil soup seasoned with oregano (see page 223) or butternut squash soup dotted with red adzuki beans and yellow corn and topped with an optional dollop of nonfat yogurt might be suggested as an introductory course, or in a larger portion along with a hearty whole grain bread and salad as a nourishing main course.

Soups filled with whole grains and their products including pastas, garden vegetables, low-fat dairy products, and cholesterol-free eggs are likely to be popular with health-conscious diners too. It will be difficult to make a choice when soups like Oriental-style vegetable and egg drop soup, black mushroom and pearl barley soup, and fresh corn soup in a light creamy broth accented with cumin (see page 196) are on the list.

SALADS

The salad list is a potential source of selections well suited to vegetarian diners too. Combinations of legumes with grains and their products, nuts, or seeds may exist; creamy dressings prepared without eggs; macaroni salads offered with or without cheese; or the chicken and ham on chef's salads replaced with additional low-fat cheeses. Most molded salads contain gelatin, an ingredient of animal origin. Watch out for marshmallows too; they contain gelatin.

Spinach salad with garlic croutons is a good illustration of a salad which might be promoted as an appetizer or main course salad for vegetarians. Prepared with crisp, garlicky croutons, sauteed in olive oil; tender, iron-rich, fresh spinach greens; vibrant, crunchy, red bell peppers; sweet onion rings and sliced mushrooms—the contrast in colors, flavors and textures is delightful. It might be served to lacto-ovo vegetarians garnished with sliced, hard-cooked eggs, while both lacto and lacto-ovo vegetarians might enjoy the medley tossed with a light dressing accented with feta cheese.

Caesar salads are popular on many menus. Keep in mind, even if the anchovies are omitted, the dressing still contains eggs.

For vegans and non-dairy-eating diners, a selection of dressings prepared without dairy products should be offered, perhaps a fruit-flavored vinaigrette or chunky vegetable salsa.

DESSERTS

The dessert menu might serve sweets appropriate for vegetarians but also contain the ingredients needed for a fruit and cheese plate. Along with a basket of bread, a lacto-ovo or lacto vegetarian might be perfectly satisfied to make a meal out of the combination. The same fruit might be transformed into a lunchtime fruit plate along with a scoop of nonfat frozen yogurt from the dessert menu and a muffin from the breakfast menu. Fruit compotes and sauces on the dessert menu can also double as appetizer fruit soups, and with a few modifications become sauces for main course vegetarian selections.

BREAKFAST SELECTIONS

Egg dishes made from both whole eggs and whites only are favorite breakfast selections. They might also be suggested as vegetarian main course lunch or dinner offerings. For example, an Italian country omelet, filled with sauteed red onions, bell peppers, mushrooms, zucchini, and herbs along with a low-fat, blueberry bran muffin is tasty any time of the day.

SIDE DISHES

Main course selections might also be created by combining side dishes currently on the menu, maybe a vegetable plate from a variety of vegetable and grain side dishes. For example, an attractive vegetable main course plate might include carrot, parsnip and leek bundles, grilled eggplant with marinara sauce, green beans and yellow pepper stew, spicy pinto beans and barley pilaf with scallions and pine nuts.

Similarly, a cold main course plate might be created from a selection of side salads. A plate featuring a colorful melange of salads— bulgur salad peppered with garden vegetables; potato, kidney bean, and bell pepper salad (see page 226); chili pasta salad tossed with slivered, toasted almonds; broccoli marinated in rice wine vinaigrette; and fresh fruit cubes, accompanied by a basket of sesame seed bread sticks and walnut biscuits, could make an impressive offering.

Nutrient-Dense Vegetarian Selections

Vegetarian dishes should be prepared from nutrient-dense foods or those that are nutritious without excessive calories rather than from those which offer little nutrition but lots of calories.

A spinach and carrot torta rustica is an example of a meat-, seafood-, and poultry-free dish that is rich in nutrients, yet can be prepared without excessive calories. Fill a double-crusted, deep dish tart with multicolored dark green, orange, and cream colored layers of spinach, carrots, skim-milk parmesan and nonfat farmer cheeses and bind with egg whites to create a dish rich in beta-carotene, B vitamins, iron, protein, and fiber and low in fat which yields as few as 350 calories per serving. Another nutrient-dense, low-fat, low-calorie option might be a brown rice pizza with a crust prepared from a mixture of brown rice, part-skim mozzarella cheese, and egg whites, and topped with Italian tomato sauce, shredded low-fat cheese, and a medley of vegetables including broccoli and cauliflower florets and sliced zucchini, mushrooms, and onions.

For vegans, a couscous casserole combining black beans, corn, water chestnuts, jalapeno peppers, and a sprinkle of slivered almonds might be suggested as a tasty, colorful, meatless entree containing complementary vegetable proteins.

Whether diners are concerned about nutrition or not, a selection like a whole wheat calzone packed with garden-fresh vegetables sauteed in a nonstick skillet, and part-skim mozzarella and skim-milk parmesan cheeses is likely to be popular with diners of all ages. At the same time, for those who care, it's nutrient-dense.

When planning vegetarian dishes, they should appeal to guests who eat meat as well as those who don't. While many guests may eat meat, it is likely many of them are eating less than previously. These are some illustrations of dishes that might appeal to both groups of diners: stuffed bell peppers layered with wheat berries, brown rice, a chunky tomato sauce, low-fat cheddar cheese, and toasted macadamia nuts; basmati brown rice pilaf decorated with vegetables and topped with toasted cashews; or Cuban black bean soup seasoned with cumin and oregano along with rye-barley flatbread.

Summary—Planning Vegetarian Selections

Many factors have been discussed which can make planning vegetarian selections easy. The following are key strategies which might be employed to create tasty menu fare suitable for all types of vegetarians.

1. Offer dishes containing no foods of animal origin for vegans, no foods of animal origin except dairy products for lacto vegetarians, and dishes with no foods of animal origin except eggs and dairy products for lacto-ovo vegetarians.

2. Keep in mind semi-vegetarians may eat seafood and poultry selections.

3. Offer nonalcoholic and decaffeinated beverages and dishes prepared with unprocessed and "organic" foods.

4. Read food labels to identify ingredients of animal origin.

5. Offer dishes containing complementary proteins—animal + vegetable proteins—or two complementary vegetable proteins—legumes + grains or their products, or legumes + seeds or nuts.

6. Include a variety of legumes in dishes on the menu, ideally combined with grains or their products, nuts, or seeds.

7. Serve soybean products, including soy milk, cheese, and ice cream, tofu, and tempeh, ideally along with grains, nuts, or seeds.

8. Select hard or medium-firm tofu for dishes in which the tofu should hold its shape, and soft tofu in blended dishes.

9. Add textured vegetable protein or meat analogs produced from soy protein to combination dishes rich in flavor.

10. Offer small amounts of high-fat nuts and seeds in selections, preferably with grains and their products, or legumes.

11. Create and promote recipes with whole grains and their products, ideally combined with nuts, seeds, or legumes.

12. Use a wide variety of vegetables in dishes throughout the menu.

13. Promote dishes currently on the menu containing only plant foods, eggs, dairy products, seafood, and poultry to non-red-meat-eating diners.

14. Develop nutrient-dense vegetarian offerings.

15. Plan vegetarian selections that will appeal to both meat and nonmeat eaters.

Protein Activities

1. List which types of vegetarians would be likely to eat each of the following items. Explain why. See Appendix 8 for a sample of correct answers.

  A. Shrimp Salad on a Bed of Salad Greens with Vegetables

  B. Granola

  C. Pecan Pie

  D. Bran Muffin

  E. Frozen Yogurt Sundae

  F. Fruited Strawberry Gelatin

  G. Cherry Pie

  H. Fried Chicken with Mashed Potatoes

2. Describe each item listed below so that one or more types of vegetarian would eat it and then identify the types of vegetarian. See Appendix 8 for a sample of correct answers.

  A. Vegetable Soup

  B. Corn on the Cob

  C. Coleslaw

  D. Turkey Hot Dogs with the Works

  E. Fresh Fruit Coated with Honey

  F. Vegetable Stir-Fry

  G. Potato Chips

  H. Stuffed Baked Potato

  I. Rice Pilaf

  J. Fettuccine Alfredo

DIRECTIONS
Complete the next three activities with a specific operation in mind, ideally one you are currently involved with. See instructor to check your responses.

3. Identify all the items on your menu that might be promoted to your non-red-meat-eating guests. For each item identified, list the types of vegetarians who might order it.

4. Identify components of your existing selections that might be offered together as vegetarian selections. For example, a rice pilaf cooked in vegetable stock, garnished with toasted cashews, and flavored with vegetables, herbs, and spices might presently be served with your grilled pork chops. It might be combined to form a vegetable plate with other grain and vegetable dishes currently accompanying meat, seafood, and poultry main course selections.

5. List and describe other items that could be added to your menu for your non-red-meat-eating guests. Consider factors such as your operation's theme, price range, clientele, method of service, and the equipment and labor required to prepare them.

Spinach and Swiss Cheese Phyllo Strudel

Phyllo leaves, also spelled filo, are tissue-thin pastry sheets, prepared by kneading wheat flour and water together and stretching. In fact, the dough is stretched very thin, making it difficult and time consuming to make in one's own kitchen.

Traditionally, several layers of phyllo leaves were liberally coated with melted butter and baked filled with ingredients to form crisp, flaky wrappers for turnovers and other baked dishes. In this recipe, the dough sheets are lightly coated with butter-flavored cooking spray rather than butter to form light packets for their vegetarian filling.

Servings: 24
Serving Size: 2 1-inch wide pieces
Yield: 3 17-inch strudels

Filling:
Vegetable cooking spray, butter-flavored
Onions, minced   12 ounces
Garlic, minced   1 tablespoon
Spinach, leaves, washed, chopped coarsely   2 pounds
Salt   To taste
Pepper, freshly ground   To taste
Swiss cheese, low-fat, shredded   6 ounces
Parmesan cheese, freshly grated, part-skim milk   3 ounces
Bread crumbs, whole wheat, dried, corn flake, or wheat flake
    cereal crumbs or wheat germ   1 ounce

Dough:
Phyllo dough sheets, frozen, thawed (12 × 17 inches)
    12 ounces (18)
Vegetable cooking spray, butter-flavored, 3-second sprays   18
Bread crumbs, whole wheat, dried, corn flake, or wheat flake
    cereal crumbs or wheat germ (divided)   2 ounces

1. Coat a nonstick skillet with cooking spray. Add the onions and garlic. Cook until tender without browning.
2. Add the spinach; cook until wilted, or about 3 minutes. Drain, pressing off any excess liquid.
3. Season with salt and pepper to taste. Toss with the Swiss and parmesan cheeses and the 1 ounce of bread crumbs.
4. Unfold the sheets of phyllo dough so that they lie flat. Cover with plastic wrap and then a damp towel to keep them from drying.

5. Spread a large piece of parchment paper or plastic wrap on a work surface. Spread 1 dough sheet on the parchment or plastic lined work surface with the longest side nearest. Coat the dough with a 3-second spray of cooking spray. Sprinkle about 1 teaspoon of the crumbs over the dough. Repeat 5 times by placing another sheet of dough over and coating with cooking spray and crumbs.

6. Spread ⅓ of the filling on top of the dough leaving a 1½-inch border of dough uncovered.

7. Lift the longest edge of the dough nearest with the parchment or plastic to fold over the dough. Replace the parchment or plastic and roll up like a jelly roll.

8. Seal the dough seam with water. Do not seal the ends. Place seam side down on a baking sheet coated with cooking spray.

9. Repeat steps 5–8 two more times.

10. Bake in a 375° F (190° C) oven until golden brown, or about 35 minutes. Let stand 10 minutes to firm up. Slice each role into 16 1-inch slices. Serve as an appetizer or main course offering.

Servings	Calories	Protein (g/%)	Fat (g/%)	Cholesterol (mg)	Carbo-hydrates (g/%)	Fiber (g)	Sodium (mg)
1	97	6 g/24%	2.5 g/23%	4.9	13 g/53%	1.6	205

Brown Lentil Soup Seasoned with Oregano

During the cold winter months, this thick and hearty soup is ideal for warming the body. It is prepared by simmering tiny, round, dried brown lentils with vegetables and spices.

Servings: 32
Serving Size: 1 cup
Yield: 2 gallons

Lentils, brown   2 ¼ pounds
Onions, minced   2 pounds
Carrots, washed, small dice   12 ounces
Celery, small dice   10 ounces
Garlic, minced   2 tablespoons
Flavorful Vegetable Stock (recipe follows) or Rich White Chicken
*   Stock (see page 78) (divided)   1 ½ gallons*
Bay leaf   1
Oregano, minced or dried   3 tablespoons or 1 tablespoon
Tomatoes, peeled, coarsely pureed   ½ pound
Parsley, minced   ½ cup
Salt   To taste
Pepper, freshly ground   To taste

1. Wash the lentils; soak in 2 gallons of cold water for about 30 minutes; discard any lentils that float to the surface; drain and rinse with cold water.
2. Add the onions, carrots, celery, and garlic and 1 pint of the vegetable stock or as needed to a sauce pot; simmer, stirring until they are partially tender.
3. Add the lentils, bay leaf, remaining stock and oregano if using dried; heat to a boil; reduce the heat to very low; cover and simmer until the lentils and vegetables are partially tender, or about 45 minutes.
4. Add the tomatoes and continue simmering until the lentils and vegetables are tender, or about 20 minutes longer. To adjust the consistency, reduce the soup to thicken and add stock or water to thin. Add the parsley, oregano, if fresh, and salt and pepper to taste. Simmer a few minutes longer. Remove the bay leaf; serve in heated soup cups or bowls along with whole wheat tortillas prepared without lard.

Servings	Calories	Protein (g/%)	Fat (g/%)	Cholesterol (mg)	Carbo-hydrates (g/%)	Fiber (g)	Sodium (mg)
1	214	17.8 g/32%	2.1 g/9%	0	32.3 g/59%	7.1	96.1

Flavorful Vegetable Stock

A vegetable stock will only be as good as the vegetables it is made from. For a flavorful stock, select high-quality vegetables at their freshest. The best vegetables to use when producing a vegetable stock are carrots, onions, celery, potatoes, parsnips, sweet potatoes, and squash. Strongly flavored vegetables from the cabbage family like broccoli, cauliflower, turnips, and rutabagas should be used with discretion. Green peppers, eggplant, and the dark outer leaves of celery should be avoided. They can make the stock bitter. In this recipe, a small amount of fresh pear is added to lightly sweeten the stock.

Use this stock as a base for soups such as brown lentil soup, or vegetarian minestrone soup, sauces, braised dishes and stews, and as a cooking medium for grains and vegetables such as pinto beans simmered in vegetable broth.

Servings: 24
Serving Size: 6 ounces
Yield: 1⅛ gallons

Celery, washed, trimmed, coarsely chopped   6 ounces
Parsnips, washed, trimmed, coarsely chopped   6 ounces
Onions, coarsely chopped   4 ounces
Leeks, green and white parts, coarsely chopped   4 ounces
Carrots, washed, trimmed, coarsely chopped   4 ounces
Pear, washed, cored, coarsely chopped   4 ounces
Tomato, coarsely chopped   4 ounces
Water (divided)   1¼ gallons
Sachet:
  Bay leaf   1
  Thyme, sprigs or dried   4 or ¼ teaspoon
  Peppercorns   ¼ teaspoon
  Parsley stems   8
  Cloves, whole   2
  Fennel seeds   ½ teaspoon

1. In a stock pot, place the celery and next 6 ingredients. Place over medium-high heat; braise-deglaze with water as needed until tender.
2. Add the remaining water and sachet. Heat to a boil; reduce the heat to low; simmer for 45 minutes. Skim the froth as needed.
3. Strain through a china cap lined with several layers of cheese-cloth. Discard the solids.

4. Cool, vented, in a cold water bath. Store refrigerated. Prior to using, skim any impurities from the stock's surface.

The following nutrition analysis is based on the ingredients used in this recipe. It does not reflect that the pulp is strained from the stock before using. As a result, likely the calories and nutrients are much less than the listed figures.

Servings	Calories	Protein (g/%)	Fat (g/%)	Cholesterol (mg)	Carbo-hydrates (g/%)	Fiber (g)	Sodium (mg)
1	18	0.4 g/8%	0.1 g/6%	0	4.1 g/86%	1	16.3

Potato, Kidney Bean, and Bell Pepper Salad in a Fat-Free Vinaigrette

The varied shapes, contrasting textures, rainbow of colors, and balance of flavors in this potato and kidney bean salad make it a pleasure to the eye and palate. It works well as a separate course salad, sandwich accompaniment, or side dish with meat, fish, or poultry selections.

Servings: 24
Serving Size: ¾ cup
Yield: 1⅛ gallons

Potatoes, new, very small, red-skinned   3 pounds
Kidney beans, canned with 50% less salt, drained, rinsed with
*   water or dried, cooked without salt   1 pound or 7 ounces*
Peppers, bell, red, green, yellow, cut into matchstick strips
*   ½ pound each*
Onions, thin slices   ½ pound
Vegetable-Thickened, Oil-Free Vinaigrette, heated (recipe
*   follows)   1 recipe*

1. Steam the potatoes or boil in unsalted water until tender, or about 10–15 minutes. Drain; place on a sheet tray to cool.
2. When cool, cut the potatoes into quarters or bite-size pieces.
3. In a bowl, combine the potatoes, kidney beans, bell peppers, and sliced onions.
4. Pour the dressing over the vegetables; toss to coat. Serve at room temperature or chilled.

Servings	Calories	Protein (g/%)	Fat (g/%)	Cholesterol (mg)	Carbo-hydrates (g/%)	Fiber (g)	Sodium (mg)
1	91	3.6 g/15%	0.3 g/2%	0	19.7 g/82%	3.7	10.8

Vegetable-Thickened, Oil-Free Vinaigrette

For this nearly fat-free tasty vinaigrette, vegetables are simmered in a flavorful vegetable stock, pureed, and mixed with red wine vinegar, a splash of lemon juice, and freshly minced herbs. Serve over vegetable salads such as potato, kidney bean, and bell pepper salad.

Servings: 24
Serving Size: 1½ tablespoon
Yield: 2¼ cups

*Flavorful Vegetable Stock (see page 224) or Rich White Chicken
    Stock (see page 78)   1 pint*
Onions, coarsely chopped   3 ounces
Celery and carrots, coarsely chopped   2 ounces each
Mushrooms, coarsely chopped   1 ounce
Vinegar, red wine   ¼ cup + 2 tablespoons
Lemon juice, freshly squeezed   ¼ cup + 2 tablespoons
Parsley, minced   ¼ cup + 2 tablespoons
Chives, minced or dried   3 tablespoons or 1 tablespoon
Garlic, minced   1 tablespoon
Salt   To taste
Pepper, freshly ground   To taste

1. Place the stock, onions, celery, carrots, and mushrooms in a saucepan; heat to a boil; boil until the vegetables are tender and the broth reduced to 1 cup, or about 15 minutes.
2. Transfer the vegetables and broth to a blender or food processor; blend until the mixture is smooth.
3. Add the vinegar, lemon juice, and seasonings to the mixture; blend well.

Servings	Calories	Protein (g/%)	Fat (g/%)	Cholesterol (mg)	Carbo-hydrates (g/%)	Fiber (g)	Sodium (mg)
1	7	0.2 g/10%	<0.1 g/5%	0	1.9 g/85%	0.4	5.5

6

Make Calories Count

Counting calories is almost part of the American lifestyle. Considering today's emphasis on leanness, it's not surprising that most people in this country are either on a weight reduction diet, have been on and off several diets, or have a guilty conscience about not dieting.

Estimating Ideal Weight

The ultimate goal for most Americans is to attain and maintain their ideal weight. There are many techniques that can be used to determine this number (see Table 6.1).

Height and Weight Tables

One of the most common references is the height and weight charts such as those issued by The Metropolitan Life Insurance Company (see Table 6.2) and those derived from the National Research Council. They offer a rough guide to determine ideal weight for an individual based on sex, height, and body frame size.

Calories

This text uses the term calorie, as most people do, to mean the energy in carbohydrates, fat, protein, and alcohol. Technically, this energy unit is a kilocalorie, a unit of 1,000 calories.

TABLE 6.1

CALCULATING IDEAL WEIGHT

A simple calculation is another quick technique to estimate one's approximate ideal weight. To perform this method, begin by determining frame size. Women with wrists measuring 6 inches and men 7 inches indicate a medium frame. Measurements smaller than this mean a person has a small frame, and larger wrist sizes reveal a large frame.

Females—Medium Frame

For females with medium frames, allow 100 pounds for the first 5 feet of height. Add 5 pounds for each inch over 5 feet and subtract 5 for each inch under 5 feet.
Example: Medium-frame female
      Height = 5 feet 5 inches
      100 pounds for the first 5 feet
      5 pounds per inch or 5 pounds per
      inch × 5 inches = 25 pounds
      100 pounds + 25 pounds = 125
      pounds approximate ideal weight

Females—Small and Large Frame

For females with small frames, subtract 10% from the weight for females of the same height with medium frames, and add 10% to this weight for females with large frames.

TABLE 6.1

Continued

Example: Small- and large-frame female
        Height = 5 feet 5 inches
        Approximate ideal weight for
        medium frame = 125 pounds
        125 pounds × .10 = 12.5 pounds
        125 pounds − 12.5 pounds = 112.5
        pounds approximate ideal weight for
        a small-frame female
        125 pounds + 12.5 pounds = 137.5
        pounds approximate ideal weight for
        a large-frame female

Males—Medium Frame

For males with medium frames, allow 106
pounds for the first 5 feet of height. Add 6
pounds for each inch over 5 feet and subtract
6 pounds for each inch under 5 feet.
Example: Medium-frame male
        Height = 6 feet
        106 pounds for the first 5 feet
        6 pounds per inch or 6 pounds per
        inch × 12 inches = 72 pounds
        106 pounds + 72 pounds = 178
        pounds approximate ideal weight

Males—Small and Large Frame

For males with small frames, subtract 10%
from the weight for males of the same height
with medium frames, and add 10% to this
weight for males with large frames.
Example: Small- and large-frame males
        Height = 6 feet
        Approximate ideal weight for
        medium frame = 178 pounds
        178 pounds − 17.8 pounds = 160
        pounds approximate ideal weight for
        small frame
        178 pounds + 17.8 pounds = 196
        pounds approximate ideal weight for
        large frame

**ESTIMATING CALORIE
REQUIREMENTS**

There are also a variety of techniques that
can be used to estimate calorie requirements.
A quick estimate of calorie needs or energy
expenditure can be made by multiplying

Calories Required to Lose Weight

Now assume the 178-pound male in the example with the approximate 2937 daily calorie energy requirement (Table 6.1) would like to lose 1 pound per week. The dieter would need to cut his calorie intake or increase his calorie expenditure or a combination of the two by 3500, or the number of calories in one pound, over the course of 7 days.

In other words, 3500 calories divided by 7 days would require 500 calories to be eliminated per day. It might be accomplished by cutting caloric intake or increasing caloric expenditure. Thus, a maintenance calorie level per day of 2937 minus 500 equals 2437 calories per day to lose one pound per week. This assumes activity level remains the same.

For the 125-pound female in the example to lose one pound per week without increasing energy expenditure, she should consume approximately 1375 calories per day, or 1875 maintenance calories per day minus 500.

Reducing caloric intake to less than 1200 calories per day is not advised for most dieters. It is too difficult to obtain the nutrients needed from food at such low levels of calories.

Strategies to Accommodate Calorie-Conscious Diners

Now the question, how can restaurants accommodate calorie-conscious diners? The key to pleasing dieters who are reducing healthfully is to offer nutrient dense foods or those rich in nutrients compared to calories.

Reduce Sugar in Dishes

Foods with few or no nutrients in comparison to their calories are considered empty calories. Sugar is basically empty calories, 45 calories per tablespoon. Thus, it goes without saying, when reducing calories, this is a good place to cut them (see Chapter 3). Even Aunt Jemima has done it. Her light syrup has one-half the sugar (no artificial sweeteners) of its counterpart. And if Aunt Jemima can do it in a product with such high brand recognition and succeed, it's likely most food service operations can too.

This doesn't mean no desserts for dieters, rather ones without the empty calories of sugar. The obvious solution is naturally sweet, high-fiber, low-fat, cholesterol-free and vitamin- and mineral-rich fruit. It might be as simple as fresh fruit, maybe a goblet of sliced fruit featuring oranges, cherries, and raspberries lightly coated in a cherry-flavored syrup, a scalloped melon shell filled with cantaloupe balls laced with licorice-flavored fruit syrup, or a small taste of many ripe, juicy fruits in season. A fruit plate is always a lovely way to end a meal, perhaps an eye-catching arrangement for two of red, orange, and pink colored fruits, including cherries, strawberries, figs, watermelon, nectarines, red plums, and seedless grapes.

Ripe and flavorful fruit selections might be steamed, baked, broiled, poached, or made into compotes too. For example, fresh pear halves might be poached in a light fruit juice syrup and finished with a splash of vanilla; baked bananas coated in graham cracker crumbs and napped with orange-pineapple yogurt sauce; or dried apricots simmered in a light fruit juice syrup. Further, fruits can be made into low-calorie one-crust pies, tarts, souffles, mousses, crepes, cobblers, and crisps. Apple crisp is a favorite of all age groups. It might be offered sprinkled with a crumbly oat topping, or for a picturesque but light dessert, a melange of fresh fruit might be attractively arranged in a phyllo pastry shell and coated with a mimosa sauce.

Frozen desserts like sorbets, reduced-fat ice cream (ice milk), and frozen yogurts and drinks from them like shakes and smoothies are popular year round. They can be prepared from a single fruit or combinations of fruits in season. For example, papaya sherbet might be prepared from ripe papaya puree and lightly sweetened with unsweetened fruit juice concentrate. It makes a light refreshing dessert for under 150 calories. On the other hand, a fruit smoothie blended from nonfat vanilla frozen yogurt, strawberries, bananas, oranges, and papaya can be suggested when a low-calorie nutrient-dense snack is desired.

Cut Fat in Recipes

Fat is a concentrated source of calories and a nutrient most Americans eat too much of. Recall that it provides more than double the number of calories in carbohydrates and protein, 9 per gram versus 4 (see Table 6.3). This equates to 9 times the 0 calories in water.

To reduce calories, fat should be reduced in dishes when possible (see Chapter 1). For example, sauteing ingredients like onions and garlic in 2 tablespoons of oil adds 240 calories to the dish. Braise-deglazing (see page 33) them in water adds zero calories. Similarly, for every tablespoon of butter eliminated from a dish, the calories will drop by 108. Likewise, replacing a glass of

TABLE 6.1
Continued

current weight by 15. For example, a 178-pound male would require approximately 2670 (178 × 15 = 2670) calories to maintain his weight, and a 125-pound female, approximately 1875 (125 × 15 = 1875) calories to maintain her weight.

This is still only an approximation, but a more accurate estimate of calorie needs can be calculated by the following procedure. (A) Determine basal metabolic rate (BMR)

BMR of Males = 11 × weight in pounds
BMR of Females = 10 × weight in pounds

(B) Determine activity calories expended

BMR × activity level = activity calories

	Activity Levels
Males:	sedentary = 25–40%
	lightly active 50–70 %
	moderately active 65–80 %
	very active 90–120 %
Females:	sedentary 25–30 %
	lightly active 40—60 %
	moderately active 50–70 %
	very active 80–100 %

(C) Total energy = A + B

Male Example
178-pound male who is lightly active

(A) 178 pounds × 11 = 1958 BMR
(B) 1958 BMR × 50% = 979 activity calories
(C) 1958 BMR + 979 activity calories = 2937 approximate total energy calories required

Female Example
125-pound female who is moderately active

(A) 125 pounds × 10 = 1250 BMR
(B) 1250 BMR × 50% = 625 activity calories
(C) 1250 BMR + 625 activity calories = 1875 approximate total energy calories required

TABLE 6.2

Standard Body Weights Based on Insurance Data*

Height	Standard Body Weight in Pounds	
	Women	Men
4 feet 9 inches	94–106	
4 10	97–109	
4 11	100–112	
5 0	103–115	
5 1	106–118	111–122
5 2	109–122	114–126
5 3	112–126	117–129
5 4	116–131	120–132
5 5	120–135	123–136
5 6	124–139	127–140
5 7	128–143	131–145
5 8	132–147	135–149
5 9	136–151	139–153
5 10	140–155	143–158
5 11	144–159	147–163
6 0		151–168
6 1		155–173
6 2		160–178
6 3		165–183

1983 Metropolitan height and weight tables. (1983). Metropolitan Life Foundation *Statistical Bulletin*, 64, 2–9.
*Weight of insured persons in the United States and Canada associated with the longest life expectancy. Values listed are for persons with medium frame and aged 25 years and over. Heights and weights are measured without shoes or other clothing.

whole milk with one of 2% milk will remove 29 calories, with a glass of 1% milk, 48 calories, and with a glass of skim milk, will remove 64 calories. It is all a matter of cutting down on fat.

Offer Selections High in Water

Since water contains no calories, it only makes sense to offer dieters selections high in water and low in fat and sugar.

BEVERAGES
Beverages likely come to mind. Some low-calorie options include the obvious bottled waters (see Table 3.5), coffees, vegetable juices, teas, and artificially sweetened sodas.

Bottled spring, well, carbonated- and sparkling waters may contain added carbonation and be prepared with added flavors, extracts, and/or essences but contain no sweeteners. Seltzers, on the other hand, contain sweeteners which add calories, about 140 per 12-ounce bottle in comparison to around 156 in the same amount of soft drink.

Fruit juices may be good sources of vitamins and minerals but because they contain so much natural sugar, most are not low-calorie drinks. For example, 8 ounces of orange juice has the same number of calories as an equivalent portion of regular cola. On the other hand, small amounts of fruit juices combined with low-calorie or calorie-free beverages make refreshing low-calorie options. For example, calorie-conscious diners won't need to worry about their diet when they are sipping on a sparkling orange cooler, a tumbler filled with ice and a blend of one-fourth orange juice and three-fourths club soda and garnished with a skewer of fresh fruit sections. By replacing the orange juice with wine, this same technique can be used to make low-calorie alcohol wine spritzers.

For a hot, low-calorie, tasty and nutritious beverage alternative to coffee, fruit juice might be combined with tea. For example, a peachy tea can be prepared by mixing peach nectar with noncaloric, cinnamon herb tea, brewed from sparkling mineral water. The outcome is a nutritious, flavorful, low-calorie beverage.

SOUPS
Broths, bouillons, and consommés garnished with attractively cut vegetables and clear soups filled primarily with diced or sliced vegetables, legumes, some whole grains or their products, and/or small amounts of lean meat, fish, and poultry are other good choices high in water. They fill the stomach without adding many calo-

ries. They may appeal to dieters as a between-meal snack or as lunch or dinner appetizer courses.

A cup of curry-flavored chicken, brown rice, and vegetable soup (see page 251) might be promoted to diners with more adventurous palates, while an Oriental-style vegetable egg drop soup with bean sprouts and snow peas and prepared with only egg whites might be suggested as a first course along with a stir-fry entree.

Warm seasoned vegetable juices make inviting low-calorie alternatives to broths too. For example, a tangy tomato warmer, made from tomato juice, low-sodium worcestershire sauce, lemon juice, garlic, and a tad of hot sauce can be offered for only 38 calories per cup.

Serve Water- and Fiber-Rich Selections

Calories can be kept to a minimum by offering dishes low in fat and refined, white sugar and rich in both water and fiber. Fruits and vegetables are two ingredients which often meet these criteria. Both are popular with dieters because they fill their stomachs without adding excess calories. Nutritionally, fruits and vegetables are cholesterol-free and rich in vitamins and minerals too.

For example, a diner can enjoy a half-cup of raw snow peas for only 32 calories and a half-cup of raw carrots for a mere 33 calories. What a vegetable plate for under 200 calories when the two are combined with cauliflower florets, tender asparagus spears, sliced summer squash, and garnished with a creamy, low-fat ranch-style dip (see page 253).

There are many opportunities to cut calories by offering more selections made from fruits and vegetables throughout the menu.

HORS D'OEUVRES AND APPETIZERS
Fruits and vegetables can add appeal to every course of the meal. Rather than a terrine made from high-cholesterol, high-fat, high-calorie meats, the meal might begin with one made from vegetables. For example, a roasted sweet pepper and eggplant terrine garnished with fresh basil leaves makes a spectacular, low-calorie appetizer course.

Or, stuffed mushrooms, easy to eat, bite-sized, finger foods might be served along with a predinner cocktail. Dieters won't feel guilty eating the fleshy caps when they are filled with a chunky mixture of sauteed, fresh vegetables rather than high-fat ground meats and cheeses and refined, white bread crumbs.

TABLE 6.3

Caloric Value of the Energy Nutrients and Alcohol

	Calories per Gram
Carbohydrates	4
Protein	4
Fat	9
Alcohol	7

TABLE 6.4

Salad Greens

Name	Description
Arugula	green-colored, very perishable, round and slightly elongated leaves with bitterish flavor; also known as rugula or rocket.
Belgian Endive	small, narrow, pointed, spearhead-like leaves, white to pale green in color with a slightly bitter flavor and waxy texture.
Bibb Lettuce	highly prized and similar to Boston lettuce but more delicate and smaller in size; an entire head is usually only a few inches across; also called Limestone.
Boston Lettuce	sweet, soft, buttery-textured lettuce with small, round, loosely formed heads.
Chicory or Curly Endive	firm, bitter-tasting green leaves with very curly jagged edges; often used as a salad base or served cooked.
Escarole or Broad-Leaf Endive	also of the endive family with broad, slightly curved, pale green leaves and a mild, bitter flavor.
Frisee	a small version of curly endive with bittersweet feathery leaves ranging from ivory to lime green in color.
Iceberg Lettuce	crisp, round compact heads with pale green leaves and rather bland flavor; Americans' favorite.
Lamb's Lettuce	narrow, dark green and tender leaves with a tangy, nut-like flavor; also known as Field or Corn Salad and Mache.
Looseleaf Lettuce	mild-flavored, ranging in color from medium to dark green and shades of red with soft, ruffle-edged leaves that form loose bunches; popular types are Red, Green and Oak Leaf and Salad Bowl Lettuces.

(continued)

SALADS

Salads are well-known favorites of the calorie conscious. They can be offered as both main courses and side dishes coated with low-calorie dressings or high-calorie ones on the side. For example, a crab and cucumber salad comprised of delicate crab tossed with crunchy cucumbers and radishes, dressed with just a whisper of sesame oil blended with rice vinegar, low-sodium soy sauce, minced ginger, and garlic and garnished with toasted sesame seeds, or an Oriental chicken salad—a bed of shredded, napa cabbage and romaine lettuce, gently tossed with julienne strips of grilled, skinless chicken breast meat, lots of colorful vegetables and an orange-pineapple soy dressing—might be highlighted as light, sophisticated lunch entrees. Either certainly beats a high-calorie sandwich loaded with high-fat, high-cholesterol cheeses, meats, or mayonnaise-rich fillings.

Green salads are well known for being low in calories and thus, popular first courses for many dieters. While iceberg is tried and tested, there are many other salad greens to pick from. They come in a whole spectrum of colors, shapes, textures, and flavors. They range from cream to deep burgundy in color and are curly to flat and thin to wide in leaf shape, tender to crisp in texture, and earthy and strong to mild and sweet in taste.

In addition to their low calorie counts, most salad greens are good sources of fiber, vitamins including vitamin C, vitamin A's precursor—beta carotene, and folacin, and minerals including iron and calcium. Nutritionally, iceberg rates lowest of the salad greens. For example, by weight, loose leaf lettuce has about 3 times more calcium than iceberg and 5 times more vitamin C and vitamin A value. Likewise, romaine is estimated to provide more than 3 times the folacin and 7 times the vitamin C and vitamin A value of iceberg. This is one more reason to compose salads with a variety of greens.

Some of the more fashionable greens (see Table 6.4) found on restaurant menus today are arugula, Belgian endive, bibb lettuce, Boston lettuce, chicory or curly endive, escarole or endive, frisee, looseleaf lettuce, radicchio, and romaine lettuce.

For a light and harmonious combination, bite-sized pieces of delicate Boston lettuce and peppery, mustard flavored arugula might be tossed with thin slices of zucchini, strips of sweet, red and green bell peppers, and tomato wedges, and dressed with a low-fat saffron and basil vinaigrette. Salads make good starter courses for weight reducers but work well as main course accompaniments too. A jicama and orange salad splashed with freshly squeezed lime juice and a sprinkle of chili powder might provide a nice contrast in flavor and texture to a grilled chicken breast sandwich, while grilled summer vegetables coated in a balsamic rice vinegar dressing can make a great match with citrus flavored pan broiled pork chops.

Fruit salads are a delightful and healthy way to end a meal. It might be as easy as gently tossing a few naturally sweet fruits together, perhaps sliced strawberries and kiwis, orange sections, and pineapple cubes. Served chilled in stemmed goblets, this colorful medley looks and tastes good.

SAUCES

Rich cream and butter sauces taste great, but so do fruit and vegetable garnishes, sauces, salsas, chutneys, coulis, and relishes. For example, a high-calorie gravy might be replaced on pan broiled pork chops with a ginger sauce and garnish of sliced pears; roasted veal sirloin might be napped with a light, creamy sauce thickened with a puree of cooked vegetables and enhanced with a vodka reduction rather than one thickened with a butter and flour roux and finished with cream; or a marinated, broiled fillet of shark might be garnished with a papaya mango salsa instead of a rich, mayonnaise tartar sauce.

MAIN COURSE SELECTIONS

By preparing main course selections with larger portions of nutrient-rich, colorful fruits and vegetables and smaller ones of more caloric white, cream, caramel, and brown-colored meat, seafood, and poultry selections, low-calorie, flavorful, texturally and visually pleasing offerings can be created.

For example, a tasty stew might be made by combining small amounts of meat, seafood, or poultry with an array of vegetables and simmering in a lightly thickened broth. Which dieter could resist a homestyle beef stew made of tender, lean beef cubes simmered in a chunky tomato-based sauce with tiny, red-skinned potato halves, kelly green peas, and cubes of lime green celery, bright orange carrots and cream-colored turnips? Or perhaps they might choose a provencal fish stew, bursting with potato cubes, corn kernels, diced tomatoes, sliced zucchini, mussels, and fish fillets in a lightly thickened fish fumet (broth). Because both are made with lots of high-fiber vegetables and water, they don't add lots of calories. Similarly, consider 3-ounce portions of grilled meat, fish, or poultry cubes on skewers. They neither look nor are filling, but when rounded out with fruits and/or vegetables, this changes. For example, to create hearty portions out of skewers with 3 ounces of shark steak, add whole mushrooms, yellow, red,

TABLE 6.4

Continued

Name	Description
Radicchio	generally found in the United States in small, round heads with burgundy red leaves and white ribs and a Belgian endive-like taste and texture.
Romaine	crisp, slightly bitter, dark green, elongated leaves, typically used to make Caesar salad.

Sources: S. T. Herbst, 1990. *Food Lover's Companion*. Hauppauge, New York: Barron's Educational Series. P. Dowell and A. Bailey. 1980. *Cooks' Ingredients*. New York: William Morrow and Co., pp. 62–65, 238–40. E. Schneider. March 1993. "Chickory & company." *Food Arts*, pp. 68–71. E. Schneider. September 1988. "Newfangled old-fashioned salad greens." *Gourmet*, pp. 83–85, 130–38. W. Gisslen. 1995. *Professional Cooking*. New York: John Wiley & Sons. S. Labensky and A. M. Hause. 1995. *On Cooking*. Englewood Cliffs, NJ: Prentice Hall, pp. 662–66.

and green bell pepper strips, and pineapple cubes for only a few extra calories.

Main course vegetarian selections featuring primarily vegetables can make low-calorie offerings too. Choices might change weekly or even daily depending on what vegetables are in season, available locally, and their price. Imagine how exciting a vegetarian plate would be which included a taste of four different vegetable dishes and one grain, maybe greens with freshly ground peanuts, cauliflower florets with cilantro and onions, oven-steamed cream style corn, carrot and parsnip puree accented with ginger and chives, and barley risotto with mushrooms and spinach (see page 254).

SIDE COURSE DISHES

Fruits and vegetables make excellent low-calorie side dishes served alone or in combinations, seasoned with herbs, spices, or other flavoring agents, or coated with low-fat sauces and cooked by a variety of methods. Careful matches with main course selections can make knockout meals.

For an East meets West low-fat, low-calorie meal, steamed sea bass topped with black bean sauce on a bed of brown basmati rice might be featured, rounded out with stir-fried Chinese broccoli with wine.

Or, if the occasion calls for an Indian-inspired light meal, cauliflower florets, stir-fried with tomatoes and accented with turmeric, freshly grated ginger, and minced cilantro and potato cubes, sauteed with freshly minced ginger and garlic and fennel seeds, can make an exotic meal out of grilled chicken drumsticks Tandoori style (see page 80).

Most dieters won't be able to fit too many meals of fried chicken, mashed potatoes, gravy and scalloped corn into their daily calorie allotments, but would be delighted to have crispy baked mustard chicken breasts with rosemary-seasoned oven-roasted potato wedges and beets glazed in orange and red wine vinegar sauce.

While fruits and vegetables are not typically paired in American cuisine, German chefs do it successfully all the time. For example, baby carrots might be joined by apple slices. Lightly glazed, this mixture might be combined with simple, roasted or grilled lean meat, poultry, or game selections and new red potatoes adorned with herbs. The outcome is a visually pleasing and tasty low-calorie meal. The naturally sweet flavors of roasted, baked, stir-fried, grilled, steamed, or microwaved fruits make distinctive, low-fat, low-calorie additions to smaller portions of lean meat, seafood, and poultry too. For example, a 3-ounce portion of sliced, roasted tenderloin of pork with fennel seeds will look ample when complemented by chunky Granny Smith and McIntosh apple-sauce, grilled corn on the cob, and steamed, tender green beans.

CRUCIFEROUS VEGETABLES

In addition to being good sources of fiber and water, low in fat and calories, rich in vitamins and minerals and cholesterol-free, cruciferous vegetables provide another benefit. This group of vegetables, which derives its name from its cross-shaped blossoms, has been shown to protect against cancer in laboratory animals. Vegetables in this group, including broccoli; brussels sprouts; all varieties of cabbage; cauliflower; collard, mustard, and turnip greens; kale; kohlrabi; rutabagas and turnip roots, contain compounds that activate enzymes which destroy carcinogens.

Cruciferous vegetables can be featured alone in dishes, flavored in endless styles or combined with other ingredients. For example, split mung beans and spinach might be offered as a main course vegetarian selection with cauliflower florets. But cauliflower might also serve as a vegetable side dish coated with generous quantities of garlic, cilantro, and hot pepper sauce, Algerian-style, or stir-fried with cruciferous broccoli and Chinese cabbage and carrots, bamboo shoots, and water chestnuts.

As the Irish well know, cabbage is tasty blended into mashed potatoes, but in the United States is more commonly featured as a salad. For example, shredded cabbage might be turned into a healthy offering by coating with a low-fat, buttermilk ranch-style dressing or by tossing with corn and bell peppers and coating in a pineapple tofu dressing. Served with a sandwich or grilled meat, seafood, or poultry, either option makes a delicious alternative to deep-fried potatoes.

BETA CAROTENE-RICH FRUITS AND VEGETABLES

Fruits and vegetables rich in beta carotene, vitamin A's precursor, may slow down the development of heart disease and play a protective role against cancer too. The choices include the dark green vegetables such as broccoli and spinach and deep orange fruits and vegetables like carrots and apricots (see Table 6.5). Recommendations state diners should eat dark green or deep orange fruits and vegetables at least every other day.

Beta carotene-rich fruits and vegetables can be incorporated into low-calorie offerings throughout the menu. For example, in lieu of baked Russet potatoes, baked sweet potatoes might be offered for a nice change. Or once cooked, sweet potatoes might be

TABLE 6.5

Beta Carotene-Rich Fruits and Vegetables

Apricots

Asparagus

Broccoli

Cantaloupe

Carrots

Green Onions

Greens (all varieties)

Lettuces (dark green ones)

Mangoes

Oriental Cabbages

Papayas

Parsley

Pumpkin

Spinach

Sweet Potatoes

Winter Squashes

Yams

shaped into patties, coated in a crisp wheat flake cereal crumb crust, and sauteed in a lightly oiled nonstick pan (see page 250) for a more elaborate sweet potato dish.

Likewise, apricots are delicious as well as nutritious when simply chilled in a light, fruit juice syrup, but make flavorful additions pureed and blended into sweet, light, egg white souffles too.

HANDLING FRUITS AND VEGETABLES

By employing careful selection, storage, preparation, and cooking techniques, the nutritional attributes of fruits and vegetables along with their vivid colors, crisp textures, and fresh flavors can be preserved.

Fruits and vegetables are available fresh, frozen, canned, and dried. Generally, fresh produce is preferred over other forms and frozen rather than canned or dried. In cases where fruits or vegetables are needed for dishes and are no longer in season locally, good quality frozen or canned products may be more desirable than ones lacking in flavor, color, and texture which have been engineered to survive early picking, ripening rooms, and long-distance shipping. Tomatoes, common ingredients in healthy commercial kitchens, are an example. When not in season, canned whole tomatoes may produce better tasting sauces, soups, and stews than their fresh, flavorless counterparts.

Deliveries should be planned so that the produce used in dishes is as fresh as possible. The nutritional value and quality of fruits and vegetables begins dropping immediately after harvesting and continues to decline until cooked or eaten. Any damaged, bruised or wilted produce should be refused or returned. Rough handling of fruits and vegetables not only may cause bruising but vitamin loss.

To retain the moisture content of fruits and vegetables and keep fragile ones like salad greens and herbs fresh, they are best stored in containers. In the case of frozen fruits and vegetables, sanitation and safety codes require freezers be kept at 0° F ($-18°$ C) or less. This practice promotes nutrient retention in frozen fruits and vegetables as well. Higher temperatures can encourage loss of nutrients in frozen produce.

Fruits and vegetables should be washed only when ready to use to conserve C and B vitamins, and should not be soaked in water unless they, like potatoes, discolor when exposed to air. This will prevent nutrients from being extracted into the water. Similarly, fruits and vegetables should be trimmed and cut as close to cooking and serving times as possible to avoid exposure to air and light. Both conditions promote nutrient loss. If fruits and vegetables must be cut in advance, they should be stored wrapped tightly.

When fruits and vegetables are to be cut, larger pieces are better than smaller ones. The larger the surface area exposed to air, the greater the loss of vitamins A (value), C, and E, some B vitamins, and the mineral selenium.

Cooking fruits and vegetables to order or preparing several small batches during the service period will help them to look and taste good as well as retain their valuable nutrients. Furthermore, waste will be reduced because only smaller amounts of vegetables and fruits will be cooked as needed. Steaming, stir-frying, broiling, grilling, and microwaving are preferred healthy cooking methods for fruits and vegetables. These techniques require little or no fat while preserving nutrients. Baking and roasting are two other good choices. Fruits and vegetables can be roasted or baked whole in their skins without added fat. Boiling may require no fat but draws water-soluble vitamins B and C and minerals such as selenium and potassium from the fruits and vegetables into the liquid. If fruits and vegetables are boiled in water, their nutrient-enriched cooking liquids can be used in lieu of water when preparing juices, soups, sauces, gravies, and braised dishes.

Overcooking fruits and vegetables destroys nutrients and results in unnecessary loss of flavor, color, and texture. Fruits and vegetables should be cooked only until crisp-tender or no longer than necessary to reach their desired degree of doneness. Deep frying is an obvious no-no. It adds unnecessary fat and destroys vitamins E, K, and A. Similarly, baking soda should never be added to the cooking liquids for fruits or vegetables. While it may enhance green-colored fruits and vegetables, the alkalinity of baking soda destroys vitamin C and the B vitamins, thiamine and riboflavin.

Heat, light, soaking in water, mechanically injuring, processing, preserving with acidic or alkaline ingredients, and very dry holding environments can all harm the nutritional value of fruits and vegetables. If possible, they should not be exposed to these conditions.

Eliminate Unnecessary Alcohol Calories

Alcohol is a source of empty calories, 7 per gram. It should be used discreetly in cooking. Previously, it was believed that with cooking, a beverage's alcohol would evaporate and leave its flavor behind without its alcohol and calories. It is now known that this is not the case. Researchers have found that cooking produces some but not total loss of alcohol, anywhere from 15% to 85% (J. Augustin, E. Augustin, R. L. Cutrufelli, S. R. Hagen, and C. Teitzel, 1992. "Alcohol Retention in Food Preparation." *Journal of the*

American Dietetic Association 92, 486–88). For example, after dishes prepared tableside, such as crepes Suzette or bananas Foster, are flamed, they may retain more alcohol than they lose. One study with cherries jubilee showed 77–78% alcohol retention. With flaming, alcohol loss is primarily a result of alcohol combustion. The alcohol continues to burn as long as minimum alcohol vapor pressure is maintained. Once this vapor pressure is reduced below a certain point, alcohol ceases to burn. This occurs during flaming and accounts for the relatively high retention of alcohol during the process.

The extent of loss will depend on several factors: type of heat (baking, boiling), source of alcohol (brandy, wine), type of cooking vessel (saute pan, roasting pan), length of cooking (15 minutes, 3 hours) and storage after cooking (2-inch, half counter pan, 4-inch, full counter pan), or any other factors favoring evaporation. For example, if a dish containing wine is covered with bread crumbs, alcohol evaporation will be affected.

ALCOHOLIC BEVERAGE SUBSTITUTES

One option to serving or flavoring dishes with alcoholic beers and wines is replacing them with nonalcoholic versions. A variety of products are available today. Their qualities range from good to poor. Thus, it's essential that each operation try them to determine if they are appropriate for their use. When the flavor of an alcoholic beverage is desired without its alcohol content, these are some other possible substitutions.

♦ Replace a tablespoon of rum, brandy, or sherry with one teaspoon of vanilla. If more than 2 tablespoons of the alcohol are needed, use fruit juice to make up the volume difference. Rum-flavored extract may be substituted for rum also.

♦ Use one-half teaspoon grated orange zest and equal amounts of orange juice, orange-flavored extract, or orange juice concentrate for orange liqueur.

♦ Replace kirsch or amaretto with a dash of almond extract blended with peach or apricot nectar to equal the amount.

♦ Finish dishes calling for sweet dessert wines such as madeira or port with an equal amount of fruit juice the color of the wine.

♦ Add 2 tablespoons of red or white wine vinegar and stock to equal one cup in lieu of red or white wine.

♦ In recipes listing liqueurs, sprinkle a few drops of the corresponding extract (mint, banana, strawberry, cherry, anise) with water or juice to equal the amount. Be aware though, extracts are alcohol-based.

Control Portions

CORRECT PORTION SIZE

One of the first steps in controlling portion size is to make sure that the kitchen staff are serving the measure of food specified. One method that might help them to visualize serving sizes of foods accurately is to equate them to common household items. These are some examples.

Measure of Food	Common Item
3 ounces meat, fish, or poultry	deck of cards cassette tape
1 ounce of cheese	pair of dice thumb of a hand
1 cup of potatoes, rice, or pasta	fist of a hand tennis ball
1 medium fruit	fist of a hand

REDUCED-SIZE PORTIONS

Portion control is essential when serving reduced-calorie items. For example, one medium-sized apple, about 5 ounces, is 84 calories. This doesn't mean all apples including jumbo-sized ones that each weigh 10 ounces contain this number of calories. Bagels are another example. Many healthy diners believe they can save calories by replacing their standard morning sweet roll, doughnut, or muffin with a bagel. In fact, a look in their calorie book probably says a bagel has 150 calories. The only problem is that many varieties of bagels weigh 4 to 5 ounces or more, not the 2 ounces assumed in the calorie count.

Cutting portion size is often an easy way to reduce calories from menu items. For example, it might be as simple as offering a medium-sized banana rather than a large one, serving one pork chop rather than two, or cutting the bread thinner. The menu might promote items in more than one size too, such as a cup or bowl of soup or a half or whole sandwich. Likely, a dieter would not order both a bowl of soup and whole sandwich for lunch but be delighted with a cup of soup and half sandwich. For example, a cup of gingered carrot bisque along with a half turkey sandwich (thinly sliced turkey, smoked on premise, and shredded iceberg lettuce layered between stone ground mustard coated rye bread slices) may hit the spot without adding too many calories.

A slice of bread is naturally eliminated from a sandwich when served open-face. For example, a toasted, open-face, vegetable and melted low-fat cheese sandwich at only 159 calories can easily be served with a bowl of vegetable soup and a light dessert and still keep lunch around 400 calories. Or, rather than serving a whole, grilled, marinated, skinless chicken breast between 2 slices of toast, calories can be cut by presenting a half breast on a toasted whole wheat crouton and garnishing with low-calorie, carotene-rich spinach leaves, vitamin C-filled, ripe tomato slices, and a spoon of piquant salsa combining the flavors of tart green apples, cherry tomatoes, and yellow bell peppers.

Likewise, pies can be prepared with one crust rather than two. For example, there's no need for a top crust when the filling is an apricot orange souffle—a slightly tart, light textured mixture with an intense apricot flavor.

Who says when pies and pastries are prepared with only one crust, it goes on the bottom? Why not the top instead? For example, calories can be dropped in a savory pie like an old fashioned, American pot pie by topping with prebaked, crispy pastry cutouts at service rather than baking enclosed in two high-fat, high-calorie crusts.

Tarts are reported to be one of restaurants' most popular desserts. Weight reducers will appreciate ones prepared with single crusts too. For example, baked, fresh ripe fruit like sliced peaches might be featured on thin, round, flat, low-fat and cholesterol-free oat pastry crusts.

SHARING SELECTIONS

In the case of appetizers and desserts, dieters may feel too guilty to eat a whole one alone but happily share one and feel proud they had the will power to resist the other half. Restaurants can accommodate dieters by offering extra plates and spoons for other members at the table to taste with.

As far as main course offerings, a small charge might be added for splitting portions. For example, diners requesting that a chef salad be divided and half served with balsamic rice vinegar dressing and the other half with low-calorie, citrus-flavored cranberry vinaigrette might be charged a few dollars extra.

HALF PORTIONS

Dieters look favorably on ordering half portions of items too. Many dishes are relatively easy to serve in smaller portions, for example, pastas or combination dishes like stews or stir-fries. It is more difficult to reduce the portion size of other items, for example, a steak or lobster tail. In these cases, diners should be assured doggie bags are available. Half the item can be eaten and the other half packed to go.

APPETIZERS AND SIDE DISHES AS MAIN COURSES

Low-calorie meals might also be created from selections currently on the menu but typically served at other times of the day or as other courses in the meal. For example, a light and healthy lunch or dinner might be created by serving a first course bow tie pasta primavera topped with freshly grated, skim-milk parmesan cheese as a main course and finishing with a cup of fresh, sliced summer fruit from the salad list.

Meals don't need to be limited to one or two courses to be low in calories either. For example, a five-course meal might begin with a cup of chicken consomme garnished with a brunoise (very small dice) of vegetables and whole wheat bread sticks. Next, a skewer of grilled, marinated, jumbo shrimp from the appetizer menu might be served on a cracked wheat pilaf from the side dish list and accompanied by another side dish—steamed asparagus (replace the hollandaise with a lemon wedge). There's still plenty of calories remaining for a salad of tender greens dressed with a light blueberry and lime vinaigrette, and of course, dessert—why not try a strawberry sorbet sweetened with fruit juice? After all this delicious food eaten in a leisurely fashion, a hot cup of amaretto-flavored, decaffeinated coffee makes the meal complete.

Present Healthy Selections Attractively

When planning reduced portion sized selections, presentation is an important factor. Diners, dieting or not, eat first with their eyes. Foods can be cut, shaped, and arranged on plates to minimize smaller portions of higher calorie items and maximize larger ones of lower calorie selections.

Consider the cantaloupe. This fruit can be cut, shaped, and arranged on a plate in numerous designs. It might be cut in halves or quarters (scalloped or straight); sliced and served on or off the rind; cubed in large or small sections; or shaped into balls of varied sizes, to name a few.

The choice of how to shape and arrange items will depend on the number and types of items to be served together and their portion sizes, as well as the shapes and sizes of the serving containers selected to hold them. For example, when a half of a cantaloupe in its shell is presented solo on a large, round, rimless dinner plate, it looks lost. But, if peeled, sliced, and presented fanned out from a single point on a large, round, rimmed dinner plate, portion size loses its significance.

Garnishing with fruits, vegetables, fresh herbs, and flowers is another method to enhance healthy menu selections without increasing their calorie counts substantially. For example, a lettuce salad will look like more than basic rabbit food when the leaves are decorated with nasturtium blossoms and leaves, chive blossoms, and pansies.

Make Special Accommodations for Dieters

Weight watchers will appreciate being informed of any special services designed to meet their needs—sauces and dressings on the side, items cooked with no or less fat, low-calorie substitutions offered for high-calorie ingredients, and special, low-calorie products available. For example, a restaurant might suggest dieters try its low-fat, low-calorie ranch-style salad dressing or its vegetable-thickened fat-free vinaigrette with the house green salad as a first course, or promote its freshly prepared, low-fat, frozen banana-strawberry yogurt or pineapple sherbet for a light dessert.

When meat, seafood, and poultry selections can be grilled as well as pan fried, potatoes roasted rather than fried, or cafe au lait made with nonfat rather than whole milk, dieters won't need to ask if it's listed on the menu or described by the wait staff.

Offer Low-Calorie and Reduced-Calorie Commercial Products

In addition to preparing low- and reduced-calorie dishes in house, there's a variety of such products available commercially and the number continues to grow. Some of them are well accepted by weight reducers and may meet an operation's needs. It is important that they be tried and evaluated before being added to the menu.

Several terms (Collier, Shannon, Rill, and Scott, 1993. *1993 Nutrition Labeling Regulations.* Washington, DC: Collier, Shannon, Rill & Scott) might indicate a product contains fewer calories than an equivalent portion of its traditional counterpart or is low in calories. Note, the term "light/lite" can indicate that a product contains one-third fewer calories than the regular food but can also be describing its reduced fat or sodium content or such properties as its texture and color as long as the label explains the intent. For example, "light" brown sugar is light in color, not lower in calories than dark brown sugar.

The terms "reduced," "fewer," or "lower" in calories indicate that a food will contain 25% less calories per standardized serving than the regular food. This claim cannot be made, however, if the food already meets the requirement for being "low in calories."

Foods labeled "low-calorie" will contain 40 calories or less per standardized serving, while "calorie-free" foods contain less than 5 calories per standardized serving. When using these terms to describe items on the menu, whether obtained from commercial sources or prepared on premise, these guidelines should be followed.

Creating Menus for Weight Watchers

A good rule of thumb for weight watchers' selections is to limit the calories in entrees or main course offerings to 350 or fewer- and appetizers, side dishes, soups, and vegetable salads to 100 to 150.

Since typical reducing diets are 1200 calories for females and 1800 for males, the following calorie allotments can be used as a guide per meal:

	Calories	
	Females	*Males*
Breakfast	200	350
Lunch	450	600
Dinner	550	850

Summary—Reducing Calories in the Menu

Many techniques have been discussed to reduce the calories in dishes. In brief, the following are key strategies that can be employed to meet diners' demand for low-calorie, tasty menu fare.

1. Cut calories in recipes by reducing the most concentrated source of them—fat—and omitting the empty calories from sugar and alcohol.
2. Offer foods low in fat and sugar but high in water like bottled waters, vegetable juices, coffees, teas, broths, bouillons, and consommes.
3. Replace more caloric foods with low-fat, low-sugar, and low-calorie and high-water, high-fiber fruits and vegetables. They should be handled properly to retain their vitamins and minerals.

4. Cut calories in menu selections by reducing portion sizes, for example, serve open face or half sandwiches, thinly sliced bread, and a cup rather than bowl of soup.

5. Arrange smaller portions of high-calorie items so that they appear to be large and larger ones of low-calorie selections so that they receive all the appreciation they deserve.

6. Encourage dieters to order half portions, create main courses out of items from the appetizer menu, or to share selections.

7. Inform weight watchers of special services designed to help them adhere to their eating plans, such as dressings or sauces on the side, items cooked with no or less fat and low-calorie products offered.

8. Substitute reduced-calorie commercial products for more caloric ones only if they provide the qualities desired.

9. As a general rule, when creating or modifying recipes for weight reducers, limit the calories of entrees to 350 or less and appetizers or side dishes to 100 to 150.

Calorie Activities

1. Select the items from the list below that would likely be acceptable to a weight watcher trying to eat healthfully. Describe how the calories of the other items on the list could be reduced or maintained while increasing their nutritional value. See Appendix 9 for a sample of correct answers.

   A. Turkey Hot Dogs with Ketchup and Mustard on Wheat Buns

   B. Roasted Chicken and Mashed Potatoes Topped with Gravy

   C. Steamed Carrots Glazed in Honey

   D. Jumbo Bran Muffin Studded with Raisins and Coated with Margarine

   E. Granola Topped with Low-Fat Milk

   F. Egg White Omelet Filled with Sliced Avocados, Diced Tomatoes, and Onions

   G. Raisin Bread French Toast Topped with Melted Margarine and Maple Syrup

   H. Freshly Squeezed Orange Juice

   I. Linguini Tossed with Olive Oil, Parmesan Cheese, and Seafood

J. New England Clam Chowder with Whole Wheat Crackers

K. Grilled Quarter Pound Burger on Whole Wheat Bun Topped with Shredded Lettuce, Tomato Slices, and Thousand Island Dressing

L. Chef's Salad with Low-Fat Ranch Dressing

M. Wild Rice Pilaf with Bacon Bits, Toasted Almonds, and Sauteed Wild Mushrooms

N. Freshly Baked Apple Pie Topped with a Scoop of Low-Fat Frozen Vanilla Yogurt

DIRECTIONS

Complete the following activities with a specific operation in mind, ideally one you are currently involved with. See instructor to check your responses.

2. Identify the items on your menu that could be recommended to weight reducers.

3. Describe how five items on your menu could be modified to become acceptable to your calorie-conscious guests.

4. Explain how smaller portions of items concentrated in calories on your menu could be presented to appeal to calorie counters.

5. What are five new menu items that could be offered on your menu to appeal to weight watchers? They should be compatible with your restaurant's theme, price range, equipment, cook's abilities, etc.

6. What special services could your restaurant promote to attract dieters?

Freshly Prepared Spicy Tomato Cocktail

With everyone being so health conscious, this recipe is ideal at breakfast or brunch but equally as good for a nutritious pre-lunch or dinner cocktail. Offer it chilled in frosted stemmed glasses, garnished with a rib of crisp celery.

Servings: 24
Serving Size: 1 cup
Yield: 1 ½ gallons

Tomatoes, ripe, quarters   24 pounds
Water   1 pint
Onion, 2-inch pieces   2 pounds
Celery, coarsely chopped   1 pound
Carrots, washed, 1-inch pieces   1 pound
Bay leaves   2
Parsley sprigs   2 ounces
Garlic cloves, peeled   1 ounce
Worcestershire sauce, very low sodium   1 ½ tablespoons
Apple juice concentrate, unsweetened   1 tablespoon
Salt   To taste
Pepper, freshly ground   To taste
Hot pepper sauce   To taste

1. Simmer the tomatoes with the next 7 ingredients until the vegetables are very tender, or about 30 minutes.
2. Remove the bay leaves. Puree in a food processor or blender until smooth. Strain through a china cap, stirring and pressing to extract all but the very fibrous vegetable components. Discard the remaining vegetable pulp or reserve for another use. To adjust the consistency, add water to thin and reduce to thicken.
3. Season with the remaining ingredients. Serve warm or chilled garnished with lemon slices or celery sticks.

*The following nutrition analysis is based on the ingredients used in this recipe. It does not reflect that the pulp is strained from the cocktail before serving. As a result, likely the calories and nutrients are much less than the listed figures.

Servings	Calories	Protein (g/%)	Fat (g/%)	Cholesterol (mg)	Carbohydrates (g/%)	Fiber (g)	Sodium (mg)
1	125	4.8 g/13%	1 g/10%	0	27.9 g/77%	7.6	70.9

Hot Fudge Pudding Cake

There's no need to prepare a frosting for this low-fat, low-cholesterol chocolate cake. During baking, a creamy fudge pudding forms on the bottom of the cake. Upon inverting it becomes the cake's delicious topping.

Servings: 24
Serving Size: 3 × 3⅓-inch piece
Yield: 1 12 × 20 × 2-inch counter pan

Sugar, granulated   1 pound
Margarine, unsalted, corn oil   4 ounces
Milk, nonfat   1 pint
Vanilla extract   1 tablespoon
Flour, cake   1 pound
Cocoa powder (divided)   4½ ounces
Baking powder   1 ounce
Walnuts, chopped   4 ounces
Vegetable cooking spray, butter-flavored
Sugar, brown   1¼ pounds
Water, boiling   1¾ quarts

1. In a mixing bowl, cream the granulated sugar and margarine.
2. Add the milk and vanilla extract; mix well.
3. Sift the flour, 1½ ounces of the cocoa, and baking powder into another bowl. Add to the sugar-margarine mixture, mix well.
4. Stir in the walnuts. Pour the batter into a 12 × 20 × 2-inch counter pan coated with cooking spray.
5. Mix the brown sugar and remaining 3 ounces of cocoa together; sprinkle over the batter.
6. Pour the boiling water over the batter. Bake in a 350° F (175° C) oven until the cake springs back when touched lightly, or about 45 minutes. Cool the cake. Cut the cake 4 × 6 into 24 3 × 3⅓-inch pieces. Serve upside down with the hot fudge sauce spooned over the cake.

Servings	Calories	Protein (g/%)	Fat (g/%)	Cholesterol (mg)	Carbohydrates (g/%)	Fiber (g)	Sodium (mg)
1	314	4 g/5%	9.6 g/26%	0.8	57.4 g/69%	2	212

Sweet Potato Patties with Hints of Orange

Soft on the inside and crisp on the outside, the natural sweetness of these low-fat, beta carotene (vitamin A) patties is accented with hints of orange and nutmeg. Unlike most croquettes, these are coated with wheat flake cereal crumbs and browned in a nonstick skillet or baked on a sheet pan rather than deep fried.

Servings: 24
Serving Size: 2 patties
Yield: 48 patties

Sweet potatoes, cooked without salt, peeled, mashed   4 pounds
Flour, whole wheat   4 ounces
Sugar, brown   4 ounces
Orange zest, finely grated   2 tablespoons
Nutmeg, freshly ground   2 teaspoons
Salt   To taste
Wheat flake cereal, crumbs   6 ounces
Vegetable cooking spray, butter-flavored

1. In a bowl, mix the sweet potatoes, flour, sugar, orange zest, nutmeg, and salt. Refrigerate until chilled.
2. Shape the sweet potato mixture into 48 small (1½-ounce) patties.
3. Place the cereal crumbs in a container for dredging.
4. Dip the patties into the cereal crumbs to evenly coat.
5. Coat a nonstick skillet with cooking spray. Place over medium heat until hot. Add the patties in batches; cook until brown on each side and heated through, or about 4 minutes per side. The patties can also be baked on a sheet pan coated with cooking spray in a 350° F (175° C) oven, turning once. Serve as a vegetable side dish with meat, fish, and poultry dishes or as an appetizer course.

Servings	Calories	Protein (g/%)	Fat (g/%)	Cholesterol (mg)	Carbo-hydrates (g/%)	Fiber (g)	Sodium (mg)
1	139	2.6 g/7%	0.5 g/3%	0	32.3 g/90%	3.6	79.4

Chicken Brown Rice and Vegetable Soup Flavored with Curry

When planning your "weight watchers" specials, begin with a cup of this or another light soup. Studies show that a cup of soup before a meal slows the rate of eating and fills the stomach.

Servings: 24
Serving Size: 1 cup
Yield: 1½ gallons

Chicken, breasts, skinless   3 pounds
Sachet:
    Bay leaf   1
    Thyme, dried   ¼ teaspoon
    Peppercorns   ⅛ teaspoon
    Parsley stems   6
    Cloves, whole   2
Rich White Chicken Stock (see page 78)   1½ gallons
Onions, coarsely chopped   8 ounces
Carrots, coarsely chopped   4 ounces
Celery, coarsely chopped   4 ounces
Vegetable cooking spray
Onions, minced   1½ pounds
Garlic, minced   1½ teaspoons
Curry powder   2 tablespoons
Red pepper, ground   To taste or ⅛ teaspoon
Carrots, washed, small dice   12 ounces
Peas, fresh, shelled, or frozen   12 ounces
*Brown rice, long-grain, cooked without salt   1½ pounds
    (7 ounces as purchased)
Milk, evaporated, skim   1 quart
Lemon juice, freshly squeezed   2 teaspoons
Salt   To taste
Pepper, freshly ground   To taste

1. Place the chicken, sachet, and stock in a sauce pot. Heat to a boil. Reduce the heat to low; simmer until the chicken is tender, or about 45 minutes. In the final 20 minutes of cooking add the onions, carrots, and celery. Skim the froth as needed.
2. Remove the chicken from the broth. Remove the bones from the chicken; discard. Cut into medium dice; set aside.
3. Strain the stock. Discard the sachet. Skim the fat from the

broth. Puree the vegetables in a food processor or blender until smooth. Return to the stock.

4. Coat a nonstick skillet with cooking spray. Place over medium heat until hot. Add the minced onions and garlic; cook until tender without browning. Add the curry powder and red pepper; cook a few minutes longer.

5. Add the onion mixture to the broth. Simmer until tender and the flavor is mellowed, or about 15 minutes.

6. Add the diced carrots and peas (if fresh); simmer until tender, or about 10 minutes.

7. Stir in the chicken, brown rice, peas (if frozen), and evaporated milk. Heat through.

8. Blend in the lemon juice and salt and pepper to taste. Serve as an appetizer or main course offering with whole grain biscuits, tortillas (no lard), or bread sticks.

*Boiled brown rice—place 7 ounces of brown rice in 2⅓ cups of water. Heat to a boil. Stir. Cover and cook over low heat until done, or about 45 minutes. Cook a few minutes longer if necessary.

Servings	Calories	Protein (g/%)	Fat (g/%)	Cholesterol (mg)	Carbo-hydrates (g/%)	Fiber (g)	Sodium (mg)
1	178	22.2 g/51%	2.5 g/12%	32.8	15.8 g/37%	2.4	169

Ranch-Style Chip Dip

While the flavor and creaminess of this dip mirrors that of typical mayonnaise- and sour cream-based chip dips, its fat and cholesterol content is substantially less. It can be prepared by blending nonfat sour cream with chopped green onions, minced garlic, and fresh herbs.

Serve this dip with raw vegetables or chips such as roasted Idaho potato chips.

Servings: 24
Serving Size: 1⅓ tablespoons
Yield: 2 cups

Sour cream, nonfat   1 lb
Lemon juice, freshly squeezed   2 teaspoons
Green onions, chopped, reserve tops for garnish   3 ounces
Parsley, minced   3 tablespoons
Garlic, minced   2 teaspoons
Basil, minced or dried   1½ teaspoons or ½ teaspoon
Oregano, minced or dried   1½ teaspoons or ½ teaspoon
Tarragon, minced or dried   ¾ teaspoon or ¼ teaspoon
Salt   To taste
Pepper, freshly ground   To taste

1. Mix the sour cream with all the remaining ingredients in a storage container.
2. Chill to blend the flavors, at least 3 hours.
3. Slice the green onion tops thin. Sprinkle over the dip.

Servings	Calories	Protein (g/%)	Fat (g/%)	Cholesterol (mg)	Carbo-hydrates (g/%)	Fiber (g)	Sodium (mg)
1	14	1.4 g/36%	.02 g/1%	0	2.5 g/62%	0.1	14.2

Barley Risotto with Exotic Mushrooms and Spinach

Italian risotto is a classic dish made with special varieties of short-grain rice, most commonly arborio. As the rice simmers, it is constantly stirred so that it gradually absorbs its cooking broth and releases starch. The finished dish is a creamy mixture, wonderful as a first or main course, or as an accompaniment to meat, seafood, or poultry entrees. For an innovative touch with a slightly more chewy texture, the traditional rice has been replaced with barley in this recipe.

Serve as an appetizer, starch accompaniment with poultry, fish, or meat such as sauteed beef sirloin steak with red pepper tomato sauce, and vegetable, perhaps steamed green beans or zucchini sauteed with garlic and seasoned with fresh herbs, or as an item on a vegetable plate.

Servings: 24

Serving Size: ⅔ cup

Yield: 1 gallon

Vegetable cooking spray, olive-flavored

Mushrooms, shiitake, fresh, cleaned, sliced, stems removed and reserved for another use 1 ¼ pounds

Shallots, minced 4 ounces

Garlic, minced 1 ½ tablespoons

Wine, dry, white 1 cup

Barley, pearl 1 ½ pounds

Flavorful Vegetable Stock (see page 224) or Rich White Chicken Stock (see page 78) 2 ½ quarts

Spinach leaves, fresh, chopped, washed 8 ounces

Salt To taste

Pepper, freshly ground To taste

Parmesan cheese, freshly grated, part-skim milk Optional (8 ounces)

1. Coat a saucepan with cooking spray. Place over medium heat until hot. Add the mushrooms. Saute until light brown, or about 5 minutes. Transfer to a container using a slotted spoon.
2. Add the shallots and garlic to the pan; cook until tender, or about 5 minutes.
3. Add the wine. Increase the heat to a boil; cook until slightly syrupy. Reduce the heat to medium-low; add the barley and mushrooms.

4. Meanwhile, in another saucepan, heat the stock to a boil. Reduce the heat to low; keep at a low simmer while cooking the risotto.

5. Slowly add 1 pint of the hot stock to the barley, stirring constantly. Continue to stir, allowing the barley to simmer. When the stock has been absorbed, slowly add another pint of stock. Simmer, stirring frequently, until all the liquid has been absorbed. Add a third pint of stock following the same procedure.

6. Stir in the spinach. Continue slowly adding the remaining stock, 1 pint at a time, stirring and cooking until all the liquid is absorbed and the barley is slightly creamy and tender. If the mixture is too wet in the end, increase the heat slightly. If additional liquid is needed, add more stock.

Servings	Calories	Protein (g/%)	Fat (g/%)	Cholesterol (mg)	Carbo-hydrates (g/%)	Fiber (g)	Sodium (mg)
1	123	3.6 g/11%	0.5 g/3%	0	27 g/85%	5.3	20.5

7

Making Magic with Recipe Modifications

Recipe "Makeovers"

Nearly every menu has dishes that are bogged down with unnecessary fat, cholesterol, or calories, could use a boost of starch or fiber, or are suffering from a sodium or sugar overdose, or worse yet, vitamin or mineral malnourishment. Chapters 1 through 6 have described ingredient substitutions and cooking techniques that can take care of these ailments and still serve up great taste.

In the following pages, 10 homestyle, traditional recipes (from my Mom's recipe file) will receive nutritional "makeovers" to address these concerns. Each of the 10 traditional recipes is presented

in its original form followed by a description of adjustments in ingredients and cooking methods that can reduce the recipe's total fat, saturated fat, cholesterol, sodium, or calories or increase its complex carbohydrates. Taste is always the foremost consideration.

These 10 recipe "makeovers" are designed to illustrate the principles of creating healthy cuisine. Studying these examples and trying out the strategies recommended can help you to acquire the skills necessary to cook healthfully. Once you've mastered these and are ready to modify your own traditional favorites, the following steps are recommended.

Steps to Modify Recipes

1. Define the recipe's uses in the food service operation. This is significant because the qualities desired may vary according to the role the selection plays in the menu. For example, the qualities diners expect in a soup served along with a sandwich at lunch may be different than those they expect in a soup when it's served as an appetizer course for dinner.

2. List the physical attributes of the dish produced in the traditional recipe. For example, one attribute of a cream soup might be its creamy consistency.

3. List the traditional recipe's nutritional strengths and weaknesses. For example, a weakness of a cream soup might be its high fat level and a strength might be its high protein content.

4. List the objectives to be achieved or the outcomes desired following the recipe's "makeover." These should include the physical characteristics and nutritional composition desired in the recipe (product) after it has been modified. Steps 1–3 should provide the basis for setting the objectives.

   For example, the outcomes desired in a recipe for a cream soup to be served along with a sandwich at lunch might include a creamy consistency with less than 30% of its calories from fat.

5. List the possible ingredient substitutions and/or changes in cooking methods that could be made to achieve the objectives listed in step 4. These strategies should yield a product with the nutritional composition and physical characteristics specified in the objectives.

   For example, a traditional recipe for cream soup might be modified by replacing its whole milk with evaporated skim milk and braise-deglazing its mushrooms in white wine rather than sauteing in butter.

6. Describe the anticipated results when each of the modifications suggested in step 5 are implemented either singly or in combination.

    For example, replacing whole milk with evaporated skim milk in the cream soup might cut the fat in the recipe from 50% to 40% while maintaining the soup's creamy consistency.

7. Create the action plan. From the strategies proposed in step 5 and their analysis in step 6, select the actions which singly or in combination with others will best produce the outcomes desired.

8. Try out the recipe modifications; evaluate the results. Does the modified recipe (product) meet the objectives set earlier in step 4? Were the outcomes desired achieved?

    Do not be disappointed if the first modification of the traditional recipe does not produce outstanding results. Even professionals who have much experience with healthy cooking will go through several recipe revisions before healthy dishes are created that meet the standards of their operations. But when they do, it's a win-win situation for everyone.

Modification Isn't for Every Dish

Finally, because a dish is high in fat, cholesterol, sugar, sodium, or calories and contains only small amounts of fiber, vitamins, or minerals does not make it bad and require that it be modified to be healthy. There are no good or bad foods. For example, flavored oils are almost 100% fat. This does not mean a garlic-flavored olive oil should not be offered along with a basket of whole grain breads. Moderation is what healthy eating is all about. A small portion or occasional serving of a high-cholesterol or high-fat dish like a flavored oil is acceptable on the healthy menu.

Further, some items simply do not lend themselves well to modification. Those selections in which it is difficult to modify the ingredients or cooking techniques and still maintain their integrity are ones in which the offending ingredient is the primary ingredient. Flavored oils are an example.

Other options to modifying dishes that do not meet specified nutritional standards are to create new, completely different, more healthy dishes to replace the unsatisfactory ones or promote nutrient-dense dishes already on the menu that can serve the purposes of the offending dishes. For example, as an alternative to the garlic oil, an item already on the menu such as a chunky Mediterranean mushroom dip might be offered.

1

Cream of Mushroom Soup

Yield: 6 servings

3 tablespoons butter
1 small onion, chopped
2 cups finely chopped mushrooms
2 tablespoons flour
5 cups chicken stock
Salt to taste
Pepper to taste
1 bay leaf
1 ½ cups scalded cream
2 tablespoons finely chopped parsley

1. Melt the butter in a saucepan. Add the onions and mushrooms; cover and cook gently for 5 minutes. Stir in the flour and continue cooking for another 2 minutes. Gradually add the chicken stock; bring to a boil, stirring. Add the salt, pepper, and bay leaf. Lower the heat, half cover; simmer for 20 minutes.
2. Before serving, remove the bay leaf and adjust the seasonings. Stir in the cream and top each bowl of soup with a sprinkle of parsley.

To reduce the saturated and/or total fat and/or cholesterol

1. Begin by replacing the butter to saute the onions and mushrooms with polyunsaturated margarine and reduce the amount from 3 tablespoons to 2 tablespoons. Better yet, omit the butter or margarine and simmer or braise-deglaze the onions and mushrooms in fat-free stock or dry white wine or cook them in a nonstick pan lightly coated with butter-flavored vegetable cooking spray. If no fat is used to cook the mushrooms and onions, a small amount of polyunsaturated margarine or butter might be melted over the soup at service for flavor.
2. To prevent the flour from lumping when using no fat or less fat, make a slurry by mixing the flour with a small amount of cold water. Add the slurry to the simmering stock while stirring. To remove the raw taste of the flour and enrich its flavor, brown it until golden without fat in the oven or in a nonstick pan on the range before mixing it with the cold water. Another low-fat option is to skip the flour and thicken with a puree of cooked vegetables.
3. Use less cream or replace it with a smaller amount of whole milk. Better yet, substitute evaporated, low-fat or skim milk, or low-fat or nonfat milk for the cream. For added flavor without fat, any of the reduced-fat milks might be enriched with nonfat milk powder. Be aware, nonfat milk powder does contain calories.
4. To enhance the soup's flavor without fat, replace the chicken stock with double strength, fat-free stock and finish with a splash of sherry. To accommodate nonmeat, seafood, and poultry eaters, the soup might be made with a double strength vegetable stock.
5. To further enhance the soup's flavor, replace the pepper with freshly ground white or black pepper and add a pinch of freshly ground nutmeg at service.
6. Flavor might also be added to the soup without fat by pureeing the chopped mushrooms and onions after simmering in the broth for 20 minutes; straining the soup through a china cap while pressing the flavors from the vegetables; discarding the vegetables; and simmering fresh, thinly sliced mushrooms and chopped onions, braise-deglazed in dry white wine or fat-free broth another 20 minutes in the soup before finishing with a reduced-fat milk of choice or less whole milk or cream.
7. See number 3 below under *To reduce the calories.*

To reduce the salt/sodium

1. Replace the raw butter with unsalted or clarified butter or unsalted or clarified margarine. Vegetable oil does not provide sodium but will not add the flavor of butter or margarine.
2. Omit or reduce the salt. For flavor without salt or high-sodium ingredients, replace the stock with double strength stock prepared in house without salt and finish the soup with a splash of drinking sherry. Salt is added to cooking sherry. A commercial low-sodium stock or broth might be used, but it will contain more sodium than a double strength, unsalted one prepared in house and likely not have its flavor or body. Sugar or one of its forms is added to some commercial, low-sodium stocks.
3. Additionally, to enhance the flavor of the soup without salt or high-sodium ingredients, see numbers 5 and 6 above under *To reduce the saturated and/or total fat and/or cholesterol*.

To increase the fiber and/or complex carbohydrates

1. Double the number of mushrooms and onions in the soup, replacing the onions with the milder-flavored shallots.
2. Serve the soup with high-fiber crackers or breadsticks or a basket filled with assorted whole grain breads and rolls or ones enriched with seeds, nuts, fruits, and/or vegetables.

To enhance presentation of the soup

1. Replace the chopped mushrooms in the soup with thinly sliced mushrooms (see number 6 above under *To reduce the saturated and/or total fat and/or cholesterol*).
2. Present the soup in a richly colored or attractively decorated, wide-rimmed soup plate and place on a complementary underliner.
3. Garnish the soup with compatible edible ingredients carefully cut and arranged, such as three thinly sliced, braise-deglazed mushroom slices overlapped in a row down the soup's center and sprinkled with finely minced parsley, or bright red, ground paprika.

To reduce the calories

1. See the suggestions above under *To reduce the saturated and/or total fat and/or cholesterol* and those under *To enhance presentation of the soup*.
2. A few calories might be cut by thickening the soup with 1 tablespoon of cornstarch rather than the 2 tablespoons of flour. Because of cornstarch's higher starch level, one-half the amount of cornstarch is required to provide comparable thickening. Be aware though, because cornstarch lacks the protein of flour, flavor will be lost when cornstarch is substituted for it. Given the strength of the other flavors in the soup, the difference will be insignificant. If cornstarch is used, it should be stirred into the soup at the end of cooking mixed with cold water or stock (slurry). It breaks down with extended heating.
3. Another method to cut calories is by reducing the soup's portion size.

To compensate for the soup's smaller portion, the portion size of low-calorie items elsewhere in the meal might be increased or the meal supplemented with additional low-calorie foods such as sliced cucumbers sprinkled with freshly squeezed lemon juice or a stir fry of Asian vegetables cooked in a nonstick skillet and seasoned with reduced-sodium soy sauce.

2

Rice Salad

Yield: 8 servings

Salad:
1 cup cooked long-grain rice
1 ¼ cups drained canned corn
1 cup boiled green beans
2 celery ribs, chopped
1 green pepper, chopped
4 tomatoes, skinned, seeded, chopped

Dressing:
1 tablespoon Dijon mustard
2 tablespoons boiling water
⅔ cup olive oil
2 tablespoons chopped parsley
Salt to taste
Pepper to taste

1. Place the rice and corn in a bowl. Stir to mix. Stir in the beans, celery, and green pepper. Add the tomatoes last. Cover and chill until required.
2. Put the mustard in a small mixing bowl; beat in the water gradually. Then add the oil, drop by drop, beating until the dressing is thick. Stir in the chopped parsley and salt and pepper to taste. Chill until required.
3. Pour the dressing over the salad; fold in, being careful not to break the vegetables. Serve.

To reduce the total and/or saturated fat and/or cholesterol

1. Replace the dressing with a commercial low-fat, low-cholesterol dressing or prepare one in house (see number 2 following). The dressing should supply the vibrant flavors needed to awaken the subtle characteristics of the salad. The dressing should complement and blend with not mask the salad ingredients.
2. When creating low-fat, low-cholesterol salad dressings, it can be difficult to find low-fat, low-cholesterol ingredients with attributes similar to those in traditional high-fat and cholesterol versions. Egg yolks and oil are examples. Rather than attempting to simulate the original dressings, another option is to develop reduced-fat and cholesterol dressings which complement the salad ingredients but with characteristics (i.e. flavor, consistency) different from those in the original dressings.

   For example, part of the oil in salad dressings might be replaced with low-fat or nonfat yogurt, a naturally low-fat soft cheese, fruit or vegetable puree, juice or juice concentrate, reduced-fat tofu, assertive vinegar, reduced, double strength stock and/or a combination of these. Whatever oil is added in the dressing, it should have a rich flavor.

   As discussed in Chapter 1, for body without fat, salad dressing can be thickened by cooking with arrowroot or cornstarch slurries or blending with smooth purees of soft or cooked fruits or vegetables. To compensate for flavor loss, small amounts of high-fat ingredients like tahini (sesame paste) can be added along with low-fat flavoring agents, including condiments like reduced-sodium soy sauce, sugar or sweet syrups like honey, seasoning vegetables like minced gingerroot, liqueurs like hazelnut, wines like champagne, freshly minced herbs like dill, and/or freshly ground spices, roasted if appropriate, such as cumin.

   In this case, rather than making the dressing from nearly all oil, begin with a base of freshly squeezed orange juice and reduced, double strength, fat-free, chicken stock made in house. To accommodate vegetarians, use a reduced, double strength vegetable stock. Thicken the liquids by simmering briefly with an arrowroot or cornstarch slurry. Chill the thickened liquids and blend in a small amount of unsweetened orange juice concentrate. This will intensify the orange flavor of the dressing and add a light sweetness. Flavor this mixture with Dijon mustard, minced green onions and garlic, grated orange zest, salt, freshly minced green herbs like tarragon and basil, and a small amount of white wine vinegar and extra virgin olive oil.

3. Another method to cut the salad's fat is to reduce the amount of high-fat dressing and extend it with a low-fat liquid such as reduced, fat-free, double strength stock.

4. To increase the salad's flavor without fat, replace the canned corn with fresh or frozen corn. Further, the flavor of all the vegetables in the salad might be intensified without fat by roasting or grilling them. The bell pepper, tomatoes, and celery can be roasted or grilled raw. The beans and corn should be blanched first.

5. For other methods to heighten flavor without fat, see number 1 below under *To increase the fiber and/or complex carbohydrates*, number 4 under *To reduce the salt/sodium*, and number 2 under *To reduce the calories*.

To increase the fiber and/or complex carbohydrates

1. Replace the refined rice with brown basmati (extra long grain) rice or other whole grain, possibly bulgur or barley.
2. Retain the peel and seeds in the tomatoes.
3. Increase the serving size of the salad. The salad's vegetables and rice are rich in fiber, not the dressing.

To reduce the salt/sodium

1. Steam or boil the rice or other grain used and green beans in unsalted water or salt-free, double strength stock made on premise.
2. Rinse the canned corn with water or replace with fresh or frozen corn cooked without salt.
3. Omit the salt in the dressing and salad completely. To produce maximum flavor with a small amount of salt, sprinkle it over the salad at service.
4. Add flavor to the dressing without salt or other high-sodium ingredients by seasoning with additional freshly minced herbs like summer savory, marjoram, and cilantro, freshly ground spices like clove berries or pink peppercorns, or diced vegetables like green or red bell peppers.
5. Do not alter the amount of Dijon mustard used in the recipe. While prepared mustard contains sodium, the recipe calls for only 1 tablespoon.
6. Replace the pepper with freshly ground pepper.
7. See number 3 above under *To reduce the total and/or saturated fat and/or cholesterol*.

To reduce the calories

1. See the suggestions above under *To reduce the total and/or saturated fat and/or cholesterol*.
2. Reduce the portion size of both the salad and dressing. For a visually pleasing presentation, mound on a bed of lettuce and attractively arrange some of the salad's neatly cut vegetables on top or garnish with fresh herbs or colorful flowers like nasturtiums.

3

Chicken Crisps

Yield: 2 servings

2 tablespoons butter
2 tablespoons flour
1 cup milk
8 mushrooms, sliced
1 tablespoon butter
8 ounces cooked chicken, diced
½ cup canned, drained peas
Salt to taste
Pepper to taste
5 thick slices white bread
1 cup oil
1 tablespoon butter
1 tablespoon chopped parsley

1. Melt the 2 tablespoons of butter in a saucepan; blend in the flour. Gradually add the milk, heating to a boil and stirring. Boil for 3 minutes. Cool slightly.
2. Cook the mushrooms in the 1 tablespoon of butter until tender. Mix in the chicken and peas. Add this mixture to the white sauce; season with salt and pepper; heat through; keep warm.
3. Remove the crusts from 4 slices of the bread. With a small cutter, cut 4 crescent-shaped pieces from the fifth slice. Heat the cup of oil in a saucepan; add the 1 tablespoon of butter. When foaming, fry the bread slices until golden on both sides. Also fry the 4 small crescents. Drain on paper towels.
4. Arrange the fried squares on serving plates. Spoon the hot chicken mixture onto the squares; decorate with the crescents and chopped parsley.

To reduce the saturated and/or total fat and/or cholesterol

1. Replace the 2 tablespoons of butter blended with the flour to make the roux with polyunsaturated margarine. A large reduction in the polyunsaturated margarine, butter, or other fat is not an option if a roux is to be made. The purpose of the fat in the roux is to separate the flour's starch granules. If there is not adequate fat to perform this function, lumps will form in the sauce and it won't get thick.
2. To thicken the sauce when using no or less fat, blend the milk with a puree of cooked vegetables like mushrooms, carrots, corn, and onions braise-deglazed in fat-free stock or stir a flour, cornstarch, or arrowroot slurry into the warm milk. Make the slurry by mixing the flour or other starch with a small amount of the cold milk or water. If thickening with a flour slurry, remove the raw taste of the flour and enrich its taste before mixing with the cold liquid by roasting without fat and with low heat until golden in the oven on a sheet pan or cooking on the range in a nonstick pan. If no fat is used in the sauce, melt a small amount of butter or polyunsaturated margarine on top of the sauce at service for flavor.
3. Rather than frying the bread in oil and butter, toast it until golden brown. Better yet, grill the bread on a lightly oiled grid for a smoky flavor as well as crisp texture.
4. Replace the whole milk with low-fat or skim evaporated milk or low-fat or nonfat milk, a combination of skim evaporated milk and fat-free, double strength chicken stock, or simply double strength, fat-free chicken stock. Nonfat milk powder might be added to any of the reduced-fat milks to enrich their flavor without much fat.
5. Use breast meat for the chicken; cook it without fat by grilling, broiling, simmering, baking, or poaching; and remove the chicken's skin before dicing.
6. Reduce the portion of chicken from 4 ounces cooked per serving to

3 ounces or less. To compensate for the loss, increase the mushrooms from 4 to 6 or more per serving and the peas from 4 to 6 tablespoons or more per serving.

7. To add flavor without fat, replace the canned peas with fresh or frozen peas and the white bread with a more interesting bread like cracked wheat and oat English muffins.

8. Rather than sauteing the mushrooms in butter, braise-deglaze them in dry white wine or fat-free stock.

9. Replace the cultivated mushrooms with part or all exotic ones. They will intensify flavor and add interest to the soup. For example, in the case of shiitakes, they will add a bosky flavor to the soup, while morels add an earthy-smoky-nutty flavor.

To increase the complex carbohydrates and/or fiber

1. Replace the white bread with a high-fiber one like multigrain bread, a whole grain like basmati (extra long grain) brown rice or barley, or a whole grain pasta like whole wheat fettuccine.

2. Increase the quantity of peas and mushrooms in the dish and supplement with nuts like toasted, slivered almonds. If fat and calories are of concern too, skip the nuts. Chicken is not a source of fiber. If its portion is reduced this will not affect the fiber content of the dish.

3. Thicken the sauce with a vegetable puree or whole white wheat flour (see page 101) roux or slurry instead of a refined wheat flour roux or slurry.

To reduce the salt/sodium

1. Rinse the canned peas with water or replace with fresh or frozen ones cooked without salt.

2. Omit the salt in the dish completely or sprinkle a small amount over at service. Diners' first bite will have a great impact on their perceptions of the dish.

3. Cook either fresh or fresh frozen chicken without salt. Don't use canned or precooked chicken. It likely has added sodium.

4. Replace the milk with unsalted, double strength chicken stock made on premise and finished with a small amount of cream or add flavor to the white sauce without salt by simmering with an onion pique (a small peeled onion with a bay leaf attached by a clove). Remove the onion pique before serving.

5. Finish the sauce with freshly ground nutmeg and black or white pepper and a splash of drinking sherry, not cooking sherry. It contains salt.

6. Replace the raw butter with unsalted or clarified butter or unsalted or clarified polyunsaturated margarine.

To reduce the calories

1. See the suggestions above under *To reduce the saturated and/or total fat and/or cholesterol.*

2. Replace the thick bread with thin or reduced-calorie bread or a

smaller portion of another grain product (preferably whole grain for fiber).

3. Calories can also be reduced by reducing the size of the entire portion. For adults trying to monitor their calories as well as eat healthfully, the portion of chicken crisps served after implementing the suggestions under *To reduce the saturated and/or total fat and/or cholesterol* is reasonable as a main course.

4

Veal Stew

Yield: 4 servings

2 pounds veal breast
4 tablespoons butter
1 onion, quartered
3 carrots, cubes
2 tablespoons flour
3 cups chicken stock
3 parsley stems
1 bay leaf
⅛ teaspoon dried thyme
12 button mushrooms
12 canned, drained pearl onions
1 cup cream
2 egg yolks
½ teaspoon lemon juice
Salt and pepper to taste
1½ pints buttered and seasoned
     mashed potatoes

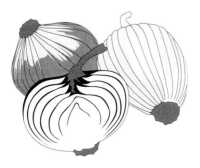

1. Cut the veal into about 1¼-inch cubes. Put into a saucepan with enough cold water to cover and a little salt. Bring to a boil; cook for 5 minutes. Skim off the scum that rises to the surface. Drain the meat; wash well with cold water. Dry.
2. Melt 3 tablespoons of the butter in a pan; cook the veal cubes slowly together with the quartered onion and carrots, shaking frequently and not allowing them to brown at all. Stir in the flour; add the stock, stirring to blend. Add the parsley, bay leaf, and thyme. Bring to a boil; simmer for 1–1½ hours or until the veal is tender.
3. Melt the remaining 1 tablespoon of butter in a saute pan; cook the mushrooms for a few minutes. Add the pearl onions.
4. Remove the saucepan with the veal from the range; place the meat in another dish, adding the carrots, mushrooms, and pearl onions. Strain the cooking liquid; boil to reduce the quantity slightly. Remove from the heat; cool slightly. Beat the egg yolks with the cream in a small bowl; add a little of the heated sauce to this; strain into the sauce. Add the lemon juice. Do not boil. Season with salt and pepper. Pour over the meat and vegetables. Serve at once with the mashed potatoes.

To reduce the saturated and/or total fat and/or cholesterol

1. Reduce the veal to 1 pound for 4 servings. Trim the meat of any visible fat. Double the portion of carrots, mushrooms, and pearl onions to compensate for the loss. Cut the veal into ¾-inch cubes rather than 1¼-inch pieces to balance the larger quantity of vegetables.
2. Replace the cream with skim or low-fat, evaporated milk or low-fat or nonfat milk or double strength, fat-free, chicken stock. Whole milk is lower in fat than cream but still high in fat. Another option is to reduce the 1 cup cream to ½ cup and replace the 3 cups stock with 3 ½ cups double strength stock.
3. Omit the butter or replace with less butter or less polyunsaturated margarine (see numbers 5 and 6 following).
4. Omit the egg yolks; their primary function is to enrich the sauce.
5. Delete the first step—simmering the veal in water. This will prevent flavor loss. Rather, begin by braise-deglazing the veal in dry white wine or fat-free stock or browning in a nonstick skillet coated lightly with butter-flavored vegetable cooking spray. Browning the meat will add flavor without fat to the stew.
6. Rather than cooking the carrot cubes, mushrooms, and quartered onions in butter in steps 2 and 3, blanch the carrots and braise-deglaze the quartered onions and mushrooms in fat-free stock. Omit cooking the canned pearl onions. Add the carrots, pearl onions, and mushrooms to the stew a few minutes before serving. This will pre-

serve their crisp-tender texture, bright orange color, and garden-fresh flavor. Add the quartered onions to the stew as specified in the recipe. Their flavor will mellow as they simmer and flavor the sauce. For a fuller flavor, simmer celery and additional carrots with the meat and quartered onions. They will be discarded along with the quartered onions before serving the stew. Note, the carrots, mushrooms, and pearl onions (if fresh) to be served in the stew are best cooked separately.

7. For better flavor without fat, replace the canned pearl onions with fresh ones. Blanch them and add to the stew a few minutes before serving.
8. To thicken the sauce without butter, use a cooked vegetable puree, bread crumbs, or mix the flour with cold water to form a slurry. Stir the slurry into the stock and cook with the simmering meat. Before mixing with the cold water, remove the raw taste of the flour and enrich its flavor by cooking in a nonstick pan without fat over low heat, stirring, until golden.
9. See number 7 below under *To reduce the salt/sodium* for low-fat mashed potato cooking procedures but skip the unsalted butter or margarine.
10. See number 1 below under *To increase the fiber and/or complex carbohydrates.*

To reduce the salt/sodium

1. Delete the first step of simmering the veal in water. This will help retain flavor in the meat. Either way, skip the salt.
2. Replace the butter with clarified or unsalted butter or clarified or unsalted margarine. Oil is an option but lacks the flavor of butter or margarine.
3. Replace the chicken stock with double strength, unsalted stock made in house. A commercial, low-sodium stock or broth might be used, but it will contain more sodium than one prepared in house.
4. Rinse the canned pearl onions, or preferably, replace with fresh ones blanched without salt.
5. To preserve the vegetables' flavors and colors and prevent them from becoming overcooked, blanch the pearl onions (if fresh) and carrot cubes without salt. Simmer in the stew a few minutes before serving.
6. Omit the salt or use less. If salt is to be added, sprinkle a small amount over the dish at service. To enhance the recipe's flavor, specify that the lemon juice be freshly squeezed. Season without salt or high-sodium ingredients by flavoring during cooking with a sachet of dried herbs and whole spices and near the end of cooking with freshly minced herbs like parsley, thyme, or tarragon, freshly ground spices or a spice blend like curry powder. Replace the pepper with freshly ground white or black pepper. Season with a pinch of freshly ground nutmeg if complementary herbs or spices are added with the pepper.
7. Prepare the mashed potatoes from fresh potatoes boiled without salt and seasoned with unsalted butter or unsalted polyunsaturated margarine, freshly ground pepper, a tad of freshly ground nutmeg or minced garlic or onions braise-deglazed in dry white drinking wine or salt-free stock. Cooking wine contains salt. Boiling the potatoes with

an onion pique (bay leaf attached to an onion with a clove) is another technique to heighten the potatoes' flavor without salt.

To increase the fiber and/or complex carbohydrates

1. Serve the stew with buttery flavored potatoes like yukon golds, mashed, boiled, or roasted with their skins; unrefined rice like brown; whole grain like quinoa; whole grain pasta like lupin fettuccine made with bean flour; or whole grain bread like oat and barley buns. If fat and/or salt are a concern also, omit these ingredients when preparing the accompaniments.
2. Increase the amount of carrots, mushrooms, and pearl onions in the stew. Wash rather than peel the carrots.
3. Thicken the stew with a puree of cooked vegetables like corn, carrots, onions, and mushrooms, whole grain bread crumbs like oat bran bread or a slurry or roux made from whole white wheat flour.

To reduce the calories

1. See the suggestions under *To reduce the saturated and/or total fat and/or cholesterol.*
2. Replace the buttered mashed potatoes with a whole grain or one of its products like a multigrain roll. While there will only be a small reduction in calories, the 6 to 11 servings recommended daily of grain products will be partially satisfied. If the vegetables are doubled in the stew to compensate for the reduced meat portion, they will provide 2 of the 3–4 servings of vegetables recommended daily.

5

Monte Cristo Sandwich

Yield: 4 servings

8 slices white bread
2 large eggs
½ cup milk
½ teaspoon salt
Pinch of pepper
8 ounces thinly sliced cooked chicken
4 ounces thinly sliced ham
4 ounces thinly sliced Gruyere cheese
4 teaspoons prepared mustard
¼ cup butter

1. Cut the crusts from the bread.
2. Beat the eggs, milk, salt and pepper together. Dip the slices of bread in the mixture; allow them to soak well, then drain.
3. Arrange the chicken on 4 slices of bread. Cover with the ham; top with the cheese. Spread the remaining slices of bread lightly with mustard. Cover the topping. Press down well.
4. Heat the butter in a frying pan. Fry the sandwiches until brown and crisp, turning once. Serve hot, cut in half.

To reduce the total and/or saturated fat and/or cholesterol

1. Replace the 2 eggs with 4 egg whites or a cholesterol-free egg substitute and the whole milk with low fat or skim, evaporated milk or low-fat or nonfat milk.
2. Replace the cooked chicken with skinless, breast meat cooked without fat.
3. Reduce the ham by half and replace with extra lean ham trimmed of fat and cooked without fat or low-fat, turkey ham.
4. Reduce the gruyere cheese by half. Grate and sprinkle it evenly over the ham. It is possible to replace the gruyere with a lower fat cheese like skim mozzarella or commercial low-fat Swiss cheese but there will be a critical loss of flavor.
5. Bake the sandwiches on a nonstick baking pan or one lightly coated with butter-flavored, vegetable cooking spray rather than frying in butter.
6. To compensate for the reduction in meat and cheese, another option is to serve the sandwiches cold, filled with smaller portions of the ham and cheese and minus the butter, eggs, and milk. Supplement with crisp vegetables like shredded lettuce, bean sprouts and bell pepper strips. Coat them lightly with a low-fat, low-cholesterol salad dressing.
7. Also, instead of serving the sandwich fried, the chicken might be layered with a reduced portion of ham and cheese on a grilled or toasted English muffin or bagel half; placed in a hot oven to melt the cheese and heat the meat through; and served topped with another toasted or grilled muffin or bagel half.
8. Add flavor without fat by replacing the white bread with a more interesting bread product like rye buns or fat-free corn tortillas.
9. See numbers 2 and 3 below under *To increase the fiber and/or complex carbohydrates*.

To increase the fiber and/or complex carbohydrates

1. Replace the white bread with a whole grain bread or one enriched with nuts, seeds, or vegetables, like oat and rye berry bread or barley bread with caraway seeds.
2. Add a layer of grilled vegetables (skin on) like zucchini, onions, and

bell peppers to a reduced portion of the chicken, ham, and cheese or in addition to the existing amount. Chicken, ham, and cheese add no fiber, so their amount does not affect its count.
3. Completely replace the chicken, ham, and cheese with a grilled vegetable medley, legume patty, or textured vegetable protein analog.

To reduce the salt/sodium

1. Replace the ham with reduced-sodium ham or meat smoked on premise without salt or sodium-containing ingredients. The meat to be smoked might be lean pork trimmed of fat, skinless turkey breast, or other low-fat meat or poultry if fat is a concern too.
2. Omit or reduce the amount of gruyere cheese. It is possible to replace it with a commercial low-sodium cheese, but there will be a loss in flavor.
3. Replace the butter with unsalted butter or unsalted margarine.
4. Soak the bread in eggs thinned with unsalted chicken stock made on premise, or use water rather than milk.
5. Omit the prepared mustard, reduce by half or replace with a sauce flavored with dry mustard or one made on premise without salt or other high-sodium ingredients. It might be a salt-free vinaigrette flavored with herbs and spices including mustard powder, or salt-free mayonnaise made on premise flavored with mustard powder.
6. Replace the pepper with freshly ground pepper.
7. To keep the sandwich flavorful and the sodium low, the chicken and ham might also be marinated in a low-sodium marinade. Chicken might be marinated before or after cooking, but the ham would work best if marinated after cooking. The marinade might be as simple as an herb vinaigrette.

To reduce the calories

1. See the suggestions above under *To reduce the total and/or saturated fat and/or cholesterol.*
2. Omit one slice of the bread and/or replace one or both slices with thinner and/or reduced-calorie bread.
3. Calories could also be cut by serving a half rather than whole sandwich accompanied by a low-calorie clear vegetable soup or green salad with a low-calorie dressing.

6

Braised Pheasant in Cream Sauce

Yield: 4 servings

2 2- to 3-pound pheasants cut into
    pieces
Salt to taste
Pepper to taste
2 tablespoons butter
1 tablespoon flour
1 pint heavy cream
½ cup white wine
1 cup sour cream

1. Season the pheasant pieces with salt and pepper. Melt the butter in a large frying pan. Add the pheasant and cook until brown on all sides. Add the flour. Stir to cook a few minutes. Stir in the cream, blending to mix. Simmer covered until tender, basting and turning the pieces often. Add more cream and butter as needed.

2. When done, remove the pheasant; set aside, keeping warm. Pour off the fat from the pan. Add the wine. Heat the sauce to a boil, stirring constantly. Let reduce slightly. Remove from the heat; add the sour cream; pour over the pheasant and serve.

To reduce the total and/or saturated fat and/or cholesterol

1. Replace the sour cream with low-fat or nonfat yogurt, low-fat or nonfat commercial sour cream or low-fat or nonfat sour cream made on premise from evaporated, skim milk or low-fat milk. If replacing the sour cream with 1 cup of yogurt, blend 1 tablespoon of cornstarch into the yogurt before mixing it into the sauce. This will help prevent it from curdling.

2. Omit the butter or replace with less butter or less polyunsaturated margarine. Another option is to brown the pheasant in a nonstick pan lightly coated with butter-flavored vegetable cooking spray. (See number 4 following.)

3. Replace the heavy cream with low-fat or skim evaporated milk, double strength, fat-free stock or half double strength, fat-free stock and half low-fat or skim evaporated milk. For added flavor without fat, the evaporated milk can be enriched with nonfat milk powder. Be aware, the milk powder does contain calories.

4. Remove the skin from the pheasants before or after preliminary browning. If the skin is to be removed before browning, the pheasant might be cooked by poaching or simmering in fat-free stock. This will add flavor while keeping the pheasant moist and juicy.

5. Simmer the pheasants in a chunky low-fat vegetable sauce like chunky Mediterranean-style sauce instead of the cream sauce.

6. Reduce the portion size of the pheasant from 4 pieces to 2 or 3 depending on the size of the birds (1½ pound, raw, skinless pheasant with bones should serve 4); or replace with 4-ounce portions of raw, skinless, boneless, breast meat only.

7. To thicken the sauce without fat, mix the flour with cold water until smooth to form a slurry. Blend it into the sauce after removing the pheasant. Prior to mixing with water, roast the flour on a sheet pan in the oven or in a nonstick pan on the range using low heat and no added fat, cooking until golden. Cooking will remove the raw taste of the flour and enrich its taste.

8. Prepare the pheasants by another cooking method using little or no

fat, like grilling, and accompany with a fat-free sauce like a tropical fruit salsa. Remove their skins before serving.

Another option is to roast the pheasants. Remove their skins and nap with their au jus, skimmed of fat, thickened with a cooked vegetable puree, and finished with a splash of madeira.

9. See numbers 2 and 4 below under *To reduce the salt/sodium* and number 3 below under *To increase the fiber and/or complex carbohydrates.* These are other methods to intensify flavor with little fat and/or cholesterol.

To reduce the salt/sodium

1. Skip the salt or sprinkle a small amount over each portion at service. Season the sauce with freshly minced herbs like thyme and/or additional spices, possibly a pinch of freshly ground nutmeg or curry powder.
2. For extra flavor, simmer seasoning vegetables (with or without spices) in the sauce and strain out before serving or finishing with sour cream. For example, minced, braise-deglazed onions and paprika might be reduced in white drinking wine (cooking wine contains salt), simmered in the sauce, and strained out before finishing with sour cream. Whether the sauce is made from unsalted stock, cream, milk, and/or sour cream, this flavoring method might be used.
3. Replace the butter with unsalted or clarified butter or unsalted or clarified margarine.
4. Replace the pepper with freshly ground pepper.
5. See number 5 above under *To reduce the total and/or saturated fat and/or cholesterol.*
6. Replace the heavy cream with unsalted stock made on premise. Further, omit the sour cream and replace with more of the stock-based sauce.

To reduce the calories

1. Reduce the wine separately by half to concentrate its flavors while eliminating its alcohol calories.
2. See the suggestions above under *To reduce the total and/or saturated fat and/or cholesterol.*
3. Calories might be reduced by decreasing the size of the entire portion. To compensate, the dish might be accompanied by a large portion of one or several low-fat vegetable dishes or a grain prepared with little or no fat.

To increase the fiber and/or complex carbohydrates

1. Serve the pheasant on a bed or base of unrefined rice like wild rice, whole grain like cracked wheat, whole grain pasta like whole wheat spaghetti noodles, a whole grain bread like multigrain crouton, or unpeeled, cooked vegetables like asparagus.
2. Braise the pheasant in a chunky vegetable sauce instead of the cream sauce.
3. Supplement the same or a reduced portion of the pheasant with

mushrooms and onions or add other types of vegetables like zucchini and corn. Pheasant contains no fiber.

4. Thicken the sauce with a cooked vegetable puree, whole grain bread crumbs, or a roux or slurry from whole wheat white flour (see page 101).

7

Minced Beef Curry

Yield: 6 servings

2 thick slices white bread
1 cup milk
3 small onions, chopped
2 tablespoons butter
2 tablespoons curry powder
2 pounds ground beef
1 teaspoon sugar
Salt to taste
¼ cup lemon juice
10 almonds
3 eggs
¼ cup strong beef stock
2 bay leaves
¼ cup chopped parsley

1. Soak the bread in ½ cup of the milk. Squeeze until dry, reserving the milk.
2. Fry the onions in the butter. Add the curry powder; fry for another minute. Add the meat, sugar, salt, lemon juice, and almonds. Beat the eggs; add half to the meat mixture. Whisk the other half into the remaining milk. Mix the soaked bread into the meat mixture thoroughly. Add the stock.
3. Put the meat mixture into a buttered casserole dish; smooth the top. Pour the egg and milk mixture over and add two bay leaves. Cook in a 350° F (175° C) oven for 30–40 minutes, or until set.
4. Remove from the oven. Remove the bay leaves. Decorate with chopped parsley. Serve with plain boiled rice and chutney.

To reduce the total and/or saturated fat and/or cholesterol

1. Reduce the serving size of the raw meat to 4 ounces per portion or divide the recipe into 8 rather than 6 servings.
2. Present the beef curry with larger portions of vegetable and/or starch dishes. Cut the meat into two thin slices and place overlapping one another mounded against the starch or vegetables. In order to form slices with the meat, shape it into a loaf before baking. These strategies will draw attention away from the reduced-portion size of the beef curry.
3. Replace the regular ground beef with extra lean ground beef, ground round (beef), ground lean veal, or ground, skinless turkey or skinless chicken breast meat.
4. Replace the 3 eggs with 6 egg whites or a cholesterol-free egg substitute.
5. Replace the whole milk with evaporated, skim or low-fat milk or low or nonfat milk. Another option is to soak the bread in ½ cup milk combined with ½ cup fat-free stock rather than the 1 cup of milk.
6. Omit the almonds; replace with vegetables like diced bell peppers or dried fruits like chopped dried apricots or a small amount of toasted slivered almonds attractively arranged on top (visibly) of the meat loaf.
7. Omit the butter. Brown the onions in a nonstick pan coated with butter-flavored vegetable cooking spray or braise-deglaze them in fat-free stock or red wine.
8. Refrigerate the beef stock and skim off the fat before using.
9. For fat-free meat extenders, see number 1 below under *To increase the fiber and/or complex carbohydrates*.
10. Bake the meat mixture in a special self-draining pan, a nonstick baking pan or one lightly coated with cooking spray.
11. Remove any fat accumulating during the cooking process from the beef curry.

To reduce the salt/sodium

1. Replace the butter with unsalted or clarified butter or unsalted or clarified polyunsaturated margarine. Vegetable or canola oil is acceptable but is less flavorful. Nut and olive oils can be very flavorful. They don't contain cholesterol like butter and are rich in monounsaturated fats. Either might be mixed with a blander vegetable oil or clarified butter.
2. Replace the stock with salt-free stock made on premise or commercial low-sodium stock. Commercial low-sodium stock contains more sodium than salt-free stock made on premise and likely is not as flavorful.
3. Soak the bread in water or unsalted stock made on premise rather than milk.
4. Replace the bread with low-sodium bread like cornbread leavened with eggs, low-sodium cereal like long cooking oats or one of the following high-starch ingredients cooked without salt: grains such as millet, rice like the reddish-brown waheni rice, legumes such as brown lentils or high-starch vegetables like corn or potatoes.
5. Omit the salt or sprinkle a small amount over the curry at service; add flavor by serving with a low-sodium sauce such as a spicy tomato chutney, or incorporating more seasoning vegetables like diced bell peppers or minced garlic and/or herbs like freshly minced cilantro into the curry.
6. For richer flavor without sodium, replace the white sugar with brown, prepare the curry powder in house from freshly roasted and ground spices, substitute toasted, slivered almonds, for the whole almonds and for fresher flavor without sodium, freshly squeeze the lemon juice.

To increase the fiber and/or complex carbohydrates

1. Replace the white bread with a larger portion of whole grains like triticale berries or their products like barley and rye bread, legumes like red lentils, or vegetables such as sweet potatoes. The ½ cup of milk required to soak the bread can be omitted if a bread product is not used. Milk like other animal products adds no fiber.
2. Blend diced vegetables like bell peppers or tomatoes or dried fruits like chopped dried peaches or golden raisins with the meat. More almonds, seeds or other nuts could be added to increase the curry's fiber content, but this will increase the fat content too.
3. Accompany the meat curry with a fruit or vegetable sauce like a cold mango and mint chutney.
4. Serve the meat with a whole grain or one of its products like whole wheat flat bread or quinoa pilaf rather than refined rice.
5. See number 2 above under *To reduce the total and/or saturated fat and/or cholesterol.*

To reduce the calories

1. See the suggestions above under *To reduce the total and/or saturated fat and/or cholesterol.*

8

Green Beans with Bacon

Yield: 4 servings

10 ounces frozen green beans
2 tablespoons butter
¼ cup chopped green onions
4 ounces chopped bacon
Salt to taste
Pepper to taste
¼ cup heavy cream
1 tablespoon chopped parsley

1. Cook the beans according to the package directions.
2. Meanwhile, melt the butter in a frying pan. Add the onions and bacon; fry until the onions are golden and the bacon pieces are crisp. Stir in the drained beans; season to taste with salt and pepper. Heat through, stirring constantly. Stir in the cream and parsley. Serve immediately.

To reduce the total and/or saturated fat and/or cholesterol

1. Skip the butter; instead, braise-deglaze the onions in fat-free stock and broil the bacon on a rack until crisp or pan broil it, removing the fat as it accumulates.
2. Replace the bacon with low-fat turkey bacon or lean ham or Canadian bacon trimmed of visible fat.
3. Reduce the amount of bacon or other meat and sprinkle over the beans at service. To compensate for less bacon or other meat, toss the green beans with sliced mushrooms, braise-deglazed in white wine or fat-free stock.
4. Omit the cream, reduce the amount, or replace with evaporated, low-fat or skim milk or double strength, fat-free stock.
5. To add flavor without fat, see numbers 1, 2, and 4 below under *To reduce the salt/sodium.*
6. Omit the cream, butter, and bacon and season with other low-fat ingredients like reduced-sodium soy sauce and/or braise-deglazed minced ginger, garlic, green onions, and/or sliced mushrooms.

To reduce the salt/sodium

1. Replace the frozen green beans with tender, fresh ones steamed or boiled without salt until al dente. The intent is to serve produce so naturally flavorful there will be less need for salt.
2. Replace the bacon with lean meat or poultry smoked on premise without salt or other high-sodium ingredients. If the choice is bacon or other high-sodium meat, reduce the amount and sprinkle it over at service. This will maximize its presence.
3. Replace the butter with clarified or unsalted butter or clarified or unsalted, polyunsaturated margarine.
4. Replace the pepper with freshly ground pepper.
5. Omit the cream, reduce the amount, or replace it with double strength, salt-free stock.
6. Omit the salt or sprinkle a reduced amount over the vegetables at service. It will be tasted immediately and its presence felt.
7. Rather than bacon and cream, combine the beans with flavorful, low-sodium ingredients like orange zest; dried cherries; toasted, unsalted pumpkin seeds or slivered almonds; minced garlic, chopped shallots or sliced mushrooms sauteed in unsalted butter; or chunky raw or cooked, fresh tomato and onion herb sauce.

8. Replace the parsley with more interesting freshly minced herbs like summer savory, tarragon, basil, or oregano or a combination of these herbs.

To increase the fiber and/or complex carbohydrates

1. Replace the bacon and cream with toasted nuts or seeds, sliced fruits or diced vegetables. For example, the beans might be tossed with a mixture of sauteed ginger and green onions and reduced-sodium soy sauce and sprinkled with toasted sesame seeds.
2. Increase the portion of the beans served.

To reduce the calories

1. See the suggestions above under *To reduce the total and/or saturated fat and/or cholesterol.*

9

Au Gratin Potatoes

Yield: 4 servings

2 tablespoons butter, softened
2 pounds potatoes as purchased,
*   peeled, sliced into thin rounds*
1 large onion, minced
1 pint grated Gruyere cheese
Salt to taste
Pepper to taste
⅔ cup heavy cream

1. Brush the bottom and sides of a casserole with part of the butter. Put a layer of potato slices, overlapping in the bottom of the casserole. Dot with more butter and sprinkle with some of the onion, cheese, and salt and pepper to taste. Pour over about ¼ of the cream. Continue with the layers until all the ingredients are used up, finishing with a layer of cheese and pouring the remaining cream over the top.
2. Cover; bake in a 375° F (190° C) oven for 1 hour, or until the potatoes are tender when pierced with a skewer. Broil for 5 minutes or until the top layer of cheese is brown and bubbling. Serve.

To reduce the total and/or saturated fat and/or cholesterol

1. Replace the heavy cream with evaporated, low-fat or skim milk, double strength, fat-free stock, or half double strength, fat-free stock and half cream or evaporated, low-fat or skim milk. Whole milk, but preferably low-fat or nonfat milk might also be substituted for the cream.
2. Another option to reduce the fat in the dish is to prepare a thin white sauce from nonfat milk. The roux used in the thickening of the white sauce will add some fat, but the end result will be a lower fat dish than if prepared with cream. If this procedure is followed, replace the ⅔ cup of cream with 1½ cups of nonfat milk. Add it to a white roux made from 2½ tablespoons of flour and 2 tablespoons of polyunsaturated margarine. Simmer the mixture with an onion pique (bay leaf attached to a peeled onion with a clove) for at least 15 minutes. Strain the sauce and season it to use.
3. When preparing the potatoes with a reduced-fat milk, a thick and creamy dish might also be produced by modifying the cooking technique. Begin by simmering the sliced potatoes and onions in low-fat or nonfat milk to cover until nearly soft, or about 30 minutes. In addition to the onion flavor, fat-free flavor might be added to the potatoes by simmering with seasonings such as freshly minced thyme or garlic. The seasonings should be selected to complement and reinforce the creamy cheese potato taste of the dish. Finally, bake the potatoes layered with the cheese and onions in a casserole dish until browned and crusty, or about 45 minutes at 375° F (190° C). This method will require more low-fat or nonfat milk than the recipe specifies of cream. The amount will vary depending on the type of milk used. For example, about 1 pint of low-fat milk could replace the ⅔ cup of cream listed in the recipe.
4. To enhance the flavor of reduced-fat milks with little fat, enrich them with nonfat milk powder. Be aware, the nonfat milk powder does contain calories.
5. Prepare the dish from buttery-tasting potatoes like yukon golds.
6. Bake the potatoes in a nonstick or other baking pan lightly coated with butter-flavored, vegetable cooking spray.

7. Reduce the amount of Gruyere cheese or replace it with an equal or smaller amount of skim mozzarella or a low-fat, commercial Swiss cheese. Sprinkle half of the cheese over the potatoes at the end of cooking so it melts over the top. Because the flavor of an aged natural cheese like Gruyere will taste better than a low-fat cheese, a smaller amount of the high-fat cheese is often a better choice than more of the lower fat cheese.

8. Omit the cheese or use less of any cheese and bake, topped with bread crumbs sprinkled with paprika and tossed with a small amount of polyunsaturated, melted margarine.

9. Replace the pepper with freshly ground white or black pepper and add a pinch of freshly ground nutmeg for additional flavor.

10. Make the potatoes into an entirely different dish calling for lower fat ingredients and cooking methods. For example, roast unpeeled baby new potatoes lightly coated with olive oil and sprinkled with fresh rosemary or steam the potato slices en papillotte with fresh Italian-style herbs.

11. See number 3 under *To increase the fiber and complex carbohydrates* below.

12. Reduce the portion size of the potatoes by increasing the recipe's yield from 4 to 6 servings.

To reduce the salt/sodium

1. Coat the baking pan with unsalted butter or margarine or vegetable oil.

2. Replace the Gruyere cheese with commercial, low-sodium Swiss cheese or use less of either melted on top of the potatoes.

3. Use less or no cheese layered in the potatoes and bake topped with unsalted bread crumbs coated with unsalted butter or unsalted polyunsaturated margarine.

4. Replace all or part of the heavy cream with double strength, unsalted stock made on premise.

5. Omit the salt or sprinkle less over the potatoes at service. Its presence will be felt more.

6. Season with freshly ground black or white pepper instead of ground pepper, a pinch of freshly ground nutmeg, and/or freshly minced, green herbs of choice like chives.

To increase the fiber and/or complex carbohydrates

1. Prepare the dish from unpeeled, red waxy or buttery flavored potatoes.

2. Bake the potatoes topped with a layer of whole grain browned bread, cereal or cracker crumbs.

3. Cook the potatoes in a chunky vegetable sauce like a spicy, hearty tomato, bell pepper and onion sauce rather than the cream sauce.

4. Increase the serving size of the dish.

To reduce the calories

1. See the suggestions above under *To reduce the total and/or saturated fat and/or cholesterol.*

10

Rice Pudding

Yield: 6 servings

½ cup raw rice
¼ cup sugar
½ teaspoon salt
1 quart milk
1 cinnamon stick
2 tablespoons butter

1. Put the rice, sugar, and salt in a buttered, shallow, ovenproof dish. Pour on the milk; add the cinnamon and butter.
2. Bake in a 275° F (135° C) oven until the pudding is soft and creamy, or about 3 hours. Stir frequently during the first hour of cooking. Remove the cinnamon stick. Serve from the baking dish.

To reduce the saturated and/or total fat and/or cholesterol

1. Omit the butter or replace with less butter or less polyunsaturated margarine melted over the pudding at service.
2. Replace the whole milk with evaporated, skim milk or low-fat milk. Enrich with nonfat milk powder if desired.
3. Bake the pudding in a nonstick baking dish lightly coated with butter-flavored, vegetable cooking spray.
4. To compensate for the loss of flavor due to less or no butter and a lower fat milk, blend dried fruits like raisins, currants, or dried cherries, cranberries, or diced apricots into the pudding, or top with a sweet, fat-free, cholesterol-free fruit sauce like a clear orange and cranberry or mixed berry sauce.
5. See number 2 below under *To reduce the calories*.

To increase the fiber and/or complex carbohydrates

1. Replace the refined rice with a whole grain rice like brown or a whole grain like cracked wheat. Adjust the pudding's cooking time accordingly.
2. See number 4 above under *To reduce the total and/or saturated fat and/or cholesterol*.
3. Increase the serving size of the pudding.

To reduce the refined sugar

1. Replace the table sugar with a smaller amount of brown sugar or unsweetened fruit juice concentrate, honey, or malt, maple, or rice syrup and a reduced amount of milk.
2. Serve the pudding warm or flavored with additional sweet spices like freshly ground nutmeg or extracts like vanilla. The perception of sweetness will be increased.
3. Replace part of the sugar by blending with dried, naturally sweet fruits or topping with a naturally sweet fruit sauce.

To reduce the calories

1. See the suggestions above under *To reduce the total and/or saturated fat and/or cholesterol* and *To reduce the refined sugar*.
2. Reduce the serving size of the pudding. To compensate for the reduced portion, garnish the pudding with attractively cut or whole, colorful,

high-fiber and high-water, low-calorie fruits like strawberries or flowers like violets or layer the pudding in a stemmed parfait glass with the fruit and place on a complementary plate liner. For a lovely presentation, the pudding might also be molded into an interesting shape, placed on a base of vibrantly colored fruit sauce like raspberry-orange and garnished with a fresh herb leaf like mint.

APPENDIX 1

Substitutes to Reduce the Total and/or Saturated Fat and/or Cholesterol

Dairy

Whipped cream
- Whipped, chilled, evaporated low-fat or skim milk
- Whipped tofu or skim ricotta cheese with a tad of oil, and if to be sweetened, honey and vanilla to taste
- Frozen low-fat or nonfat yogurt

Whole milk or half and half
- Evaporated low-fat or skim milk or low-fat or nonfat milk
- Reduced-fat milks enriched with nonfat milk powder

Ice cream
- Frozen, low-fat or nonfat yogurt, granita, sorbet, sherbert, or reduced-fat ice cream (ice milk) like layered raspberry, lime and orange sherbert parfait

Ice cream bars or cones
- Popsicles, frozen low-fat or nonfat yogurt sicles or sherbert or reduced-fat ice cream bars

Ice cream shakes or malts
- Fruit smoothies like banana strawberry whip or low-fat or nonfat yogurt or low-fat or nonfat frozen yogurt, sherbert, or reduced-fat ice cream (ice milk) shakes like peach melba shake

Coffee cream
- Milk prepared from triple strength nonfat dry milk powder
- Evaporated low-fat or skim milk

Sour cream
- Low-fat or nonfat yogurt (1 cup yogurt blended with 1 tablespoon cornstarch if to be cooked)
- "Lite" sour cream
- Low-fat or nonfat sour cream made on premise from skim, or low-fat evaporated milk, or low-fat or nonfat milk
- Low-fat or nonfat fresh cheeses like cottage or farmer whipped with lemon juice or low-fat or nonfat milk or low-fat or nonfat buttermilk

Whole milk cheeses like cheddar, Swiss, cream, and colby
- Less whole milk cheese but visible
- Part-skim mozzarella, pot, farmer, sapsago, or hoop cheeses
- "Lite" cream or neufchatel cheeses
- Low-fat or nonfat cheeses like cottage, ricotta or processed cheeses
- Fresh low-fat or nonfat cheeses made on premise like yogurt, paneer, or white cheeses

Meat, Seafood, Poultry, and Eggs

Dark poultry meat with skin
- Poultry breast meat with skin removed before or after cooking
- Poultry simulated textured vegetable protein products

Packaged chicken parts
- Packaged poultry meat labeled without skin

Duck, goose, or squab
- Duck, goose, or squab cooked without fat and served without skin like roast duck melon and mango salad
- Pheasant, quail, cornish game hen, or chicken cooked without fat and served without skin

Fried fish or chicken
- Lean fish or skinless chicken breast meat preferably:
  - baked with a low-fat crust, like skinless chicken breasts baked in ginger-flavored mashed sweet potatoes
  - roasted with seasoning agents like whole chicken roasted with lemon, garlic, and rosemary with skin removed before serving
  - grilled or broiled flavored with a dry rub or low-fat marinade like scallops marinated in a raspberry peppercorn glaze and grilled on skewers with vegetables

- poached in flavorful broth or wrapped in plastic with sea-sonings like monkfish poached wrapped in plastic with thyme, orange zest, fennel seeds, and Dijon mustard
- steamed or cooked in parchment like red snapper steamed with ginger, green onions, garlic, and low-sodium soy sauce
- simmered in flavorful stock skimmed of fat and later thickened with a fat-free starch slurry, bread or other crumbs or vegetable purees like blanquette of skinless chicken legs and mushroom caps braise-deglazed in madeira wine and served in reduced fat-free cooking juices thickened with a slurry of browned flour and finished with evaporated skim milk and a tad of butter
- Lean fish and skinless breast meat of chicken deep fried in veg-etable oil rather than hydrogenated vegetable oil (shortening)

Tuna packed in oil
- Tuna packed in water
- Fresh tuna cooked without fat

Prime grades of beef
- Lower grades of beef like choice or select

Regular ground beef
- Ground lean veal or skinless turkey or chicken breast meat
- Extra lean ground beef or ground round
- One of the above meats extended with grains, vegetables, bread or low-fat cracker crumbs, legumes, textured vegetable protein, or other very low-fat ingredients like meat loaf stud-ded with potato cubes and grated beets
- Ground beef analogs

Beef, pork, and lamb cuts
- Lean cuts of the listed meats trimmed of fat, cooked to no more than medium to prevent drying, marinated with low-fat mix-tures or dry rubs for flavor, or cooked by moist methods
- Veal and low-fat game, skinless white poultry, meat, or lean fish
- Reduced portion sizes of the listed meats served with more veg-etables and grains like lamb kebobs with mushrooms, red bell peppers and zucchini
- Dried bean, pea, or lentil selections like Egyptian fava bean patties or lentil and brown rice salad with green onions and to-matoes
- Beef or pork analogs

Bacon
- Low-fat turkey bacon or lean Canadian bacon or ham
- Less bacon but more visible

Cold cuts
- Fresh lean meat trimmed of fat and cooked without fat or skinless poultry breast meat cooked without fat

Whole eggs
- Two egg whites per whole egg
- Two egg whites and 1 whole egg per two whole eggs
- Cholesterol-free, fat-free egg substitute
- Leaven baked goods with yeast, baking powder or baking soda

Fats and Oils

Butter, lard, or shortening

In general use
- Whipped butter or polyunsaturated margarine
- Vegetable oil and butter blend
- Margarine (softest best)
- Poly- or monounsaturated oil (substitute ¾ tablespoon oil/ 1 tablespoon butter)
- Less butter or margarine but added at the end of cooking or browned first

As spread on bread products
- Jelly, jam, marmalade, honey, syrup, cinnamon and sugar, margarine or butter whipped with fruit puree and/or one of the previous sweeteners like strawberry butter
- Braise-deglazed, minced seasoning vegetables like glazed onions
- Roasted or grilled, flavorful vegetables like garlic
- Low-fat condiments like mustard, relish, or salsa
- Seasoned, whipped, low-fat or nonfat fresh cheese like farmer
- A flavorful oil, like extra-virgin olive, ideally extended with a flavorful vinegar like raspberry
- Spreads from vegetables or legumes like grilled eggplant and red pepper spread or from flavorful ingredients high in unsaturated fats like tapenade (olive) or tahini (sesame seed)

To prevent sticking in pans
- Ingredients simmered in liquids like stock or braise-deglazed instead of sauteed like wild mushroom leek compote
- Nonstick pans
- Vegetable cooking spray or vegetable oil sprayed from bottles

In cakes and baked goods
- Fruit purees like dried plum (prune)
- Light or dark corn syrup

- Fruit purees, fruit butters, and corn syrup with a small amount of oil

Flavoring on cooked vegetables
- Vegetables roasted or grilled for flavor like zucchini
- Freshly minced herbs and freshly ground spices or low-fat condiments like low-sodium soy sauce
- Butter or other flavored, vegetable cooking spray
- Butter substitute powder
- Small amounts of high-fat ingredients like toasted seeds or chopped browned nuts made visible

Salad dressings
- A splash of citrus juice, vinegar, and/or sprinkle of herbs and spices
- Dressings with oil reduced to 1–2 tablespoons/cup
- Assertive vinegars like balsamic and flavorful oils like macadamia nut in low-fat dressings
- Dressings extended with minced, raw, and roasted fruits and vegetables, their purees, juices, dried pulps, and juice concentrates, wines, liqueurs, sweet syrups, double strength stocks or low-fat condiments like chili sauce
- Dressings from low-fat or nonfat yogurt, cheese, milk, or buttermilk like herbed cottage cheese dressing
- Dressings in which oil is replaced with small amounts of mashed olives or anchovies, olive juice, tofu, black bean paste, or ground nuts
- Low-fat dressings with body from starches or fruit or vegetable purees
- High-fat dressings thinned with juice or stock
- Low-fat commercial dressings
- Reduced amounts of dressing sprayed on salads at service
- Low-fat salad dressings with vibrant flavoring agents like grated ginger or horseradish, minced garlic, or citrus zest
- Dressings offered on the side

Mayonnaise
- Low-fat or nonfat yogurt
- "Lite" commercial mayonnaise or other low-fat, low-cholesterol commercial or freshly prepared salad dressing
- Mayonnaise extended with low-fat ingredients like skim buttermilk
- Cholesterol-free and low-fat condiments like vinegar, chili sauce or pepper jam

- Blended tofu (high-fat, no cholesterol) or low-fat or nonfat fresh cheeses seasoned without fat
- Cold fruit or vegetable sauces like pineapple, papaya, onion, ginger, and cilantro salsa
- Salad dressing (thickened with starch not egg yolks so cholesterol-free but high in total fat)

Miscellaneous

Pan-fried, deep-fried, or sauteed ingredients
- Ingredients braised, poached, simmered, or boiled with fat skimmed from cooking liquids like poached eggs served on baked black bean patties with tomato jalepeno salsa
- Ingredients broiled, grilled, or roasted on racks or grids
- Ingredients baked, braise- deglazed, microwaved, or pan-broiled without fat and any formed during cooking removed
- Items baked coated in low-fat ingredients like zucchini slices baked coated in cereal crumbs like oat flakes for crisp crusts

High total and/or saturated fat and/or cholesterol crusts
- Pastries made with no or 1 crust like vegetarian pot pie topped with pastry cut outs
- Low-fat crumb, phyllo, bread, or meringue crusts like turkey tamale pie on cornbread crust
- Crusts with shortening, lard, butter, or margarine replaced with vegetable oil or frozen vegetable oil

Coconut
- Coconut extract
- Reduced amounts of freshly grated coconut toasted if appropriate to enhance flavor

Cream soups
- Clear soups filled with vegetables, grains, and small amounts of lean meat, seafood, or poultry like consomme brunnoise (very small diced vegetables)
- Cream-style soups prepared with low-fat or skim evaporated milk or low-fat or nonfat milk or low-fat or nonfat yogurt and thickened with vegetable purees or starch slurries like cream of potato and leek soup thickened with potato puree

Gravies and high-fat sauces
- Fruit and vegetable sauces like tomato ginger preserve
- Items flavored with low-fat marinades or dry rubs
- Sauces thickened with starch slurries, crumbs, vegetable purees,

or by reduction like cassoulet cooking broth thickened with cornbread crumbs
- Low-cholesterol and/or low-fat sauces finished with a tad of butter and/or polyunsaturated margarine
- Sauces prepared from fat-free stocks, wines, beers, liqueurs, or low-fat or nonfat milk, buttermilk, or yogurt like a red grape and zinfandel sauce
- Cooking juices reduced and skimmed of fat (refrigerate to solidify the fat and remove easily)

Frostings and high-fat toppings
- Fresh fruits, their purees or sauces or fruits baked on the bottom or top of cakes like peach upside down cake or gingerbread cake topped with bananas
- Frostings or toppings prepared with marshmallow creme, mostly sugar and little or no fat like powdered sugar and orange juice glaze, or an egg white base like meringue
- Hard candy chips like peppermints
- Sprinkle of confectioners', brown or granulated sugar mixed with sweet spices like cinnamon if appropriate
- "Light" sweet syrups
- Reduced amounts or no frostings or toppings
- Frozen low-fat desserts like nonfat frozen yogurt

Chocolate
- 3 tablespoons cocoa or carob powder and ¾ tablespoon vegetable oil or 1 tablespoon margarine for each ounce of chocolate like hot fudge (cocoa) pudding cake

Nuts or seeds
- Reduced amounts of nuts or seeds made visible, toasted to enhance flavor and chopped to spread further if appropriate
- Nugget-style cereals like Grape Nuts
- Dried fruits like currants and banana chips

Desserts with egg yolks
- Desserts made from egg whites like floating islands and angel cake
- Desserts made from fruits or primarily sugar without eggs like plum compote with caramel crackle

APPENDIX 2

Substitutes to Reduce Sodium/Salt

Meat, Meat Substitutes, and Cheese

Sardines, anchovies, caviar, herring, smoked salmon, salt cod, smoked trout, or other smoked, canned, cured, or pickled fish

- Fresh or fresh frozen fish, canned tuna, salmon or crab, or shell-fish cooked without salt like scallops poached in plastic with minced ginger, garlic and cilantro, grated orange zest, and a splash of drinking sherry
- Fish smoked or pickled on premise without salt or other high-sodium ingredients
- Canned, salt-free fish
- Smaller portions of the listed items made visible or served with larger ones of low-sodium grains or their products, vegetables, or fruits

Imitation crabmeat (surimi)

- Fresh or fresh frozen crabmeat cooked without salt or other high-sodium ingredients

Bacon; bacon bits; Canadian bacon; salt pork; canned or cured ham; corned, chipped, or dried beef; bologna; luncheon meat; pastrami; pickled pig's feet; or other kosher, canned, cured, pickled, or smoked meats or poultry

- Smaller amounts of the listed items made visible or served with larger ones of low-sodium grains or their products, vegetables, or fruits
- Fresh or fresh frozen meat or poultry cooked without salt or other high-sodium ingredients

- Meat or poultry smoked or pickled on premise without salt or other high-sodium ingredients
- Dried beans, peas, or lentils cooked without salt or other high-sodium ingredients, unsalted nuts or seeds or selections made from these ingredients

Hot dogs, bratwursts, or sausages from pork, beef, poultry, or other ingredients

- Sausages made on premise without salt or other high-sodium ingredients
- Fresh or fresh frozen meats or poultry cooked without salt or other high-sodium ingredients
- Smaller portions of the listed items made visible or served with larger ones of grains or their products, fruits or vegetables

Low-cholesterol and/or low-calorie processed cheeses, blue cheese, or cheese spreads or sauces

- Smaller amounts of the listed cheeses made visible or served with larger ones of low-sodium ingredients
- Fresh, unsalted low-fat or nonfat cheeses
- Equal or smaller amounts of aged cheeses
- Commercial reduced-sodium cheeses

Aged cheeses like provolone or gouda

- Smaller amounts of aged cheeses made visible
- Grated tofu

Chip dips

- Dips or sauces prepared on premise from fresh fruits or vegetables or dried legumes cooked without salt like guacamole or red and white bean salsa with bell peppers
- Commercial low-sodium dips

Canned, packaged or frozen, main course dishes including breaded meat, fish, or poultry

- Main course dishes cooked from fresh ingredients without salt or other high-sodium ingredients

Canned soups or dehydrated soup mixes

- Soups made without salt from fresh ingredients, freshly prepared, salt-free stock or low-sodium, commercial stock
- Commercial, reduced-sodium, or salt-free soups

Soy protein products

- Products cooked without salt, made from dried beans, peas, or lentils, grains or their products, or vegetables, fruit, or unsalted nuts or seeds like kidney beans simmered in spicy tomato broth garnished with bell peppers, carrots, and celery

Vegetables and their Juices

Canned lima beans, peas, corn, or sauerkraut
- Smaller portions of the listed vegetables rinsed with water or lower-sodium, canned vegetables rinsed with water
- Frozen lima beans, peas, or corn or better yet, these vegetables, fresh cooked without salt

Canned tomato, sauerkraut, or vegetable juices
- Fresh vegetable juices seasoned without salt or high-sodium condiments such as a garden vegetable juice
- Fruit juices or bottled waters
- Iced teas or coffees

Canned tomato sauce and other tomato products
- Tomato sauce or other tomato products made from fresh tomatoes without salt or from unsalted canned tomatoes
- Unsalted, commercial tomato sauce or other salt-free cooked or flavored tomato products

Canned legumes like kidney beans
- Dried legumes cooked without salt
- Canned legumes rinsed with water

Canned baked beans
- Baked beans made from dried beans, fresh tomatoes, no or less salt, and without salt pork or bacon (could smoke bacon on premise without salt or high-sodium ingredients or replace bacon with fresh meat)

Potato chips or other packaged potato products like instant mashed
- Potato chips or other potato dishes made from fresh preferably, or frozen potato products with no added salt like mashed potato pancakes accented with onion and garlic

Breads and Grains

Commercial bread stuffing
- Stuffings made on premise without salt from low-sodium breads, grains boiled without salt, fruits or vegetables

Mixes for grain dishes
- Grain dishes prepared on premise without salt

Most commercial dry cereals or instant hot cereals
- Low-sodium, dry cereals like puffed wheat or rice or shredded wheat or regular or quick cooking hot cereals

Salted snack foods
- Unsalted forms of snack foods like unsalted pretzels or salt-free popcorn
- Snacks prepared on premise without salt and low-sodium or sodium-free baking powder
- Naturally low-sodium snacks like rice cakes, melba toast, or raw fruits or vegetables

Mixes for quick breads, cakes, cookies, or pastries
- Quick breads or other baked goods prepared on premise without salt and leavened with eggs or low-sodium or sodium-free baking powder

Chow mein noodles
- Rice steamed or boiled without salt
- Crispy noodles deep fried in vegetable oil (high fat) on premise without salt
- Soft noodles made and boiled without salt

Seasoned bread crumbs
- Bread crumbs made on premise without salt from low-sodium bread

Flavoring and Leavening Agents, Condiments, and Other Processed Foods

Salt or seasoned, flavored, or lite salt
- Herbs, fresh preferred
- Spices, freshly ground preferred
- Herb and spice blends made on premise without salt and whole spices toasted to enhance flavor if appropriate such as Caribbean curry powder
- Splash of angostura bitters, vinegar, wine or citrus juice
- Commercial low-sodium seasoning blends like pumpkin pie seasoning
- Equivalent amounts of condiments with less sodium than table salt like soy sauce or low-sodium soy sauce
- Citrus zests in sauces or dressings
- See substitutions for condiments like worcestershire, etc. in chart below
- Ground dried fruit and vegetable pulp like beet, pineapple, ginger and pepper with roasted game hen

Baking powder
- Low-sodium commercial baking powder
- Sodium-free baking powder made on premise
- Eggs

Cooking wine
- Drinking wine
- Fruit juices like tangerine-pineapple juice
- Flavor extracts like orange or almond extract

Monosodium glutamate (MSG) or Accent
- Herbs or spices
- Seasoning vegetables like lemongrass
- Splash of vinegar, lemon juice, or other acidic ingredient like grapefruit-orange-strawberry juice
- Sprinkle of sugar like powdered
- Flavor extracts like banana extract

Pickles, olives, or pickle relish
- Freshly chopped or sliced vegetables or fruits
- Chunky fruit or vegetable sauces made in house like mango chutney or corn relish

Commercial chili sauce
- Chili sauce made from fresh tomatoes seasoned with dried, fresh chilies, chili flakes, or ground red pepper

Condiments like worcestershire, soy or teriyaki sauces, ketchup, or mustard
- Fruit, legume, or vegetable sauces made on premise like black-eyed pea and shallot relish or cranberry ketchup
- Minced seasoning vegetables cooked without salt like onions and garlic braise-deglazed in white wine
- Marinades or dry rubs prepared without salt or high-sodium ingredients like a southwestern dry rub for lean beef of cilantro, garlic, hot chili pepper, cumin, pepper, and a tad of olive oil and lime juice
- See substitutions for salt, etc., in chart above
- Low-sodium commercial forms of condiments like ketchup with no salt added

Horseradish sauce
- Freshly grated horseradish root or spicy radish like daikon

Meat tenderizer
- Meats cooked by moist methods like marinated spicy pot roast with gingersnap gravy
- Meats marinated in mixtures made in house without salt from low-sodium acidic and other ingredients like vinegars, wines, citrus juices, oils, herbs and spices; skip the dairy products like yogurt
- Meats with connective tissues broken down by mechanical methods like pounding, cubing, or grinding

- Meats with visible connective tissues like silverskin removed
- Tender meats which require no tenderizing

Bouillon or stock bases
- Stocks or bouillons made in house from raw ingredients without salt
- Commercial, low-sodium stocks or broths

Commercial barbecue sauce
- Barbecue sauce prepared from fresh tomatoes without salt or unsalted, canned tomato products
- Marinades or dry rubs made from low-sodium ingredients like wine, vinegar, lemon juice, oils, herbs, or spices like tropical marinade, or spicy cajun rub
- Fruit, vegetable or herb sauces like jalepeno-cilantro lime salsa

Commercial salad dressings or ones made from mixes
- Salad dressings made from fresh, nondairy ingredients and seasoned with herbs, spices, sugars, sweet syrups, and/or seasoning vegetables like very garlicky warm sherry vinaigrette

Commercial spaghetti or pizza sauces
- Spaghetti or pizza sauces made from fresh tomatoes or unsalted, canned ones and herbs and spices
- Freshly made spaghetti or pizza sauce toppings without salt or tomatoes like cheese-free basil and pine nut pesto

Salted seeds or nuts
- Unsalted seeds or nuts
- Dried fruits such as cranberries or blueberries

Margarine or butter
- Unsalted butter or margarine
- Jams, jellies, marmalades
- Vegetable or nut oils like canola or pistachio
- Reduced portions of margarine or butter or reduced portions flavored with low-sodium seasoning agents like herbs or honey

Saccharin
- Sugar or one of its forms, sorghum molasses, honey, rice syrup, malt syrup, or fruit juice concentrates

Instant cocoa mix
- Low-fat or nonfat milk with chocolate syrup
- Chocolate drink

Pudding mix

- Pudding made in house without salt and unsalted butter or margarine and less or no milk like semolina pudding with raspberry sauce

Gravy mix

- Gravy made without salt from low-sodium stock freshly prepared without salt and an unsalted butter or margarine roux or thickened with a salt-free flour and water slurry or cooked vegetable puree
- Sauce made from fruits, vegetables, or legumes cooked without salt like apple cider sauce for pork

Gelatin mix

- Gelatins made from unsweetened, commercial gelatin, fruits, their juices or purees and sugar if needed
- Chilled, fresh, canned, or cooked fruit selections like a fruit palette of pureed plums, grapes, bananas, strawberries, blueberries, and tangerines or other seasonal fruits

APPENDIX 3

Substitutes to Increase Fiber

Grains

White rice
- Unrefined rices like fluffy brown wild pecan or whole grains like rye berries

Wheat (white) flour
- Whole white wheat flour
- White flour + wheat germ, whole grain flours, whole grains, nuts, or seeds
- 1 pound whole wheat flour = about 14 ounces white flour

Wheat (white) cake flour
- Whole wheat pastry flour

Wheat (white) bread crumbs
- Whole grain bread, cake, cracker, or cereal crumbs, oats, wheat germ or chopped nuts or seeds

Pasta from wheat flour
- Whole grain pastas
- Lupin pasta made with one-third bean flour
- Pastas topped, tossed, or filled with vegetables, seeds, or nuts or sauces made from them like pasta primavera
- Unrefined rices or whole grains like triticale berries

Refined wheat quick or yeast breads, rolls, or crackers
- Whole grain breads, rolls, or crackers like whole wheat tortillas, chive flecked barley muffins, or graham crackers
- Breads, rolls, or crackers enriched with vegetables, fruits, seeds,

or nuts like onion and garlic oat bread, pumpkin bread with walnuts, or pumpernickel raisin bread

Cereals from refined grains
- Cereals topped or enriched with dried, fresh, frozen, or canned fruits, preferably unpeeled
- Whole grain cooked or dry cereals like oatmeal or bran flakes
- Granola

Refined wheat cakes or other sweet baked goods
- Cakes baked with whole grain flours like whole wheat apple spice cake with coffee glaze
- Cakes with fat replaced by fruit purees like chocolate applesauce cupcakes
- Baked goods enriched with fruits, whole grains, vegetables, nuts, or seeds like chocolate zucchini cake or peanut butter oatmeal cookies
- Fresh, canned, frozen, or dried fruits preferably unpeeled, or desserts made from them like peach crisp with oat topping
- Cakes napped with fruit sauces, garnished with fresh fruit, or served with fruit on top like pineapple rum upside down cake

Pastry crusts
- Whole grain cracker, cookie, cake, or cereal crumb crusts like graham cracker, whole wheat phyllo crusts or crusts made from doughs with ground nuts or whole grain flours

Stuffings
- Stuffings prepared from whole grains or their breads or enriched with vegetables, dried fruits, and small amounts of nuts like bulgur stuffing with toasted walnuts, mixed dried fruit and dried mushrooms

Fruits and Vegetables

Peeled fruits
- Unpeeled fresh, cooked, dried, or canned fruits like poached plums and cherries
- Fruits cooked, stuffed, or topped with seeds, nuts, or whole grains like baked apples stuffed with dried, mixed fruits and chopped nuts
- Fruits, cooked coated in whole grain cereal, cake, bread, or cracker crumbs, chopped nuts, seeds, or whole grain flour batters or doughs like banana slices rolled in peanut butter granola cookie crumbs and frozen

- Fruits served on crusts made from whole grain flours, cookies or crackers, cereals, cakes or their crumbs or chopped nuts or seeds like whole wheat gingersnap fruit pizzas

Peeled fruit sauces
- Sauces made from unpeeled fruits like rhubarb or whole plums

Peeled potato dishes like mashed
- Baked, boiled, steamed, mashed, or roasted potatoes with their skins or cooked skins only

Fruit juices like grape or orange
- Fresh, canned, or dried fruits like grapes or sliced oranges (with membranes)

Raw or cooked peeled vegetables
- Unpeeled, cooked, fresh, frozen, or canned vegetables like steamed broccoli or asparagus with unpeeled stems
- Raw vegetables served unpeeled like cucumbers or combined with whole grains or their products like tomato and 3 whole grain bread salad
- Vegetables cooked, coated, or topped with whole grain flours; cereal, bread, or cracker crumbs; chopped nuts; seeds or whole grain flour batters like Mexican ratatouille topped with cubes of blue corn and flax seed bread

Meat, Fish, Poultry, and Dairy

Ice cream or other frozen desserts
- Ice cream or frozen desserts topped, coated, or enriched with fruit chunks or their purees, seeds, nuts, whole grain, sweet cereal, cracker or cake crumbs, or chunks of whole grain cookies (oatmeal raisin) or their doughs such as frozen low-fat yogurt balls rolled in whole grain gingersnap crumbs

Milk shakes and malts
- Shakes or malts from frozen yogurt, ice milk, or sherbert containing nuts, whole grain cookies or fruits like cinnamon apple yogurt shake
- Fruit smoothies like nutty banana shake

Meat and cheese sandwiches
- Sandwiches made with increased amounts of raw vegetables and whole grain breads
- Nut butter sandwiches on whole grain breads topped with fruits or vegetables

- Sandwiches with dried bean, pea, or lentils, or their spreads or patties like whole wheat tortillas with refried beans
- Sandwiches seasoned with fruit, vegetable, or legume chutneys, relishes, salsas, coulis or sauces like mango mustard on a turkey ham sandwich
- High-protein salads emphasizing vegetables, legumes, fruits, nuts, or seeds like chicken salad with almonds, water chestnuts, celery, onions, and dried apricots in a whole wheat pita pocket

Entrees featuring meat, seafood, poultry, cheese, or eggs

- Entrees featuring increased amounts of whole grains, their pastas or breads, or vegetables like:
    Stir-fries
    Casseroles
    Soups
    Main course salads
    Stews
    Pizzas
    Pasta dishes
    Sandwiches
    Hot pots
    Ragouts
    Risottos
- Traditional entree plates with larger portions of grains and vegetables
- Vegetable or fruit plates
- Meat, seafood, or poultry rolled, enriched, or filled with whole grains or vegetables like lettuce-wrapped spring rolls
- Entrees featuring dried beans, peas, lentils, nuts, or seeds along with vegetables and whole grains like black-eyed peas and barley casserole
- Meat, seafood, poultry, eggs, or cheese cooked, coated in whole grain bread, cereal, or cracker crumbs or doughs or batters made from whole grain flours like chicken sausage quiche in whole wheat crepe cups
- Meat, seafood, poultry, cheese, or egg entrees served with fruit or vegetable sauces like cumin mushroom sauce or sauces thickened with vegetable or fruit purees

APPENDIX 4

Substitutes to Reduce Calories or Add Nutrients or Increase Portion Size without Calories

High-Fat Items

- See Appendix 1

Alcoholic Beverages

  In Cooking

Rum, brandy, or sherry
- One teaspoon vanilla/tablespoon alcohol for first 2 tablespoons alcohol and then fruit juice to equal

Orange liqueur
- One-half teaspoon orange zest and orange juice to equal the volume of the listed liqueur

Kirsch or amaretto
- Dash of almond extract and peach or apricot nectar to equal the volume of the listed liqueur

Sweet dessert wine
- Fruit juice of the same color

Red or white wine
- Two tablespoons red or white wine vinegar and 7 fluid ounces stock for a cup of wine

In Cooking or Drinking

Beers or wines
- Nonalcoholic versions of beers and wines
- Light beers
- Beer blended with vegetable juices like tomato
- Wines blended with fruit juices like mimosas with peach and tangerine juices and orange-flavored sparkling water
- See the substitutions for sodas following

Nonalcoholic Sweet Beverages

Sodas
- Fresh or bottled waters
- Hot or cold, regular or decaffeinated, flavored or unflavored teas or coffees like minted iced tea slush
- Bouillons, consommes, or broths
- Bottled waters blended with fruit juices like melonade sipper
- Artificially sweetened sodas
- Vegetable juices
- Low-fat or nonfat milk or fruit juices (comparable in calories to sodas but more nutritious) like fresh citrus cooler

Fruit juices
- See the preceding substitutions listed for sodas
- Fruit itself such as half grapefruit for grapefruit juice (more filling because negligible calories from its fiber)

Ingredients High in Sugar

Presweetened breakfast cereal
- Cooked or dry sugar-free cereals sprinkled with sweet spices like cinnamon, reduced amounts of sugar, artificial sweetener, or sweet, ripe fresh or canned fruit packed without sugar
- Cereals high in volume but low in weight like puffed rice (perception of more created)

Jams, jellies, marmalades or syrups
- Smaller portions of jams, jellies, marmalades, or syrups

- "Light" or low-calorie jams, jellies, marmalades, or syrups, or ones flavored with artificial sweeteners
- Naturally sweet high-fiber and/or water fruit toppings like strawberry puree or pear and apple salsa

Sweet desserts

- Smaller dessert portions
- Desserts artificially sweetened
- Desserts with less sugar served warm or at room temperature like bread pudding with rum-flavored sauce
- Desserts deriving part of their perceived sweet flavor from sweet spices like nutmeg or extracts such as vanilla
- Decaffeinated or regular coffees flavored with sweet spices or extracts
- Naturally sweet fruits high in water and/or fiber like cantaloupe
- High-fiber and/or water fruits perceived to be sweeter by sprinkling with salt or an acid like lemon juice such as watermelon, cantaloupe, or apples
- A high-calorie dessert shared with another diner

Fruits, Vegetables, and Grains

High-starch vegetables

- Vegetables high in fiber and water like broccoli for corn

High-starch fruits

- Fruits high in fiber and water like honeydew melon for banana

Grains or dishes made from them

- Grains or dishes made from them replaced with smaller portions of grains and larger ones of high-fiber and water fruits and vegetables like open-face sandwiches topped with lots of shredded vegetables or stir-fried rice with lots of vegetables and a smaller amount of rice

Flour as a thickening agent

- Cornstarch or arrowroot (thickening power of 1 tablespoon cornstarch or arrowroot = 2 tablespoons flour and calories similar)
- Fruit or vegetable purees

APPENDIX 5

Sample Answers to Chapter 1 Activities

Note: The following answers are not the only correct responses. They are a sample of the possible correct responses. You are encouraged to supplement them with your own.

Number 1

A. Roasted chicken with bread stuffing laced with ground pork and seasoning vegetables could be a good choice for diners monitoring their fat and cholesterol intakes. The secret is to serve a smaller portion (2½ ounces) of the skinless roasted chicken breast meat with a larger serving of the stuffing. To minimize the stuffing's fat and cholesterol (1) use no more than ½ ounce of cooked, very lean ground pork per serving; (2) cook the stuffing's seasoning vegetables without fat (braise-deglaze in stock); (3) moisten the stuffing with fat-free flavorful stock; and (4) add no egg yolks or fat to the stuffing.

   The stuffing's fat and cholesterol could be reduced further by replacing the ground pork with more vegetables such as diced bell peppers or corn kernels, dried fruits like raisins or dried apricot bits, more bread, or a combination of these.

B. The whole wheat pizza topped with shrimp, bell peppers, onions, and melted mozzarella cheese would not be recommended to fat- and cholesterol-conscious diners if it is made in the traditional manner. The mozzarella cheese is rich in fat and cholesterol and the shrimp is high in cholesterol.

Whole wheat pizza crust can and often is made without added fat or a small amount of a flavorful, monounsaturated fat-rich oil such as extra-virgin olive oil. Bell peppers and onions contain no cholesterol or fat. They might be added to the pizza raw or cooked without fat by a method such as braise-deglazing in stock or roasting.

While shrimp is very low in fat, a 2-ounce portion provides about 85 milligrams of cholesterol. When 2 ounces of part-skim-milk mozzarella cheese are combined with the shrimp, the cholesterol increases by about 16 milligrams and the fat by around 9 grams. Nutritionists recommend cholesterol intake be limited to 300 milligrams per day and fat to no more than 30% of calories. The 30% fat level is about 67 grams per 2,000 calories.

The fat and cholesterol content of this pizza could be reduced while retaining its flavor by first, making the pizza crust without fat, and second, covering it with a layer of spicy, fat-free Italian tomato sauce, followed by braise-deglazed vegetables such as sliced bell peppers, onions, and mushrooms and a small amount of shrimp and cheese. For a nearly fat-free, cholesterol-free pizza, the shrimp and mozzarella cheese could be omitted and the crust topped with only tomato sauce and vegetables.

Other options include (1) replace the mozzarella cheese with a low-fat and low-cholesterol processed cheese, (2) substitute a surimi product (imitation shrimp from white-fleshed fish) for the shrimp, or (3) reduce the portion size of the pizza. Another nearly fat-free alternative is (4) a double-crusted pizza (top and bottom) filled with layers of fat-free, well-seasoned tomato sauce and roasted, grilled, or braise-deglazed vegetables such as zucchini, spinach, onions, and carrots.

C. Cream of tomato soup, made by simmering tomatoes in a roux (butter and flour) thickened whole milk white sauce and finishing with cream is rich in both fat and cholesterol. When the soup's basil croutons are prepared by sauteing cubes of bread in butter, the soup's cholesterol and fat count increases further.

The fat and cholesterol could be reduced in the soup by preparing its white sauce with nonfat milk or evaporated skim milk, thickening the white sauce with a flour and water slurry or margarine and flour roux, and omitting the cream. To flavor the white sauce without fat, it could be simmered with an onion pique (onion with bay leaf attached by a clove) and seasoned with a pinch of nutmeg. If desired, a small piece of butter or cholesterol-free margarine might be swirled over the soup at service.

Another method to reduce the fat and cholesterol in the soup is simmering the tomatoes in a flavorful white stock thickened with a margarine and flour roux and finishing with evaporated skim milk. If desired, a tad of butter or margarine could be melted over the soup's top.

Although the basil-seasoned croutons make a tasty garnish for the soup, similar results could be achieved by accompanying it with crisp, basil-seasoned breadsticks prepared without fat. Sauteing the croutons in a small amount of butter-flavored vegetable spray or margarine or replacing the croutons with a sprinkle of freshly minced basil are other methods to reduce the topping's fat and cholesterol.

D. Spaghetti is low in fat and a good source of B vitamins and starch. The new Food Guide Pyramid recommends Americans eat 6–11 servings from the bread, cereal, rice, and pasta group daily. When tossed with olive oil, bacon bits, and parmesan cheese, this high-starch favorite becomes loaded with fat and cholesterol.

Pasta dishes do not need to be high in fat and cholesterol to taste good. Proof is spaghetti noodles topped with a flavorful, fat-free, Italian-style tomato sauce strewn with a 3-ounce portion of slivered, grilled skinless chicken breast meat or extra-lean sausage balls made on premise. Equally delicious and healthy are spaghetti noodles lightly coated with extra-virgin olive oil, tossed with a medley of grilled vegetables, and lightly sprinkled with very lean, crisp turkey bacon bits or strips of very lean ham and freshly grated skim-milk parmesan cheese or other low-fat cheese.

E. A cup of old-fashioned potato salad, prepared by coating cubes of boiled potatoes, chunks of hard-cooked eggs, and diced celery and onions in mayonnaise could add a sizable amount of fat and cholesterol to the diet. Some chefs raise the salad's fat content further by marinating the potatoes in French dressing (oil and vinegar) prior to blending with the other ingredients.

Several strategies could be employed to reduce the fat and cholesterol in this salad while keeping its flavor.

First, the salad could be made with more potatoes, celery, and onions, and less or no whole eggs or with egg whites only. If desired, other vegetables like bell peppers, green beans, and carrots could be tossed with the potatoes. They will add flavor and texture to the salad without fat.

Second, flavorful potatoes like buttery-tasting Yukon Golds or unpeeled red-skinned baby new potatoes could be selected.

Third, the potatoes could be boiled in fat-free chicken or vegetable stock rather than water. The flavor added to the potatoes during boiling will reduce their need for dressing.

Fourth, the mayonnaise could be replaced with a (1) reduced-fat commercial mayonnaise flavored with fat-free, cholesterol-free seasoning agents like chopped parsley, minced chives, hot sauce, and prepared mustard, or (2) smaller amount of high-fat mayonnaise extended with nonfat yogurt and prepared mustard and seasoned with minced parsley and chives. If the integrity of the potato salad is not of concern, it could be dressed in (3) a starch-thickened juice or stock vinaigrette, (4) reduced-fat mayonnaise flavored with nontraditional seasoning agents like curry powder and dried cherries, (5) a low-fat ranch-style dressing, or (6) a fruit, vegetable, or herb sauce like reduced-fat parsley pesto or mint chutney.

Fifth, the potatoes could be baked for the salad, their shells hollowed out and filled with a smaller portion of potato salad, encouraging diners to eat the shells too.

F. A marinara-coated meatball sandwich could be acceptable for diners monitoring their fat and cholesterol intakes if it is prepared as follows: (1) Make the meatballs with extra-lean ground beef or ground skinless chicken or turkey breast meat and extend them with bread crumbs, a legume puree like kidney been, and/or vegetables like chopped bell peppers and onions. (2) Shape the meatballs smaller so that a 3-ounce cooked portion will cover a large sandwich bun, and (3) pan broil them in a nonstick skillet removing any fat that accumulates. (4) Omit the fat in the marinara sauce. There's no need for any. (5) Spread the meatballs over the whole wheat bun, ladle a hearty portion of marinara sauce over, and dash with a few squirts of red wine vinegar. (6) Omit the mozzarella cheese or replace some of the meatballs with shredded skim-milk mozzarella cheese. (7) Top the sandwich with lots of shredded lettuce tossed with thinly sliced onions and green and red bell peppers. Skip the ripe olives. (8) Cover the meatballs with the whole wheat bun top and the sandwich is ready to eat.

G. Beets in sweet and sour sauce would be acceptable for cholesterol- and fat-conscious diners to eat unless a large portion of butter or other fat is added to the recipe. A traditional methods for making this dish and one that makes it cholesterol- and fat-free is coating cooked beets in a cornstarch-thickened sauce made of sugar and vinegar.

H. Peach crisp with low-fat vanilla frozen yogurt could be prepared and served in a fashion that would keep it low in fat and cholesterol. The primary ingredient in this dish is peaches. They are both fat- and cholesterol-free. For a healthy offering, the crisp could be made by coating a thick layer of sliced peaches in starch-thickened sugar syrup, topping with a mixture of rolled oats, flour, sugar, and a small amount of melted polyunsaturated margarine, and baking. The warm crisp could be presented with a melon ball scoop of low-fat frozen yogurt melting over its top.

I. Baked potatoes topped with chives are low in fat and cholesterol. The sour cream is not. Omit it from the menu or offer it on the side along with a choice of other fat- and cholesterol-free toppings. They might include one or more of the following: chunky tomato salsa, diced bell peppers, garlic powder, minced green onions and stems, caramelized shallot marmalade, fresh herb blend, braise-deglazed mushrooms, low-fat buttermilk ranch potato topping, butter-flavored powder, fat-free marinara sauce, and freshly ground pepper.

J. Deep-fried items of all types including these cod fillets are high in fat, and tartar sauce made with mayonnaise is high in both fat and cholesterol. A lower fat and cholesterol method of preparation would be to bake the cod fillets in a crisp cereal or bread crumb crust. For flavor and to help the crumbs adhere, the cod might first be briefly marinated in a mixture of nonfat yogurt, prepared mustard, and orange zest, then rolled in corn flake crumbs, and finally, baked on a sheet pan until golden. Topped with a chunky fruit sauce like chilled mango, red onion, and pineapple salsa, and served with roasted potato wedges splashed with balsamic vinegar, this low-fat white fish selection might be promoted as heart-healthy fish and chips.

K. The lemony whipped cream on this fresh fruit makes this dessert high in fat and cholesterol. To reduce both, the fruit might be served lightly coated in (1) sugar or honey, (2) a starch-thickened fruit juice sauce, (3) a creamy fruit yogurt sauce made by blending nonfat yogurt with a fruit spread and/or fruit puree, or (4) a creamy sauce made from evaporated skim milk thickened with gelatin and flavored and sweetened with fruit spread and powdered sugar.

L. Macaroni and cheese with ham and buttered bread crumbs is traditionally high in fat and cholesterol. The butter, whole milk, and cheese in the cheese sauce, the ham, and the butter in the bread crumb topping are the sources of fat and cholesterol in this dish. A healthier version of the macaroni and cheese could be created by making the cheese sauce with evaporated skim milk, thickening it with a margarine and flour roux, and reducing the amount of high-fat cheddar cheese or replacing part of it with low-fat, low-cholesterol cheddar cheese. A small amount of very lean ham or low-fat turkey ham might be diced and added to the dish, but if the ham is omitted or replaced with blanched vegetables like peas, corn kernels, or diced carrots, no fat or cholesterol would be added. The butter can be omitted from the bread crumb topping or replaced with polyunsaturated margarine. A flavorful whole grain bread or ready-to-eat cereal like corn flakes is recommended if the crumb topping is to be made without fat. The macaroni and bread crumbs are not a source of fat or cholesterol.

Another healthy alternative to the macaroni and cheese is to serve pasta topped with a fat-free marinara sauce or tossed with vegetables primavera style. The fat and cholesterol content of both of these dishes would still be acceptable if a small amount of freshly grated skim-milk parmesan cheese and/or very lean diced ham is added.

M. Vegetable beef soup is likely low in fat and cholesterol. These are indicators that the soup is low in both: (1) a clear broth skimmed of fat, (2) lots of vegetables, and (3) small amounts of lean beef.

N. Lamb stew with vegetables can contain substantial amounts of fat and cholesterol when prepared by traditional methods. There's no need. These few changes in the recipe can make the stew into a healthy choice. Begin with very lean lamb, allowing 4 ounces raw per portion. Trim the lamb of any visible fat; cut it into small cubes; and brown it in a nonstick skillet lightly coated with vegetable cooking spray. Simmer the browned lamb cubes in very flavorful broth along with onions, bay leaf, and other seasoning agents until very tender. Skim the fat from the cooking juices and thicken them with a browned flour slurry. Boil a variety of colorful vegetables separately, until tender. Add them to the stew only to heat through. Serve the stew over a whole grain, a whole grain product like pasta or bread, or mashed potatoes prepared without whole milk, butter, or other fat.

O. Banana nut cake with cream cheese frosting is almost certain to be high in fat and cholesterol. For half the amount of both fat and cholesterol, diners might be recommended to share a slice with a companion or eat half and save the rest for another day.

These are some recipe modifications that can be made to reduce the fat and cholesterol in the cake: replace the butter in the cake with a puree of ripe or baked bananas and dates; omit the nuts; substitute two egg whites for each whole egg; and top with powdered sugar frosting prepared with nonfat milk. Note, the cake is no longer a banana nut cake but a tasty low-fat, low-cholesterol banana date cake.

P. Pork fried rice can unknowingly be high in fat and cholesterol. While pork fried rice contains only a small amount of pork, the rice may be stir-fried in a large amount of oil and whole eggs blended into the dish at the end of cooking. By using very lean pork trimmed of fat, stir-frying in a small amount of oil, and replacing each whole egg with two egg whites, the fat and cholesterol in this dish can be minimized.

APPENDIX 6

Sample Answers to Chapter 2 Activities

Note: The following answers are not the only correct responses. They are a sample of possible responses. You are encouraged to supplement them with your own.

Number 1

A. The refined wheat buns on the turkey hot dogs with ketchup and mustard are a good source of the complex carbohydrate, starch. To increase the fiber of this selection, the hot dog could be served on a whole grain bun and the ketchup and mustard supplemented with red bean chili, lots of shredded vegetables, and pickle relish.

B. Roasted potato chips sprinkled with herbs are rich in the complex carbohydrate, starch. To increase the starch and fiber content of this dish, the potatoes' fiber-rich skins could be retained and the chips offered with a high-fiber salsa like herb and garlic tomato or a starch- and fiber-rich bean dip like spicy black bean, bell pepper, and tomato.

C. Granola, made from high-fiber, high-starch whole grains and fiber-rich nuts, seeds, and dried fruits, is a good source of complex carbohydrates. To increase the complex carbohydrates in the granola, a larger portion could be served. For a high nutritional score in all areas, the granola could be created with a hearty portion of vitamin-, mineral-, and protein-rich whole grains and a small amount of high-fat nuts and seeds and naturally sweet dried fruits.

D. Bran muffins are good sources of fiber and starch. To maximize the amount of both in the bran muffins, these quick breads could be made with whole wheat pastry flour and enriched with bran or other whole grains like oats; dried fruits like raisins and currants; or fruit purees like date or banana. High-fiber nuts and seeds could be blended into the muffins, but because they are concentrated sources of fat, small amounts are recommended.

Honey is high in the simple carbohydrate, sugar. It should be used sparingly in the healthy diet.

E. Apples are good sources of fiber and so is the sauce made from them. For example, the fiber in ¾ cup of applesauce is comparable to the fiber in a slice of whole grain bread. To increase the sauce's fiber content further, it could be made from a puree of unpeeled apples and, if desired, garnished with fresh sliced or dried fruits such as raisins.

F. Buckwheat waffles, made from all whole grain flours or a combination of whole grain and refined flours, are good sources of the complex carbohydrates, fiber and starch. The waffles' fiber and/or starch content might be increased by (1) increasing their portion size; (2) blending dried fruits like dates or cherries, purees of fruits like ripe banana, or cooked vegetables like pumpkin or sweet potato, into their batter; (3) replacing the honey yogurt topping with a fruit compote; or (4) supplementing the honey yogurt with sliced fresh fruit.

G. The noodles and vegetables in the chicken noodle soup add both starch and fiber to the diet. To raise the soup's fiber content, the soup could be prepared with whole wheat noodles and offered with whole grain crackers or whole grain breadsticks.

H. Stuffed baked potatoes with diced roasted bell peppers are good sources of starch and fiber. To increase the fiber content of this dish, diners could be encouraged to eat the potato's stuffing along with its shell and the peeled roasted bell peppers replaced with unpeeled, diced, raw bell peppers.

I. Corn is a good source of fiber and starch. Margarine is a concentrated source of fat. Nevertheless, a light coat on the corn will add flavor and is acceptable as part of a healthy eating plan. For good taste without added fat, the corn could be roasted and served sprinkled with freshly squeezed lime juice and fresh herbs.

J. Frozen yogurt with strawberry sauce is not a good source of complex carbohydrates. To increase the frozen yogurt's fiber and/or starch, (1) replace its clear strained strawberry sauce with sliced fresh fruit, a sweetened puree of fresh strawberries, or cooked strawberry sauce filled with berries; (2) blend fruits, nuts, seeds, or whole grains or their products like granola or oatmeal cookies into the frozen yogurt; (3) offer the frozen yogurt garnished with a whole grain or fruit-filled cookie; or (4) present the frozen yogurt on a slice of whole grain or fruit-filled cake.

K. The spinach fettucine is rich in starch and a source of fiber. The light Swiss cheese sauce, like other foods of animal origin, is not a source of fiber. While the cheese sauce may be thickened with a flour-based roux, the amount of starch this yields per serving will be minimal.

Spinach fettucine has more fiber than pasta made with refined semolina wheat flour. Methods to further increase the complex carbohydrate content of the fettucine are (1) replace the cheese sauce with a vegetable, legume, and/or nut sauce such as chunky tomato, bell pepper sauce or low-fat sun-dried tomato and herb pesto, (2) add vegetables such as broccoli or bell peppers to the cheese sauce, (3) toss vegetables and/or legumes with the pasta before topping with a light cheese sauce, (4) increase the portion size of the fettucine, and (5) accompany the pasta with a basket of whole grain breads.

APPENDIX 7

Sample Answers to Chapter 4 Activities

Note: The following answers are not the only correct responses. They are only a sample of the possible correct responses. You are encouraged to supplement them with your own.

Number 1

None of the items on this list appears to be low in sodium.

A. Hot dogs made from beef, pork, or turkey are high in sodium. Ketchup and mustard contain sodium, but because a small amount of these condiments is used, their sodium contribution to the total diet is insignificant. Salt is required to control leavening in "home-made" hot dog buns and other yeast breads. Commercial breads often contain additional sodium-derived additives.

A better choice for a sodium-conscious diner would be turkey sausages made on premises without salt or other high-sodium ingredients, topped with chopped onions and salt-free, fresh, spicy tomato salsa, and served on toasted "home-made," low-sodium wheat buns.

Diners might also be encouraged to order other types of low-sodium sandwiches such as a grilled skinless chicken breast on whole wheat toast garnished with a fruit chutney or a broiled burger topped with sliced tomatoes, onions, and lettuce—ketchup and mustard on the side.

B. Commercial frozen waffles and those made from mixes

generally contain salt as well as sodium additives. Honey is a good choice for sodium-conscious diners, but dairy products of all types including yogurt are natural sources of sodium. However, since the honey orange yogurt topping is only a dollop, its sodium contribution to the diet is of little concern.

The sodium could be reduced in this dish by preparing the waffles from scratch without salt and topping them with sliced fresh fruit, a fruit sauce, or warm honey or maple syrup. Unsalted butter and unsalted margarine are low-sodium spreads but they will add fat and calories to the waffles. For convenience, low-sodium waffles could be made during slow periods and frozen for later use.

C. Fresh fettucine noodles contain some sodium but the cheese, cream, and melted butter in their sauce put this dish in the very high-sodium category.

The sodium could be reduced in the fettucine by omitting the salt in the pasta's dough and boiling the noodles in unsalted water. Similarly, a very low-sodium sauce could be created by preparing one without salt, from fresh ingredients, and with no or small amounts of dairy products. For example, the fettucine might be topped with spicy tomato sauce and lean meatballs or lightly coated in olive oil and tossed with roasted vegetables, julienne strips of marinated, grilled, skinless chicken breast, and minced herbs. Freshly grated, skim-milk parmesan cheese could be offered on the side.

D. Freshly roasted potatoes are low-sodium choices but the parmesan cheese, garlic salt, and low-fat sour cream dip are not.

A lower sodium choice could be created by lightly coating the potatoes during roasting with olive oil, seasoning with freshly minced garlic, garlic powder, or minced herbs, and offering with a freshly prepared, salt-free sauce like chunky tomato salsa, mint chutney, or garbanzo bean and bell pepper dip. By omitting the parmesan cheese and replacing the sour cream dip with one of these very low-fat dips, the fat content of the selection will decrease too.

E. Ham, cheese, mayonnaise, and dill pickles are all high-sodium ingredients.

Instead, sandwiches might be recommended filled with salt-free, freshly roasted or grilled, sliced, lean meats like beef, pork, lamb, or skinless chicken or turkey breast and topped with fresh vegetables such as shredded lettuce, sliced cucumbers and tomatoes, and a "home-made," salt-free sauce such as pineapple chutney or herb vinaigrette.

Diners might also be encouraged to order other low-sodium sandwiches such as salt-free, pan-broiled, lean turkey, chicken, or beef burgers on seven-grain buns; stir-fried, marinated, lean beef steak strips in whole wheat pitas; or grilled fresh fish rolled in whole wheat tortillas. To moisten and add texture and flavor to these sandwiches with minimal sodium, they might be filled with fresh vegetables such as shredded purple cabbage and carrots, sliced onions, bell pepper strips, or bean sprouts and either a small amount of a high-sodium sauce like ketchup or tartar sauce or a large amount of a freshly prepared low-sodium sauce such as roasted corn relish, Italian tomato sauce, or tart apple and ginger salsa.

Sodium could be reduced further in all of these sandwiches by offering them on breads or buns prepared on premise with less salt.

F. In addition to the baking soda and/or powder and salt (sodium chloride) in "home-made" bran muffins, commercial muffins often contain additional sodium additives. The bran muffins' salted margarine increases their sodium content further.

By making the muffins from scratch or purchasing them from a local baker, their salt could be omitted, and if very low-sodium muffins are desired, eggs or sodium-free baking powder could be used as leaveners. The list of low-sodium spreads might include unsalted margarine, unsalted butter, honey, jelly, jam, or fruit spread.

G. Soy sauce is the high-sodium ingredient in this dish. A lower sodium choice would be steamed green beans, fresh, not frozen or canned, tossed with toasted sesame seeds, sesame oil, and if desired, low-sodium soy sauce.

The green beans could also be prepared in another low-sodium-style such as sauteed in unsalted margarine or canola oil with sliced mushrooms and onions.

H. Dairy products including frozen yogurt are natural sources of sodium. Generally, sodium-containing additives are also ingredients in commercial frozen dairy desserts. Since the frozen yogurt would be topped with only a few tablespoons of commercial strawberry sauce, it would add minimal sodium (10 milligrams/2 tablespoons) to the dish and be of little concern.

By making the frozen yogurt from fresh yogurt, its sodium-derived additives could be eliminated. The frozen yogurt's sodium could be reduced further by blending sodium-free ingredients like fruits into it and reducing its portion size. Fresh strawberries in a light sugar or honey syrup or a freshly prepared strawberry sauce could be offered as sodium-free toppings.

Fruit-flavored (dairy-free) sorbets and granitas could be suggested as other naturally low-sodium frozen dessert alternatives.

I. Assuming the noodles are boiled, the vegetables blanched, and the chicken poached in water without salt, the stock is the only high-sodium ingredient in the chicken noodle soup.

Ideally, the stock would be made on premise without salt. A commercial, reduced-sodium stock or broth is another choice. These products may contain sugar.

J. The vegetables and boiled egg wedges in this green salad are naturally low in sodium. The canned garbanzo beans, turkey salami, and commercial dressing increase the salad's sodium content.

Sodium-free garbanzo beans could be made by cooking dried garbanzo beans in unsalted water. More convenient low-sodium options for the beans are rinsing the canned beans in water or purchasing low-sodium, canned garbanzo beans.

Fresh skinless chicken or turkey breast or lean meat sausages seasoned without salt or high-sodium ingredients and smoked on premise are low-sodium alternatives to the turkey salami. To reduce the sodium in the ranch-style dressing, it might be made from fresh ingredients without salt. However, buttermilk, one of its primary ingredients, is naturally high in sodium. Better choices for sodium-conscious diners would be dressings made in house without dairy products, salt, or other high-sodium ingredients such as honey citrus and poppy seed dressing, an herbed chunky fresh tomato dressing, or a raspberry vinaigrette.

APPENDIX 8

Sample Answers to Chapter 5 Activities

Note: The following answers are not the only correct responses. They are a sample of the possible correct responses. You are encouraged to supplement them with your own.

Number 1

A. No vegetarians. Vegetarians do not eat shellfish such as shrimp.
B. All types of vegetarians. The grains, dried fruits, seeds, and nuts in granola are acceptable to serve to vegetarians if they are coated with a sweetener of nonanimal origin such as fruit juice concentrate, brown sugar, or brown rice syrup, and the granola is made with no fat or a vegetable fat such as oil.
C. Lacto-ovo vegetarians. Lacto-ovo vegetarians eat eggs, one of the ingredients found in pecan pie. These vegetarian diners also eat dairy products. Therefore, they could enjoy their pie topped with a small scoop of nonfat frozen yogurt or along with a glass of nonfat skim milk if they desired. Traditionally, pie crusts were made with lard. No longer. Today they are more commonly made with vegetable fats such as shortening and vegetable oil, and thus, appropriate to serve to vegetarian diners of all types.
D. Lacto-ovo vegetarians. These vegetarians eat eggs, an ingredient often found in bran muffins.

E. Lacto and lacto-ovo vegetarians but not vegans. Lacto and lacto-ovo vegetarians eat dairy products such as yogurt. Vegans eat no foods of animal origin.

F. No vegetarians. Gelatin is an animal by-product.

G. All types of vegetarians. Cherry pie is generally made from cherries, a sweetening agent (sugar), and starch thickener (cornstarch). Since pie crusts are made from flour, salt, water, and a solid fat, one could be made from vegetable shortening to accommodate vegetarian diners.

H. No vegetarians. Vegetarians do not eat poultry. If the mashed potatoes are made with butter and/or milk, lacto-ovo and lacto vegetarians would find them acceptable but not vegans.

Number 2

A. A medley of al dente vegetables simmered in a flavorful vegetable broth.

    All types of vegetarians.

    If the soup is prepared with chicken stock, it would not be appropriate to serve to any types of vegetarians.

B. Freshly grilled corn on the cob lightly coated with extra-virgin olive oil and freshly squeezed lime juice accompanied with salt and a selection of herbs for sprinkling.

    All types of vegetarians.

    If the corn is coated with butter, it would be acceptable to serve to lacto and lacto-ovo vegetarians but not vegans.

C. Crisp, shredded green cabbage dotted with diced red and green peppers and grilled corn kernels gently tossed in a creamy tofu mayonnaise dressing.

    All types of vegetarians. The salad contains no foods of animal origin.

    Another dressing for this salad that would be accepted by all types of vegetarians is a standard oil and vinegar French dressing. The cabbage salad would not be suitable to serve to vegans and lacto vegetarians if it is coated with an egg yolk emulsified dressing like mayonnaise.

D. Grilled turkey flavored vegetable and grain hot dog on a toasted whole wheat bun topped with a choice of ketchup, mustard, pickle relish, red bean chili, and melted soy cheese.

    The hot dog would be acceptable to all vegetarians because it contains no foods of animal origin.

E. A medley of ripe, fresh strawberries, sliced kiwi, cantaloupe balls, pineapple cubes, and blueberries, lightly coated with honey, and presented in a gold-rimmed goblet.

Honey is a product of animal origin. For this reason, it may be avoided by vegetarians.

An alternative that would be accepted by all types of vegetarians is the fruit lightly sweetened with brown or white sugar, fruit juice or its concentrate, or brown rice or maple syrup, or best yet, glazed in its own naturally sweet juices.

F. Stir-fried broccoli florets, baby corn, red and green bell pepper cubes, cloud ear mushrooms, sliced carrots, and onions seasoned with garlic, soy sauce, and sesame oil.

All types of vegetarians.

G. Your favorite brand (name) of reduced-fat and salt-free crisp ripple-style potato chips.

All types of vegetarians would find these chips acceptable if fried in vegetable oil or vegetable shortening. However, many of these diners might avoid them because of their additives or they might prefer their potatoes prepared in a healthier fashion such as baked or roasted.

H. Freshly baked russet potatoes stuffed with creamy mashed potatoes whipped with milk, fresh butter, freshly ground pepper, and sea salt and topped with a sprinkle of freshly minced chives.

Lacto and lacto-ovo vegetarians but not vegans. Omit the milk and the butter, and the potatoes would be appropriate for vegans too.

I. Brown basmati rice simmered in flavorful chicken broth dotted with small dices of red, green, and yellow bell peppers and sliced green onions.

No vegetarians.

Prepared with vegetable broth, the pilaf would be suitable for all types of vegetarians.

J. Fresh spinach fettucine noodles coated in a creamy sauce made from reduced cream, butter, and freshly grated parmesan cheese.

Lacto and lacto-ovo vegetarians but not vegans. Lacto and lacto-ovo vegetarians eat dairy products including cream, butter, and parmesan cheese. Vegans eat no foods of animal origin.

APPENDIX 9

Sample Answers to Chapter 6 Activities

Note: The following answers are not the only correct responses. They are a sample of the possible responses. You are encouraged to supplement them with your own.

Number 1

A. A standard turkey hot dog on a refined wheat (white) bun with ketchup and mustard is about 275 calories. For most calorie counters, this item would be an acceptable choice for a quick lunch along with some vegetable sticks, a glass of nonfat milk, and a piece of fresh fruit.

   While turkey hot dogs are around 100 calories each, their fat content tends to be very high, often around 70% of each dog's calories. Served with an unbuttered bun and the condiments, the fat in the combination drops to around 35%. Along with a nearly fat-free vegetable and fruit side dish and nonfat milk, the amount of fat in the meal would drop to less than 30%.

   For comparable calories, a grilled, skinless, half chicken breast on a toasted whole grain bun with shredded lettuce, onions, and bell peppers and a chunky vegetable salsa would be more filling and nutritionally would be a better choice than the hot dog. The chicken breast contains minimal fat, about 20% of its calories come from fat and the whole grain bun provides more fiber, vitamins, and minerals than the refined wheat bun. Similarly, the shredded vegetables and salsa are nutritionally superior to the hot dog's ketchup and mustard.

B. Roasted chicken and mashed potatoes topped with gravy is a high-fat, high-calorie selection. It would not be acceptable to most dieters.

To reduce the fat, and thus, calories in the roasted (whole) chicken, chicken breasts could be roasted with their skins on but removed before serving.

The gravy topping the mashed potatoes and the butter and whole milk whipped into them add fat and unnecessary calories. Mashed potatoes whipped with skim milk or evaporated skim milk and topped with a sauce made from fat-free, flavorful pan juices thickened with a cooked vegetable puree and a slurry of cornstarch would be more appropriate for calorie-conscious diners. For mashed potatoes with a buttery flavor but without the fat, cholesterol, and calories of butter, butter-flavored powder could be blended into the mashed potatoes.

Baked potatoes topped with diced bell peppers and a dollop of herb-flavored, nonfat yogurt or roasted, baby, new potatoes (skins on) seasoned with minced fresh herbs are two other higher-fiber, reduced-fat, reduced-calorie potato selections that might replace the butter- and whole milk-filled mashed potatoes with gravy.

C. Steamed carrots glazed in honey would not be acceptable to most dieters.

The carrots in this dish are well recognized as healthy choices by calorie counters. Carrots are composed primarily of calorie-free water and fiber and are good sources of beta-carotene. Likewise, steaming the carrots is a calorie-free cooking method. However, the honey on the carrots provides empty calories. While the amount of honey in each portion may be small, and thus, add limited calories, a better choice would be a larger portion of naturally sweet, steamed carrots sprinkled with fresh herbs.

D. A jumbo bran muffin studded with raisins and coated with margarine would yield more than one third of some dieters' daily calorie allotment.

Bran muffins are rich in fiber and B vitamins but also fat and sugar, and thus, calories. Margarine, of course, is a concentrated source of calories. It contains about 100 calories per tablespoon.

Reducing the size of the muffins and omitting the margarine or replacing it with a low-sugar fruit spread or whipped margarine would reduce the calories in this selection substantially.

A whole grain bagel with a small amount of low-fat cream cheese or toasted, whole grain English muffin with a low-sugar fruit spread are other lower-calorie, nutrient-dense options. Like the bran muffins, they make an easy-to-eat breakfast on the run.

E. Granola is typically a mixture of whole grain cereals such as rolled oats dotted with nuts, seeds, and dried fruits, baked, coated in oil. Whole grain cereals are rich in B vitamins and minerals and good sources of the complex carbohydrates, starch and fiber. They provide about 100 calories per uncooked half cup. Nuts and seeds, however, are very high in fat and are concentrated sources of calories. For example, an ounce of cashews with about 70% fat provides 165 calories, while a tablespoon of sesame seeds with about 85% fat yields 50 calories. Similarly, dried fruits are sources of fiber, and many are rich in minerals, but small amounts can yield substantial calories. For example, there are about 150 calories in ⅓ cup of seedless raisins and around 40 calories in 5 dried apricot halves. The oil coating the granola is another concentrated source of calories. At about 120 calories per tablespoon, many calorie counters would prefer to obtain their fat in other forms. The low-fat milk topping the granola contains less fat and fewer calories than whole milk but more than nonfat milk.

A more desirable option might be "home-made" granola prepared from whole grain cereals baked without oil and topped with sliced fresh fruit and nonfat milk. A ready-to-eat whole grain cereal might also be recommended as an alternative to the granola.

F. An egg white omelette is high in protein and low in fat and calories. It could be recommended to weight reducers as a main course breakfast, lunch, or diner selection. Filling with fruits and vegetables is generally a good method to add flavor to the omelette without much fat or many calories. This is true for the onions and tomatoes in this omelet, but the avocados are an exception. They are high in both fat and calories. Flavorful vegetables such as bell peppers or zucchini might be substituted for the avocados at only a tad of the calories.

Also, omelettes whether made with whole eggs or egg whites only are cooked by frying in fat. Whether the choice is butter, margarine, or oil, a tablespoon will add another 100 or more calories to the omelette. To minimize the amount of fat and calories, the omelette might be cooked in a nonstick omelette pan lightly sprayed with butter-flavored vegetable oil.

G. Most weight reducers will find it difficult to fit raisin bread French toast topped with margarine and maple syrup in a low-calorie healthy menu plan.

French toast is traditionally made by coating bread in a batter of whole eggs and whole milk and frying in melted butter. A nutritious, yet flavorful, lower-calorie option might be made by coating whole grain bread with or without raisins in a batter of evaporated skim milk, egg whites, and freshly ground cinnamon and browning in a nonstick pan lightly sprayed with butter-flavored vegetable oil. The margarine and syrup topping the French toast might be replaced with a naturally sweet fruit spread, fruit sauce such as smooth apple sauce, reduced sugar maple syrup, a sprinkle of powdered sugar and sliced fresh fruit, or a small portion of margarine whipped with a sweet fruit sauce.

The raisins in the bread add fiber, vitamins, and minerals, iron in particular, to the French toast. While raisins are concentrated sources of natural sugar, raisin bread contains only a few more calories than wheat or whole grain bread.

H. Both orange juice and the fresh fruit it is squeezed from are good choices for weight reducers. The new Food Guide Pyramid recommends diners eat 2–4 servings from the fruit group daily.

Many dieters would prefer an orange to its juice only. Peeling the orange and eating its fibrous pulp while savoring its tart, sweet juice is a more fulfilling dining experience for many weight reducers.

I. Linguine tossed with olive oil, parmesan cheese, and seafood could be a good choice for dieters if the linguine is paired with small amounts of oil, cheese, and seafood. For example, a healthy version of this dish might be 1½ cups of whole wheat linguine (boiled without added oil) coated with a teaspoon of olive oil, tossed with freshly minced herbs, 3 ounces of grilled shrimp and scallops, and a colorful mixture of grilled vegetables. Freshly grated skim-milk parmesan cheese might be offered on the side for those who would like to indulge.

J. Briefly, New England clam chowder is prepared by simmering cubes of potatoes and clams in broth, thickening with a butter and flour roux, and finishing with whole milk and cream. Calories in a 1-cup portion are 200 or more. Most calorie-conscious diners would be better served with a lower fat and calorie soup.

Examples of lower fat and calorie soups that might be offered are vegetable soup with no meat or small amounts, Manhattan clam chowder (tomato-based), gazpacho (chilled tomato soup), consommé garnished with lean meat or vegetables, or French onion soup minus the high-fat cheese. Lentil and dried bean soups and clear soups with rice or noodles provide more calories than vegetable-filled soups but are also nutritious choices for calorie counters.

A reduced-calorie, low-fat New England clam chowder could be prepared in house by replacing the soup's whole milk and cream with evaporated skim milk and thickening the soup with a puree of cooked potatoes.

Whole wheat crackers can be good accompaniments to soups for dieters. Their fat and calorie contents vary greatly from product to product. To determine if crackers are appropriate for weight watchers, their fat and calorie counts can be obtained from their labels. For comparison, a slice of bread has 1 gram of fat and 70 calories.

K. A quarter-pound burger with thousand island dressing would take a substantial bite out of a dieter's daily calorie allowance. The bun, lettuce, and tomato would be better choices if they were offered with a smaller portion of a lower fat and calorie meat, seafood, or poultry sandwich filling and topping.

The quarter-pound burger might be replaced with a 3 ounce portion of (1) baked skinless chicken or turkey breast, (2) roasted lean beef or pork, (3) canned salmon or tuna packed in water, (4) grilled turkey patty from skinless ground breast meat, or (5) broiled lean fish fillet. A fat-free fruit or vegetable sauce such as mango and pineapple salsa or sweet and sour corn relish could moisten and add flavor to the filling with only a tad of the calories in the thousand island dressing.

Another low-calorie option is to reduce the burger's beef patty to 3 ounces of grilled, very lean, ground beef such as ground round and replace the thousand island dressing with mustard, ketchup, and a few dill pickle spears. Calories could also be saved by serving the burger or other sandwiches open-faced, using a single slice of bread or half of a bun.

L. Chef's salads, heavy on the salad greens, light on the meat, cheese, and eggs, and drizzled lightly with low-fat dressings can be good selections for calorie counters.

A description for a weight watchers' chef's salad might be a heaping plate of lettuce and vegetables tossed with ½ ounce each of low-fat Swiss and low-fat cheddar cheeses, 1 ounce of grilled, skinless, chicken breast meat, and 1 ounce of extra-lean ham, all lightly coated with low-fat ranch dressing. The dressing could be served on the side if desired. For variety, a smaller portion of chicken and ham might be combined with ½ boiled egg cut into wedges.

M. Wild rice contains about twice the protein of refined rice and significantly more B vitamins. When cooked in water, its nutty rich flavor can be enjoyed by weight reducers at 80 or so calories per ½ cup.

Here, the wild rice is served pilaf-style flavored with high-fat bacon bits, toasted almonds, and sauteed mushrooms (likely in butter). Grains cooked pilaf-style are sauteed in fat first and then simmered in stock alone or with additional flavoring ingredients. Sauteing the wild rice in fat and combining with bacon bits, toasted almonds, and sauteed mushrooms might enhance its flavor but it also adds concentrated calories, the factor weight reducers are trying to moderate.

A wild rice dish with less fat and calories could be created with a few modifications. (1) Omit sauteing the grains in fat; simply simmer them in a rich, fat-free stock. (2) Add the mushrooms to the pilaf but braise-deglaze them in reduced red wine. (3) Skip or reduce the amount of bacon bits and toasted almonds in the pilaf. (4) To compensate for their smaller portion, add extra mushrooms, another kind of mushrooms, or shallots. (5) If adding a reduced amount of bacon bits, select an extra-lean product like turkey bacon and broil it until crisp. (6) Sprinkle both the bacon bits and almonds visibly over the dish at service. In a traditional wild rice pilaf, the almonds will be browned in a skillet without fat. The same procedure should be followed in the reduced-calorie version of the recipe.

N. A piece of apple pie, with or without the frozen yogurt, will add unnecessary calories to the diet in the form of sugar and fat. For a more nutrient-dense apple dessert, a baked apple or small square of apple crisp with a low-fat whole grain topping might be offered. Other lower calorie apple desserts are apple pie filling ladled over a small scoop of nonfat frozen yogurt, a small scoop of reduced-fat ice cream on a base of apple pie filling, an apple tart with a low-fat whole wheat phyllo shell, or best yet, a bright red or green, crisp, raw apple. Another option is to recommend that the weight watcher share a piece of the apple pie with another diner.

Recipe Index

Subject Index